Hollywood Math and Aftermath

Hollywood Math and Aftermath

The Economic Image and the Digital Recession

J.D. Connor

BLOOMSBURY ACADEMIC
NEW YORK · LONDON · OXFORD · NEW DELHI · SYDNEY

BLOOMSBURY ACADEMIC
Bloomsbury Publishing Inc
1385 Broadway, New York, NY 10018, USA
50 Bedford Square, London, WC1B 3DP, UK

BLOOMSBURY, BLOOMSBURY ACADEMIC and the Diana logo
are trademarks of Bloomsbury Publishing Plc

First published in United States of America 2018
Paperback edition first published 2020

Cover design: Eleanor Rose
Cover image © Film, Déjà Vu (2006) Washington, Denzel, 2006,
Director: Scott, Tony
[Touchstone / The Kobal Collection]

Library of Congress Cataloging-in-Publication Data
Names: Connor, J. D. author.
Title: Hollywood math and aftermath: the economic image
and the digital recession / J. D. Connor. Description: New York :
Bloomsbury Academic, 2018. | Includes bibliographical
references and index. Identifiers:LCCN2017061 140 (print) |
LCCN 2018000056 (ebook) | ISBN 9781501314407 (epDF) |
ISBN 9781501314391 (ePUB) | ISBN 9781501314384 (hardback :
alk. paper) Subjects: LCSH: Money in motion pictures. |
Motion picture industry–Economic aspects–United States. |
Motion pictures–United States–History–20th century. Classifi cation:
LCC PN1995.9.M59 (ebook) | LCC PN1995.9.M59 C56 2018 (print) |
DDC 384/.830973–dc23 LC record available at https://lccn.loc.gov/2017061140

ISBN: HB: 978-1-5013-1438-4
PB: 978-1-5013-6224-8
ePDF: 978-1-5013-1440-7
eBook: 978-1-5013-1439-1

Series: Bloomsbury Ethics, 1234567X, volume 6

Typeset by Deanta Global Publishing Services, Chennai, India

To find out more about our authors and books visit
www.bloomsbury.com and sign up for our newsletters.

For my parents

CONTENTS

ACKNOWLEDGMENTS

This project began as a set of explorations of representations of the economy in a business that is notorious for both its publicity and its opacity. It was also an attempt to go beneath and beyond my prior project on the recent history of the Hollywood studios by exploring their economic bases. The project came into initial shape while I was at Yale. Throughout that portion of the process, the Film and Media Studies Program was always deeply supportive, as were some members of the art history department, where my appointment lay. After the others—let's call them the non-supportive members of the department—voted against my promotion to non-tenured associate professor, a different rhythm took hold. For better or worse, that difference is legible in the introduction and latter chapters. Those were written as a kind of saving throw as I was moving into the Division of Cinema and Media Studies in USC's School of Cinematic Arts.

Underlying those tonal and argumentative differences I have continuously benefitted from the help of a host of knowledge professionals. The staff at the Margaret Herrick Library was terrifically helpful in working through the earlier materials. Business librarians at Harvard and Yale helped me track and understand corporate reports. My wife, Lisa Giglio Connor, and my friend, Ben Sheffner, were tremendously helpful in guiding me through the legal research process necessary to tell the stories of Relativity and *The United States of America v. The Wolf of Wall Street*. A former student who wished to remain anonymous was crucial to helping me understand the effects of tax credit financing on other aspects of the production and distribution process.

I have also benefitted from the chance to work through a great deal of the project in public. I presented parts of the introduction and the first and final chapters at USC and King's College London, a very early version of some material from the second chapter at Binghamton, the third at SCMS, the fourth at the University of Toronto's Centre for the Study of the United States and at the University of California, Irvine, the sixth at Yale. Some material has been previously published in other forms. Parts of Chapter 4 appeared in *Reading Capitalist Realism*, edited by Leigh Claire LeBerge and Alison Shonkwiler. Parts of Chapter 5 first appeared in the *Blackwell History of American Cinema*, vol. 4, edited by Roy Grundmann, Cyndi Lucia, and Art Simon. The introduction to Part II combines material from an essay published at Post45 and one from a special issue on "Contemporary Cuts" in the *Journal of Visual Culture*, edited by Lanfranco Aceti. I am grateful to the close work by all these editors and the anonymous referees who have tried to get me to make clear what it is that I think I am doing and to do it better. Less anonymous, but far more numerous, have been those undergraduates and graduates who have tried to take up certain ideas and shape them to their own ends, or who have pushed back on lectures or seminars where badly thought through versions first came to light. In return, this project bears the particular imprint of work by Annie Berke, Jordan Brower, Kirsty Dootson, Zelda Roland, Annie Schweikert, and Maddie Whittle. Finally, faced with the prospect of a book that might drift off into technicality, it has been a boon to the writing to be able to publish occasional pieces with the *L.A. Review of Books*. None of that material is included here, but I need to thank my editors, Elliott Eglash and Anna Shechtman.

As usual, I owe my greatest intellectual debt to the slowly rotating cast of characters of Post45, who have influenced the project directly and indirectly, by becoming the chorus of interlocutors I hear whenever I set down to revise. Alongside/inside/outside that group, I should also express my gratitude to Jordan Bear, Joseph Clarke, Victor Fan, Andy Hoberek, Amy Hungerford, Brian Kane, Akira Lippit, Michael Szalay, and Haidee Wasson for support intellectual and material. At USC, my new colleagues have been re-energizing, but I want to single out Nitin Govil for managing my tenure case, a process that required him to become perhaps the most intensive and comprehensive reader of my work in the world. Jerome Christensen continues to be a source of challenge and inspiration.

The folks at Bloomsbury have been a joy to work with as the project ended up extended by circumstance. I want to thank Katie Gallof, Erin Duffy, and Susan Krogulski for understanding and assiduity throughout.

As it happens, the conceptual narrative of collapse and reconsolidation that I trace in the book mirrored all too closely my own career path during its composition. It didn't have to work out that way—I am certainly not too big to fail—and I am beyond lucky that things resolved as they did. Moreover, I am beyond lucky that my family has been willing to suffer through the grinding crisis of this book's production. They deserved much better, as almost everyone does, and I am grateful to them for sticking it out. For them, publication is no real compensation; any reparations will have to be paid outside these pages.

Introduction:

The equation of pictures

The equation

Money is Hollywood's great theme—but money laundered into something else, something more. Money can be given a particular occasion and career, as box office receipts, casino winnings, tax credits, salaries, lotteries, inheritances. Or money can become number, and numbers can be anything: carbon footprints, pixels, votes, likes. Within money, Hollywood finds potential stories, and they are fungible. Within money, Hollywood finds an escape from stories, into a realm less bound by material objects. This zone where numerical intensity overlaps with questions of storytelling is Hollywood math. Yet Hollywood math is always in crisis, beset by innovations in financing and distribution, transformations in the mediascape, and, ultimately, upheavals in the economy and ecology of the world. The industry maintains its preeminence by turning those crises into stories—in advance or after the fact—and turning those story-solutions into possible models for future work. Every film is greenlit knowing that it will be released into a world that does not yet exist; every movie is a bet that the world in which it appears will be a world that wants it. This is Hollywood aftermath. Math and aftermath transpire within a zone, an open arena for work, a place where there seems to be both freedom and boundedness, a place where problems can appear and solutions, however innovative, seem to emerge from the same set of considerations, now reconfigured and reconsidered.[1]

The passage from the seeming bedrock of the cash nexus to the lofty abstractions of number-as-such is complex. One of Hollywood's long-standing myths about itself is that despite the complexity of the system, somewhere, someone knows how it actually works. The most famous statement of this principle of occult knowledge is F. Scott Fitzgerald's encomium to Monroe Stahr in (*The Love of*) *The Last Tycoon*, that Stahr was one of "not half a dozen men" who "have been able to keep the whole equation of pictures in their heads." Stahr, and the supervising producers he exemplifies, become admirable metonyms for the industry as a whole, metonyms to which cinema studies recurs. Mark Lynn Anderson has recently chided Thomas Schatz for, in essence, believing the myth, "recapitulat[ing] the equation of the studio executive's intellection with the mystified value of the production system."[2] By "whole equation," Fitzgerald and Schatz, like David Thomson, have meant the process in toto.[3] The mastery is mastery of the whole. It is not that this handful of executives chooses the best pictures or tells the best stories or makes the most money. It is that they get it—all of it. For Anderson, though, Fitzgerald's equation is quickly joined by another—the equation of intellection with "mystified value." This second equation is even more occult than the first, a secret within a complexity, and the only proper response to it is to cast aside the myth and return to the production process itself, something complex enough.

But if we retain the mythic dimension of Hollywood strategy alongside a focus on the production process, the complexity doesn't compound. Instead, the compounding simplifies things by giving us a sense of how it is that knowledge is put into practice, how it comes to ground. Knowledge here is no single thing—it ranges from formal economic training and modeling to accounting standards to business intelligence to rules of thumb and hunches. Those levels of formality collide and cohere and find themselves given practical valence in all sort of ways that themselves collide and cohere. To get at the ways knowledge and practice interact through various movie projects, I want to read slightly against the grain of Fitzgerald's aphorism. What makes Stahr and his fellow moguls the geniuses of the system is *not* their ability to understand the system in all its details, but rather their ability to retain a comprehensive *model* of that system, a model that even in the 1930s is somehow both mathematical and imagistic: an equation of pictures—a formula for making, an equation between, an equation composed of pictures.

In practice, that equation requires choices, and the process of making choices—that is, strategy—depends on an equation between at least two possibilities. John O. Thompson suggested a linguistic analogy for this equation in his foundational essays on the "commutation test" and Hollywood acting. Just as one might imagine substituting one word for another in order to capture subtle differences in meaning, so he suggested imaginatively substituting one star for another—Ava Gardner for Grace Kelly—or even one performance element—their smiles—to reveal the same thing. A star might read as more or less American, more or less mobile, more or less natural, and so on, and those differences would change the meaning of the film. Thompson's work was dedicated to the isolation of such meanings, but late in the essay, he turned to the ways in which those meanings took on practical bearings in "the history of casting" and "actual casting practice."[4] The commutation test, then, is not simply an instance of how criticism might make use of such strategic considerations, but a way in which the consideration of meaning might lead criticism back toward the practice of strategy. As Thompson's work implies, by expanding the realm of strategic or quasi-strategic choice, new practices become important alongside the producer's labor: not only casting but the crafts of screenwriting and production design and sound design, the intertextual management of a star's career, and the design and execution of slate-driven strategies within a particular funder. Choices add up to become data, and the practice of strategy shifts.

The model

In Thompson's delimited realms of commutation, it would still be possible to keep track of all the choices that go into a project. Economist Arthur De Vany suggests that even if players in the system *do* behave this way, they should not; attention to individual stories or individual choices is a fundamental distraction from the actual economics of the project. On his account, the ultimate fate of any film is unknowable—unknowable at conception, unknowable in production, unknowable until release—because all the things that supposedly predict results or mitigate risk do not. The box office tournament is fundamentally chaotic and unpredictable. In contrast, "The choices inside the studio tend to be driven by playing out alternative movies as scenarios. This is story-telling, not good decision logic, and it is prone to errors of all sorts."[5] I've argued against that claim in my previous book, *The Studios after the Studios*, but here, rather than argue against it, I want to ask why people in Hollywood would believe De Vany's argument and what would happen if you tried to put it into action.

The companies that have come closest to putting De Vany's guidance into operation have been hedge fund–style slate underwriters such as Thomas Tull's Legendary Pictures and Relativity Media. I discuss Tull's complicated relationships with Warner Bros. and with China in Chapter 7; here I concentrate on Relativity Media. Hollywood studios have a long-standing—and in many cases deserved—reputation for taking advantage of their funding partners through creative accounting or restricting them to less favorable projects. The problem is a version of the more general "principal/agent" dilemma where asymmetric information allows the agent to make decisions that serve its interests rather than those of the principal. As economist Kay H. Hofmann has demonstrated, the slate funding system does in general work to the detriment of slate funders.[6] In order to overcome that problem, the funding principals need to balance out the information asymmetry at its heart. The usual route is to become knowledgeable enough about the moviemaking process to be able to enter independent production. But Relativity pursued a different route. The funder began as an almost pure example of De Vanian indifference to stories. It used a much-touted, proprietary form of Monte Carlo analysis to choose particular projects to co-finance, usually with Columbia and Universal. Those projects were chosen not because of any belief in their merit or quality, or because of any supposition about the desires of the audience, but (ostensibly) because the martingale suggested a high likelihood of success *regardless of the causal relations among the variables it tracked*. The slate Relativity was underwriting, then, was a subset of Hollywood's overall production and (ideally) not the result of a particular corporation's decisions. At the same time, the formula would be constantly updated with ever more variables and ever more complex simulations. Here, the principal had information about its agent's projects that the agent itself lacked. It sounded like a radical innovation, and while Relativity might have been greeted as just another sucker on the verge of getting fleeced by Hollywood insiders, it was not. Instead, in keeping with the widespread cultural overestimation of financial prowess, coverage was credulous, as in this piece from *Esquire*'s Chris Jones:

> "What I first see is a bunch of numbers," says Ramon Wilson, Relativity's thirty-year-old executive vice-president of business development. A former investment banker, Wilson leads a team of young-turk statisticians—Hollywood's equivalent of Moneyballers—who occupy a cramped, windowless back room littered with empty cans of Diet Coke. . . . Before Relativity commits to financing a particular movie—either through its slate deals with Sony and Universal or on its own—it's fed into an elaborate Monte Carlo simulation, a risk-assessment algorithm normally used to evaluate financial instruments based on the past performance of similar products. Enough variables are included in the Monte Carlo for Wilson and his team to have reached the limits of their Excel's sixty-five thousand rows of data: principal actor, director, genre, budget, release date, rating, and so on. After running the movie through ten thousand combinations of variables (in marathon overnight sessions), the computers will churn out a few hundred pages that culminate in two critical numbers: the percentage of time the movie will be profitable, and the average profit for each profitable run. The computers will also calculate the best weekend for the movie to be released, whether Russell Crowe will earn his salary or Sam Worthington will be good enough, and the box-office effect of an R rating versus PG-13. But for Kavanaugh, those are secondary considerations: Unless the movie shows the distinct probability of a return—no one at Relativity will reveal the precise green-light figure, but it's something like 70 percent—the script gets shredded. "Everything has to run on the principle of profit," Kavanaugh says. "We'll never let creative decisions rule our business decisions. If it doesn't fit the model, it doesn't get done."[7]

As these things happen, a combination of ego and failure forced Relativity to abandon its strategy of piggybacking on supposedly sure things. Its principal backer, Elliott Management, took control of the co-financing deal and Relativity responded by expanding, first into production, then in 2010 by purchasing Starz's Overture films distribution arm and becoming a proper "minimajor" studio. (It became its own agent in the principal agent problem.) Despite obvious signals that its films were not profitable, Relativity continued to push into new arenas and was regularly able to draw on new sources of capital. As it moved away from simply putting its money where its model told it to, the company began to engage in something precariously close to "scenario thinking" with *Limitless* (Neil Burger, Relativity, 2011). Still, Relativity's higher overhead became unsustainable and it was forced into bankruptcy in 2015. Kavanaugh and Wilson managed to bring the company out of Chapter 11, but it was broken up and sold for parts shortly thereafter. In its last throes, the movie arm, Relativity Studios, left "the model" behind. The studio was to be led by Dana Brunetti and Kevin Spacey and decidedly executive-driven.[8]

This is a great story of hubris, and was reported with great glee. *New York* magazine's Vulture.com ran a postmortem headlined, "The epic fail of Hollywood's hottest algorithm"; *Variety* commissioned a cover by Sam Spratt of a crumbling marble bust of Kavanaugh headed "Relativity in ruins."[9] But however familiar the ending of the corporate story, there was within it a crucial change: with the digital turn in strategy, the equation of pictures was no longer kept in a single person's head. Instead, strategists made a show of binding themselves, Odysseus-like, to "the model" and avoiding the siren song of "relationships." This antisentimental spectacle was tailored for the bro-culture of quasi-athletes and traders, but, as I will describe in the next chapter, it was not *quite* their exclusive purview.

The method

Despite De Vany's warnings, then, even the most numerically driven, model-bound versions of Hollywood may founder on the rocks of story. Numbers are nested in cultures.[10] And in Hollywood every story about their occult power—*The Number 23, A Beautiful Mind, Numb3rs*—speaks to ruthless financial pressure or risk-averse decision-making. Woody Allen famously noted that if show business weren't a business, it would be called show show. But the corollary also holds: If it didn't depend deeply on the aesthetic artifacts it produces, it would be called business business. In this sense numbers are never enough. To avoid becoming simply business business, something has to happen to turn the numbers into stories. Elevated into a cultural theory, though, and this argument runs the risk of banality: Hollywood thinks about capitalism by telling stories about money.

Seen this way, then, the "argument" of this book is both banal and right up-front. The version in the next chapter is, admittedly, slightly more complex:

While the industry conceives of its relation to the economy in many ways, at different levels of practice and abstraction, there is a condensed image of that thinking that has become essential to Hollywood production and has remained so. I call that image, after Gilles Deleuze, an economic image, and I explain how it emerges from a particularly fraught passage in the second volume of his study of cinema. The rest of the chapters would then simply be essays in the application of that idea, attempts to find yet further instances of an economic image, in other decades or genres or media. By these lights, there is no particular reason for the book to detail the cases it does since, if the claim is valid, the supporting cases should be fungible. Given that contingency, reading this book can simply become a matter of sufficiency: How much persuading is sufficient? Or, to put it more negatively, *we get it*.

Seen another way, though, the project is properly historical, and the chapters are necessary to a story of consolidation, collapse, and recovery. That history unfolds in two dimensions: chronologically and topically. Chronologically, it moves from the accretion of representational authority in the form of the reinvigorated studio in the 1970s (here, Warner Bros.) through the Great Recession and its aftermath. Topically, it includes studies of several studios and their funding regimes; of themes and genres; of adaptations and industrial rhetoric. That diversity of topics can give the work its essayistic feel, can make it seem that there is no systematic project on offer.

What makes it harder to see evolving logic of the project is that the subject of this history is not a typical category (like a studio, theme, genre, etc.) or even a broad field (Hollywood economics) but Hollywood's capacity for abstraction in the face of material constraints. That may itself sound abstract, and at times it is. But more often it is a matter of trying to determine just how to measure or come to terms with or judge what we are already familiar with (Hollywood). Think of a road. How fast can traffic safely drive on it? Ordinarily, we take our cue from a speed limit sign, and that limit has been set by the interaction of features of the landscape with technical factors (engineering conventions) and social and political principles (a statutory limit for highway travel, relative traffic density, the desires of residents of the surrounding neighborhood, and many others). Now imagine we did not have the speed limit sign. We might determine the road's capacity by observing those same phenomena and drawing conclusions: we would watch traffic, survey the area, get a sense of the landscape and the climate, examine the surface of the road, pay attention to accidents and close calls, and so on. To determine Hollywood's capacity for abstraction we would observe the constitutive interactions of the industry in operation and go searching for its constraints. Along the way, we would adduce its conventions and principles.[11]

What sort of principles or conventions are those? In this book, I try to work in three directions, to find strategic principles and formal conventions that are responsive to three subdisciplines: media industry economics, media industries studies, and what is usually called film-philosophy. Those three approaches do not sit easily together. Their relationships to reading diverge: the first tends to be inimical to readings of individual movies or series, the second less interested in readings than in ethnography, and the last largely at ease with the long-standing traditions of close reading. Correlatively, they are interested in different forms of generality: The first grapples almost exclusively with large numbers of cases, searching for systemic patterns; the second is open to studies of large patterns of, say, craft labor, but comfortable with case studies of a franchise or a television series that capture a general form of interaction; the last aspires to the generality of concepts rather than the generality of the survey.

In this project, I hope to reach that final sort of generality by casting individual readings of motion pictures against the most conceptual aspects of their production. That is, by examining how these stories emerge in light of their economic and strategic and labor contexts. It may be merely a matter of personal preference that the concepts I begin from are frequently derived from philosophy, as in the discussion in Chapter 2 of the fixation of corporate belief at Warner Bros. But in that case, I am tracing how philosophy becomes finance. In Chapter 6, the reverse is the case. Beginning from Myron Scholes's account of stock pricing, I investigate how that might be deployed for art. Finally, in Chapter 8, the priority is re-reversed as I interrogate a problem of ostensive definition from Wittgenstein in light of cinematic and painterly versions of the same: "This poor schmuck"; "This painting."

This project would not be possible without the substantial work done by all three of those disciplines. The next chapter is a prime example. As I attempt to delineate the economic image, I draw on the work of Jonathan Beller and David Rodowick, both of whom have found fruitful ways of putting Deleuze to work to explain aspects of the contemporary system of cinematic images. Less present there, but just as fruitful, have been studies of the digital aesthetics by Sean Cubitt and the interplay of image and affect by Eugenie Brinkema.[12] Both are superb readers of cases; both have generated conceptual architectures that can seem, in retrospect, inevitable. Similarly, the discussion of *Moneyball* depends on the scholarly work on Hollywood's managerial accounting practices and their relationship to other forms of economic thinking that businesses engage in. The foundational work of Michael Pokorny and John Sedgwick, De Vany, S. Abraham Ravid, and others has examined cofinancing, screenplay sales, star power, ad content, and other aspects of distribution in order to determine, as Ravid puts in one article, "Are they all crazy or just risk averse?"[13] Beyond this is Harold L. Vogel's still-standard guide to the industry's economics and Charles C. Moul's edited volume that surveys its various aspects.[14] Pokorny and Sedgwick in particular have demonstrated that despite the industry's general unwillingness to disclose crucial financial data, with sufficient attention to archives or other datasets, it is possible to mount rigorous economic studies of critical features of the industry's history. The final strand, media industries studies, appears in that case study in the analysis of the industrial discourse surrounding the upheavals in the project when director Steven Soderbergh was fired at the last minute. That approach is perhaps most similar to Derek Johnson's work on Marvel. Other avenues into the study of media industries are more indebted to traditions of political economy (Janet Wasko, Douglas Kellner), or to studies ranging from state and interstate regulation and cultural policy to more local investigations of reception.[15]

What holds that case (and the dozen or so that follow it) together, ultimately, is not a heretofore undetected rapport between wildly varying strands of cinema studies. Each would likely find it lacking or worse—a quadruple mystification. First, for economists it mystifies by overemphasizing the particular case at the expense of the economics of dozens of comparable movies made by Sony and its competitors. Second, for media industries scholars it is overly attentive to studio executives' (and stars') intellection at the expense of either the work of everyone else (a fetish for capitalists rather than laborers) or the power of the system outside the choices and controls of any of its participants (as Anderson chided Schatz). Third, for a broad swath of scholarship that regards meaning as the collaborative product of interpretive communities it mystifies by focusing on a (private) reading of the project rather than on its actual readers (its audiences), whether those be participants in the industry or more broadly. And finally, for film-philosophers it mystifies by ventriloquizing its concepts through players and not taking ownership of them.

Instead, what holds these cases together is the claim that the links between these disparate strands of cinema studies lie, first and foremost, in the cases themselves—that movies and television series are the occasions for and the results of the interactions among such levels of attention and such forces of meaning-making. More particularly, I am claiming that one of Hollywood's signal strengths—its literalism, its commitment to making things stand for themselves—is the communicating channel between the material and the abstract; the pragmatic and the conceptual. Hollywood thinks through agency and authenticity by telling stories about mergers and counterfeiting (*Performance* and *The In-Laws* in Chapter 2); it thinks through duration and futures markets by telling stories about playing hooky and time-travel (*Ferris Bueller* and *Déjà Vu* in Chapters 3 and 4); it thinks through populations and audiences by telling stories about airplane passengers and casualty rates (*Lost* and *Contagion* in Chapters 6 and 7).

Chapter by chapter, my approach will be familiar: I have chosen what I take to be illustrative cases and attempted to unfurl them. The presumptions here are that Hollywood movies—at least *some* Hollywood movies—narrate their way through conceptual or theoretical or economic difficulties with far more precision than they are given credit for, and that it requires patient explication to reveal that precision. Within that general approach, though, there is something more methodological. By saying these movies narrate their way through difficulties, I mean something more intentional than they *embody* or *register* or *display* those difficulties. Such symptomatic readings usually fail to raise the question of how much credit the movies and their creators deserve and instead quickly substitute a far more totalizing and unintended account of cultural significance. Approaches such as systems theory, political economy, and even psychoanalysis make whatever analytic headway they make by intentionally evacuating central social institutions and practices. Those analytic reductions do not seem accidental but rather essential to the enterprise. By restoring those categories, I make the case for a more embedded account of cultural production. So in *The Studios after the Studios* the evacuated institution was the studio itself—often understood as the mere corporate epiphenomenon of the system in general, as a stand-in for capital, or, when taken semi-seriously, as the projection of the personality of its mogul, and only rarely as a social form. Here, the evacuated category is abstract reflection. Where we find relatively durable institutions, there it becomes possible to imagine a politics of participation that is not entirely conflictual, not entirely a matter of false consciousness, not entirely without the chance to petition for a redress of grievances. And even when the lived experience of such participation is at its worst, when the world of work becomes a pit of conflict, delusion, and alienation, it is still possible to imagine that relatively abstract reflections on that situation are meaningful, and, perhaps, utopian.

The impetus to reground critical theories within the institutions they describe has diverse origins spanning from Karl Polanyi's initial work on embedded institutions to Harold Garfinkel's ethnomethodology to John Thornton Caldwell's delineations of "production culture." Within film studies, the de-scaling of "film theory" looks like a hard-won victory over academic abstractions, the answer to long-standing calls for a sociological turn.[16] "In this pragmatic process-driven inductive approach to theorizing film form and effect, practitioners enact a kind of theory that scholars like David Bordwell and Noel Carroll have called for—namely, 'middle-level theorizing' that is workmanlike, specific, delimited, and local."[17] That contextualized thinking is to the good, and it helps explain why an idea in a movie might also be an idea about working in the movies. But there is no reason to limit the effective scope of those theories in advance. Long traditions of industrial self-reflection, combined with the inherent need of Hollywood movies to be *about* things help push movie-thinking beyond its occasions. It counts as criticism to determine where that thinking began; but neither criticism nor thinking stops there.

The culture

Nor should it. The equation of pictures is more than simply a model of Hollywood and its own self-understandings. Figuring out Hollywood amounts to figuring out culture as a whole—not because culture begins and ends with Hollywood, but because the *whole* of the equation of pictures prompts us to investigate both culture's capacities and its limits. As products made for large and diverse global audiences who have access to fitfully public production histories and financial details, movies endlessly raise questions of cultural participation and value: Were the time and money spent worth it (for me, for its makers)? Is the system supportable? Are there alternatives within it (for me, for us)? While in principle, anything from an investment bank to a school curriculum to the cut of a pant leg might exemplify advanced capitalist culture, with a movie, that exemplification becomes explicit. Of course, that explicitness is fugitive, now appearing in the narrative, now in the discursive and institutional surround, but wherever it comes to the fore, it is both marked as cultural and commoditized.

Surely part of the reason Fitzgerald wrote as much as he did about Hollywood was his sense that it constituted the center of gravity for cultural production as such.[18] By the twenty-first century, though, cultural production seems decentered. Yet Hollywood retains its capacity to map cultural production both because it offers itself as a paradigm of universally accessible narration and because it remains industrially expansive. When it comes to Hollywood, we know, or could quickly find out, more about the interface of these movies with their financial contexts. In many other hierarchical industries of cultural production—design, fashion, publishing—financial contexts are not part of their ordinary consumption. There are exceptions. Architecture, professional sports, and the art market increasingly solicit intense audience interest in their economics. In contrast, among the newly disintermediated cultural products of the internet, there are indeed vast metrics—view counts, vine loops, numbers of followers—but the network-inflected discourses of virality and reality (however qualified) have not yet not fully supplanted older models of cultural production that required greater objectification or aesthetic distance.

The sense that Hollywood no longer stands in for culture-making, or that it soon will cede that primacy to individuals, disrupters, startup culture, or unforeseen new media casts the industry as the old-fashioned player in the mediascape. While Hollywood labor seems to be an early avatar of the "gig economy," where employment shifted from long-term contracts to run-of-show or less, it is also exceptional and atavistic in the continuing importance of unions to the industry. (Here, again, professional sports are similar.) But if we regard this long-standing feature of the industry as merely residual, we underestimate the importance of metonymic participation within a culture that combines political liberalism with advanced capitalism. If the operations of the state or the social class are too distant or too diffuse to comprehend, participation within a studio, or a guild, or an audience brings that metonymy closer. As I argued in *The Studios after the Studios*, under certain conditions, the studio itself constitutes the privileged zone of contact between individuals and the industry. It is both a social form and a target for thinking about the practices of moviemaking. There are other such zones. The individual production can sometimes suffice even without aspiring to industry-defining status; the guilds connect (or connect by excluding) workers by craft; suprastudio trade groups such as the Motion Picture Association of America and the Academy of Motion Picture Arts and Sciences theorize about the meaning of the movies in public. These publics or quasi-publics open up those questions of individual participation in cultural collectivities I raised above.

The halves

Economic images permeate this book, but the book itself is divided into two large sections, Precession and Recession. The first covers a period when the Hollywood system was dominated by the sort of problem→solution thinking that could take place within the zone of math and aftermath. New solutions are precessive: they emerge as causally or logically prior to the usual operations of the industry.[19] In the face of a newly-assertive talent agency oligopoly, for example, studios might shift to a mode of storytelling that would be relatively immune to the lures of stardom—high concept. As I will show with regard to *Titanic*, its allegorical attention to the system as it existed in the 1990s was underpinned by a stable economy of economies— of risk, responsibility, and attention—itself underpinned by a broadly financialized capitalism and given a particular piquancy by Hollywood's own semi-autonomous traditions of financing. When that meta-relation destabilized—when the risks were no longer individual but systemic, when responsibility for that system could no longer be meaningfully anchored internally in individual or even collective agency, and when the moral emplacement of Hollywood's own finances within the more broadly financialized economy required attention of its own—the usual rebalancing efforts and the industry's precessive competence yielded to a sense of incalculability. The zone of math and aftermath itself seemed to slip away.

There are fewer economic images in the second half of the book, and so it might seem that the argument is falling apart. But if I am right, what has fallen apart is the stable relationship between small solutions to the representational problem—the economic image—and the supervening tiers of production consciousness—the production as a whole, the slate, the studio's position within the conglomerate, the industrialized production of culture. Which is to say that the economic image is not simply a thing that appears willy-nilly but is evidence of the current state of the order of composition—its coherence, expansiveness, dominance, and pliability.

By digital recession, then, I mean to do more than describe the period or to qualify this particular economic crisis by its relation to a general technoscape—to the digital turns in production (cinematography), distribution (HDTV), exhibition (streaming), or strategy (the Moneyball Initiative). I want to convey a more general sense that the historical pivot from precession to recession was grounded in the conviction that something like the temporary withdrawal or decomposition of the familiar world had taken hold. The allegorical engine of neoclassical Hollywood sputtered. In response to that sense the industry scrambled to gather the world nearer or to piece it together. That piecing together did not seriously attempt to undo the digital turns; instead, it presumed that such decomposition was a necessary precursor to its reassemblage. Pixellation preceded reembodiment. Only a new kind of insistence might rebalance this meta-economy. In *The Big Short*, this looks like scolding; in Chapter 8, it looks like pointing.

In order to keep the book to reasonable length, I have left it to the reader to decide whether to (re)watch the central films in each chapter or simply read the exceptionally useful plot summaries at the American Film Insititute catalog (catalog.afi.com). I do, though, strive to provide very precise descriptions of those narrative moments that might otherwise be missed in the happy unrolling of generic beats. Something similar holds for the studio and corporate histories at play, although I usually provide both an outline of the major corporate events and a more detailed account of the executive machinations when those are relevant.

I have discussed the first chapter above, as an example of the sorts of methodological crossings at work throughout. Beyond that, individual chapters can be read separately and worked through in relation to their central cases. In contrast, the introductions to the two larger sections—on *Titanic* and *Where the Wild Things Are*—are more speculative. While still grounded in particular cases, they are structured less as arguments than as diagrams of the conceptual leaps that are made stepwise in the meatier chapters. In discussing *Titanic*, the key piece of evidence is a behind-the-scenes moment when Cameron is making a cut, that most ordinary of post-production tasks, but the questions are much larger—how art and industry are balanced and who balances them. In discussing *Where the Wild Things Are*, the key evidence is the teaser trailer but the question is how we ought to understand the synchronization of cultural products with political and economic contexts in light of their overarching media environment. That context is the onset of the Obama administration, the solidification of the opposition to his signature legislative efforts, and two rather typical photo opportunities.

In Chapter 2, I look at Warner Bros. in the 1970s, when the studio was most intensively reimagining its place within the changed macroeconomy of the Nixon and Carter years. There are four crucial examples—*Performance, The Exorcist, All the President's Men,* and *The In-Laws*—and each revolves around a particular economic phenomenon—extortion, leasing, forensic accounting, and counterfeiting. In Chapter 3, I attempt to determine what the culture of the Chicago School of Economics might look like. The Tax Reform Act of 1986 was the landmark legislative achievement of Ronald Reagan's second term and the last time the U.S. government attempted to tax capital at the same rate as labor. Unsexy as the subject might be, tax fairness and Chicago-style free markets became the subject of two widely popular films, *Ferris Bueller's Day Off* and *The Untouchables.* In the final chapter of the section on precession, I investigate the system of tax credit–based financing that came to dominate movie production in the new millennium. Credits—refunds that increase based on expenditures—appear on screen as second chances and time loops in films such as *Déjà Vu* and *Source Code.* Time travel films amount to a particular approach to financial recovery, and Hollywood's mastery of that approach suggests that the industry was operating on a post-crisis footing even before the financial meltdown.

The second half begins with the reading of the beginning of the Obama era. From Obama, I turn to the indie collapse of 2008 in order to look at the ways the major studios assimilated the "indie" spirit to such blockbusters as *WALL•E* and *Incredible Hulk.* They share an obsession with libraries—a "bibliotechnological" imaginary—that seemed to offer a way out of the crisis by turning movies into stories of value. While much has been made of the digital convergence of different media into a new, multiscreen, TV-centered ecology, the actual political management of that process—the boring and botched rollout of HDTV in the United States—has not inspired much criticism. In Chapter 6, I aim to correct that through a case study of J.J. Abrams's work on *Lost.* The landmark ABC series turns on questions of resolution, analogy, and digitization, making sense of the "digital turn" across different media. In Chapter 7, I look at the strange relationship between materiality and belief in three films: *Contagion, Pacific Rim,* and *Upstream Color.* If the culture of the Great Recession began by exploring financial panic and foreclosure, years of stalled recovery and grinding austerity left Hollywood even less certain. The question these movies ask is: How is any society possible at all? The final chapter turns to narrower questions: the elusiveness of justice and the place of number in the configuration of social desert. As usual, the occasion for that abstract interest is a specific case; here, a literal case, *The United States of America v. The Wolf of Wall Street.* With such literalism it may be that math and aftermath have returned. Finally, in the conclusion I tally the possible conceptual yield of the project.

Notes

1 It is worth noting at the start that while I am interested in math as a theme, I am not interested in mathematics-as-a-discipline as a theme or the use of movies to teach math. For those, see Jessica K. Sklar and Elizabeth S. Sklar, eds., *Mathematics in Popular Culture: Essays on Appearances in Film, Fiction, Games, Television and Other Media* (Jefferson, NC: McFarland, 2012); Burkard Polster and Marty Ross, *Math Goes to the Movies* (Baltimore: Johns Hopkins, 2012); and the lively Simon Singh, *The Simpsons and their Mathematical Secrets* (London: Bloomsbury, 2013).

2 Marc Lynn Anderson, "The Silent Screen, 1895–1927," in *Producing*, ed. Jon Lewis (New Brunswick, NJ: Rutgers University Press, 2016), 15–35, 35.

3 David Thomson, *The Whole Equation* (New York: Knopf, 2004).

4 John O. Thompson, "Screen Acting and the Commutation Test," in *Stardom: Industry of Desire*, ed. Christine Gledhill (New York: Routledge, 1991), 186–200, 197.

5 Arthur De Vany, *Hollywood Economics: How Extreme Uncertainty Shapes the Film Industry* (New York: Routledge, 2003), 269. In addition to the behavioral objections I discuss below, see John Sedgwick's review which indicates three further grounds for critique: The persistent stability of the movie production oligopoly despite the underlying chaos; the lack of attention to downstream markets, particularly television; and the interindustry corporate relations that make the study of motion pictures less unique than it might once have been, John Sedgwick, *Economic Record*, 81 no. 255 (December 2005): 446–48.

6 Kay H. Hofmann, *Co-Financing Hollywood Film Productions with Outside Investors: An Economic Analysis of Principal Agent Relationships in the U.S. Motion Picture Industry* (Wiesbaden: Springer Gabler, 2013).

7 Chris Jones, "Ryan Kavanaugh uses Math to Make Movies," *Esquire*, November 2009, http://www.esquire.com/news-politics/a6641/ryan-kavanaugh-1209/.

8 Relativity's emergence as a stand-alone studio after bankruptcy was only temporary. Initially, Singaporean media company YuuZoo would have taken a controlling interest, but that deal foundered. Shiwen Yap, "Singapore: YuuZoo calls off $150m investment in U.S.-based Relativity Media," *Deal Street Asia*, March 1, 2017, https://www.dealstreetasia.com/stories/66289-66289/. Ryan Faughnder, "Relativity Media Struggles to Come Back from Bankruptcy," *Los Angeles Times*, November 4, 2016, http://www.latimes.com/business/hollywood/la-fi-ct-relativity-bankruptcy-20161102-story.html. The television division became Critical Content, Joshua Rich, "Relativity Television rebrands as Critical Content, post-bankruptcy," *The Wrap*, January 26, 2016, https://www.thewrap.com/relativity-television-rebrands-as-critical-content-post-bankruptcy/.

9 Alas, neither outlet would grant permission to reproduce their crucial images. See Benjamin Wallace, "The Epic Fail of Hollywood's Hottest Algorithm," *Vulture*, January 2016, http://www.vulture.com/2016/01/relativity-media-ryan-kavanaugh-c-v-r.html; James Rainey and Brent Lang, "Relativity in

ruins: Is it too late for Ryan Kavanaugh to save his studio?" *Variety*, July 28, 2015, http://variety.com/2015/film/news/relativity-financial-troubles-ryan-kavanaugh-1201549697/.

10 Not simply in Hollywood. For a look at the comparable operation of number in Indian cinema, see Nitin Govil, "Size Matters," *BioScope: South Asian Screen Studies* 1, no. 2 (2010): 105–09 and the follow-up, "Recognizing 'Industry,'" *Cinema Journal* 52, no. 3 (2013): 172–76.

11 This inductive model is a revamped version of the railroad-network mapping problem laid out in George Kubler's *The Shape of Time* and ported into film studies in the opening pages of David Bordwell, Janet Staiger, and Kristin Thompson's *The Classical Hollywood Cinema*. I discuss the limits of their reading in *The Studios* 326–27, note 17.

12 Sean Cubitt, *Digital Aesthetics* (Thousand Oaks, CA: SAGE, 1998); Eugenie Brinkema, *The Forms of the Affects* (Durham, NC: Duke University Press, 2014).

13 John Sedgwick and Michael Pokorny, *An Economic History of Film* (New York: Routledge, 2004); S. Abraham Ravid, "Are they all Crazy or just Risk Averse?: Some Movie Puzzles and Possible Solutions," *Contributions to Economic Analysis* 260 (2003), 33–47. That special issue of *CEA*, edited by Victor Ginsburgh, contains essential contributions.

14 Harold L. Vogel, *Entertainment Industry Economics: A Guide for Financial Analysis*, 8th ed. (Cambridge: Cambridge University Press, 2011); Charles C. Moul, *A Short Handbook of Movie Industry Economics* (Cambridge: Cambridge University Press, 2005).

15 Central anthologies include Jennifer Holt and Alisa Perren, *Media Industries* (Malden, MA: Blackwell, 2009); Vicki Mayer, Miranda J. Banks, and John Thornton Caldwell, *Production Studies* (New York: Routledge, 2009); and Timothy Havens and Amanda Lotz, *Understanding Media Industries*, 2nd ed. (Oxford: Oxford University Press, 2016).

16 Dudley Andrew, "Adaptation," in *Concepts in Film Theory* (Oxford: Oxford University Press, 1984), 96–106.

17 John Thornton Caldwell, *Production Culture* (Durham, NC: Duke University Press, 2008), 25.

18 Jordan Brower, "'Written with the Movies in Mind': Twentieth-century American Literature and Transmedial Possibility," *MLQ* 78, no. 2 (2017), 243–73.

19 Bill Grantham discusses the obverse of this process in his overview of Hollywood finance history. He shows "how models of film financing have evolved . . . adapted and fluctuated as parties have alternatively accepted risk or declined to do so, and have sought to shift risk to other participants in the financial chain," "Motion Picture Finance and Risk in the United States," in *Film and Risk*, ed. Mette Hjort (Detroit: Wayne State, 2012), 197–208, 197–98.

1

The economic image: Hollywood dataculture and the moneyball of *Moneyball*

The economic image

What makes the equation of pictures possible? Ordinarily, the question has a practical bearing, and the answer is money, a universal solvent of differences, differences that might reemerge as questions of labor, time, ideas, and so on. But when the answer to that question is number as such, the grand old debates of the philosophy of mathematics rush in. What makes equation *as such* possible?

For Hollywood, even asking the question invites suspicion. The turn away from practicality toward a pure abstraction or a pure materiality leads toward madness or conspiracy, and madness and conspiracy are the signs of money's pervasive influence. Surprisingly, perhaps, Gilles Deleuze makes a similar point in *Cinema 2: The Time-Image*:

> The cinema as art itself lives in a direct relation with a permanent plot [*complot*], an international conspiracy which conditions it from within, as the most intimate and most indispensable enemy. This conspiracy is that of money; what defines industrial art is not mechanical reproduction but the internalized relation with money. . . . Money is the obverse of all the images that the cinema shows and sets in place, so that films about money are already, if implicitly, films within the film or about the film.[1]

The eruption of economic critique where we would expect an argument about medium specificity is striking. In the midst of his taxonomy of images—a taxonomy that leans heavily on the semiotics of Charles Sanders Peirce and the philosophy of Henri Bergson—production context surprisingly returns.

In the opening sentence of the cinema books, Deleuze had apparently cast aside history—"This study is not a history of cinema." But just as quickly he reinstated the sorts of contingency and consistency out of which a cinema history might be made. Directors—and Deleuze's cinema remains crucially a directors' art—are artists but also thinkers. If they produce "rubbish" that is merely because they are "more vulnerable—it is infinitely easier to prevent them from doing their work" than other thinkers. Those concessions to the constraints of industrial artistry quickly take a back seat to the ramifying taxonomy. At the highest level, there are the movement-image, typical of classical Hollywood, and the time-image, typical of the global art cinemas of the postwar period. But there are also forerunners, subtypes, and complexes; perception-images (POV shots are examples), affection-images (think of a Dietrich closeup), action-images (a stagecoach in a landscape). Now, midway through the second volume, when the grand transition from movement-image to time-image is underway, the directors' vulnerabilities return and are grounded in the limitations of money. It feels as though an earlier Deleuze, the writer of *Anti-Oedipus*, has suddenly taken over, and has knocked the argument and the type sideways. And so he will say, all in italics, *"the cinema confronts its most internal presupposition, money, and the movement-image makes way for the time-image in one and the same operation."*[2] Once it has been knocked off-kilter in this confrontation, film "endlessly relaunches" a "dissymmetrical" exchange: "The film is movement, but the film within the film is money, is time."[3]

To be sure, Deleuze's turn to economy is not as specific as Thompson's turn to the ideology of casting, and it will take some patience to understand what importance it might hold for a study of contemporary Hollywood. Here, Deleuze invokes the basic Marxist equation, the "tricked, dissymmetrical exchange" of Money for Commodity for Money (M-C-M) as the ground or the analogue or both for the dissymmetrical exchange of the time-image. The principal alternative, again, is the movement-image, one built on equivalence, or, as Deleuze puts it here, C-M-C. But if the time-image is the dissymmetrical obverse of the symmetrical movement-image, it also seems to be the movement-image's successor in a history of cinema. The equivalence of the movement-image "makes way" for the dissymmetry of the time-image; Hollywood gives way to Europe (and Japan, and elsewhere). The passage from the one to the other—the crisis of the movement-image—gives rise to (or *seems* to give rise to) a self-reflexivity, of "films within the film." The crisis thus generates a kind of "special" image, a crystal-image, "giving image for money, giving time for images, converting time, the transparent side, and money, the opaque side, like a spinning top on its end."[4]

Anne Friedberg describes this chapter as the "most promising and yet undeveloped section of the book."[5] Few critics have taken up this passage, or even the formal-financial transition it implies. David Rodowick, in a characteristically incisive footnote, explains the importance of the dissymmetry between time and money that comes with the advent of the time-image. Gone is the parallel between the fungibility of images and commodities. In place of that parallel, there is now only a "struggle between the image and capital to see who will be exhausted first."[6] For Jonathan Beller, the parallel between images and capital continues to operate, only the time-image amounts to a new "representational paradigm," which accords with the shift "from monopoly to multinational capitalism."[7] For Beller, the changes in representational paradigm happen to cinema in general; there is no canon of films whose resistance to capitalist equivalence emerges from their access to direct images of time. In contrast, for Rodowick, time-images constitute a profound form of resistance to the economic order, even if the outcome of that struggle is up for grabs.

Rodowick and Beller, then, offer potentially incommensurable ways of understanding the critical transition in Deleuze's writing on cinema. Deleuze locates that transition after the Second World War, but there is simply no way for the uneven and at least apparently historical shift from the movement-image to the time-image to occur in the postwar period if the crucial event or aspect of that shift is a confrontation with financial scarcity. Such a confrontation was baked into the movement-image from the moment the patent trust was busted. Indeed, Deleuze's authority for the decisive effects of what we might call first-stage financialization on cinema is a lecture by Marcel L'Herbier delivered in 1926. Beller, then, takes Deleuze's point to be, implicitly, that the time-image marks the emergence of a new accord between cinema and the mode of production. What appear to be strategies of resistance through formal innovation are, instead, further elaborations of the "representational paradigms" belonging to monopoly (movement-image) and multinational (time-image) capitalism. Beller saves Deleuze's history by rejiggering his account of capital. For Rodowick, in contrast, the too-early arrival of the confrontation with money suggests the logical possibility of an earlier, *forced* disequivalence between time and money under the regime of the movement-image, emblematized not by a proto-time-image but by montage. Rodowick saves Deleuze's history by rejiggering his notion of form. Neither manages (or, really, attempts) to save Deleuze's account of the eruption of money as an event *within* the postwar history of film.

And what are we to do with Hollywood cinema in the wake of the transition to the time-image? Does it constitute a retrograde departure from the advanced cinema of the time-image, and can it amount to a historical deviation despite its overwhelming importance to the market and its global social reach? Perhaps the "operation" that both constitutes the confrontation with money and launches the time-image is something more like a material trope—a transition that happens within narrative and that is supported by a host of filmmaking practices that could be impinged upon by such a shift, but a transition that nevertheless retains the abstraction, formality, and iterability of a storytelling function.

If that is the case, it would explain why Deleuze's apparently historical argument gives way to his assertion of disequivalence between the motion of the film and the eruption within those films of time. In other words, this apparently historical transition may operate materially or formally, depending upon one's analysis of the relative predominance of industry or art within the contest for supremacy. When the confrontation with money occurs in the cinema that will be dominated by the time-image, that relationship is internalized in such a way that the results create the appearance of time liberated from the logic of equivalence and exchange, the logic of capital. Time is the transparent side; money, the opaque. In that case the Rodowickian struggle ensues. But for the cinema that remained within the movement-image—that is, for Hollywood—the challenge of money—that is, time—is one that is met through the assertion of symmetry. And for a cinema that confronts money within a realm of forced equivalence, money is no longer the opaque side of the crystal. Instead, the economic image replaces the crystal-image. Or, to put it in less grandiose terms, and to shift from criticism back to practice, if you make industrial art, you will find at different moments that the scale is tipped either toward the art or the industry. Whether and how you decide to right that balance is a calculation that has both aesthetic and economic aspects. The discourse both within and outside the film will find itself divided between those aspects, rippling along a faultline of a mutual allegorization. The economic image is the system's epicenter.

On Deleuze's account, films about money are films about film. "Analyzing the films where money plays an important role, we encounter as it were naturally, the theme of the film reflected in the film." About-ness is the simplest allegory, the sort of thing that makes a heist movie like *Ocean's 11* (Soderbergh, Warner Bros., 2001) the projection of its own backstory, the display of its own process of assembly. But the converse of Deleuze's point should be available as well, that is, that films about time are films about money—or that they might be, if that fundamental dissymmetry can be jerked back into a place of rough equivalence. This is, I will argue, what *Déjà Vu* does, and it is what I am saying the neoclassical Hollywood project amounted to. Faced with a cinema headed formally and materially along a schizoid trajectory, the great aesthetic undertaking of the major studios was to successfully revitalize the classical canons of balance, proportion, causality, and intention. As epigones of the classical studios, they inevitably performed this counter-operation at one remove, carrying within them the quasi-historical scar of their own reorigination.

The economic image displays the internalized relation of the film to money, to people and institutions, to the times and places—actual and virtual, literal and conventional—of its production, distribution, and exhibition. "Displays" here is meant to include as wide a range of modalities of presentation as possible: allegory, explicit reflection, metonymy, description, depiction, insinuation. In calling these "economic images" I want to stress not only the Deleuzian roots of the idea, but the difficulty of justifying the importance of those images within a project that is more properly historical. Reading Deleuze on the transition to the time-image, I find the necessary specifics lacking. In the case of the economic images I will highlight, the specifics seem overwhelming. It will not be a matter of sidestepping history for taxonomy but of attempting to refound history on these instances that make the equation of pictures possible.

Still, one might reasonably object that my emphasis on the historical-ish elements of Deleuze's account is partial and that it too readily grounds a multifaceted transition in but one of its aspects. If the standard account of the time-image insists on two-sidedness, the two sides are not time and money but the time of the film's presentation (its real time) and the time of the events it has captured (its virtual time). The shift from the movement-image to the time-image is properly formal and is founded on the gap, the interstice, between real and virtual. One emblem for that gap is the cut between two shots (or between an image and a sound). Here, Deleuze reaches for a kind of rigor he associates with mathematical abstraction. "Cinema and mathematics are the same here: sometimes the cut, so-called *rational*, forms part of one of the two sets which it separates (end of one or beginning of the other). This is the case with 'classical' cinema. Sometimes, as in modern cinema, the cut has become the interstice, *it is irrational and does not form part of either set . . .* a frontier which belongs to neither one nor the other."[8] The irrational cut is an abstract emblem of the time-image, or, in his terms, "The direct time-image effectively has as noosigns the irrational cut between non-linked (but always relinked) images."[9] If my argument is correct, and the economic image holds as important a place in contemporary Hollywood as the time-image does in Deleuze's "modern" cinema, then as the forced equivalence between dissymmetries it should also have an emblem in the cut. If the irrational cut stands as an outside to the unlinked shots on either side of it, this cut should efficiently rationalize away the dissymmetry between shots—not in the sense that it makes those shots actually equivalent, but in the sense that it hypothetically suspends the disequivalence they continue to bear. Since we expect from Hollywood a higher degree of continuity between shots than from, say, the cinema of Alain Resnais, I will take a term from finance economics and call these Efficient Market Hypothesis cuts or EMH cuts.

The moneyball of *Moneyball*

To see that difference in practice, let us take as our pivotal example the adaptation of Michael Lewis's *Moneyball*, a nonfiction account of the rise of statistical techniques in baseball management. Seen one way, it was the feel-good, underdog story of Billy Beane, who washed out as a professional ballplayer before becoming the general manager of the Oakland A's, a scrappy team trying to compete against clubs spending five times as much. From the beginning the movie was a tricky project. It combined two very dangerous topics: baseball, which is geographically limited in its appeal to the Americas and a handful of Asian countries, and statistics, which are limited in their appeal to "people who are interested in statistics." Worse, the general popularity of baseball in the United States had been eroding for decades, both in absolute terms and relative to other professional sports.[10] But with Brad Pitt set to star, Steven Zaillian writing the script, and Steven Soderbergh directing, the project went ahead. In June 2009, as Chris Jones was researching his puff piece on Relativity, and just days before *Moneyball* was to begin shooting, Sony pulled the plug.[11] Soderbergh's final draft had scared them off—it began with him saying "an important part of this film will be written in the editing room. This isn't a cop-out; it's just a fact, and entirely by design." This version *Moneyball* was going to mix interviews with the actual players and managers into the fictional story. It was, he said publicly, going to be the baseball version of *Reds*. All that authenticity threatened to undermine the clear narrative thread, and despite having sunk $10 million into development, the project was in danger of falling apart.

The studio reassembled *Moneyball* by first locking down Pitt, who was elevated to producer, and bringing in producer Scott Rudin. At the same time, they stepped away from Soderbergh's docufictional approach and hired Aaron Sorkin to rewrite alongside Zaillian. Everyone tried to play nice. Pascal said calming things about Soderbergh—"It was hard making that decision. It was really hard making it OK with Brad. I feel terrible because I think Steven Soderbergh is a wonderful director." Pitt said calming things such as: "I understood that the numbers didn't add up for what Steven wanted to do with it," and "the studio is the one writing the check, so I don't take offense to that." And Zaillian tried to say nice things about being forced to work with Sorkin, although, as he put it, "when I asked him what he'd do if I was calling to tell him [that I would be rewriting long stretches of his script]. Without much hesitation, [Aaron] said, 'I'd burn the studio down.'"

They obviously didn't burn the studio down. Instead, they approached the project as, they said, a "character-driven" story—the tale of Billy Beane—and Pitt promised new director Bennett Miller that the movie would be "a Trojan horse. We will give them the gift of a Hollywood movie starring Brad Pitt that's going to be real entertainment, but inside it is some cargo that is not really accepted in a vintage way, something that they don't anticipate." However important Trojan Horses might be to the Pitt brand, it may nonetheless seem bizarre for one of a movie's producers and its director to be discussing their secret scheming against the studio with *The Hollywood Reporter*. Yet as I discuss in Chapter 5, such public subversion is a trope in the discourse of Hollywood independence. Trojan horse or no, *Moneyball* is both an instance of and a rejoinder to the model-first sort of thinking that backstopped Relativity in its heyday. On the one hand, "the numbers didn't add up," Pitt says, deflecting responsibility; on the other, in order to get the project back on track, much more had to change besides the budget. Something—something secret or mystified or unanticipated—had to be generated to convince "notoriously picky" Miller to agree to direct. And it is that reliance on occult meaning that will define not only this project but the Oakland A's.

The subtitle of Michael Lewis's book is "The Art of Winning an Unfair Game," and what makes the game unfair is the steep gradient between the salaries the A's pay and the salaries of teams like the Yankees and the Dodgers. This appealed to Pitt: "I'm a sucker for injustice stories," . . . "and wanting to right the injustice."[12] Righting the injustice in the absence of money means having an idea, preferably a secret one. Pitt's Beane has hired a young statistics whiz, Peter Brand (Jonah Hill) to better evaluate players. As Brand works through the model, we see numbers on various screens—a whiteboard, a spreadsheet, and eventually, an illegible combination of numbers and other characters. "What's this?" Brad Pitt asks. Jonah Hill answers: "This is the code that I've written for our year-to-year projections." The code is illegible, but it will work, and in *Moneyball* working means that it will enable the A's to field a winning baseball team. To make *that* happen, the code will churn through an enormous database, sorting and comparing things, "getting things down to one number." The movie calls this reading: "Using stats the way we read them, we can find value in players that nobody else can see." The rest of baseball, in this model, "undervalues" certain players for "biased reasons." The A's will capitalize on that, assemble a team of "misfit toys," and win.

That expository dialogue was a late addition to *Moneyball*. It is not in Steve Zaillian's December 1, 2008, draft. Nor is it in the much-altered Soderbergh shooting draft of June 2009. It is not in those versions because as long as Soderbergh is involved, the character of Billy Beane is not a naïf, but someone who is groping his way toward the revolution. But even once Soderbergh is fired and Sorkin comes on and Beane increasingly becomes the stand-in for an audience who doesn't understand the new approach to baseball, the scene is never that bald. Location shooting had begun in July 2010, and principal photography later that summer, yet as late as the October 15 "3rd Blue Revisions," no one was discussing unseen value. Only during the marathon postproduction—thirty-six weeks—did Miller, Zaillian, Sorkin, and the producers settle on the exposition, and only then did they settle on the happy ending.

The movie's happy ending will not be the A's winning the World Series—they did not. Nor will it be Brad Pitt's Billy Beane becoming the highest paid general manager in baseball—he rejected the Red Sox' offer. The happy ending, for Beane, will be winning enough games that he can keep his job and stay in Oakland near his daughter. At the same time, the movie's happy ending will decidedly *not* be the players discovering that they are undervalued and successfully demanding their rightful compensation. Baseball players, and subsequently professional athletes in most other major sports, have since used "statistics the way we read them" to do just that.[13] But no one in *Moneyball* has any interest in wising up the players lest the arbitrage possibility disappear, leaving the A's back in the cellar. (They would be there in 2015.) Stripped of Pitt's stardom, and this relationship looks like exploitation, and in *Moneyball*, we are supposed to root for it.

The relationship between Beane and pitcher Chad Bradford has all the makings of a bad conscience. "You knew I was worth $3 million and you thought you could get away with paying me $237,000," Bradford might say. Instead, he thanks Beane for the opportunity to play and says he'll pray for him and his family. In order to allay—or at least defer—the eruption of a demand for something like justice, the movie turns to its real, chiasmic project: convincing the numberjockey to understand the human costs of his reduction of people to numbers and convincing the subjects of that reduction to willingly enlist themselves in the project.

Watching Jonah Hill's Brand (a fictionalized version of Paul DePodesta) explain to Carlos Peña that he's been traded—again, a scene that is offscreen in the Zaillian draft and not in the Soderbergh draft—the scene carries much of Amy Pascal's affect: "It was really hard . . . ." The eruption of the personal within the cold logic of moneyball sets up a complementary sequence, a montage in which Brand and Beane explain to players that they need to look for "their pitch." By maximizing what they do best and forcing opposing pitchers to throw more pitches, they will contribute more to the team while improving the odds for everyone who follows them in the lineup. In this sequence, players willingly adopt the high strategic arts of moneyball rather than pursue more traditional, skill-based coaching. The point is not to improve timing, bat speed, or vision, but to rebalance the *odds* in the hitters' favor. "This is a process. It's a process. It's a process," Beane intones. Hailed by the ideological sports apparatus, the players do their jobs and the team cruises into the playoffs. By incorporating its own backstory— firing Soderbergh—*Moneyball* becomes more structurally sound and more ideologically coherent. The dual alibi at the heart of *Moneyball* absolves management of paying fair wages because the market as a whole is unfair and because by arbitraging it they are, in fact, coming closer to the meritocracy that the market professes to believe in.

With the invocation of market meritocracy, the much broader context comes rushing back. That linkage is not simply ideological. Instead, the material infrastructure that made possible the moneyball revolution in sports lay at the basis for the transformation of popular dataculture. The Society for American Baseball Research, and its statistical offshoot, sabermetrics, became the paradigm for advanced statistical analysis of sports. That statistical analysis initially supported the massive expansion of the fantasy sports industry and its concomitant transformation of sports gambling. In time sabermetrics transformed the management *and play* of those sports themselves. Further, the dataculture of sports led, in direct ways, to a similar revolution in political prognostication. Nate Silver, of fivethirtyeight.com, began as a baseball stats person, developing a particularly nifty fantasy stat called PECOTA, a backronym for Player Empirical Comparison and Optimization Test Algorithm, before he became the most famous poll aggregator in the United States. What Silver brought to political analysis was the combination of a new, simulation-driven account of how different possibilities would play out and, thought this is often forgotten, a commitment to the close study of political ground-games, visiting local offices, tallying get-out-the-vote calls, and so on—the equivalent of scouting. Silver parlayed his remarkable success in forecasting the 2008 U.S. election— he was *exactly right*—into the premier data-journalism job in the United States, at the *New York Times*, before departing the *Times* and returning to a more hybrid sports-and-politics gig at ESPN.

Data journalism in various forms has taken its place alongside phenomena such as the rock-star status of Edward Tufte and his data visualization precepts in the reshaping of news. New technological capacities for data processing and visualization, mobilized by individual skills and given an impetus by the grinding industrial transformation of newsmedia have transformed facticity in both its appearance and its relation to authority. Tufte's "small multiples" began to appear everywhere, and readers, trained by sports coverage or not, have come to understand them.[14] At the same time, the deployment of *Moneyball*-derived approaches in politics has changed candidate strategies from inflected centrism to base-maximizing. You don't want to offer a policy with the broadest appeal; you want the most delegates. The success of the Obama campaign's 2008 strategy in the caucuses vindicated their approach.

This reconfiguration of popular dataculture has importance across a host of media, yet it is not part of the baseline cinematic attempt to come to terms with big data. Simulations and small multiples are still, ordinarily, less important to film and television than lotteries and metonyms. Dataculture is a zone where the new old media of news and the new old media of cinema part company. As Stephanie Ricker Schulte has shown, representations of the internet have progressed through phases, beginning with thematics of asymmetry and connection and growing more interested in surveillance capabilities.[15] Big data thematics, though, are more than simply the extension of the panopticon, important as that idea remains. Iterations appear as the management of selection criteria, and we are asked to identify with the pathos of the general manager in, for example, *Under the Skin* (Jonathan Glazer, Film4/A24, 2013) and *Snowpiercer* (Bong Joon-Ho, RADiUS-TWC, 2013). Or, in other cases, instead of iterations, we find scenarios that seem to be driven by outliers—by luck—only to discover that there has not been any luck in the process at all; these are lotteries that are not lotteries (*Ex Machina* [Alex Garland, DNA/A24, 2015]; *The Hunger Games* [Gary Ross, Color Force/Lionsgate, 2012]).

In the work of Michael Lewis—in both the sports books *Moneyball* and *The Blind Side*, and in his histories of high finance such as *Liar's Poker, The Big Short, Flash Boys,* and his account of Long-Term Capital Management—the interplay of arbitrage and exploitation looks like the oscillation between an idea and a person.[16] The arbitrageurs are forever attempting to isolate themselves from the consequences of their actions by reducing what they do to "strategy," but because the central phenomenon of their strategy is the trade, the equation of one thing with another, when their trades become a traffic in people, the brutal legacies of actual human traffic rise up through the rhetoric. This helps explain some of the difficult reckonings with race in Lewis, and some of his interest in situations of self-exploitation, where the idea, and not the power relation, can take center stage.

So when John Meriwether pioneers bond arbitrage at Salomon Brothers, Lewis describes him as setting up "a sort of underground railroad that ran from the finest graduate finance and math programs directly onto the Salomon trading floor."[17] These intellectuals replace mere traders like Lewis, who now "belonged to a new semi-informed breed who could 'pass' as experts on the new financial complexity without possessing true understanding."[18] Lewis, not happy "passing," remains jealous of his hyperwealthy former colleagues until they are wiped out. The 1998 disaster spawned by Meriwether's Long-Term Capital Management came the closest to breaking the contemporary financial system before the 2008 crash. In addition to everything else it did, it liberated Lewis from his aspirations to untold wealth. "I demanded no further reparations. I was once again satisfied to be paid by the word."[19] Underground railroads, new breeds, folks who are passing and demanding reparations—the racial configuration remains, just barely, subtextual.

Once the traders are no longer trading themselves, though, exploitation comes roaring back. In *Moneyball*, the complex salary system imposed by the league underpays high-value rookies. Initially this allows the A's to compete by drafting well. Lewis immediately, and without hesitation, links the moment of free agency to the rights of individuals under capitalism: "Not until . . . he had been in the big leagues for six years, would Barry Zito, like any other citizen of the republic, be allowed to auction his services to the highest bidder. At which point, of course, the Oakland A's would no longer be able to afford Barry Zito. That's why it was important to find Barry Zito here, in the draft room, and obtain him for the period of his career when he could be paid the baseball equivalent of slave's wages."[20]

Lewis's rhetoric here matters not simply because he has been central to the writing of capitalist culture but because his attempts to grapple with the moral consequences of market arrangements are both analogue and source for much of Brad Pitt's corporate-auteur persona. It is Pitt who keeps the *Moneyball* project going at Columbia for moral reasons, and it is Pitt who, five years later, pushes to get *The Big Short* made. In between, he will appear in movies about contract killing (*Killing Them Softly,* Andrew Dominik, Plan B/Annapurna, 2012), contagion (*World War Z,* Marc Forster, Plan B/Paramount, 2013), and what we might call the material display of the liquidation of a position, the Second World War tank movie *Fury* (David Ayer, Plan B/Warner Bros., 2014). But none of these intervening works is as important as *12 Years a Slave* (Steve McQueen, Plan B/Fox Searchlight, 2013), in which he casts himself as a creative worker called to moral account.

What he creates in *12 Years* is a gazebo, a small offshoot of the Epps plantation house, fulfilling his long-standing desire to be an architect. This architectural imaginary has regularly shaped the films Pitt has appeared in. In *Ocean's 13*, his Rusty gets to geek out about attacking Al Pacino's casino, explaining that Pacino's character had "fired Gehry, Gwathmey, Meier, four others just so he could say he designed the hotel himself. What this means to us: There's no set of unified plans." At the same time that he was complaining about ego-driven gaming moguls, he was setting up "Make it Right," a nonprofit foundation that would eventually build more than a hundred LEED Platinum–certified homes for low-income residents in New Orleans's hurricane-devastated Lower Ninth Ward.[21] So when Pitt the gazebo-builder shows up outside New Orleans in *12 Years*, he is glad of his contract but ready to acknowledge that liberating Solomon Northup "will be more than a pleasure. It will have been my duty."

Pitt's recent career arc demonstrates cutting-edge star persona management, but one leverageable across projects at wildly different scales— from *World War Z* to *Killing Them Softly*—and no longer understandable as part of a clean one-for-them, one-for-me alteration. Paul McDonald has combed through the projects undertaken by various star production shingles (Pitt's is called Plan B) in an effort to extract an account of star strategy today.[22] What he finds is a sorting of star involvement and visible presence into what we might call "risk buckets," where the presence of the star is thought to be, at least at greenlight, downside protection. Here, the reliance on Pitt's star power helps projects with domestic or at least limited cultural relevance—a baseball movie—enter other markets. In the case of *12 Years*, where then-conventional wisdom about the limited appeal of African-American historical subjects meets up with other limitations—the R-rating, the commitment to a set of indie narrative strategies (at least in the opening reel), and the general riskiness of avowedly Oscar-bait-y projects— Pitt's willingness to cast himself in a minor role was likely essential to getting the film to greenlight even if that role happened to accord entirely with his own carefully crafted persona as moral, architectural, and contractual conscience. Once cast as the actual creative worker, Pitt's image could then

FIGURE 1.1 *Brad Pitt, Louisiana Architect.* 12 Years a Slave, *McQueen, Plan B/
New Regency/Summit, 2013.*

be exploited in ways that were antithetical to the project's *other* socio-
contractual commitments, namely to the film's Black actors, writer, and
director.

Pitt's Bass prizes his freedom to contract. "My freedom is everything. The
fact that I can walk out of here tomorrow brings me great pleasure." The
perversion of that freedom sets *12 Years* in motion. "We are on our way
to rejoin the company having left for a short time to make a small profit
from our own exhibitions," Northup's captors explain, before detailing
his compensation package. The system they describe is one of small-
scale independent productions ("small profit . . . our own exhibitions")
alternating with larger enterprises ("the company," "a spectacle unlike most
have ever witnessed"). They are able to make him the offer because "men
of true talents are seemingly in short supply." Yet we never see Northup
accept. Instead, the moment of consent and contract—like virtually every
other bureaucratic moment in the film—is elided in an EMH cut. We jump
from the gazebo on the town green where the offer is made to Washington,
DC. The gazebo-construction scenes later in the film, then, not only offer
Pitt the opportunity to play the righteous white man, but also restore the
utopian promise of contract altogether. Such a restoration will require
reconstruction, ideological and literal.

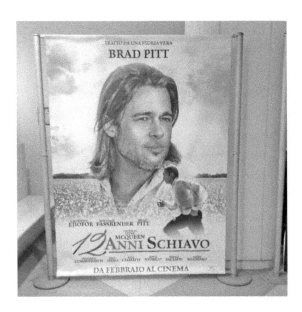

FIGURE 1.2 *Brad Pitt, overseer.* 12 Years a Slave *poster via BIM Distribuzione.*

Pitt's fascination with contracts, housing, and moral rectitude reaches one peak in *12 Years a Slave*, where the stakes are floridly corporeal, but that fascination reaches another peak in 2015's *The Big Short* (Adam McKay, Plan B/Paramount), where the stakes seem to be utterly numerical—at least until Pitt's character, Ben Rickert, arrives to bind the model back to its underlying reality. The arbitrage here is between the risk that mortgage-backed securities carried in the market and the actual risk that those mortgages would default. Capturing that value amounted to betting against the housing market. Late in the film, two relatively novice investors are congratulating themselves for realizing that the rot in the housing market will not be confined to the marginal borrowers who will lose their homes first, but that it will spread upward, taking out the "A Tranches." As they celebrate "the deal of our lifetimes" and dance goofily across a casino floor, Pitt talks them down: "Don't do that. Stop. Stop. Stop that. Stop it. STOP. . . . Do you have any idea what you just did?" Rickert is a mild version of a doomsday prepper, traveling in a surgical mask and laying up stocks of seeds, but in this scene he is, essentially, a scold:

If we're right, if we're right, people lose homes; people lose jobs; people lose retirement savings; people lose pensions. You know what I hate about fucking banking? It reduces people to numbers. Here's a number: every one percent unemployment goes up, 40,000 people die. Did you know that? Did you know that? . . . Just don't fucking dance.

What excuses his participation in the scheme, given his moral priors, is not the moneyball-style enlistment of the borrowers in their own arbitrage but the assertion that the system was so expansive that no individual investor could meaningfully change it. The crisis was baked in.

Moneyball is the story of an asymmetric oligopoly—A's versus Yankees and Red Sox—while The Big Short is the story of "a few outsiders and wierdos" against an oligopolistic banking system incomparably more vast. But however different the scale, and however different the balance between the individual and the system, in The Big Short, what matters is, again, reading. Ryan Gosling's character explains that those weirdos "saw what no one else could . . . by doing something the rest of the suckers never thought to do. They looked." Christian Bale's Michael Burry explains his strategy to Lawrence Fields, his principal financial backer, on speakerphone:

> Burry: It's only a matter of time before someone else sees this investment. [Pounding desk:] We have to act now.
> Fields: How do you know the bonds are worthless? Aren't they filled with fucking thousands of [Cut to Burry] pages of mortgages?
> Burry: I read them.
> Fields (still offscreen): You read them?
> Burry: I rea, yeah—yes.
> Fields: No one reads them—only the lawyers who put them together read them.
> Burry (grabbing handset): I don't think they even know what they've made.

In The Big Short there are other ways of learning about the impending economic collapse. Traders visit Florida subdivisions and Las Vegas trade shows in order to discover just how epically clueless real estate agents, mortgage brokers, and the packagers of complex mortgage-backed securities actually are. But those anecdotes, compelling as they are, follow Burry's initial plunge into the numbers, just as the gut-wrenching player trades in Moneyball follow Peter Brand's initial tour of the white board.

At the heart of that tour is a state-of-the-art montage version of an economic image now on the verge of becoming cliché.[23] The montage emerged to solve a particular cinematic problem: Watching people typing or looking at spreadsheets or texting is fundamentally boring in ways that watching people talk on the phone is not. The phone gives us both a voice and a body, and it cleaves them in ways that compound rather than reduce our potential objects of attention. Watching Billy Beane talk through a trade, a flickering glance or a raised eyebrow or a mouthed word can throw the entire conversation into relief. Watching Michael Burry snatch up his phone so that he is no longer on speaker conveys a jump in intimacy far greater than the minor action implies. In place of the telephonic, which divides our attention while anchoring us in a particular time and place, the *Moneyball* montage dislodges us in time and space, giving us a variety of screens and boards in a variety of locations within the A's offices. As we learn that we should learn to read statistics, we are brought closer and closer to the screen, and the number goes granular, pixellates, and eventually is swapped out for the on-screen version of the old-fashioned halftone image of a person.

In *The Big Short*, before Michael Burry explains that he has read the bonds, we see him do something very like that. In this reading, the numbers are accompanied by a sotto voce self-narration and flashes to the scenes of homeownership that the numbers in the bond represent. Reading, here, is both a far more private experience than in *Moneyball* in that only Michael is reading and he is only reading to himself, and more public in that the other employees at Scion Capital are able to witness the scene. In *The Big Short*, the on-screen numbers grow larger and pixellate before being swapped out not for the halftone image of a person but for the image of a person behaving rhythmically—doing pushups, situps, brushing his teeth, drumming.[24]

These economic images allocate our interest first to abstraction then to bodies, stressing the material underpinnings of their own digital evanescence. This is an old habit of cinema, of course, given new impetus by the digitization of cinematography. Still, the regular invocation of a real, actual body can seem to be the formal equivalent of Pitt's scolding. ("You know what I hate about digital photography? It reduces people to numbers. . .") Once the sequence becomes standardized, it can be comically disavowed, as

FIGURE 1.3 *Value no one else can see: the economic image as coded montage.* Moneyball, *Miller, Columbia, 2011.*

it usually is in *The Big Short*; it can be expanded until its occult significance swallows the world, as in *Lost* (see Chapter 6); or it can be taken to an unimagined extreme, where the duck-rabbit game such montages play with formalism and materialism can continue to undergird an aesthetic proper to late capitalist society, an aesthetic that nonetheless intimates the world to come, as in Michael Mann's *Blackhat* (see Chapter 8). But however such scenes of digital reading appear to us, they solicit further reading on our part, and those readings ask us to understand both the art and the industry in each other's terms.

The Moneyball Initiative

One way to justify the continuing importance of close-reading practices, then, would be to do what I have been doing here: to show how narrative styles and standards *are*, at a given moment; to elicit the look and feel of these movies. But to justify the continuing importance of close reading to the study of media industries one would need to demonstrate that the reading of those movies is important to the industry itself, to demonstrate that such texts play an essential role within the equation of pictures. Such demonstrations are, alas, usually kept behind the veil of corporate secrecy. In the case of Sony Pictures, though, the late-2014 hack and the subsequent posting of the hacked materials on Wikileaks has opened a window onto the practice of corporate strategy after the digital turn. There, we find that in the fall of 2013, Sony undertook what it called "The Moneyball Initiative," an effort to extend to motion picture production an analytics-driven approach. The goal was to "create a model to improve decisions in the planning process." To reach that goal, the studio would first have to clean up its data to make them useful. The project would cost $424,000 for phase I and $243,000 for phase II.[25] The relevant executives signed off on the project on January 6 and 7, 2014, coincident with their viewing of a PowerPoint presentation.

The Moneyball Initiative would unite Sony's development-tracking analytics platform called "Concept-to-Camera" (C2) with its performance-tracking. The presentation notes that despite "the emerging, cross-industry focus on 'Big Data,'" "the only company utilizing a similar approach is Relativity Media"[26] That may seem ironic today, but perhaps less so than the presentation's assertion that the initiative will adhere to Sony's usual high standards of data integrity. At the bottom of the Moneyball Initiative inception charter is the signal quotation from Peter Brand: "It's about getting down to the numbers. Using stats the way we read them, we'll find value that no one else can see."[27] The quotation is wrong. Brand actually says "It's about getting things down to *one* number"—not *the numbers*—and they are searching for "value *in players* that *nobody* else can see." There is a conservation of misreading here: the one in "one number" is pushed later in the sentence into the one of "no one" and, in an inversion of Lewis's usual direction, the bodies that go missing in "value in *players*" and "no*body* else" have already been incorporated into the plural "number*s*" But what the quotation does not get wrong is the commitment to reading statistics.

Here, then, we find one part of the studio—the part that is, at that very moment, attempting to move the studio away from the practice of close-reading projects toward a more "holistic" approach—reading one of its films, more or less closely, in order to lobby for its own project. Whether that reading is part of an actual commitment on the part of the IT group or whether they believe that carrying out such readings is necessary to persuade those top-level executives they refer to as "readers of reports" is unclear. But whatever combination of reasons lies behind the quotation, the whole project amounts to an exercise in internal branding that would be, even *should be* unnecessary given the studio's commitment to the project. The point of the exercise will be to escape the confines of De Vanian "scenario thinking" and replace it with a more clear-eyed approach. It doesn't need to be called "the Moneyball Initiative"—"Motion Picture Analytics" is what it is, and its aim is consistent with other efforts in the industry to improve "business intelligence." But it *is* called the Moneyball Initiative, and it is sold with a misquotation from the film.

The kinds of forces that drive a studio to undertake something like the Moneyball Initiative have diverse, even contradictory motivations. There are broad, cultural occasions such as the availability and prominence of new forms of data analysis. There are persistent economic conditions at the macro level—low interest rates—and dramatic changes in financing arrangements. There is the seemingly ever-present need for key decision-makers to establish their right to their positions of power, both by fitting into industry-wide trends and the decision and taste habits of the very small group of executives they might consider their peers *and* by distinguishing themselves somehow, thereby burnishing their brands and cultivating among their bosses a sense that they are not interchangeable with those peers. There is the bubbling turmoil beneath those decision-makers as producers, heads of marketing, financial analysts, and others compete for authority within the studio. The temptation is strong to assume that in this complex contest, the production, much less the analysis, of individual motion pictures is beside the point. And yet: and yet that is not how, in at least this case, this studio behaved.

Whatever transpired in the pitch meeting for the Moneyball Initiative, or in the meetings leading up to the pitch meeting, there was to be a central scene where the project of a "data-driven" look at the financial record of the studio and its competitors over time would be on the table. Making sense of that pitch required that the numbers be, as I described above, encultured. The culture at hand was the culture the studio had made for itself. And it had made that culture not simply by drafting off the broader culture's increasing fascination with big data but by reshaping the story of the coming of big data along the lines of the studio's own attempts to understand the interplay of "the model" and "relationships." In authorizing the Moneyball Initiative, Columbia was authorizing itself. But it was a self that only came to be through a process of close reading its own position in the precession of culture.

Notes

1 Gilles Deleuze, *Cinema 2: The Time Image*, trans. Hugh Tomlinson (Minneapolis: University of Minnesota Press, 1989), 77.

2 The French reads: "Bref, *c'est dans une même opération que le cinéma affronte son présupposé le plus intérieur, l'argent, et que l'image-mouvement cède la place à l'image-temps.*" *Cinéma 2: L'Image-Temps* (Paris: Les Éditions de Minuit, 1985), 105; the English verison appears on 78.

3 Deleuze, *Cinema 2*, 78.

4 Ibid.

5 Anne Friedberg, *Window Shopping: Cinema and the Postmodern* (Berkeley, CA: University of California Press, 1994), 129.

6 D.N. Rodowick, *Gilles Deleuze's Time Machine* (Durham, NC: Duke University Press, 1997), 236–37, n13.

7 Jonathan Beller, *The Cinematic Mode of Production: Attention Economy and the Society of the Spectacle* (Hanover, NH: Dartmouth, 2006), 19. See also n1 235: "Not coincidentally, this shift from one representational paradigm to another coincides, historically speaking, with the break . . . between the movement-image and the time-image."

8 Deleuze, *Cinema 2*, 181.

9 Ibid., 278.

10 Ratings data for the All-Star Game and World Series can be found at Baseball Almanac, http://www.baseball-almanac.com/asgbox/asgtv.shtml, http://www.baseball-almanac.com/ws/wstv.shtml (via Jeff Sharon, http://www.jeffsharon.net/?p=412). For a comparative view, see McNabb or Kolb, "The Meteoric Rise of Other Football," (http://mcnabborkolb.com/blog/819180034).

11 The timing is somewhat unclear. The public reports that the project was being put in turnaround appeared on June 21, 2009; the film was scheduled to begin shooting the next day. Pascal's decision was made as late as June 19. (Michael Fleming and Peter Bart, "Sony Scraps Soderbergh's 'Moneyball,'" *Variety*, June 21, 2009, http://variety.com/2009/film/features/sony-scraps-soderbergh-s-moneyball-1118005208/).

12 Alex Ben Block, "Brad Pitt Reveals What he, Sony did to Save 'Moneyball,'" *The Hollywood Reporter*, December 16, 2011, http://www.hollywoodreporter.com/news/moneyball-making-brad-pitt-bennett-miller-274738.

13 To his credit, Lewis (and Beane and DePodesta) knew that players and their agents would quickly adopt new metrics for evaluation in order to maximize their value in the marketplace, Michael Lewis, *Moneyball* (New York: Norton, 2004), 274.

14 Here, I intended to reproduce a typical section of a page from the *New York Times*, featuring a number of "small multiples." Their fee was $514. Readers are invited to visit the *Times* website on their own; more effective examples can be found using the page-facsimile features of the "Times Machine."

15 Stephanie Ricker Schulte, *Cached: Decoding the Internet in Global Popular Culture* (New York: New York University Press, 2013).

16 Lewis, *Moneyball*; Michael Lewis, *The Blind Side* (New York: Norton, 2007); Michael Lewis, *Liar's Poker, 25th Anniversary Edition* (New York: Norton, 2011); Michael Lewis, *The Big Short* (New York: Norton, 2011); Michael Lewis, *Flash Boys* (New York: Norton, 2015); and Michael Lewis, "How the Eggheads Cracked," *The New York Times Magazine*, January 24, 1999, 24ff., http://www.nytimes.com/1999/01/24/magazine/how-the-eggheads-cracked.html.

17 Lewis, "How the Eggheads Cracked."

18 Ibid.

19 Ibid.

20 Lewis, *Moneyball*, 22.

21 Make it Right, makeitright.org.

22 Paul McDonald, *Hollywood Stardom* (Malden, MA: Wiley-Blackwell, 2013), 109ff.

23 The cliché was solidified in *The Accountant* (Gavin O'Connor, Warner Bros., 2016).

24 These scenes of number-reading have analogues in other depictions of mental acuity crossed with neurodiversity—Burry, who has Asperger's, joins Russell Crowe's John Nash in *A Beautiful Mind*, Dustin Hoffman's *Rain Man*, Scarlett Johansson's *Lucy*, David Krumholz's Charlie Eppes in *NUMB3RS*, and Ben Affleck's accountant in *The Accountant*. Neurodiversity here functions to minoritize the usually white and usually male protagonist in the scene, allowing him to continue to occupy the center of the power structure while simultaneously disavowing his responsibility for it. The white guys who see through the farce of the housing market remain "outsiders and weirdos," and, by the end, they are deservedly enriched for their insightfulness.

25 Out of an abundance of caution we sought permission from Sony to reproduce the relevant pages. They responded with a cease and desist letter threatening legal action; Bloomsbury reasonably acceded. Readers are invited to peruse the key documents at the Wikileaks site. While the reliance on hacked documents is unsavory and raises ethical questions, publication of those documents is likely protected by the first amendment. I discuss some of the ethical and archival issues surrounding the hack in "The Sony Hack: Data and Decision in the Contemporary Studio," *Media Industries* 2, no. 2 (2015), https://quod. lib.umich.edu/m/mij/15031809.0002.203/--sony-hack-data-and-decision-in-the-contemporary-studio?rgn=main;view=fulltext. "IT Projects Projects

View_Final," April 7, 2014, https://wikileaks.org/sony/docs/03_02/Finance/ SPFINANCE/FY14%20Projects/FY14%20Project%20Reports/12_Mar_14/ For%20Distribution/IT%20Projects%20-%20Projects%20View_Final.pdf.

26 "Moneyball Inception Greenlight Deck v. 2," slide 8, https://wikileaks.org/sony/ docs/03_02/Finance/SPFINANCE/FY14 Projects/Green Light Decks/Moneyball Inception Greenlight Deckv2.pptx.

27 "Moneyball Project Charter," https://wikileaks.org/sony/docs/03_02/Finance/ SPFINANCE/Master%20Data%20Requests/FY14%20Project%20Request/ PSOW/Moneyball_Project%20Charter.pdf.

PART ONE

Precession

Titanic: It's all on the screen

Titanic was, for more than a decade, the biggest movie in the history of cinema—at least by the most common metric, box office unadjusted for inflation. Whatever its actual budget—$200 million was confirmed; higher numbers were likely—studio executives insisted that "we know we have a great film and people will see that all of the money is up on the screen."[1] Critics agreed, in the same terms. "Andy Jones of *TNT Rough Cut Reviews* estimated that a ticket was worth $10 for *Titanic*, since 'every cent of the $200 million plus spent in production flickers on screen.'"[2] Yet when asked about the budget, director James Cameron responded, "What do you care? It doesn't cost you or anybody else more than the price of a movie ticket?"[3]

However characteristically touchy his answer, Cameron was, for the moment, resisting the conflation of the general audience (who had no reason to care about the budget) with the studio exec (who did). He had different responsibilities to each. Still, he did not resist the idea that although Fox and Paramount financed and distributed it, *Titanic* remained his film. He would be the one standing on the stage at the Academy Awards proclaiming himself king of the world, and, in the ways that mattered to him, he would not be far wrong.

Titanic is a particularly powerful meditation on the relationship of money and value because while it was vastly bigger than the typical Hollywood movie, it was nevertheless produced, distributed, and exhibited in nearly typical ways. The process was not revolutionized; it was simply enlarged. In that inflation, the skin of the system became more transparent. Players and institutions were pushed to ask new questions and generate new knowledge about its workings. What is more, *Titanic* demonstrates the system nearly at the peak of its powers. Those powers include the ability to incorporate contingencies, even dire threats, at every stage of the moviemaking process and to make those contingencies allegorically visible within narratives. This may seem hopelessly abstract, but by plunging into a case we will see how *Titanic* both tells the story of its own production while also telling the story of its own allegorical command. At the core of that meta-story are very particular calculations, and they reveal that the relations between a given narrative and other possibilities are structured as a matter of precession. Changes at the meta level become tractable within narrative because those temporally or logically antecedent causes supervene in potentially foreseeable ways.

To return to the foundational conflict behind *Titanic*: It would be mistaken to say that the film remained Cameron's *although* Fox and Paramount distributed it rather than *because* they distributed it. Studio collaborations do tend to weaken both corporate brands because such situations highlight the salable elements that initially encouraged them to share the risk. As the corporate authorship of a coproduction wanes, other auteurs—directors, stars, the underlying property—are able to fill the gap. And to the extent that the coproduction appears to be the product of a studio's desire to mitigate its financial risk, it points up the relative vulnerability of the contemporary studio (Figure I.1).

Yet even in the paradigm case of *Titanic*, a film that seemed to mark the ascendancy of the blockbuster auteur against the studios, the evidence of coproduction finds its way into the story, into the story of the film's own immensity and danger. Perhaps the most compelling character in Act III is First Officer Murdoch, a man who, indeed, bears the name of the actual first officer on the *Titanic*, but whose whipsaw progress through all the points of the moral compass—venal, noble, negligent, vengeful, self-destructive—marks him as a stand-in for Fox's CEO (Figure I.2). Rupert Murdoch, more Captain than CEO, found himself with a picture of such budgetary excess that he was forced, he felt, to veer from his buccaneering principles and bring in a partner to share the cost. The deal has since become notorious: Fox gave Paramount domestic distribution and agreed to split the global profits 50–50 in exchange for half the film's budget. But Paramount's share was capped at $65 million, and as the film ran over budget, Fox was forced to shoulder the additional costs. It was the worst of possible worlds: Fox's risk continued to increase while its possible reward remained limited. The deal turned out to be a tremendous blunder, but what was Murdoch to

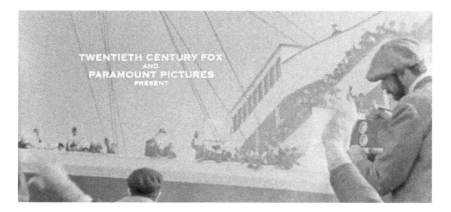

FIGURE I.1 *James Cameron mans the camera as the coproduction launches.* Titanic, *Cameron, Fox/Paramount, 1997.*

FIGURE I.2 *Mr. Murdoch takes the easy way out.* Titanic, *Cameron, Fox/Paramount, 1997.*

do? The film suggests that he had no choice. Confronting the budgetary iceberg—"Right ahead!"—he orders the ship hard to port. In retrospect the iceberg confronts Murdoch with the same stolidity Paramount showed in its negotiations over the film. The moment is one of sublimely emblematic confrontation: a frozen incarnation of the Paramount logo blankly staring down the panicky Murdoch (Figure I.3). Eventually, and regardless of historical reality, Murdoch kills himself; eventually, Fox dispatches an apologetic executive to England to attempt to appease First Officer Murdoch's surviving relatives by setting up a scholarship in his honor.[4]

Does this sort of account seem unserious? Does it seem so even though we know that Cameron has shot himself into the picture over against his distributors' credits? Is the breaking point of our conviction the idea

FIGURE I.3 *A meet and greet with your distribution partner.* Titanic, *Cameron, Fox/Paramount, 1997.*

that Murdoch is Murdoch—a delicious joke from the get-go? Or is it the appearance of Paramount, the most contingent element in the corporate backstory, in the guise of the least contingent element of the narrative? We might persist in thinking that Murdoch's avatar is real yet unimportant, but surely the iceberg is the more tendentious. The grounds of our resistance are several, but central to them is the mismatch between contingency and necessity, between the accidental and the essential. Cameron might have foreseen Murdoch's failure of will at the script stage if that is who he thought Murdoch was from the beginning; and he might have foreseen that Fox would turn to Paramount because he knew, like everyone in the industry, that Paramount was the studio to turn to when you wanted to share risk; yet he had no choice but to run the ship into the iceberg. How could he have intended anything like the confrontation I have sketched? Or, to put it another way, what gives the allegorical studio clash more than merely illustrative value? Isn't it just another bit of post-hockery?

One route to a possible answer to these last questions would require us to "go back to *Titanic*," as the film puts it. In piggybacking on the film's own success, our interpretation has the advantage of all teleologies: it puts us on notice about where we are headed and thus makes every step along the way subject to skepticism. Yet this advantage is not limited in scope. What is true for the interpretation is true for the studio and the system as a whole—that is, it is true to the extent that there is a system in the first place, the kind of system that depends on its instances for elaboration and counterpoint.

Titanic first sinks nineteen minutes into the three-hour epic (Figure I.4). The "forensic analysis" has two motivations. The immediate reason for it is that it sets up an opposition within the story between ways of knowing how something was—there are the mechanics, the things that Mr. Bodean

FIGURE I.4 *Internalized anticipation: The sinking of the digital ship, 1.0.* Titanic, Cameron, Fox/Paramount, 1997.

finds "pretty cool," and then there is "the experience of it," emblematized by Rose's reference to the smell of fresh paint. But if the film is busy warding off the easy cynicism of Bodean and Lovett ("You're so full of shit, boss") ("enough of that bullshit"), it is also opening up a space of possibility. The ship is going down: this was the unalterable given. No one who saw *Titanic* the film could have been surprised that *Titanic* the ship was going to sink. Yet by immediately opposing Bodean's computer reconstruction of the wreck to Rose's experiential one, the film lays claim to the novelty of its climax. Yes, the ship will go down, but for the audience—an audience initially figured as the crew of Lovett's fortune-hunting vessel (Figure I.5)—knowing that amounts to knowing nothing at all.

More important, though, than the philosophical distinction between these knowledges (roughly between *savoir* and *connaissance*) is their pairing. As the site within which the enunciation of *Titanic*'s fate takes place, the film is now able to claim the event. When the climactic, experiential shipwreck finally occurs, it is the payoff not of our extracinematic knowledge of history but of intra-narrative knowledge. Bodean's computer simulation is the gun in the first act that goes off in the third. The space of possibility the film opens for itself seals out history in a very particular way: whatever transpires within the film will have its origins within the film.

What I am describing as a matter of narrative structure and confidence centers on the film's reckoning with loss. As Vivian Sobchack puts it in her remarkable essay, "Bathos and the Bathysphere," "*Titanic*'s extraordinary poetic power and mass appeal are essentially tied to and emergent from its framing narrative, which 'rounds' off and fills in the loss of a past disaster." The film "isolates and seals its objects of desire within its own framing, and, as [Gaston] Bachelard notes, 'when a thing becomes isolated, it becomes

FIGURE I.5 *Internalized reaction: Audience rapture.* Titanic, Cameron, Fox/ Paramount, 1997.

round, [and] assumes a figure of being that is concentrated upon itself.'"[5] This phenomenological roundness allows the film to withstand the crushing pressures of its bathetic narrative.

Sobchack's account may seem mystical but is only the phenomenological corollary to Peter Krämer's more industrially minded claim that, "like many of the most successful products of popular culture, the film (supported by the surrounding publicity) explains itself to its audiences, offering them guidance on how to understand and enjoy *Titanic*."[6] Indeed, for Krämer, *Titanic*'s success is merely a specific version of a more general phenomenon of auto-explanation. "An important aspect of Hollywood's hold on the public imagination is its ability to generate, from within the films themselves, the very terms in which its major releases are going to be discussed."[7] On Sobchack and Krämer's accounts, the film's formal power allows it to incorporate the reactions and desires of its mass audience, but there is no reason to restrict the vector of its successful incorporation. The story reckons not only with historical fact and the audience's foreknowledge, but also, somehow, with production history and the film's extended presence within the enfotainment universe. As Justin Wyatt and Katherine Vlesmas make clear, a "drama of recoupment" occupied reporting leading up to the film's release. Would *Titanic* make money or lose money? And if the (ultimately wrong) answer seemed obvious, then the more important question was why the studio had allowed the production to spiral out of control.

To begin to answer these questions, we might attempt to better understand the peculiar role this picture played at Fox. Why impute the responsibility for *Titanic* to Murdoch? Because the system cascades in precisely that way. Art Linson, a producer who moved from Warners to Fox in 1996, explained the hierarchy of the modern media conglomerate: "The best way an outsider can understand these subtle distinctions [between executives] is by asking who has the power to say yes, maybe, or no." And that power has a series of firebreaks and feedback loops built into it:

[Newly-appointed head of film production] Tom Jacobson could say no, but if he wanted to say yes to anything, he would have to appeal to [studio head] Bill Mechanic for an approval. And even if he wanted to say no, Mechanic could overrule him, assuming you knew how to get to Mechanic. If this request was very expensive, such as the green-lighting of a fifty-million-dollar movie, Mechanic would have to appeal to [Fox Entertainment CEO Peter] Chernin for approval. If Mechanic wanted to say no, it would end there, unless you could appeal to Chernin to overrule Mechanic. If a request was very, very expensive, such as more money for a *Titanic* production that was running mercilessly out of control, Chernin would have to ask Murdoch for approval. As complicated as all this seems, it is a layered committee method designed to pass on the risks and defuse the blame.[8]

As a description of risk management, the pyramid seems eminently rational. It is designed to allocate responsibility appropriately: The riskiest decisions are made at the highest levels of the corporation and more intimate, operational decisions are made farther down. Understood that way, Linson would be wrong to call it a "method designed to pass on risks and defuse the blame."

But the corporate hierarchy interacts with the production system in complex ways. As economist Richard Caves makes clear, the option contract at the heart of creative industries provides regular occasions for the re-evaluation of a project, but those decision points do not guarantee that the project will be profitable. In fact, given the situation of the motion picture— where "costs are sunk progressively and information on the product's quality revealed gradually"—the option contract can encourage a studio to pursue films it knows will lose money. Caves calls this process "the nurture of ten-ton turkeys." It works like this:

> Suppose that the new project is expected at the outset to break even— worth doing, but no excess profit. The entrepreneur takes the first step, committing (say) 10 percent of the project's total cost. Now some components of the project—a screenplay, set designs, "dailies" . . . —are available for inspection. . . . If they fall short [of expectations], the size of the disappointment is crucial. If expected revenues are now written down by 20 percent, the project is abandoned. If they have shriveled by only 9 percent, however, expected revenues exceed the costs *remaining* to be incurred. The holder of the option chooses to continue, even though the project will appear to have run a loss when the books are ultimately closed. If expectations about the project's revenues continue to shrink, although no faster than increments of sunk cost are incurred, the last 10 percent of outlay will be authorized even if expected revenues are now only 11 percent of their original level.[9]

At each decision point, the calculation shifts further from "will this project be profitable?" to "will expected revenues be greater than remaining expenses?" Hence, "rational decision-makers can carry projects to completion that realize enormous ex post losses."[10] What is worse, the evaluative process that the option contract is designed to encourage remains mired in uncertainty. Paraphrasing William Goldman, Caves reasons from the principle that "nobody knows" whether the final project will be successful. The band of possible outcomes is wide indeed. (Economist Arthur De Vany would say that the band is absolutely undetermined.) Directors and others who might know early on that the film will not succeed nevertheless have an interest in continuing. And even if the crucial decision-makers are merely *uncertain* about the project's success, their degree of conviction and their enthusiasm "serve as a costly signal" to everyone else. This enthusiasm, in turn, clouds the decision-making process further. Caves captures the dilemma: "Even the most skilled manager will find it difficult to simultaneously fire up the team and ponder dousing it with the cold water of termination."[11]

In our terms, the uncertainties that give rise to the option contract system interact with the complex feedback loops of the risk allocation hierarchy in such a way that the entire process becomes an alibi for its failures. Directors can only be expected to maintain their enthusiasm for projects; studios can only be expected to delimit their responsibility further, and even then, what responsibility remains might be fobbed off on a worry about the signal that would be sent to the creative community should a project be cancelled.

In negotiations over *Titanic*, Cameron routinely bargained from extreme positions backward. When asked to make cuts, he treated the proposals as dire threats: "If you want to cut my film, you'll have to fire me. And to fire me, you'll have to kill me."[12] So while he eventually offered to forego his directorial salary and profit participation, he remained steadfast that the negotiations were entirely motivated by questions of quality: "Filmmaking is war. There is no other way to look at it. It's a great battle. A battle between Business and Aesthetics."[13] Or, as Caves less belligerently but more ominously phrases it, "Deficient budgetary control systems interact treacherously with *art for art's sake*."[14]

Faced with an escalating budget and an intransigent director, Fox tried and failed to bargain with Paramount. They adopted the same terms that Cameron had employed against them. "It was only about money for them. . . . It was not about getting this right. [Paramount] is risk averse. It was like being involved with somebody who didn't understand the business. They're not playing at the same level." Paramount's response came from Rob Friedman, the studio's marketing and distribution chief: "This statement does not merit comment."[15] (What would you expect the iceberg to say?) Given the ease with which Fox could take up the aesthete's argument, we might rewrite Caves's description in Wittgenstein's prose: "Where sufficient budgetary control systems are imposed, there we find *art for art's sake*." In its seemingly endless auto-narration, the system is designed to proffer aesthetic or ideological solutions to financial problems. Only then can everything— the art and the industry, the beauty and the business—end up on screen.

In the late 1990s the system, at least at Fox, was so thoroughly committed to this foundational agon that when empowered actors did not encounter corporate control systems, they solicited them. For neoclassical filmmakers the antecedent belief in the totality of representation had the potential to override other, more narrowly personal or project-specific interests. I have argued that *Jaws* converted plausible denial, up to then merely an element of contemporary political context, into an aesthetic model. Within the studio itself, plausible denial is a producer's malady, an affliction that is necessary to assure that even those productions that fall outside the risk-responsibility purview of the CEO can nevertheless be understood (the passive is crucial) as belonging to him, or to the studio, or the conglomerate, in a meaningful way. What is more, given the relative paucity of evidence of executive intention that even producers within the system can marshall, accounts of studio concern will necessarily appear as narratives, and spooky ones at that. Such narratives will also, and just as necessarily, be bathetically dismissed. Here is Linson describing his first lunch meeting with Bill Mechanic:

> As I glanced over Bill's shoulder, I accidentally made eye contact with Murdoch. I felt the chill. He didn't know who I was, but his look reflected grave disappointment, as if he foretold the next few years. It was either disappointment or gas from the dreadful commissary food.[16]

Murdoch will remain the lodestar of Linson's corporate fantasies, as if attention from the top might rescue the conglomerate from its fate. Linson believes that "with the rise of corporate vertical integration, . . . the guy at the top—in this case Murdoch—didn't care about movies any more than he cared about baseball."[17] Such statements are not new—there are examples from the classic era accusing the New York–based CEOs of the same indifference—nor are they universal—no one seems to have thought Paramount's Charlie Bluhdorn didn't *care* about movies. These remarks have their place, then, not as an analysis of the industry but as the setup to particular, deniable stories about the meanings of films within the studios that develop, finance, and distribute them.

In the triumphant version, Linson's independence within the conglomerate makes it possible for him to surprise Murdoch with an utterly unanticipated film. The example is David Fincher's *Fight Club*. Linson is drawn to Fincher early on because the director is "excited about ideas that were almost indefensible in the corporate culture that would pay for it."[18] The movie proved difficult to market and did not become a financial success until it reached DVD. Nevertheless, Linson was thrilled, largely because *Fight Club* fulfilled its role *within* the studio: It could not be ignored. "I loved the movie. It was so audacious that it couldn't be brought under control. Soon Murdoch and Chernin would be flopping around like acid-crazed carp wondering how such a thing could even have happened."[19] Was it disappointment or gas in that initial, fleeting eyeline match? Linson would do whatever he could to make it the former.

But the triumphant confrontation between producer and studio is only one narrative possibility. A bathetic lack of concern is more likely. Indeed, the presence of a film such as *Titanic* makes it almost inevitable. There is, alongside the economies of risk and responsibility, a third economy within a studio, an economy of attention. Linson describes the production of *Great Expectations*, his first film for Fox, this way:

> It was a couple of weeks before we were to start photography, and considering that costs were already bursting, the mood from Fox was

remarkably quiet. I soon learned why we seemed to be flying under the radar. A month and a half before we started photography, *Titanic* began filming. The scale and the costs of that movie were so immense that until we got into real trouble, no one at Fox paid any attention to us. . . . When the name James Cameron was uttered above a whisper, Mechanic, Rothman, et al. would jerk their heads upward and downward as if they were jolted by a fire drill. When we completed the first eight days of shooting, we were already a week behind schedule, and no one from Fox had even called us.[20]

Like the tales of uncaring CEOs, tales of "flying under the radar" are just as conventional, whether they are spun to explain the bizarrerie of a 1940s B movie or the origins of a film such as *M*A*S*H*.[21] How is this film to be rescued for studio attention? Linson suggests a possibility:

Let me take an ugly left turn for a moment, if for no other reason but to keep both of us enthused. Mechanic and Rothman didn't tell Cuarón or me that a pivotal scene in *Titanic*—one that centered the entire romance of the film—was identical to one in our movie. Whether it was a grand coincidence or an accidental stealing or something even darker, I don't know. Both main characters were burgeoning young artists hired by the rich girl to be drawn nude, resulting in love, romance, and sex. We never saw the *Titanic* script, but if you look at both movies, it would be clear that Fox had to hold our little movie from release until the monster drank first. If we had anything fresh to offer, it was preempted. We were steamrolled.[22]

At its limits, Linson's theory of the studio is supernatural and conspiratorial. But it was not wrong. When post-production delays forced Fox to push back the opening of *Titanic* from July to December 1997, the studio pushed *Great Expectations* back as well since, it was claimed, they would compete for the same, largely female, audience. [23] Cuarón was relatively accepting: "This has been a very long process, and I just wanted to be over with it. But then, after seeing *Titanic,* I was glad we weren't in its wake. We are not the iceberg that will sink that movie."[24] And while the notion that *Titanic* stole the portrait scene from *Great Expectations* does not match the available timeline, it is surprising that executives did not mention (or perhaps notice) the crucial similarity between the two films.

Critics did. David Elliott, writing for the *San Diego Union-Tribune*, dismissed *Great Expectations*' portraits (done by Francesco Clemente) as "chic piffle. . . . His 'best' doodles of Estella are just a touch better than the nude drawing in *Titanic*."[25] In *USA Today*, Susan Wloszczyna opened "Films Draw on Nudes for Artistic Expression" by noting that "movies are suddenly a-swoon with supine young actresses who doff their duds and pose for would-be Picassos."[26] In that same article, *Great Expectations'* writer Mitch Glazer called the coincidence "spooky. When I wrote my first draft in September '95 for *Great Expectations* I had no notion of the other films . . . . I wasn't even aware of the *Titanic* scene until I read a review. I immediately thought, 'Oh, my God. I wish we had a sinking boat, too.'"

Wloszczyna took the trouble to distinguish between the varieties of artistic experience. For Rose, "The key word . . . is liberation." Cameron contended that she "embraces" the situation "as a way of taking power." In *Great Expectations*, Estella "is leading the show." But her position of power is part of her own limitation, not her freedom. Glazer explained, "She doesn't know how to express herself to men except by being teasing and manipulative." Gwyneth Paltrow, who played Estella, had turned down the role Kate Winslet played in *Titanic*. She explained why the nudity in *Great Expectations* was worth doing in characterological terms entirely consistent with Glazer and Linson's understanding of the film's role within the studio: "There's a difference between being completely naked, and completely sexually explicit on screen, as opposed to using your sexuality as an intellectual weapon against somebody, and using it as part of your psychological make-up."[27]

As in most Hollywood films, the display of femininity approaches, but cannot provide, the total. It promises what only artistry can deliver. It is

FIGURE I.6 *Scenes from the artists' studio.* Titanic, *Cameron, Fox/Paramount, 1997;* Great Expectations, *Cuarón, Fox, 1998.*

FIGURE I.7 *The haptic image and the director's touch.* Titanic, Cameron, Fox/ Paramount, 1997.

romantic. But that romance takes many forms, forms decisively inflected in these cases by the woman's gaze (inviting or confronting), by lighting (amber lamplight or natural overexposure), by setting (opulent ornamentation or shabby chic; her place or his), and by the soundtrack (light piano or rock) (Figure I.6). Rose offers her body and a financial token to Jack—the money is the guarantee that her body is not entirely surrendered, else he would be paying her. ("As a paying customer, I expect to get what I want," she says.) Across the scene, the film carefully matches several inset shots, one of Jack's fine, artistic, appreciating fingers running over a Monet canvas, justifying our attention through his; another of Rose's fingers skillfully spinning the dial on the safe in which "The Heart of the Ocean" has been stored; several shots of Jack's fingers not only drawing Rose, but blending the contours of her torso (although decorously stopping at her navel). The match between the safe dial and the drawing of her nipple is all the more charged when we know that the hand drawing Rose is Cameron's own[28] (Figure I.7). In contrast, Estella asks flatly "Do you want me sitting or standing?" Finn can only say "Both." In both cases the film presents the model as incomplete, literally obscured. In *Titanic*, Jack's sketchbook blocks the view of Rose's vulva (it remains vague in the drawing as well), while in *Great Expectations*, the shallow focus gives us a clear view of the drawing of Estella's sex while the photographic Estella is lost in the bokeh (Figure I.8). Only the artist—on-screen, behind the camera, or both—can give the paying customers what, presumably, they want.

Romance aside, the drawing scenes are economic images, moments of immediate exchange between money, power, attention, and art. But when the film instead elaborates the complementarity between business and aesthetics over time, totality is figured by equal parts nostalgia and anachronism. Academic critics have consistently drawn attention to *Titanic*'s nostalgia.

FIGURE I.8 *Lost in the bokeh*. Great Expectations, *Cuarón, Fox, 1998*.

Sobchack quotes Susan Stewart, who defines it as "sadness without an object"[29] while Julian Stringer contends that "the film teaches viewers to miss the things they have never actually been denied. . . . Instead of expecting viewers to supply lived memories, they are now encouraged to bring nostalgia to an image that will supply the memory of a loss never suffered."[30] Where Stewart's (and Sobchack's) nostalgia "turns toward a future-past, a past which has only ideological reality," Stringer's turns to a past that might have actually existed but instead is "nostalgia without lived experience or collective historical memory." Yet whether the object of longing never existed or only happens not to exist in this case, *Titanic* offers pain for losses never suffered.

On Sobchack's account the film compensates for this lack through its narrative self-sealing. On Stringer's account, the compensation occurs largely outside the narrative, in the consumables the film charges with emotion, what he would call "patinated" consumption. Indeed, *Titanic* is fascinated with moral questions of selling, of being sold—"To me it was a slave ship," Rose begins; "As a paying customer," she continues—and of the worth of things unreal—whether that is the "Heart of the Ocean" itself or Jack's drawing, a work that "will be worth a lot more in the morning," Cal, Rose's cuckolded fiancé, smirks.

The complement to the audience's nostalgia and to its compensation via either narrative self-sealing or patinated consumption is the film's commitment to anachronism. At one level, this is simply the epic's wager: that the modernity or contemporaneity of the lead characters will excuse their historical inauthenticity. It is not that these spitting young people with their fully developed sense of the arbitrariness of class distinctions are out of place, but rather that they are the people who drive history forward. Hence Jack recognizes Monet and not just money; hence Rose knows that the *Demoiselles d'Avignon* is good even if it was painted by

"Something Picasso"; hence the knowing banter about "Dr. Freud" and his theories.

Nostalgia and anachronism reestablish the film's roundness at the level of its corporate or industrial self-consciousness. On the one hand, nostalgia stages the interaction of business and aesthetics from the point of view of aesthetics, where the imposition of budgetary constraints constitutes the loss while the longing is the aesthete's affect. "Cameron points to his monitor, which shows his stars . . . wading waist deep in seawater inside the ship's once-opulent dining room. 'Take a good look,' he says, 'because you're the last to see it.' And with a single deft keystroke to his editing machine, the minute-long sequence disappears. 'That's a million-dollar cut.'"[31] Ananchronism, on the other hand, stages the interaction between business and aesthetics from the point of view of business, where the imposition of the budget appears as a feeling of recognition of the present in the past, and the continuity of labor or the durability of the work constitutes art. Linson's conspiracy, like my reading of the allegory of coproduction, is an anachronistic recognition, nostalgic for a studio that had to care. Then again, so is the audience's concern with the film's budget. Why do we care about the money spent on *Titanic*? The nostalgist answers "Because it was never ours to lose." The anachronist says, "Because as paying customers, we expect to get what we want." Fox says both.

That moment of equipoise was more durable than it might seem. *Titanic* was underpinned by a stable meta-relationship between the three economies of risk, responsibility, and attention. Its allegorical form of sustained attention to the economies of the Hollywood system had evolved alongside the predominant motion picture financing regime, which itself evolved as part of the radical financialization of the U.S. economy. For, finally, *Titanic* is the story of a band of treasure hunters who abandon their search for jewels in favor of a new economy of experience. They don't quite know that is what they are doing, though, so when Rose pauses in her story, calling the narrative back into the present, the reverse shot of the transfixed crew is played for laughs. Which to say that the easy equivalence in *Titanic* between stuff and stories is a utopia of fungibility.

Notes

1   Tomas Jegeus, head of Fox's UK marketing, quoted in Justin Wyatt and Katherine Vlesmas, "The Drama of Recoupment: On the Mass Media Negotiation of *Titanic*," in *Titanic: Anatomy of a Blockbuster*, eds. Kevin S. Sandler and Gaylyn Studlar (New Brunswick, NJ: Rutgers University Press, 1999), 29–45, 36.

2   Wyatt and Vlesmas, "The Drama of Recoupment: On the Mass Media Negotiation of *Titanic*," 38.

3 Ibid., 36.

4 Anne Massey and Mike Hammond, "'It was True! How can you Laugh?' History and Memory in the Reception of *Titanic* in Britain and Southampton," in *Titanic: Anatomy of a Blockbuster*, eds. Kevin S. Sandler and Gaylyn Studlar (New Brunswick, NJ: Rutgers University Press, 1999), 239–64, 247–48.

5 Vivian Sobchack, "Bathos and Bathysphere: On Submersion, Longing, and History in *Titanic*," in *Titanic: Anatomy of a Blockbuster*, eds. Kevin S. Sandler and Gaylyn Studlar (New Brunswick, NJ: Rutgers University Press, 1999), 189–204, 202.

6 Peter Krämer, "Women First: *Titanic*, Action-Adventure Films, and Hollywood's Female Audience," in *Titanic: Anatomy of a Blockbuster*, eds. Kevin S. Sandler and Gaylyn Studlar (New Brunswick, NJ: Rutgers University Press, 1999), 108–31, 108.

7 Krämer, "Women First."

8 Art Linson, *What Just Happened? Bitter Hollywood Tales from the Front Line* (New York: Bloomsbury 2002), 24.

9 Richard Caves, *Creative Industries: Contracts Between Art and Commerce* (Cambridge: Harvard University Press, 2000), 136–37.

10 Caves, *Creative Industries*, 137.

11 Ibid.

12 Paula Parisi, "Man Overboard!" *Entertainment Weekly*, November 7, 1997, 26–37, 36, https://issuu.com/paulaparisi/docs/ew_titanic-cover-story, accessed January 20, 2017.

13 Parisi, "Man Overboard!" 37.

14 Caves, *Creative Industries*, 141.

15 Parisi, "Man Overboard!" 37.

16 Linson, *What Just Happened?* 19.

17 Ibid., 17. The integration is only sporadically vertical; at News Corp. it was predominantly horizontal. At the time, they owned the Los Angeles Dodgers, hence the remark about baseball.

18 Ibid., 143.

19 Ibid., 153.

20 Ibid., 112.

21 While at Fox, Linson would literalize his metaphor when he produced *Pushing Tin*, a Hawksian film about air traffic control. It flopped.

22 Linson, *What Just Happened?* 112.

23 Ibid., 92; John Horn, "Release Dates are a High-Stakes Gamble for Films," *Toronto Globe and Mail*, January 2, 1998, C2.

24 Linson, *What Just Happened?* 112. Cuarón has long expressed his dissatisfaction with the film. See Brent Lang, "How Alfonso Cuaron Went Back to Scratch to Rekindle his Career after 'Great Expectations,'" *Variety*,

April 20, 2016, http://variety.com/2016/film/news/alfonso-cuaron-great-expectations-1201757974/.

25 David Elliott, "Dumbed Down Dickens: New 'Great Expectations' Flunks Dickens, Aces Paltrow," *San Diego Union-Tribune*, January 29, 1988, Night and Day 15.

26 Susan Wloszczyna, "Films Draw on Nudes for Artistic Expression," *USA Today*, January 29, 1988, 7D. In addition to *Titanic,* something similar occurs in *As Good as it Gets* (James L. Brooks, Warner Bros., 1997). The parallels were also the subject of a widely syndicated article by Pamela Mitchell, "The Real Artists Behind Reel Art," *The Star-Ledger*, March 4, 1988, 61.

27 P. Fischer, "Gwyn's *Great Expectations*," *Courier Mail*, March 26, 1988, 8. Whether Paltrow knew of the parallel scenes only further complicates the issue. Brian McFarlane discusses this scene in *Screen Adaptations: Great Expectations* (London: Methuen, 2008), 122.

28 Wloszczyna, "Films Draw on Nudes."

29 Sobchack, "Bathos and the Bathysphere," 192.

30 Julian Stringer, "'The China Had Never Been Used!' On the Patina of Perfect Images in *Titanic*," in *Titanic: Anatomy of a Blockbuster*, eds. Kevin S. Sandler and Gaylyn Studlar (New Brunswick, NJ: Rutgers University Press, 1999), 205–19, 213.

31 Parisi, "Man Overboard!" 28.

2

Follow the money:

The Warner '70s

Midway through William Wyler's *How to Steal a Million* (Fox, 1966), Eli Wallach explains to Audrey Hepburn how he managed to pick such a good wine: "I own the vineyard."

Hepburn: What fun.
Wallach: It's a subsidiary of Eastern Coal & Coke.
Hepburn: Eastern Coal & Coke.
Wallach: That's a subsidiary of Western Wool & Flax.
Hepburn: Fascinating. *What's your growth factor?*
Wallach: Say, you're marvelous; you're wonderful. Usually I have
    trouble talking with girls, but with you, it's . . . it's as though you
    were a member of the board.

The gentle fun at the American's expense is an insight into the psychology of the conglomerate. Deep inside the ludicrously diversified behemoth, there are tiny companies that give the CEO something to talk about over dinner. Those companies might be vineyards, or sports franchises, or studios, but the point of them is to class up the CEO and, by extension (or, in addition), "goose" the stock price, as Transamerica CEO Jack Becket put it when discussing United Artists.[1]

It is a truism that the sixties were the age of the conglomerates. Mergers could be tax free, but there was also a stable and effective antitrust regime that prevented cross-ownership. This combination forced conglomerates to form across industrial lines. The resulting holding companies were blandly named monstrosities such as National General, TransAmerica, Commonwealth United, and Occidental. Even legendary brands like Chris-

FIGURE 2.1 *What's your growth factor? The seductions of accounting.* How to Steal a Million, *Wyler, World Wide/Fox, 1966.*

Craft (boats) diversified unrecognizably into television stations, industrial carpet and padding, and then chemicals. The Hollywood studios became baubles. United Artists was already part of TransAmerica (insurance, Budget Rent-A-Car, an airline); Paramount was part of Gulf + Western (oil, insurance, bananas) MGM, Columbia, and Fox were still independent, although conglomerates owned chunks of them. Disney and Universal were the exceptions.

However cataclysmic the era of conglomeration might have been for the creative workers at the studios, the process was, more or less, ordinary. The crises that faced decision-makers at studios—and I want to insist on a very wide ambit for that role, one that would include everyone from the CEO to below-the-line workers who might successfully imagine themselves making creative contributions to the studio's products—were crises of precession. They could be solved by recognizing the problem and engineering it out of the process at a conceptually prior moment. The mediascape had decisively altered—television was already enormously important—but the decisions about filmmaking were less inflected by television than by the need to reassure the new, deep-pocket owners of the continuing relevance of filmmaking to the overall enterprise. Those efforts differed by studio, but at no studio was the concern with the sources of funding and revenue more intense than Warner Bros. More than any other, Warners sought to alleviate its studio crises by aestheticizing the economics that underlay the system as a whole. To understand how that works on the screen, I examine two parallel phenomena: the transformation in Warner Bros. politics in the seventies and the transformation in Warner Bros. economics in the same period. If the American New Wave was replaced by the resurgent studios, the studios managed that only in concert with the broad advance of economic conservatism at the end of the seventies. Warners was the canniest.

For the diversified conglomerates of the 1970s to become the media conglomerates of the late twentieth century, an array of barriers to reintegration and recentralization had to be removed. Most obvious, strong antitrust action had to give way to a new laissez-faire. Less obvious, but still essential, the risks to deferring return on capital had to wane. The studio assembly line is quite long, and the newly ramified revenue stream is even longer. For such delays to be irrelevant in a publicly held company, one of two things has generally been true: either some other revenue stream has masked or swamped the delay (steady insurance premiums or cable subscriptions, oil or bottler revenues, or any other marker of a deep-pockets corporate parent) or the company's other products have included similar delays in order to temper investor expectations. Pharmaceuticals would be one example (although never actualized in Hollywood); consumer electronics another (tried twice, by Sony and Matsushita); other entertainment products would be a third. But whether the delay is masked or expectations are tempered, the cost must be manageable. In this aspect a world-historical shift, the monetarist revolt that broke the back of The Great Inflation of the sixties and seventies, came to the aid of the reagglomeration of the Hollywood studios. The global economy moderated its inflation expectations, and the studio system, with its tiered products, long-time horizons, and consistent, planned production, could be born again.

In the late sixties buyers targeted Warners not for the floundering studio but for its valuable recording arm. By the turn of the millennium the studio had been restored as the iconic brand in what was then the largest media company on earth. However opportunistic, even fickle, the company might seem under CEO Steve Ross, the Warners brand continued to develop, almost without surcease. Warners was more than a participant in the general resurgence of studio power. It was at the forefront of that consolidation and expansion, of the drive for synergy and the limited collapse of that outsized dream.

The 1970s portion of the larger story might be best landmarked by four, evenly spaced movies: *Performance* (1970), *The Exorcist* (1973), *All the President's Men* (1976), and *The In-Laws* (1979).[2] The release of *Performance* had a demonstration effect—for the right audience. It proved that newly installed studio head Ted Ashley was serious about reinvigorating the studio as a friend to the auteur; indeed, its release may have had more to do with making a statement about Ashley than anything else. Among his first acts at the studio, he pulled the supposedly unreleasable film off the shelf, had it recut at additional expense, and then released. *The Exorcist* was the first major project Ashley saw from acquisition to release. It constitutes the apogee of auteurism at Warner Bros. Yet it also represents the new, contingent economics and identities at heart of Warner Communications, Inc. The third film, *All the President's Men*, marked Warners at its most politically savvy, and it revealed the ideological flexibility at the heart of its corporate strategy. Where *Performance* and *The Exorcist* nested the studio in the complications of identity, *All the President's Men* rewrote those stories as identifications with bureaucracy and the state. Warners in the thirties had analogized itself with Roosevelt's New Deal. Now, in the late seventies, it attempted more.[3] In *The In-Laws*, Warners seized the moment of the impending Reagan revolution and offered a comprehensive defense of both the newly invigorated national security state and monetarist economics.

Merger

The short and decisive battle for Warner Bros.–Seven Arts in early 1969 did not presage a new mode of doing business in Hollywood. Instead, it seemed to be more of the same incremental fiddling with corporate control. The studio, which had recently been bought out by a "mere" TV distributor, was going to land inside one or another of the bizarre, diversified conglomerates of the sixties and seventies—either Commonwealth United (movies, music, oil, real estate, jukeboxes) or Kinney Service (janitorial services, publishing, parking garages, funeral homes).[4] In 1969, only Universal and Disney were parts of a broadly integrated media corporation, and that model seemed to be going nowhere.

Indeed, it had to be going nowhere for Kinney to acquire Warners. W7A had initially intended to merge with theater chain National General (which, typical for its time, owned a publisher and an insurance company). But that merger was blocked because in the late 1960s, the Department of Justice still frowned on vertical integration in the motion picture industry.[5] National General was unconcerned because its primary target was the music side of W7A (Atlantic, Reprise). Even when National General agreed to sell off the movie studio Justice blocked the deal.[6] W7A then turned to Commonwealth United only to have Kinney jump in between them and raise similar antitrust concerns. Commonwealth, it seems, already had small a production-distribution arm. Justice blocked that merger, too. This left one possibility, Kinney, which itself had to play a quick shell-game with the Ashley Famous and London International talent agencies. Since movie producers were prohibited from representing talent (one of the few antitrust provisions that remains today, largely through the efforts of the Writers Guild), Kinney sold the agencies. They became ICM, and Ted Ashley left his agency to run the new Warner Bros.[7]

Ross's Kinney Service, the acquiring company, soon renamed Kinney National Service, then National Kinney Service when it was spun off from Warner Communications, was another typical conglomerate. Kinney was formed when Ross united a chain of funeral parlors—reliably profitable, but so profitable it could not be taken public without risking an entire industry's goodwill—with a chain of parking garages—not surprisingly unprofitable given its deep mob ties. Kinney executives told Ross's biographer Connie Bruck that the skimming in the garages created a $1 million slush fund for use in bribing inspectors, paying off unions, securing lucrative leases, and so on. The garages hid the funeral profits; the funeral parlors hid the garages' backers; everyone made out.[8]

From this base, Ross was able to purchase, rather remarkably, Warner Bros.–Seven Arts. The deal for W7A went through the usual run of offers and counteroffers and their attendant PR battles. What shook it loose was a complex move by Kinney, in which they offered two different, convertible, preferred stocks. One was structured so as to provide at least a 40 percent return after five years, regardless of the performance of Kinney. Nothing remarkable in that. But in addition, Warner stockholders would receive 8/10ths of share of "Series C Preferred."

This was a novel security devised by Alan Cohen at the law firm of Paul, Weiss. Almost as soon as it had successfully financed the Warner Bros.–Seven Arts takeover, the Securities and Exchange Commission (SEC) ruled it was not stock, but a warrant, and would be immediately taxable as income. In what would be a forerunner of the Time-Warner deal two decades later, Ross's company's actions were the overriding example that compelled government regulatory action. The point here is that outlaw economics— the economics of the one-sided deal—were strictly limited. On the one hand, investors, some especially unsavory, demanded continued stock performance and that performance was required in order to leverage the kinds of deals Ross wanted to do. On the other hand, the more innovative the deal, the greater the likelihood that it would be irreproducible. Each deal had to be a hit, and each hit had to be unique. In this way, Ross's corporation embodied in its dealmaking Hollywood's one-off mode of production. Kinney was thus intellectually and organizationally ready to move to Hollywood even before it made its play for Warner Bros.

Homology aside, in Ross's conglomerate, division heads such as Ashley operated with a great deal of freedom. As William Frankel, Kinney chairman, put it: "All Kinney executives have promised not to write scripts, not to pass judgment on studio operations, not to give opinions on revenue to be grossed by pictures they have or have not seen and not to be casting directors."[9] A division head's corporate role was to replicate, at the divisional scale, the remarkable dealmaking skills that Ross exhibited at the conglomerate level. In this ramified structure, personal initiative and corporate success nourished each another. It made Kinney a company subject to drastic changes and dramatic turns.

Like other Hollywood studios in the sixties, W7A had turned to the UK in search of profits. United Artists had succeeded mightily with the James Bond films, MGM with *Blow-Up*, and Warners followed. Swinging London attracted studio capital. The fashion burn rate may have been faster than anything Hollywood studios had previously encountered, though, as one subcultural style succeeded another in a matter of months.[10] Still, fresh off the merger, the first film W7A put into production looked to be a sure thing. Ken Hyman, Warners chief in England and the son of studio boss Eliot Hyman, had given the green light to Donald Cammell and Nic Roeg's *Performance*, an organized-criminal-meets-faded-rock-star project. Mick Jagger was to star, Cammell was a bona fide member of "the scene," and the whole thing was to run £1.1 million. The pitch was so obvious, the calculation so easy, that the movie got made with almost no input from Hollywood. When the film was finished, though, Ken Hyman felt betrayed. Despite the script, he and the rest of the Warners brass were unprepared for the frankness (and endlessness) of the sex and the drugs, the extension of the violence, and, perhaps worst of all, the unconscionable delay in actually getting Jagger on the screen. The project was shelved, another failure from the youthquake era of 1968–71, another nail in the coffin of Swinging London's marketability.[11] It was a tidy example of what happens when the studio loses control to the auteurs.

When Ross, Ashley, and John Calley stepped in at Warner Bros., their first move was to write down the value of the production slate.[12] With the slate written off, there was no harm in releasing movies that might underperform because, frankly, nothing could underperform the new estimates. In any case, at a major studio, the loss on a given picture might be overridden by the need to keep the expensive distribution system flush with product.[13] So *Performance* would be recut to the new Kinney National Service standards and emerge as one of the first reliable signals of the emerging mode of operation: financial legerdemain for the business pages, strong studio control of the outgoing product, and, somehow, a commitment to the work of new or independent voices. When Warners gave Alfonso Cuarón a shot at the third Harry Potter installment or Tim Burton or Christopher Nolan the chance to direct a Batman movie, it was being true to a long-standing belief that innovative directors offer it the best chance to expand the audience for an established franchise.

In the mid-sixties, Jack Warner bought and sold and rebought his old studio. The new ownership and management at Warners replaced this decrepit business model with the thrilling business of stock manipulations, mob ties, and quickly shuffled hands of corporate poker. From Steve Ross on down, Warners intended to do whatever it took to bring the excitement they felt about the deal and merge it with the excitement they saw in, and maybe even felt about, the movies. It was pervasive.

With the arrival of Ross's new executive crew, *Performance* came off the shelf. Cammell was brought to Los Angeles to recut the picture—toning down the violence, getting Jagger in earlier and doing something, anything, about the three-way/four-way/n-way sex of the second half. Although no copy of the first version of *Performance* survives, there exists a transcript of the version directors Cammell and Roeg finished in the UK. By measuring the distance between it and the released version, which Cammell recut with Frank Mazzola in LA, we have a rare insight into exactly what differences the director and editor *thought* the studio required. We know that their choices were successful; what we will not know from this is exactly how much *less* they could have got away with; nor will we know which changes were made in response to *explicit* instructions as opposed to intuited desires. It could be that Ashley simply decided that getting *any* version of *Performance* released was critical, and that the changes made no difference. Yet this seems unlikely for two reasons: 1. Warners had only a tiny investment in the film—even less once it had been written down; 2. The decision to summon Cammell to LA and pair him with an experienced editor evinces the need to do something significant. The more logical conclusions are that Ashley saw *something* somewhere in these changes and that Warners found enough to allow it to distribute the film.

It seems clear that this was a project that could simply have been shelved. And it seems clear that Ashley did not want to do that. It also seems clear that in comparison with the preview version, the changes, while perhaps of the order to get the film into releasable shape, were not ones that fundamentally altered its nature, or if they were, that those alterations were not simply accommodations, they also introduced new complications. The opening crosscutting between gangland enforcer Chas (James Fox) having rough sex and a black Rolls Royce cruising down the road, for example, went from five alternating shots to more like fifty. A close-up of a slashed toe was removed. The young male object of mob boss Harry Flowers's lascivious gaze was cut at one point. The last cut ostensibly makes that homosexual gaze deniable (although previous shots let us know who is in the bathroom as he enters), but formally it opens the frame and makes homosexuality more pervasive, more essential.[14]

This shift from perversion to pervasion is typical of the film's reedits, and it compounds the thematic density of Cammell's original ideas. Instead of a simple opposition or a dialectic caught at a standstill, the reedited *Performance* approaches classical wholeness even in its sexual whirl. It is justly famous for its portrayal of the psychic merger of Chas and Turner (Mick Jagger). Chas is on the run from Flowers and must be suspicious that Turner will turn him over to his old boss. When Turner and Pherber (Anita Pallenberg) remake Chas, ostensibly so that his passport photo will not resemble him, they remake him both *as* Turner (as Jagger) and as "a man, male and female."

Chas initially rejects this reconfiguration of his avowed sexuality. Yet when Turner emerges in Chas's psilocybinized reverie as Harry Flowers, Chas's suspicions go by the wayside. Somehow the professional similarity between the two performers opens a channel to their shared anxieties—"He's stuck," the women say about Turner; "he's afraid of you." As confirmation, Chas gets together with Lucy (Michèle Breton), until then the most suspicious member of Turner's ménage. In the morning, when she rolls over to him in bed, we see that *she* is Turner, at least fleetingly.

FIGURE 2.2 *Chas as male and female man.* Performance, *Cammell & Roeg,*
Warner Bros., 1970.

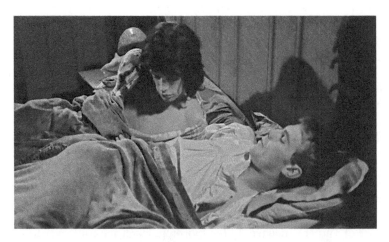

FIGURE 2.3 *Chas and Turner.* Performance, *Cammell & Roeg, Warner Bros., 1970.*

FIGURE 2.4 *Turner as Chas*. Performance, *Cammell & Roeg, Warner Bros., 1970*.

Even the promise of an open sexuality is temporary. Chas heads upstairs to get Lucy some shampoo and finds he has been discovered by Flowers's men. As he bids Turner goodbye, the paranoid possibility that Turner has ratted him out seems to reappear—Pherber takes it that way; Chas seems to at times. Yet as Chas draws a bead on Turner's bowed head and Pherber cries out, the tableau seems less the performance of a ritual of revenge than the sign of real metempsychosis. Chas kills Turner and heads off to his own death. Only then, outside in the car, do we see that Turner has—somehow— replaced Chas.

There are a number of possible sources for these magical pervasions: the mushrooms from the garden; the narrative forms of Borges (whom everyone, from the gangsters to the rockers, is reading); the open portals of a frank bisexuality; William S. Burroughs's tale of the Hashishim; a modernist aesthetic that wants to undermine the conventionality of continuity editing; even the sonic manipulations of the Moog synthesizer that Turner (and Jagger, and, unseen, Jack Nitzsche) control. All of these seem native to the Swinging London setting of the second half of the film. Left out of this list, indeed, left out of almost every discussion of the psychic mergers of the second half of *Performance*, are the corporate mergers carried out by Harry Flowers's mob in the film's first half.

Cammell and Roeg firmly tie the corporate shenanigans at the beginning of *Performance* to the sexual byplay at its end. The Rolls Royce in the opening crosscuts carries a barrister to court where he will defend one of the targets of Harry Flowers's expansion against charges of securities fraud. The fraud is that Flowers has paid a dividend of 15 percent on "the nonvoting B shares" to "expedite" a merger. The defense is that the client knew nothing about the fraud; that he acted in his interests and not out of fear. "In the fluid state of business ethics pertaining today we must protect the inalienable right of the smaller businessman to be conjoined in commercial union." The barrister moves beyond defending that inalienable right toward a defense of identity as such. There may be a "fluid state," but in the midst of that flux, "business is business and progress is progress." Things are themselves and words are not always used tendentiously. "I say 'merger,' gentlemen, not takeover. Words still have meaning even in our days of the computer." The sneering traditionalism of this last line, shared by the jury, seems appropriate to the courtroom. Yet the soundtrack has begun to burble and bleep with Moog tones. The nearly random flux of sonic data accompanies a shift in the barrister's tone. As his defense of his client rises to a defense of the system as a whole, affective dimensions come to the fore. He concludes with a paean to the sexualized economic nationalism that would be more typical of the Thatcherite/Reaganite 1980s: "Our national economy, our national survival, devolves upon the consolidation, by merger, of the smaller and weaker economic units with the larger and lustier pillars of our commercial complex." Lustier pillars: sex and capital, it turns out, suit each other. In retrospect, the initial crosscutting thus offered a question—how do the Rolls and the sex go together? The narrative's simple answer is that Chas works for Flowers, the barrister accuses Flowers, and Chas will threaten the barrister. But the more important link between sex and capital is conceptual. Early in the film, both Chas and the barrister are defenders of identity within the "fluid state" of contemporary desire.

Just as Fraser's merger was not simply the march of the market, so Flowers's mob is not simply a criminal enterprise. Flowers's own homosexuality is almost Whitmanesque in his desire for wholeness: "United we stand, divided we're lumbered." Chas shares an uncertain personal past with Joey; theirs is a childhood friendship gone wrong. The film implies that this parting of the ways had a strongly homoerotic component through Joey's violation of Chas, the graffito "Poof" painted on Chas's wall during the fight scene, and Joey's attempt to get Chas to "say it," to which Chas responds "I am . . ." before pretending to pass out. Later, during the "Memo from Turner" sequence, Turner-as-Flowers will recall meeting Chas when he was "a faggy little leather boy with a smaller piece of stick." The implied arc—from rough trade to his current rough trade—would be in keeping with Chas's extreme and defensive heterosexuality.

More important in this regard is the sequence in which the barrister appeals to the jury. His free market litany is intercut with shots of the jury in which they are not watching him but a low-end pornographic film depicting some mild s&m while a hostess serves them drinks. Any viewer who managed to hover "neutrally" through the opening crosscutting between the barrister's Rolls and Chas's mirror-aided romp is now forced to grapple with the bad faith of such an adjudicatory role. Welcome to the sordid world of the audience and its pursuit of justice, this scene says. Enjoy the performance.

Chas's problem is that he enjoys his work too much, that he makes it "double personal." Flowers (and later Turner-as-Flowers) will be adamant that Chas works for him. The first time we see Chas at work, he and his associates are wrecking the offices of a mini-cab depot that is to be merged into what Harry Flowers calls "this great democratic organization of ours." Deep in the garage, they bemoan the "inefficiencies" of the company, destroying "outdated" equipment and shaking their heads at "correspondence not answered." The extortion scheme is well in hand. The next day, Chas and his lads follow up with the barrister. They break into his garage and pour acid over his car. They tie up the chauffer and shave his head.

The film, in other words, confesses what Warner Bros. (and Ross) could not, that some deep mischief in the garage lies behind every "merger," no matter how plausible it might be to see these acquisitions as simply examples of capitalism on the march. But if *Performance* confesses, it also contends that there might yet be an art to the bare-knuckled operations of criminal capitalism. In 1966, Andy Warhol had publicly offered to endorse a wide range of products and practices, from "sound equipment" to AC-DC. In *The Philosophy of Andy Warhol* (1975), he declared that "Business Art is the step that comes after Art."[15] In *Performance*, the mixture of art and business turns on the notion of madness. Flowers says of Chas that "he's a nutcase, like all artists, but I know I can rely on him." Turner, in contrast, tells us, nearly quoting Antonin Artaud, that "the only performance that really makes it, that makes it all the way, is the one that achieves madness." As it built a conglomerate and a studio of auteurs, Warners could never know whether it was populated by reliable nutcases or performers who had crossed the line into madness. It thrived on the ambiguities of this excess.

Fixation

We come to the full possession of our power of drawing inferences the last of all our faculties, for it is not so much a natural gift as a long and difficult art.

—CHARLES SANDERS PEIRCE, "The Fixation of Belief," 1877

Performance began with the merger of sex and capital in the flickering between Chas's romp and the arrival of the Rolls Royce. Form became narrative in the barrister's paean to the "lustier pillars" of the economy. Narrative became form again when the jury was recast as the audience for a pornographic film. And so on. But if *Performance* runs through the possibilities of merger as such, *The Exorcist* is an investigation of what comes next—possession, or, even more literally, rental and tenancy. The complicated artistry of pleasure and finance that lay behind *Performance* and that pervaded its narrative pauses with *The Exorcist*. In its place, director William Friedkin constructs an aesthetic where transactions between place and person, atmosphere and ego, suffusion and identity provide evidence of power. *The Exorcist* is, not surprisingly, about belief. But it is not, as one might expect, about existential leaps of faith. Instead, it concerns itself with the more pragmatic question of "fixation."

Inside the conglomerate, fixation amounts to the determination of what exactly will be its core and how the various pieces will subsist together. In 1971, Kinney became Warner Communications and spun off or sold its other interests. "Warner Communications Inc. is engaged solely in the entertainment/ communications business," they declared in their annual report.[16] Warner began investing in cable systems, and clearly saw cable as the future.

If cable were to be the future, it was a small part of the company in 1973: 5 percent of revenues, merely 1.5 percent of profits. Recorded music was still the present. It accounted for half of WCI's revenues and half its income that same year. Nothing seemed to be able to touch the music business. In contrast, the film studio was subject to cycles of boom and bust that occasionally reflected the broader economy and occasionally did not. Turning it around, as Ashley did, would make the biggest impact on WCI's bottom line. Revenues went from $64 million in 1970 to $153 million in 1973 to $275 million in 1974, the year *The Exorcist* had its biggest effect. Income went up as well. The film studio that had lost almost $6 million in 1970 made $22 million in 1973 and $57.5 million in 1974. It accounted for more than half the company's profits that year.[17]

More than anyone, Ted Ashley was given credit for restoring the studio to profitability. Initially, profitability depended on making more hits. Warners aggressively pursued the youth market with films like *Performance* and *Woodstock* (its first big Kinney-era hit); it catered to the older viewer with films like John Wayne's *Chisum*; and managed to bridge the generations with the youth-targeted nostalgia film *Summer of '42*. The studio also ramped up its television production.

But Warner took special pride in its ability to make hits through marketing. Its 1973 Annual Report crowed:

We are very concerned with making good films. . . . But the demands of today's marketplace call for much more if a production-distribution company is to be successful. The distributor must aggressively and imaginatively market his product if he is to draw audiences to theaters.

A prime example of this imaginative marketing is a film called "Billy Jack." Almost unnoticed when it was released, it created the greatest excitement in the film industry in 1973. Together with the Taylor-Laughlin Distributing Co., Warner Bros. distributed "Billy Jack" by arranging for its exhibition in a large number of theaters simultaneously in each market and accompanied this "saturation booking" with heavy television and other advertising. In this case the results were explosive. "Billy Jack" originally released in 1971 ranked among the year's top grossing films.[18]

At the same time that it was experimenting with new, forward-looking distribution models, the studio looked to slash fixed costs both because they weighed down the bottom line and because they made the studio less nimble. Ashley's grandest scheme involved the studio plant itself. In June 1971, he and Columbia president Leo Jaffe announced that the two studios would move in together on the Warners lot. The Burbank Studios, as it would be called, would own the facilities; the studios would rent. Columbia's Gower St. studio and its Burbank ranch would be sold, and the proceeds would revert to the Burbank Studios. By sloughing off their high fixed costs, the studios would be better positioned to ride out the recession of the early seventies. (That August, the Nixon administration would impose wage and price controls in an effort to rein in inflation.)[19]

In the *Wall Street Journal*, an anonymous executive hailed the deal as "the first time in the movie business that a decision was based on economics rather than emotions."[20] This was patently false and said more about the myth of Hollywood irrationalism than the reality of studio economics. Nevertheless, the agreement emblematized a major shift away from identifying studios with places. Fox had sold its land to Alcoa to build Century City. It leased back its lot. Gulf + Western (Paramount) had sold half its lot to an Italian real estate company. And MGM had sold sixty-eight acres and was considering a further sale. "Today the economy is such that the so-called question of ego—our image—is terribly unimportant," said Leo Jaffe.[21]

Jaffe may have believed that or he may have been in denial, but Columbia nearly went bankrupt in 1973 in part because of such thinking. Only an image-unconscious studio head would think that a musical remake of Frank Capra's *Lost Horizon* (starring Liv Ullman, no less) was the appropriate way to christen the new facility. Two pilots, nestled in the mountains (or at least over the hills in the San Fernando Valley), squabble over whether to stay in Shangri-La or not. Like most of Columbia's major productions in the early seventies, it was a flop. That year, the studio lost $50 million. Investment banker Herbert Allen bought control, installed David Begelman and Alan Hirschfeld, and temporarily turned Columbia around.[22]

Ashley, in contrast, was committed to his studio's image, to remaking Warners in the Kinney image. And vice versa. Instead of seeing the sale of the Burbank lot as the loss of the studio's patrimony, the deal with Columbia confirmed that Warners was in the business of making audacious deals. That buccaneering could occasionally conflict with the emerging distribution-driven model of Warners' success. For example, at the same time they agreed to pool their studio space, Ashley and Jaffe also agreed to set up a joint distribution operation in Europe, beyond the reach of American antitrust enforcement.

In *Final Cut*, Stephen Bach points out that the key difference between United Artists and studios like Warners was not that UA had no lot but that it was "free of player and other talent contracts" and a "direct signatory to none of the unions."[23] If UA offered "independent production in an atmosphere of autonomy and creative freedom," Warner, under Ashley, was determined to offer studio production in the same atmosphere.[24] But to do so would require a greater tolerance for risk and a willingness to spend money on talent. Ashley possessed both.

The month before the Burbank deal, Harper & Row published *The Exorcist*. It sold poorly at first, but author William Peter Blatty's appearance on the Dick Cavett show changed that.[25] He was always the best salesman of his work. He had initially struck a paperback deal that allowed him to retain the film rights. Then he sold the hardcover to Harper & Row and the film rights to Warners. "I hope the deal I've just made will help make it possible for all screenwriters to participate more richly in the in the artistic and economic ends of film-making." More richly indeed: producer credit, screenplay credit, $641,000, and 35 percent of the net profits. He retained TV, sequel, and theatricalization rights.[26]

Yet despite Blatty's legendary deal, he felt the film got away from him. Between the first cut and the release version Friedkin removed twenty minutes, and in those twenty minutes, the moral of the film seemed to vanish. It had originally been there in the form of a conversation between Father Karras and Father Merrin, where the old priest answers the question: "Why this little girl?" Blatty fumed at its absence: "The audience is longing to hear that! 'Why am I being subjected to all this bestiality; what is the point?' . . . They think it was just a series of shocks with no point at all otherwise."[27] The audience is never given "the point," and Blatty cannot understand why the film is as popular as it is. Oddly, for Blatty, the moral did not disappear at the behest of the studio. In fact, what seemed most perplexing to the writer-producer was that Friedkin had almost complete control of the production and still he squandered his chance to make a statement. "The film that Billy delivered in '73 *was* highly effective. But it lacked a spiritual centre. You proceeded from shock to shock without a clear purpose. It was a rollercoaster ride whose success made me comfortably well-off, but also troubled me."[28] In the post-production rush, Friedkin eventually had two different editing teams working nearly nonstop on the film. His relationship with Blatty, who had lobbied Warners to hire him in the first place, turned so sour that Blatty found himself barred from the editing rooms. Blatty's deal seemed to guarantee him control, but in the end, the alliance of director and studio proved more powerful.

Like Blatty, who could not find the moral in the film, *New York Times* critic Vincent Canby could not discover the sort of allegory he expected. For *The Exorcist* to find its place in the director-centered New Hollywood, it had to make a personal statement, yet there was nothing there:

While watching the film the first time at a press screening, I kept trying to figure out what the movie was *really* up to. Critics are like that. They keep trying to find hidden meanings in the most explicit, bald-faced narratives. . . .

I thought it might actually be about film criticism: the possession of the child was simply a metaphor for the young critic who finds himself possessed at various points in his career by consuming passions that have emanated from the brains of others. . . .

Not at all.[29]

Canby had been one of the few critics to pan the film, and his decision to revisit his review conveys his bafflement. There was no manifest meaning; in that he agreed with Blatty. But more surprising there was no hidden meaning. Why, he wonders, would an institutionally sanctioned auteur squander such a remarkable opportunity?

Canby's mistake was to regard the metacinematic potential of the possession story as something hidden. "I love to talk film. To discuss. To *critique*." When Lt. Kinderman says this to Karras, Canby's preferred allegory obtrudes. This line, punctuated differently, appears in the novel, as do other metacinematic potentials. But throughout *The Exorcist* as it was released in 1973, Friedkin curtails this sort of dialogue. In the same scene in the novel, Kinderman will hit the nail too squarely on the head when Karras asks him if anyone has ever told him he looks like Paul Newman: "'And believe me, inside this body, Mr. Newman is struggling to get out. Too crowded. Inside,' he said, 'is also Clark Gable.'"[30] That line is missing from the film, as is a concluding, painfully parallel scene between Kinderman and Father Ryan. "'I shot that ending,' Friedkin confirms, 'and it was no fucking good at all.'"[31]

Friedkin consistently chipped away at explicit discussions of faith or cinephilia. "The first time round I was determined to eliminate any form of overstatement from *The Exorcist* and not to lay on the message at all."[32] He sensed, as his critics largely have not, that the film would have been far less shocking had there been a stable, well-articulated framework of reference into which characters might nest incomprehensible events. The problem for Friedkin was, in short, meaning. Questions of meaningfulness simply had to remain open for the film to do its work. A uniform semantics or theodicy would have undermined its effect. When Kinderman pumps Karras for information and the priest proves as cagey as Friedkin, Kinderman calls him out: "Answer the question, Father Paranoia." He does not. Discussing "The Version You've Never Seen"—a recut and remixed version from 2000— Friedkin said "Bill [Blatty] had been imploring me for years to put the film back to the way I first cut it, because he felt it had more meaning like that. So I finally agreed. . . . Viewing both versions now, I can see that the old version *is* a colder film, more dyspeptic and abstract, more like a piece of contemporary music than a classical piece. This new version is much warmer. And, I think, much better."[33] Friedkin's evaluation aside, the tradeoff is clear:

more meaning versus more abstraction. Friedkin had fought for abstraction in 1973, and he had won.

In the 1973 release version of the film, Friedkin placed a "subliminal" image of the demon, Pazuzu, in Karras's dream sequence. He added several others for "The Version You've Never Seen." The additional images were unnecessary in the original release because music played that role. As sound historian Jay Beck put it: "The music in *The Exorcist* was specifically chosen and placed in the film to function on the level of liminality, being either barely perceptible or indistinguishable from general background sounds."[34] Jack Nitzsche, who programmed and operated the Moog in *Performance*, did the music for *The Exorcist*. This element of the soundscape, along with an innovative division of labor in the sound team, constitutes the film's progressive legacy in Beck's account. Yet at the same time, the film relied on discrete, even proprietary sound effects that undermined that innovation. When the demon speaks through the girl's body, it is, at first, shocking. Consequently, Michel Chion sees *The Exorcist* as "contribut[ing] significantly to showing spectators how the cinematic voice is 'stuck on' to the cinematic body." Beck reads that moment of adhesion differently, as "the mark of transition that separates the period of experimentation during the early 1970s from the reification of recording and mixing practices that is introduced with Dolby Stereo."[35] The film's janus-faced approach to sound produces in Beck the same ambivalence that the amorality and unallusiveness of the film induced in Blatty and Canby. "'The Exorcist' is about demonic possession," Canby concludes, nothing else. It has no instructive aim. For Beck, "*The Exorcist* is a compendium of interesting sound work but without a larger system of sound usage. . . . In many ways the film becomes anti-climactic once the exorcism begins."[36]

To be disappointed in *The Exorcist*, as Blatty and Canby and Beck are, is to be disappointed that there is no unified conception behind it (what Beck will call, after Walter Murch, "design"). Yet as it proceeds "from shock to shock," as it leaves one disappointed Kinderman-critic after another in its wake, *The Exorcist* allegorizes the story of allegory, and it exorcises the search for meaning. What it installs in the place of meaning is efficacy: "It *was* effective." "I don't have a philosophy that is of any interest, even to me. I'm just trying to do stuff that I think works."[37] *The Exorcist* was built to show that there was no tradeoff between the studio and the auteur, between the popular and the personal. Ashley could take credit for seeing the film from acquisition to release; Blatty could take credit for the novel, the script, and as producer; Friedkin could use it to cement his status as a blockbuster auteur after *The French Connection* (Fox, 1971).

To believe in *The Exorcist* was not to believe in anything except that it would work. "Nobody has believed in this more than Ted Ashley," Friedkin said while still on set in April 1973. Even as the production went over budget, the increasing costs seemed to be part of the publicity. Joyce

Haber reported that because Friedkin wanted to work with his own crew, labor costs were higher. "The Washington union said that for each man we brought in we had to use a local guy. Sometimes two. That doubled the payroll."[38] Yet studio chief John Calley, who was notoriously so frightened reading the book that he demanded his dog climb in bed with him, was not scared by Friedkin's overruns. "These are the best dailies I've ever seen in my life. I think he's not wasting any money. . . . It's not a bummer situation."[39]

The Exorcist, for all its excessive display and its tremendous effectiveness, operates within Warner Bros. more philosophically, or at least at a higher level of abstraction, than *Performance*. It shares this paradigmatic quality with *Jaws, The Godfather,* and *The Conversation*, as I argue in *The Studios after the Studios*. These films seem to balance themselves between the personal filmmaking values of the New Hollywood and the renovation of classical narrative forms. Yet their historical significance lies not in their popularity but rather in their ability to posit a reciprocating framework that might routinize the transformation problem, the antinomy of popularity and authorship. Hollywood always had, and always would have, hits. What it could not find until the period from 1972 to 1975 was an understanding of the postclassical system that could be articulated at all possible moments of recursion: sequence, story, cycle, studio, and industry.[40] Studios and others might copy hit films in an effort to repeat their success; but part of that success consisted in the films' power to incarnate the model of success. Beck implicitly lays out that model when he casts *The Exorcist* as a crucial turning point in sound history. The attachment of the demon's voice to Regan's body is the pivot from experimentation to reification. In the film, this is the announcement of possession. In the life of the corporation, this is the fixation of belief.

When Canby claimed that *The Exorcist* was "not at all" about possession as a figure for film criticism, he was not entirely correct. Inside *The Exorcist* there is another film, *Crash Course*. Its role is to suggest two or three crucial emblems for the film: a framework for identity, an image of shock-inducing direction, and a reminder of the constructed or rendered nature of presence in film.

The first of these aligns identity with the notion of temporary corporate possession, an economic image that thus positions *The Exorcist* within the cutting-edge corporate finance of WCI. We know the name of the film-within-the-film from the sign on Chris's trailer. We also know that the trailer has only been leased to Warner Bros. just as the house Chris and Regan live in is a rental. ("The house was a rental," begins the second paragraph of the novel.) Part of the *Crash Course* shoot is to take place in the District, part in Burbank. The novel describes it as the corporate equivalent of *Lost Horizon*: a musical comedy remake of another famous Frank Capra/Columbia film, *Mr. Smith Goes to Washington* (1939). When she arrives home after her one day of shooting, Chris calls it "The Walt Disney version of the Ho Chi Minh story." Blatty and Canby were tempted by the thought that *The Exorcist* was

FIGURE 2.5 *Leased to Warner Bros.* The Exorcist, *Friedkin, Warner Bros., 1973.*

"*really*" about criticism (or *critique*). We might be similarly tempted by the thought that the film is "*really*" about the new joint tenancy at the Burbank Studios. It would be difficult to stabilize the analogy between *Crash Course* and Columbia, though. In addition to the Warner trailer, there is a loving shot of the Panavision Silent Reflex camera on a crane, and Panavision was part of WCI (Figure 2.6). Its business model was unequivocal: "'We do not sell cameras' [President Robert] Gottschalk says. 'Selling equipment is silly to me. The market is too small for professional equipment. It's also wrong for someone to purchase the equipment because it either becomes refined or outmoded too quickly to recoup the investment.'"[41] But if it is impossible to say that the on-screen Warner is the same as the offscreen Warner, it is possible to trace the arc of possession: from place to person; from atmosphere to ego.

FIGURE 2.6 *Leased equipment.* The Exorcist, *Friedkin, Warner Bros., 1973.*

When we first meet Burke Dennings, the director of *Crash Course*, he is illustrating a sweeping camera move up and over a crowd protesting the destruction of the philosophy building. His motion will be echoed by the shot of (not by) the Panavision camera on the crane. This swirling camera will reappear in a more extreme version in the camera that captures the images for Regan's pneumoencephalogram.

Allegories of cinema in *The Exorcist* are often accompanied by neutral, bureaucratized voices that could as soon be talking to the viewer as to Regan: "You're going to feel a little stick," "You're going to feel some pressure," "Don't move," "When I touch your forehead open your eyes . . ." In the last of these cases, "the film obeys, opening its eyes to see the haggard face of Regan," as Mark Kermode describes it.[42]

As Regan manifests further signs of possession, she is further subjected to the predations of the medical establishment and its violent cinema. In recoil, Regan's demon seizes upon the identification of the camera with her and with the audience to suggest that in the wake of Dennings's death, she will assume his role as director. And so she violently grabs the crotch of the hypnotist and drives him into the ground in full, growling p.o.v. The film has obeyed the hypnotist; now it will obey Regan.

Her extreme profanity makes her the heir to Burke's shock humor. When Chris confronts Burke with her questions of motivation and plot—why *does* the administration want to tear down the philosophy building?—he sarcastically suggests they contact the writer in France. "What's he doing there? Hiding?" "Fucking." This gets a big laugh. Later, at Chris's party, Dennings's shock-for-shock's-sake conversation crosses the line when he announces, "There seems to be an alien pubic hair in my gin." And when he is alone with the butler Karl, he accuses him of being a Nazi and calls

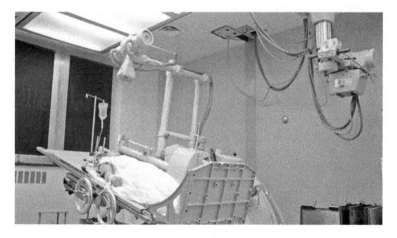

FIGURE 2.7 *The pneumo camera.* The Exorcist, *Friedkin, Warner Bros., 1973.*

him a "cunting Hun." A fight breaks out. His immediate recourse to profane, sexualized humor marks him as a lonely old man, by an iron law of Hollywood Englishness (bawdy = desperate). In contrast, Regan's ability to vocalize Burke, "Do you know what she did, your cunting daughter?" buttresses her claim to directorial power.

This arbitrary attachment of a voice to a body suits the film's soundscape as a whole. Chris's walk home from the set of *Crash Course*—from one rented space to another—is one of the film's most atmospheric sequences, in part because, as Friedkin put it, "Nothing happens," and in part (and as a consequence) because it is sonically obtrusive.[43] This is where we hear "Tubular Bells" for the first time. (Friedkin had notoriously thrown out Lalo Schifrin's complete score and replaced it with occasional music—never under dialogue unless it was diegetic.[44]) And yet because the walk is atmospheric, its role has been underestimated. Once Chris is home she will never go back on set; she will not read her script; and she will not inquire about what might become of the film after the director dies. *The Exorcist* all but drops *Crash Course* during this brief sequence. But it does not drop that film's audience. Instead, it seems to carry that audience from the set to Chris's home, as if it wanted us to shift our inevitable attraction from filmmaking to something else.

The Georgetown portion of the novel opens on April Fool's Day; in the film it is Halloween. Shifting the time from spring to fall alters the background of Chris's walk home. It also means that instead of a campus on holiday (Spring Break), it is a campus in full swing. In place of the logistical logic that would encourage a film company to film when there were fewer uncontrolled elements, the film version of *The Exorcist* follows an experimenter's logic, the high postmodern curiosity that wonders what people might be willing to watch in a world where there is always, potentially, filming.

The first line on set comes through a bullhorn and calls out for "a priest, a nun, and two students. That's what we want. That's exactly what we want." It alerts us to the constructed nature of cinematic crowds. As Chris walks home, she will be passed by a group of trick-or-treaters (two witches, a ghost, something with orange hair); then she will spy two nuns, habits billowing behind them; and then she will come across Father Karras counseling another priest: "Not a day of my life goes by I don't feel like a fraud," Chris will hear them before she sees them. She will also lose the dialogue in the sound of a passing airplane.

When we first hear the bee-buzz connected with the demon in the Iraq prologue, it obtrudes, but we cannot know, yet, whether this is because the demon itself stands out, because Father Merrin hears it this way, or because it is an expressionistic effect. Something similar applies to the distinctly material sounds of the "rats" Chris hears in the attic. (Much of this effect is lost in the move to surround sound; once the noise has a decisive spatial origin, it is harder to imagine it as originating in the mind of the on-screen listener.) The scene on set is a hubbub, but still seems representational: it says, this is what it is like to be on a crowded film set. Yet in the walk home, the soundscape is increasingly rendered, to use one of Michel Chion's oppositions. The footfalls are too punctual, the leaves too crisp as they fall from the trees, the motorcycle too throaty, the nuns' habits too billowy, the passing airplane too convenient. It may be that Chris persists in a heightened state of attention to the world around her, but whether we are supposed to share that intensity or whether we are merely subjected to it remains an open question.

A rendered soundscape or an explicitly constructed crowd raises the possibility of authorship. It opens up a space that might be filled by the director or the audience or someone else. Friedkin's candidacy was the most promising. His control over the project was remarkable for a major Hollywood production. He had just come off an Oscar-winning hit; he was working far from Burbank; his budget and shooting schedule were flexible. If there was to be such a thing as an authored Hollywood film, *The Exorcist* should have been it. Yet Friedkin's public stance throughout the process foregrounded both his pragmatism and his willingness to compromise. And by stripping out Blatty's ready moralizing and making a show of his belief in whatever works, Friedkin tempered his own authorial stance vis-à-vis the film. At the same time, he regularly made choices that increased the obviousness of those choices. If he was an auteur, he was an auteur whose private thematic was a desire to prod the audience.

We first hear the demon speak about halfway in, when Regan barks, "Stay back! The sow is mine!" and then, "Fuck me! Fuck me!" The demon is next heard in the crucifix masturbation scene ("Let Jesus fuck you!"). If the climax of the film has been the shocking discovery of this voice in this body, the rest of the film tells two parallel, investigative stories: Kinderman's search for Burke Dennings's killer, and Karras's attempt to figure out whether Regan is possessed. Kinderman's search is imagistic: he sees things; he explains that Dennings was found with his head turned "completely around." (The camera cuts across the axis at this point, highlighting the 180° rotation.) Karras's search is sonic and linguistic. His crucial tool is a tape recorder, and his investigation breaks open when he finds out that Regan speaks "English in reverse."

If we want to know what the sound *means*, we will have to play it backward. But for the film's audience, the effect of the sound is more important than the meaning. "English in reverse," at least in *The Exorcist*, sounds a good deal like the chanting Arabic of the film's Iraq prologue. If that sound is the demon's language, then the passage from Nineveh to Georgetown is a transcendent example of a voice finding a body, a process Chion calls de-acousmatization. The *acousmêtre*, the unseen sonic being, underlies one of the great narrative courses of sound film. Here, the path of the *acousmêtre* is emblematic of the film's pattern of concretization. What was *langue* is now *parole*; what was atmosphere is now ego.

What brings about this manifestation? The film's word for this unseen cause is "power." Kinderman believes that "a very powerful man" snapped Dennings's neck and threw him out the window. Regan, when possessed, eschews breaking her wrist straps because that would be "a vulgar display of power." In the end, that display of power will be announced or perhaps conjured over and over again, "The power of Christ compels you." The obscene or naked display of power in the film and the cultivation of "shock after shock" by the film muddied the ending for many audiences and gave rise to Blatty's decades of resentment.

In the end, then, we can see that *The Exorcist* tells the story of Warner Bros. in two registers. The more literal and limited allegory works through the problems and promises for the studio of temporary possession and rental. Without ownership, how does identity continue? The film's answer is to claim that all identity is temporary possession. The more general and speculative possibility liberates auteurist control and paranoia from their local economies and makes them available for use in more abstract problems of power, identity, and reification. Completing the cycle begun by *Performance, All the President's Men* puts control and paranoia back to work for the studio. Instead of sharing authorship with some mere individual, even an individual demon, Warners can now contend with the state.

Paranoia

When Chris arrives home from work, her assistant tells her she has been invited to dinner at the White House. Chris laughs it off, and, like *Crash Course*, the invitation is never mentioned again. But the mere mention of the president reminds us that Georgetown is part of the District, and that another, more earthly, power resides there.

Whatever Friedkin's personal views, by 1973 Warners' politics had become quite complicated. Outlaw economics became untenable once Ross decided to turn the company toward vertical, rather than horizontal, integration. As WCI's investment in cable television grew, Warners' politics changed to fit the new situation. No longer could it hope to remain outside the administration's eye. Broadcast networks had long been barred from producing much of their own programming. In 1973, the government (via the Office of Technology Policy) was considering extending that prohibition to owners of cable systems as well. In response, WCI made a deal with a devil of its own, Charles Colson.[45]

During part of the year between his departure from the White House and his indictment on Watergate-related charges, Colson was "on the WCI payroll as a consultant vis-à-vis cable regulation."[46] This relationship had a direct impact on the sorts of stories WCI would tell. A "former WCI executive" told investigative journalist Connie Bruck that "it was because of Colson's relationship to the company that Warner Publishing was told not to enter into a contract for the publication of a manuscript that had been submitted to the Watergate burglar James McCord in the spring of 1973. The manuscript, in which Colson was a major player, was full of revelations that would not emerge for another four to six months, in the course of the Ervin hearings. Had it been rushed to print, it would have been a publishing coup."[47]

As part of the effort to secure its vertical integration on the cable side, Warners joined a lawsuit against the major broadcast networks. And in keeping with Nixonian practice, lifelong Democrat Ted Ashley gave more than $100,000 to Nixon's reelection campaign, skirting the law by spreading the donations around to various county Republican organizations. His donations were revealed in the spring of 1974, just as Colson was indicted. Ashley resigned, telling reporters that the revelations had nothing to do with his decision and that he intended to go into politics. He did not. Instead, he returned to Warners a year later when the furor had passed.[48]

As soon as Colson was out of the picture, Warners jumped at the chance to make *All the President's Men*. It was a classic double game: Steve Ross and Robert Redford could continue to campaign for Democrat Hugh Carey in New York while Ashley was underwriting Nixon. All the while, the Republican cash-for-favors machine could slowly undermine the foundations of antitrust enforcement.[49]

In the film, this ideological dissonance appears when Redford/Bob Woodward announces that he is a Republican to Hugh Sloan. Dustin Hoffman/Carl Bernstein looks at Redford in shock and Redford returns the glance. For Woodward, it was true; but Hoffman's shock in the film is hard to place: is it that Woodward has said it? That Redford has? That it might be true of Redford? That one or the other, Woodward or Redford, is craven enough to say it knowing that there is no chance Sloan or the audience will believe that he could be a Republican? Everything is a possibility.

"You're both paranoid. She's afraid of John Mitchell and you're afraid of Walter Cronkite." When Woodward says this in *All the President's Men*, he is trying to bring Bernstein back down to the story at hand. If everyone's paranoid, then we can all just get back to work. "Boy that woman was paranoid," Bernstein has just said. "At one point I suddenly wondered how high up this thing goes and her paranoia finally got to me. I thought that what we had was so hot that any minute CBS or NBC are gonna come in the windows and take the story away." The matching cases of paranoia depend on matching conspiratorial organizations—the Nixon administration on the one hand, large media companies like the Post and CBS on the other.

The name Cronkite here is not a detail from the Watergate scandal as such—Cronkite broke no news; he does not figure in the book. Instead, Cronkite is an artifact of the screenwriting process. Writer William Goldman recounts meeting the anchor for the first time in late 1974. Cronkite's greeting? "I hear you have script trouble." As for having someone take the story away, that is Goldman's fear as well, realized when Carl Bernstein and Nora Ephron presented Redford (acting as producer) with their own version of the script.

> As a screenwriter, I test very high on paranoia. I'm always convinced of any number of things: that my work is incompetent, that I'm about to get fired, that I've already *been* fired but don't know yet that half a dozen closet writers are typing away in their offices, that I *should* be fired because I've failed, on and on.
> But all those nightmares—and on occasion they've all happened—are within the studio system. . . . But for two *outsiders*, a hotshot reporter and his girl friend, to take it upon themselves to change what I've done without telling anybody and then to turn it in to the producer—a "go" project, remember—
> —not in this world possible.[50]

In the film, then, the screenwriter's paranoia about loss of control is handed over to the writers at the *Post*, a likely enough identification. But the *Post* was also a media conglomerate with troubles similar to those facing WCI. In response to the paper's Watergate crusading, the Nixon administration attacked the *Post*'s ownership of several television stations. It was another case of content and distribution interfering with each other.[51]

This bit of Hollywood conspiracy helps nuance Fredric Jameson's otherwise bravura reading of *All the President's Men* in *The Geopolitical Aesthetic*. The film, for him, displays parallel conspiracies, organizations that operate in opposition but that ultimately further a system in which organization "as such" is the victor. Conspiracies are, for Jameson, typically degenerate totalities, representations of the total submission of the world to the imperatives of the market, yet hopeful emblems nonetheless in their socialization of what is truly social. This argument, which Jameson has been making in one form or another since his early work on Wyndham Lewis, never for a moment imagines that totality is anything but figural: it must be represented since it cannot be lived. The Woodstein movie, which looks like a political film that is actually about politics, hence, a real totality, turns out to be an allegory of itself. And in that allegory, what is represented is not politics but capitalism, emblematized in the dramatic ascending shots inside the Library of Congress and the matching shots of the radial DC streets both day and night.[52]

Yet these great moments of structural revelation are the exceptions; the aim of *All the President's Men* is to show the sort of work that goes into realizing one's place in such a network, to account for the emergence of self-awareness that would seek out such emblems in the first place. The locus of that knowledge in *All the President's Men* is twofold, but it does not map onto the opposing conspiracies. First, there is the *Post* newsroom, a poster-colored

FIGURE 2.8 *Geometric totality.* All the President's Men *and all the president's men's books, Pakula, Warner Bros., 1976.*

grid of open—we can now call them *uncubicled*—desks. Knowledge emerges there as *knowledge produced*, regathered from notes, elicited on the phone, coerced out of loyal female employees. The soundscape is dry and concussive: typewriters, telexes, bakelite handsets in their cradles, hold buttons. Many of the voices come "on-the-air" and have lost much of their treble and dynamic range; they are the self-advertisements of bureaucratized communication. Dialogue at the *Post* is nearly always in service to the *story*, its confirmation, its wording; debates are internal to the communications apparatus.

The parking garage at night is the second location of knowledge, of *knowledge imparted*. Deep Throat knows without effort; he may only confirm and hedge, but beneath that he *knows*. Here the soundscape is awash in "materializing sound indices" (msi's)—the reverberant scuff of feet on the concrete, the thickness of saliva in a smoker's mouth, the resounding flick of a lighter.[53] Since there is no work in getting the knowledge, no process, each crumb is burdened by markers of its source. The work is material; it consists of making sounds not stories. The garage sessions do not turn into debates because there is nothing debatable; there is only the truth, where to find it, what it will look like, how it will sound.

The newsroom lacks materializing sound indices with the exception of the scrub-squeak of the felt tip pens and the scritching of the pencils. Writing implements have particularly rendered sounds in the film, part of Pakula's and Warners' general commitment: "You try to orchestrate the sound track very carefully for an effect," Pakula said. "That's one of the great tools you have as a director—what you do with the sound track."[54]

FIGURE 2.9 *Gridded architecture at The Washington Post*. All the President's Men, *Pakula, Warner Bros., 1976.*

As for *why* handwriting implements in the *Post* and elsewhere have such high msi's where machine writing instruments do not, this sonic convention extends the film's general notion that any fall out of an organization and into mere personhood entails a heightened vulnerability. The individual's relationship to the collective of which he is not firmly a part must be a paranoid one. Woodward, in the film, tests very low on the paranoia scale, with the exception of one night after a meeting with Deep Throat. He walks away from the garage in a long shot, gathering speed, eventually running. When he turns, breathing hard, the camera is tight on him. No one has been following him. The paranoia is structural, and contagious: "Her paranoia got to me," "It's the way they're not talking." The more knowledge appears to be made, the less effort its materialization will require. The more it appears to be imparted, the more paranoid its scenes of exchange will become, for in those scenes the parallel conspiracies make contact through the bodies and voices of individuals acting outside the bureaucratic communication loops.

Voice, handwriting, and machine writing come together in the scenes where Woodward and Bernstein attempt to reconstruct the organizational hierarchy and informational economy of the Committee to Re-Elect the President (CREEP) from an alphabetical list. As they work through the photocopied, typewritten list, they visit and cross off each employee.

On one of their trips through the list, we will see the streets of the District pass into radial essence. This is one of those Jamesonian moments when the individual's relationship to knowledge has been totalized. But by reading the corporation out of capitalism, Jameson misses the studio pun in the sequence. As they pull away from the corner, we will hear Hoffman/

FIGURE 2.10 *Alphabetic totality: CREEP list*. All the President's Men, *Pakula, Warner Bros., 1976.*

Bernstein begin to list the names. And very quickly, Redford/Woodward will correct one pun only to replace it with another:

> Bernstein: How can you keep goin' at something past the point when you believe it?
> Woodward: We just have to start all over again.
> Bernstein: Naismith, Narrow, Ness, Nichols, Nixon
> Woodward: Ed Nixon . . . Jolson, Jones, Jordan, Jost
> Bernstein: If we could only get somebody that worked for finance to talk. I can't believe . . .
> Woodward: What about the bookkeeper?
> Bernstein: Which bookkeeper?
> Woodward: The bookkeeper that worked for both Slanz and—
> Bernstein: Oh, *you're* alright.
> Woodward: —Sloan and Stanz.
> Bernstein: I been there. I called her twice. There's no answer.
> Woodward: I say we should start again. Abbott, Addis, Agusto, Albers, Aldiss, Allessandro,
> Bernstein: Gelovsky, Glenn, Gonstel, Boyle, Brenner, Bromley
> Woodward: Jost
> Bernstein: Naismith, Narrow, Ness, Nichols . . .

A sense of replacement—of Ed Nixon for Nixon, of Redford's voice for Hoffman's—encourages us to ignore the next name, that is, Jolson. Yet to go from the Jewish actor to the WASP at the same time is to go from Jakie Rabinowitz to Jack Robin, or from Theodore Assofsky to Ted Ashley, or Steven Jay Rechnitz to Steve Ross. If the synchronization of Al Jolson's voice and lips is a landmark of classical Hollywood cinema and the foundation of the Warner Bros. myth, this scene, with its asynchronous voice-over marks a reorigination. When you no longer believe in something, you start again. The cultivation of a paranoid sensibility in which every sound or image is meaningful undermines the authorship of any individual working outside a system. In conjunction, and as part of its effort to shore up the corporate brand, Warners deploys an already corporatized history of film sound in what amounts to an audio EMH cut. That branding project is one its agents—screenwriter, director, star—all participate in.

Effects of the "spatial signature" can provide the framework for an auditory scene, as Michel Chion notes. In this case, though, it is the bifurcated spatial signature that provides the framework for a generalized auditory suspicion, for a scene where all sound can be semantic. One project of *All the President's Men* is to make that suspicious audition, the paranoid soundtrack, general. The connection between the "Jolson" we hear and the Jolson we neither see nor hear is contingent on our having ears to hear it, as they say. In the context of the emerging neoclassical Hollywood, the contingent is the essence of the aesthetic and the principle of the economic system.

Just as *All the President's Men* has a spatial signature, it possesses a racial signature. Michael Rogin wrote that *The Jazz Singer* performed the assimilation of Hollywood Jews "via the mask of the most segregated; the blackface that offers Jews mobility keeps the blacks fixed in place." Warner Bros.' studio-defining film, *The Jazz Singer* told not only the story of Al Jolson but also "the collective autobiography of the men who made Hollywood."[55] When Woodward and Bernstein visit the Library of Congress to investigate Howard Hunt's investigation of Ted Kennedy, they are told by an officious librarian that "all White House transactions are confidential." They nearly abandon their search, but Bernstein is determined to press on: "We need a

FIGURE 2.11 *Warners' vision of a friendly face: Playwright Jaye Stewart.* All the President's Men, *Pakula, Warner Bros., 1976.*

FIGURE 2.12 *"Who's Charles Colson?" Mute African-American reporters frame Woodward's ignorance. All the President's Men, Pakula, Warner Bros., 1976.*

friendly face." It is almost too pat, given Warners' history, that this face will be a black one. (It belongs to playwright Jaye Stewart.)

Similarly, when Woodward asks his boss, "Who's Charles Colson?" he is told, "You know, I'm glad you asked me that question. The reason I'm glad you asked me is because if you'd asked Simons or Bradlee they would have said, 'You know we're gonna have to fire this schmuck at once because he's so dumb.'" Their conversation is framed, as it were, by two African-American reporters—reporters we must assume do not repeat the tale of Woodward's idiocy to Bradlee. The schmuck will need Bernstein's help, but he will need his African-American colleagues' silence.

The injunction of *All the President's Men* is "Follow the money." It pairs neatly with the film's other message, Colson's motto: "When you've got 'em by the balls, their hearts and minds will follow." Both of these are stand-ins for the importance of controlling distribution or, more properly, dissemination. "You know what I never understood," Woodward tells Sloan, "how the distribution of funds worked." "Badly." All that Woodward and Bernstein do—interviewing, tracing library slips, regenerating the organizational structure of CREEP from the alphabetical phone list by driving all over the city—amounts to an attempt to duplicate what Deep Throat, the "garage freak," already knows. Faced with a choice between knowledge generated and knowledge imparted, between Jolson and Colson, Sloan or Stanz, the film, like the studio, has it both ways. Deep Throat controls the dissemination of information, the leakage from the governmental conspiracy to the newspaper conspiracy. He is an obvious figure for the man who turned his garage empire into a media empire. His charisma is the enigma of distribution. Jameson imagines that the two sides of the conspiracy are interchangeable— "You're both paranoid. She's afraid of John Mitchell and you're afraid of Walter Cronkite."—and assumes that one studio is the same as another. The alternative is to imagine that distribution makes all the difference.

Options

The In-Laws recasts *All the President's Men* as a comedy from CIA agent Howard Hunt's point of view. The relationship between these narratives is the sort Stanley Cavell calls "adjacency." For Cavell, genres are not preexisting molds into which creators pour particular instances. Rather, on his account, films declare or compete for membership in them. When a particular film negates important features of a genre it becomes part of an adjacent genre. If the heroine of a screwball comedy has children or if her mother is alive to hound her but her father is not there to coax her toward her rightful husband, then this heroine finds herself in what Cavell calls the melodrama of the unknown woman.[56] Certain films noirs compose something very like a Cavellian genre, a melodrama of male recognition. The adjacent cycle would be the Mexican chase film.

In film history, this is the function of *The Big Steal* (Don Siegel, RKO, 1949), the Mexican comedy staffed out of the same offices that made *Out of the Past* (Jacques Tourneur, RKO, 1947), both of which starred Robert Mitchum and Jane Greer. In neoclassical Hollywood, both cycles have become variations on the botched-caper film: *The In-Laws* is *The Big Chase* to *All the President's Men*. The remake of *The In-Laws* (Andrew Fleming, 2003), starring Michael Douglas and Albert Brooks, is the Mexican comedy to the remake of Warner Bros.' *Ocean's Eleven* (Steven Soderbergh, 2001), starring everybody else. Through such adjacencies, we gain a stronger sense of the range of systemic or studio options at a given point; or, more to the point, we gain a sense of where to look to find the answers to questions of collective cognition that might have eluded us.

The burglars that Woodstein track to Miami—not quite out the country— are veterans of the Bay of Pigs. These CIA operatives have been turned against domestic threats, or Republican fantasies of domestic threats, such as Ed Muskie and Gene McCarthy. "These aren't very bright guys," Deep Throat tells us. In *The In-Laws*, when Shelly (Alan Arkin) goes to Vince's (Peter Falk's) office, the safe containing the currency plates stolen from the U.S. Mint is located behind a picture of JFK. "Well at least we tried," the inscription reads. "The Bay of Pigs. That was my idea," Vince explains to Shelly at the diner.

In *The In-Laws* Vince drags Shelly (his future in-law) into his scheme to steal the plates and deliver them to the military dictator of Tijada in order to

FIGURE 2.13 *Fond memories of the Bay of Pigs.* The In-Laws, *Hiller,* Warner Bros., *1979.*

thwart the dictator's plans to flood the world with undetectable counterfeit money. It was a scheme too risky for the CIA; Vince is on his own. As he explains:

Vince: We know that these plates are going down to Central America, and these people intend to run off billions of dollars of this currency. They want to obliterate their debts.
Sheldon: What debts?
Vince: Well, all these countries, Shel, they all owe billions of dollars to the West. And they can never pay it back. They're too poor. You know that. Their only hope is a worldwide inflation. But it has to be a huge one, I mean so big that paper money's not worth anything. You use it for wallpaper. Now once they get these plates, the ones that I robbed yesterday, which is American dollars, now they're all set.
Sheldon: Set for what?
Vince: Well, what do you think's gonna happen when they start running off all this dough and suddenly there's trillions of extra dollars, francs, and marks floating around? You've got a collapse of confidence in the currency.
Sheldon: Right.
Vince: People are gonna panic.
Sheldon: Yeah.
Vince: There's gonna be gold riots, atonal music, political chaos, mass suicide, right? It's Germany before Hitler. You can see that. Jesus. I don't know what people are gonna do when a six pack of Budweiser costs $1200.
Sheldon: That would be awful.

Viewed in macroeconomic terms, *The In-Laws* is an argument in favor of secret governmental action to stave off inflation. It is a warrant for the monetarist revolution led by Paul Volcker, a revolution launched in response to a small-scale version of the economic chaos Vince Ricardo is outlining.

The fear of a country awash in indistinguishable counterfeit bills is a fear occasioned by the quantity theory of money, or by a version of that theory in which the price level closely tracks the quantity of money. That theory had new life and new importance as a result of the debate surrounding the work of Milton Friedman, who saw his monetarism as an answer to the "moneyless" nature of the reigning Keynesian orthodoxy. On a Keynesian model, there was more play in the theory. Changes in individual liquidity preferences, interest rates, and the velocity of money could temporarily "absorb" inflationary pressures. To the monetarists, velocity is more constant, and so more money means higher prices, and a flood of money means economic chaos.

The reason this debate matters for *The In-Laws* is that no studio had had stronger ties to the emergent Keynesianism of the thirties than Warner Bros. In its insurance-themed *Gold-Diggers* musicals and its general New Deal boosterism, Warners argued that the state and the studio were the sources of regulation of aggregate demand; that the problem of the depression had a Keynesian solution.[57] By the seventies, Warners had gone through the looking glass. Its fate was entirely tied up with large satchels of cash, with stock issues that were really warrants, with future earnings, with potential returns and complicated expectational mathematics. There could be no neoclassical Hollywood without the New Classical economic consensus, yet there could be nothing neo*classical* about a Hollywood that did not try to make that relationship necessary.

A moment here for intentions. Accounting for the responsible party when one offers a complicated interpretation of a film is tricky. The film industry is built with layer upon layer of intentional actors, any one of whom may reach for credit or search for deniability as the case may be. Given that recent production records are sealed as a matter of course, and that participants' accounts are unreliable *a priori* since they are always part of the system's self-promotional feedback, pinning intentions onto particular actors depends far more on feel than it should. At the same time, film studies can shuttle between accounts of Hollywood films that are nearly authorless and those that are as strongly authored as an individual literary work might be. Still, these difficulties should not prevent us from asking, "But who is thinking all of these things?" or from being on the lookout for the argumentative equivalent of handwaving.

This case, though, is far simpler. The person thinking these things is Andrew Bergman, the screenwriter of *The In-Laws*, a certified film studies scholar, who got his PhD at Wisconsin, where some of the Warner Bros. archives are located. His thesis on Hollywood's Depression-era filmmaking was published as *We're in the Money*, taking its title from the opening number of Warners' *Gold Diggers of 1933*.[58] It was built around extensive accounts of the principal Warners products of the thirties: the Busby Berkeley musicals, the transformation of the Gangster picture into the G-Man series, and the social problem film—"Warner Bros. Presents Social Conscience," is the chapter title. As part of his research, Bergman would have watched at least some of the "Brass Bancroft" Secret Service series of films that launched the career of Ronald Reagan at Warner Bros. in 1938. In the first, *Secret Service in the Air*, Reagan poses as a counterfeiter to infiltrate an illegal alien-smuggling ring; in the third, *Smashing the Money Ring*, Reagan poses as a prisoner to infiltrate a counterfeiting ring inside a penitentiary; and in the second, *Code of the Secret Service*, Reagan goes into Mexico in order to retrieve stolen U.S. Mint plates that will be used to flood the United States with counterfeit money. (The last film, *Murder in the Air*, features Reagan armed with an "inertia projector," an airborne electromagnetic ray. The device gave him the idea for Star Wars, the Strategic Defense Initiative.) Bergman would go on to write the play *Social Security*. In the 1970s, then, Andrew Bergman is the uncontested master of macroeconomic shtick: in place of David Ricardo and his pet peeve the Corn laws, we have Vincent Ricardo and his reluctant ally Sheldon Kornpett.

What is astonishing in the thoughtworld of *The In-Laws* is that it links together two aspects of the emerging Reaganite hegemony that even today are not sufficiently intertwined: the brutal structural adjustment that brought an end to The Great Inflation and the religitimization of the national security state and its rogue activities on behalf of a happily ignorant populace: "We really had to keep you in the dark," CIA honcho Ed Begley, Jr., tells Arkin. *The In-Laws* epitomizes Reagan's "Morning in America": the return of the cuddly but unfathomable CIA, the sanctioning of crime against the people in the name of a secret war that will ultimately be to their benefit, the acknowledgment and simultaneous disavowal of the imbalances of the world monetary system, and the Iran Contra–style deployment of the dialectic—give the dictator the plates in order to stop him.

As Sheldon Kornpett comes to accept the acceptability of all this, we, in the audience, are invited to as well. His enlistment has three stages. The first is outright rejection. When he hears Vince's story of life in the Guatemalan bush, the "tse-tse flies the size of eagles," complete with beaks, carrying off "brown babies" into the night, he is incredulous. Vince's story may be a complete fabrication, but given that he has been in CIA "since Eisenhower," we can hear it as a cover story for his covert actions in Guatemala. (The background to the image could either be the Arbenz coup in 1954 or the preparations for the Bay of Pigs invasion force in 1961. Howard Hunt was involved with both.) The eagles and the children recur in the second act of Kornpett's enlistment. The plates are in Vince's office, and he convinces Sheldon to steal them for him. Kornpett agrees and they take harrowing taxi ride through the city. "The eagle has landed," the cabbie announces as they screech to a halt; "Did we hit the little boy on 6th Avenue?" Sheldon immediately asks. In this phase, Kornpett willingly participates in the illicit events, but he does not know their real significance. He thinks he is just being "incredibly receptive," as he tells his daughter. The significance of his actions will emerge when he discovers that Vince planned the Bay of Pigs. Kornpett completes his conversion in Tijada. When he sees that Vince is being set up by his cabbie, Shelly leaps on top of the speeding taxi, landing spread eagle, in order to thwart the general's plan. "Sheer heroism" Vince calls it. Off they speed down United Fruit Boulevard to General Garcia's mansion.

If the film is Shelly's Reagan-era *Casablanca*, what is in it for Vince? The question of his motivation is fraught, because we are never certain what his emotional state will be: "One minute he's laughing, the next he's crying, then he almost punches Tommy in the mouth," Shelly notes with wonderment. This inability to achieve a coherent affective position links Vince to the dictator he opposes. While Ricardo is crazy, Kornpett says, "There's also something lovable about him"; while Gen. Garcia is a dictator, there is "something still very innocent about him." What is it that they have in common beyond this syntactic parallel? On the one hand, their sentimentality is nearly free-floating. On the other, they both possess a combination of macroeconomic savvy and microeconomic ignorance. Ricardo can empathize with the Latin American masses, but he has never seen the long-running tv game show "The Price is Right"—"You mean they're supposed to guess what all that crap is worth?" Garcia delivers a monologue much like Ricardo's speech on Latin American debt, yet he has paid outrageous sums for the black velvet tigers and toreadors that make up his "art collection." In order to make sense of Vince's motivations, we need to account for both the affective and the cognitive dimensions of his storytelling.

His economics are in line with Volcker's monetarism, but his emotionalism is characteristic of Volcker's predecessor, Arthur Burns. Vince's fantasy is that somehow American economic problems are or will be the product of Central American desperation—legitimate desperation, to be sure, he assures us. The opposite was the case. The problem, as the governors of the Fed saw it, was that continued inflation in the United States could get out of control. In 1974, Burns worried that "if headway were not made this year in dealing with the problem, the country would be experiencing a Latin American type of inflation, and the American people would not tolerate that for long. One way or another highly restrictive policies would become inevitable, and the nation might have to go through a long and serious contraction."[59] This had been Burns's worry from the beginning. In 1970, faced with Sen. William Proxmire's proposal to require the Fed to increase monetary growth, he thought that if it passed, "it would only be a matter of time before the Federal Reserve would find itself in the position of some Latin American central banks" that is, in the dependent position of running off money to appease political powers.[60] Global inflation was primarily an American phenomenon: "Well, the U.S. was exporting inflation to everybody by that point," Fed governor James Pierce noted.[61] By 1979 inflation *was* out of control, and only a massive intervention could stop it.[62]

The ostensible Latin Americanization of the U.S. economy and the terrible price that would have to be paid to avoid it seem to have weighed heavily on Burns. He called his 1979 Per Jacobssen lecture—one of the most important lectures an economist can give—"The Anguish of Central Banking." That anguish—or, rather, that staged anguish, if he is in fact acting Reagan acting—is legible in Vince when he tells Shelly about inflation, or when he tells the Kornpetts about the tse-tse flies. The man who readily concedes that "they can never repay these debts" is the same man who concludes his ludicrous tale of giant insects, "You can imagine the pathetic quality."

Whatever his motivation, what Vince gets out of his adventure is what Steve Ross got out of his: the chance to cash out of his seventies-era conglomerate. The door to his shabby office reads "Trans-Global Enterprises, Vincent J. Ricardo, President." Ricardo's operation fronts for the CIA, not the mob, but it still has come between him and his dream of becoming an entertainment impresario. In the late seventies, Ross was financially hamstrung by his inability to sell much of his WCI stock; Vince hosts a

FIGURE 2.14 *The pathos of the CEO: Loaded with options.* The In-Laws, *Hiller, Warner Bros., 1979.*

FIGURE 2.15 *The figure of economic narrative as such: "Serpentine!"* The In-Laws, *Hiller, Warner Bros., 1979.*

barbecue wearing an apron that reads "I'm loaded with options."[63] Vince's hands go up in victory when Shelly tells his wife that "Carmen Dragon and the Paramus Philharmonic" are tuning up to perform at the backyard wedding. Those raised hands are doubled by Dragon's raised hands as the orchestra—an institution of classicism so common even Paramus has one—begins; and Dragon's baton doubles Vince's spatula at his barbecue. What Vince wants is what Steve Ross wanted: to orchestrate things. No wonder that in the 2003 remake, Vince is renamed Steve.

The comedic centerpiece of *The In-Laws* comes as the two men first arrive in Tijada, the ruritanian banana republic at the heart of the plan to destabilize the American dollar. They come under fire from agents in the general's employ, and their contact, Jesus Braunschweiger, is killed. The dentist and the agent run, serpentine, to Braunschweiger's Mercedes Benz only to discover that the dead man still has the keys. Sheldon, fully enlisted in the rogue plot, pleads for the opportunity to run back, rummage through Braunschweiger's pockets, and return to the car. On his return trip, though, he forgets the serpentine command and makes a beeline for safety. Still he gets to the car successfully, unscathed by the bullets that kick up little fountains of Road Runner dust. All at once Ricardo barks, "Serpentine, Shelly! Serpentine!" Kornpett goes *back* into the line of fire and then retraces his path to the car, weaving. Sheldon's seemingly needless risk makes his act an instance of artistry, of pure style. If we ask why he does it, the obvious answer is that his on-screen director tells him to. And like the child who has to take an odd number of steps on his walk home from school or who must leave out the letter *e* as she spells her way through the state capitals while jumping rope, Kornpett is playing along in the spy game, now rendered juvenile and harmless.

These faux-deadly, childlike games complement the film's Americanized birds of prey. Part of the comedy of the serpentine scene rests on our knowledge that no matter *how* Arkin runs he won't get shot, because this is only a movie. The scenes of bullet tag around a New York taxi and of polyphonic pleading that thwarts their execution by firing squad are the same. The car chase on the Tijadan highway is edited in such a way as to encourage us to see the same old pickup truck out the back window on each successive pass. Even the mud fantails are not edited in continuity. These games are rule-bound, arbitrary, aesthetic.

The final scene in *The In-Laws* will again rearrange and invert the elements of the tse-tse fly infestation. Vince and Sheldon will arrive—not leave—from above, dangling beneath a helicopter. As they descend, a crane shot that reverses the glorious ascent in *All the President's Men* will remove them from the child's world of games. When we first see Vince, he is complaining about the Mets' personnel moves; in the final scene he will be apologizing for never having time to play baseball with his son, Tom. "Well, maybe this will make it up to you." Vince gives him cash—$1 million—to make up for years of paternal neglect. And it works. "I finally impressed my son."

By successfully enlisting Sheldon in his scheme, Vince is able to assume the fatherly role that he has always avoided. But what has changed from the Eisenhower and Kennedy eras is not merely the player but the game. "It used to be cowboys and Indians," Vince says, explaining his departure from CIA. "Today I almost died for the international monetary system. What the hell is that?" That is the difference between a conventional fight and a fight for a convention; that is neoclassicism. WCI had found its way through the seventies by relying on complex financial arrangements; Warner Bros. had translated those arrangements into a vision of the economy as a whole and of the studio within it.

Notes

1   Stephen Bach, *Final Cut: Art, Money, and Ego in the Making of Heaven's Gate* (New York: Newmarket, 1999), 25.

2   One might build this account around another collection of films—*Woodstock* (1970), *Billy Jack* (1971), *The Summer of '42* (1972), *The Enforcer* (1976), and *Superman* (1978) might do as well. Indeed, a corollary claim of this book (or, really, any book about a style or a period) would necessitate that there be possible alternate assemblies.

3 See the discussion of Bergman and Szalay, below.

4 Commonwealth United all but collapsed in the summer of 1969 following an article in the *L.A. Times* (John J. Goldman and Paul E. Steiger, "Disclosures Startling in Commonwealth's Proxy," July 10, 1969, B11, 15) that questioned its real estate practices. As a conglomerate, it was one of the beneficiaries of the scurrilous dealings of Investors Overseas Service. The story of IOS and the financial implosion it brought about is told by Charles Raw, Bruce Page, and Geoffrey Hodson in *Do You Sincerely Want to Be Rich?: The Full Story of Bernard Cornfeld and I.O.S.* (New York: Broadway, 2005). The discussion of Commonwealth United's troubles appears on pages 435–45. To get a fuller sense of the ways in which Hollywood was caught up in the conglomerate maelstrom, take the case of *Darling Lili*. This Julie Andrews musical was produced by Paramount, but when Commonwealth United faced a financing crunch driven in part by its attempt to buy Rexall Drugs from Dart Industries, Paramount gave the revenue stream from the musical and $12 million to Commonwealth in exchange "17–year 9½% debentures with a face value of $20 million, plus 400,000 shares of its common stock and warrants to buy 160,000 more shares at $17.25 a share," (Goldman and Steiger, B15).

5 National General had been formed when Fox was forced to divest itself of its theater chain.

6 "Proposal to Divest Warner Bros. Studio Confirmed by Officers," *Wall Street Journal*, January 3, 1969, 24.

7 "Kinney National to Sell Two Units for $12 Million to Martin Josephson," *Wall Street Journal*, July 6, 1969, 21.

8 Connie Bruck, *Master of the Game* (New York: Simon & Schuster, 1994), 36–42.

9 "Kinney National's Plan to Acquire Movie Firm Passes Holders of Both," *Wall Street Journal*, June 11, 1969, 15.

10 Andrew Walker, *Hollywood UK: The British Film Industry in the Sixties* (London: Stein and Day, 1974).

11 Walker, *Hollywood UK*.

12 "Kinney Net to Tumble in Year Ending September 30 Because of Write-Down," *Wall Street Journal*, September 16, 1969, 18.

13 This desperate need for product often lies behind legendary Hollywood bombs, as it did for *Heaven's Gate* (Michael Cimino, UA, 1980). When Arthur Krim and David Benjamin left United Artists, they left a thin slate behind. The remaining UA executives considered making a big play for a book despite production executive Chris Mankiewicz' feeling that it was an "unmitigated, irredeemable piece of *shit*." (The description indicates that the book, although unnamed, is Peter Benchley's *The Island*, the story of pirates who are responsible for the Bermuda Triangle phenomena. It was produced by Universal in 1980.) "That was never the point," Stephen Bach explained. "The point was that an alarming product shortage was looming" (*Final Cut*, 70, 73). At the same time, UA signed a deal to distribute Lorimar films in order

to mask the production gap, much in the same way Paramount under Brad Grey acquired DreamWorks to bridge "an enormous gap in the slate" in 2006. (Merissa Marr, "Pushing the Envelope: Paramount's Strategy," *Wall Street Journal*, http://online.wsj.com/article/SB116961043704085847.html, January 29, 2007, accessed January 20, 2017.)

14 Colin MacCabe notes that the shot had been cut in his remarkably useful account of the production of the film *Performance* (Bloomington, IN: BFI, 1998) and his edited version of the screenplay, Donald Cammell, *Performance*, ed. Colin MacCabe (London: Faber and Faber, 2001).

15 Andy Warhol, *The Philosophy of Andy Warhol (From A to B and Back Again)* (New York: Harcourt, 1975), 92.

16 Warner Communications 1971 Annual Report, 3.

17 Warner Communications Annual Reports. Although Ted Ashley hoped television revenues would grow alongside motion pictures, they did not.

18 Warner Communications 1973 Annual Report, 10.

19 The 1969–70 recession in Hollywood predated the broader economic downturn, but studios depended on broader capital markets for their production loans.

20 Earl C. Gottschalk, Jr., "Film Firms Mull Merging Studio Facilities, Seeking to Cut Costs, Revive the Industry," *Wall Street Journal*, July 18, 1971, 34.

21 Gottschalk, "Film Firms Mull Merging Studio Facilities, Seeking to Cut Costs, Revive the Industry."

22 For the story of Begelman's embezzlement, see David McClintick, *Indecent Exposure* (New York: Collins, 2002).

23 Bach, *Final Cut*, 48.

24 Ibid., 49.

25 Mark Kermode, *The Exorcist*, 2nd rev. ed. (London: BFI, 2003).

26 Dan Knapp, "Rendering Unto the Author What Is His," *Los Angeles Times*, January 15, 1972, K12.

27 Thomas D. Clagett, *William Friedkin, Films of Aberration, Obsession and Reality*, 2nd ed. (Los Angeles: Silman-James, 2003), 155.

28 Kermode, *The Exorcist*, 96.

29 Vincent Canby, "Why the Devil Do They Dig *The Exorcist*?" *The New York Times*, January 13, 1974, 4.

30 William Peter Blatty, *The Exorcist* (New York: Harper, 1971), 181.

31 This he told Mark Kermode before the 1997 edition of his BFI Modern Classics monograph; in 2000 he "restored" most of this scene along with much else to "The Version You've Never Seen," to the great detriment of the film.

32 Kermode, *The Exorcist*, 103.

33 Ibid., 96.

34 Jay Beck, *A Quiet Revolution: Changes in American Film Sound Practices*, (PhD Dissertation, U Iowa, 2003) vol. 2, 419.

35 Michel Chion, *Voice in Cinema*, trans. Claudia Gorbman (New York: Columbia University Press, 1999), 164; Beck, *Quiet Revolution*, 426.

36 Beck, *Quiet Revolution*, 424.

37 Friedkin, quoted in Chris Chase, "Everyone's Reading It, Billy's Filming It," *The New York Times*, August 27, 1972, D1, 9; D9.

38 Joyce Haber, "Making a Believer out of Friedkin," *Los Angeles Times*, April 26, 1973, G30. For a robust account of the anti-union class politics of the New Hollywood directors, see Derek Nystrom, *Hard Hats, Rednecks, and Macho Men: Class in 1970s American Cinema* (New York: Oxford, 2009).

39 Haber, "Making a Believer," G30.

40 This notion of levels of recursion became the subject of its own genre of Hollywood filmmaking; I discuss this in "Let's Make the Weather," in *The Studios after the Studios*.

41 It debuted its revolutionary Panaflex camera in Spielberg's *Sugarland Express* that same spring.

42 Kermode, *The Exorcist*, 61.

43 Ibid., 28–29.

44 Again, this convention has been obliterated in the rerelease.

45 Warner bought two major cable systems in 1971—TeleVision Communications and Continental Telephone—immediately making it one of the four largest cable companies in the country. Still, its subscriber base was only 175,000. "Kinney Arranging Big Acquisitions in CATV Field," *Wall Street Journal*, October 13, 1971, 12.

46 Bruck, *Master*, 70.

47 Ibid., 70–71.

48 The donation was revealed in "List of the 95 Largest Contributors to Nixon Campaign," *The New York Times*, September 29, 1973, 15. Karl Fleming profiled him in "Who is Ted Ashley? Just the King of Hollywood, Baby," *New York*, June 24, 1974, 30–35. His departure story appears in Joyce Haber, "Ted Ashley Opts for the Unknown," *Los Angeles Times*, August 28, 1974, G11; his return appears in Mary Murphy, "Ashley Back as Chief of Warner Bros. Studio," *Los Angeles Times*, December 11, 1975, H30.

49 Warner was a small fry in this process. Bigger players included ITT and the Hughes companies. See Michael Drosnin, *Citizen Hughes* (New York: Holt, Reinhart and Winston, 1985).

50 William Goldman, *Adventures in the Screen Trade* (New York: Warner Books, 1983), 239.

51 As Bob Woodward described it: "The most sinister pressure [on the reporters] was the repeated denial of the information we were publishing. The second-most sinister was the Nixon White House and re-election campaign strategy of getting people to challenge the FCC television licenses that The Washington Post Company owned. That caused the stock of The Washington

Post Company to drop significantly, and was a classic strong-arm tactic that I suspect we will not see again for many years or decades. Anyway, let's hope," transcript of Q&A on the thirty-fifth anniversary of Watergate, http://www.washingtonpost.com/wp-dyn/content/discussion/2007/06/14/DI2007061400497.html, accessed January 20, 2017.

52 Fredric Jameson, "Totality as Conspiracy," in *The Geopolitical Aesthetic: Cinema and Space in the World System* (Bloomington, IN: BFI, 1992), 9–85.

53 Michel Chion, *Audio-Vision*, trans. Claudia Gorbman (New York: Columbia University Press, 1994), 114–16.

54 Jared Brown, *Alan J. Pakula: His Films and His Life* (New York: Back Stage Books, 2005) 197.

55 Mike Rogin, *Blackface, White Noise: Jewish Immigrants in the Hollywood Melting Pot* (Berkeley: University of California Press, 1996), 112, 84.

56 Stanley Cavell, *Contesting Tears* (Chicago: University of Chicago Press, 1997), 3–46.

57 Michael Szalay, *New Deal Modernism: American Literature and the Invention of the Welfare State* (Durham, NC: Duke University Press, 2000), 233–44.

58 Andrew Bergman, *We're in the Money: Depression America and its Films* (Chicago: Ivan R. Dee, 1992).

59 Thomas Mayer, *Monetary Policy and the Great Inflation in the United States: The Federal Reserve and the Failure of Macroeconomic Policy, 1965–79* (Northampton, MA: Edward Elgar, 1999), 106.

60 Mayer, *Monetary Policy and the Great Inflation in the United States*, 82.

61 Ibid., 115.

62 At several points in the 1970s, various forces attempted to change the way the Fed chose its monetary targets from a "Money Market Conditions" approach that emphasized interest rate stability to an "Aggregates" approach that emphasized the money supply. These repeated challenges were unsuccessful until Volcker became chair. Mayer sums up the political value of this supposedly scientific revolution: "As long as the Fed focused on controlling interest rates, it took public responsibility for interest rates, and hence was blamed when interest rates rose. It was the genius of Volcker's monetarist experiment that the Fed, by saying 'we control money not interest rates', obtained the political cover that allowed interest rates to rise." *Monetary Policy*, 28–29.

63 Bruck, *Master*, 185–87.

3

High concept the Chicago way:

Dan Rostenkowski, Ferris Bueller, Eliot Ness

What would the culture of the Chicago School of Economics look like? By culture, here, I mean something more than simply the mores and tastes of the faculty and students in the economics department and their close allies in the Graduate School of Business and Law School.[1] I do not mean what novels Richard Posner or George Stigler or Gary Becker enjoyed. But I also mean something more specific than simply whatever culture attended the school's era of greatest prestige or power. That influence was, indeed, decisive. Members of the school constructed the crucial public arguments in favor of the vast deregulatory effort they would undertake in Reagan's first term. They and their acolytes served in the administration and were appointed to the federal bench, where they rewrote the parameters of U.S. communications policy, drawing up what Jennifer Holt has called the blueprints of the new media empires. In particular, the Chicago revolution in antitrust policy "would be the key to the expansion and merging of the film and cable companies throughout the rest of the 1980s and into the 1990s."[2] Without relinquishing the crucial role of political economy in shaping culture, I want to attempt to isolate its textual intermediaries. For my purposes the culture of the Chicago School would be those artists, artifacts, movements, and institutions that share or find themselves sharing both an ideological commitment to a minimal state and an analytic commitment to the exploration of the consequences of the unlimited application of economic analysis. This conception is designed to be more delimited than an unreflective account of the symptomatic relation of culture to its material base might be, and, as I hope to show, it poses and answers certain particular questions of agency and contract in both theoretical and practical domains.

Scholars do not regularly question the scope of cultural accompaniment because both very specific and extremely broad answers can seem compelling. If culture necessarily follows from socioeconomic relations at an economy-wide scale, then the scope of accompaniment is potentially universal and the relevant scholarly questions turn on issues of cultural opposition or subversion. How, in a totalized understanding of cultural production, is opposition possible? If, though, cultural production proliferates in uncountably many variations based on the biographies, situations, identities, and so on, of the individuals and institutions involved, then the scope of accompaniment contracts. In those cases, the moment when one appeals to a more totalizing idea can seem to be a great leap from the metonym to the whole. At the intermediate level, the level at which, as I noted in the introduction, much media theorizing has asked scholarship to operate, the field of examples—of exemplary examples—is constrained by the critic's taste or time, or by an external metric (ten most popular . . .). But if one believes at all that there are links between social or economic systems and aesthetic systems, then that delimitation becomes more pressing. In the case of the culture of the Chicago School, the problem of accompaniment becomes both unignorable and newly manageable because its *particular* formulation of the social contends that the *whole* of it is best understood through the application of neoclassical economic models. This peculiar universalism is the problem that confronted Fredric Jameson when he attempted to grapple with the work of Gary Becker, and despite his usual analytic confidence, he was, nonetheless, somewhat flummoxed.

The most obvious analogue, for Jameson, was almost surprising. "Only Sartre's novels . . . give any sense of what a representation of life that interpreted and narrated every human act and gesture, desire and decision in terms of Becker's maximization model would look like." They "reveal a world peculiarly without transcendence and without perspective . . . and indeed without plot in any traditional sense, since all choices would be equidistant and on the same level."[3] Yet this relentlessly planar conception of social happening is not what Jameson sees around him; it is not, in any meaningful way, the attendant culture of the contemporary economy. Instead, looking at culture, Jameson is shocked by the successful equation of business and glamour. "The most astonishing feature of this discursive development" for him is "how the dreariness of business and private property, the dustiness of entrepreneurship and the well-nigh Dickensian flavor of title and appropriation, coupon-clipping, mergers, investment banking, and other such transactions (after the close of the heroic, or robber-baron, stage of business) should in our time have proved to be so *sexy*."[4] What has saved business from its boring essence is its analogy with the media. His argument is thus consistent with his argument about *All the*

President's Men: that capital becomes sexy when it becomes media, or, in his more complex formulation: "The analogy between media and market . . . is not because the media is *like* a market. . . . Rather it is because the 'market' is as unlike its 'concept' . . . as the media is unlike its own."[5] And my critique of that argument is also consistent with my critique in Chapter 2. It is not that the market and the media are unlike their concepts—it is not that they promise a universality they necessarily fail to deliver—but rather that they are embedded in institutions through which they come to narrative. In fact, the whole of the previous chapter can be read as a demonstration that part of the reason the market remains sexy is that it routinely assimilates potentially boring economic practices to their metaphorical equivalents. Corporate merger becomes metempsychosis; leasing becomes demonic possession, and structural adjustment becomes a story of rogue spies and counterfeiters.

This form of literalization is, as I have contended, one of Hollywood's great enduring strengths. In the eighties, it was yoked to a broadly Reaganite admixture of amped-up Cold War anxiety, hypermasculinity, and extreme gloss in films such as *Top Gun* (Scott, Paramount 1986). *Top Gun* was a paradigm of high-concept filmmaking in ways beyond its stylishness. As a mode, high concept prioritized design over characterological complexity, a shift that helped movie studios wrest control from powerful auteurs and agencies while simultaneously allowing movie studios to argue for their centrality within the media conglomerates only then emerging. Seen this way, high-concept moviemaking is simultaneously a collection of practices within culture very broadly defined ("Reaganism") and the product of a set of largely intra-industrial logics, a precessive move within Hollywood. To bring those registers into closer contact—to ask how movies become the shuttle between them—and to return to the Chicago School, I turn to a specific moment late in the Reagan era when market ideology had to be recalibrated.

Well into the Reagan administration, film financing often relied on complex tax avoidance strategies.[6] The most important of these was the limited partnership. Delphi was, for a time, the most prominent of the limited partnership shops, and it can illustrate the system. Through successive rounds, it raised $50 million or more for Columbia and TriStar. It raised money for TriStar's first hit, *The Natural* (Barry Levinson, 1984), and it raised money for the terminal flop that ended TriStar's independence, *Ishtar* (Elaine May, 1987). Like other intermediaries, in the mid-1980s, Delphi would enter production more directly, partnering with POS and Paramount refugee Frank Yablans. And like most other indies, that role was unsustainable. The agreement was dissolved and Delphi merged with TriStar in 1986.

Like nearly all limited partnerships, Delphi's were designed to lose money, but to lose money in very particular ways. An outgrowth of the baroque tax system, LPs in motion picture production but also in real estate and oil and gas offered investors in high income tax brackets the chance to suffer "passive losses" that could then dramatically lower their tax liabilities. Say a studio needs to raise money for a slate of films. It might simply borrow that money, at terms, from a bank. By the early 1980s, though, the Volcker/Reagan recession had driven interest rates to nearly 20 percent. Instead of directly borrowing to fund production, then, a studio might also offer ordinary investors the opportunity to purchase a share of the revenue stream from those films. For the first years of the partnership, those investments would lose money on paper as the films were developed and produced. Investors could then realize swift and substantial losses that would reduce their other tax burdens. Eventually, the films' revenues might make the investment profitable, but for high-net-worth individuals—generally referred to as "Long Island Dentists"—the combination of tax advantages and industry sizzle made such investments attractive. In exchange, the studios received what were, in effect, interest-free loans. What is more, the payouts could be structured so that the studio always won—hefty distribution fees could be built in, for example. Some limited partnerships, particularly Disney's, were profitable, but even when they were not, everyone benefited.

In the early years of the partnership, interest expenses and depreciations would result in significant paper losses. Such shelters, often abused, might generate tax advantages several times the value of the initial investment. Delphi II, for example, was "expected to generate a tax loss of between $27,500,000 and $41,500,000" in 1983 alone. "For a limited partner in the 50% tax bracket, this would be equivalent to a deduction of roughly 70% of his partnership investment." When the partnership wound down, any profits would be taxed as capital gains. The strategy was wildly popular: between 1980 and 1986, public sales spiked from $2.9 billion to $13.1 billion.[7]

Delphi might have been an independent company, but that independence was contingent. And in 1986, Delphi and TriStar concluded that the investment manager made more sense inside the firm rather than outside it. That change was inspired, in part, by changes in the tax laws. Under the Tax Reform Act of 1986 (TRA86), passive losses could no longer offset income from salaries unless one liquidated the entire position.[8] The demand for pass-through losses dried up. In the new regime, investors would be upset with a studio that did not offer substantial positive returns. As a result, prospectuses increasingly emphasized the regularity of a studio's output. The two shifts operated in tandem: investors went from demanding easy-to-generate losses to hard-to-guarantee profits.

Roland Betts, who helped pioneer LP motion picture financing, made the double move. Betts's first Silver Screen Partners, like the Delphi LPs, underwrote production at the new TriStar. There, its investors were backstopped by a unique relation with HBO and agreements TriStar had with CBS. After the 1986 tax reform, Delphi closed up shop, but Silver Screen Partners grew. The first incarnation, Silver Screen Partners, had raised

$82 million and helped fund seven films; SSP II would raise $192 million for ten. At the same time, it moved from TriStar to Disney.

> The difference between the two deals is control, Betts says. With HBO, the partnership participated in the film-making process, from approving properties to negotiating with Tri-Star for release dates. With Disney, he says, Silver Screen will be a passive partner.
> "We feel the stature of the new management team at Disney is so strong, we didn't need to be involved (in creative decisions)," Betts says. "We were interested in Disney because the name is terrific, but we wouldn't have gone there if Michael Eisner (former head of Paramount Pictures) and Frank Wells (former head of Warner Bros.) hadn't gone over there first."[9]

As the new Disney solidified, the alliance continued: SSP III raised $300 million for nineteen movies; SSP IV, $400 million for thirty-three.

Disney elaborated on Betts's expansive vision. Eisner explained that he and Wells

> shared the view that we needed to protect our financial downside even as we moved forward aggressively. By raising financing from outside sources, our balance sheet could be protected from any sudden, significant losses in the event that we had a bad run with our movies. Unfortunately, the tax-shelter money that we raised so successfully at Paramount had essentially dried up, largely because the IRS codes permitting such investments had been significantly tightened. It was Frank who found an alternative. . . . In effect, we had interest-free financing, which allowed Frank and me to sleep better at night. Silver Screen's investors split revenues on the movies.[10]

The shift from loss-generating limited partnerships suited to a high-interest, high-tax environment in the early 1980s to profit-generating limited partnerships suited to the relatively low-interest, relatively tax-neutral environment of the late 1980s might seem to be a minor blip in the political economy of the industry. But a studio was only able to make use of the latter sort of LP to the extent that it could persuade small-scale investors that its film strategy was coherent, that is, to the extent that the studio had a convincing brand. Disney did, and the covers to its offering documents featured Mickey Mouse casting a magic, money-making spell. At the same time, the sort of self-reflection that such retail investment presentations inspired reinforced the much broader effort to cultivate corporate identity. In the wake of TRA86, whether a studio absorbed its funder (as Columbia/TriStar did), or grew close to it (as Disney did), or avoided such outside obligations by funding itself through the proceeds of its deconglomeration (as Paramount did), was a matter of calculation: Which sources of funding would be most articulable to its executives, its shareholders or other investors, and the range of market intermediaries?

Left undiscussed in most cultural histories of the 1980s, the bipartisan Tax Reform Act of 1986 seems out of place in a country consumed by the more emblematic, late–Reagan Era Iran-Contra hearings. Yet the rewriting of the tax code exerted a decisive force on the motion picture industry, which profoundly changed its mode of financing as a result. *Ferris Bueller's Day Off* (John Hughes, Paramount 1986) and *The Untouchables* (Brian De Palma, Paramount 1987) constitute two major thematizations of that change. Like their fellow high-concept films, particularly those from Paramount, *Bueller* and *Untouchables* are stylish; their characters dwell in designworlds enabled by financial success. Where they part company with, say, *Beverly Hills Cop*, is in the scope of their reflection on the mechanics of that success. *Bueller* and *Untouchables* share a fascination with technologies of market freedom, in particular the discovery of the power of accounting to realize moral ends.

Chicago had been the epicenter for the laissez-faire ideology that took power in what we now usually call the Reagan revolution. In the University of Chicago economics department, and at the law and business schools, seemingly no sector of economic thought went untouched, and no sector of thought more broadly. In macroeconomics, "moneyless" Keynesian homeostasis seemed less and less tenable in light of new models of regulatory capture, inevitable deficits, and Milton Friedman's monetarist account of the Great Depression. Both Keynesians and Chicago School economists could explain how the Paul Volcker/Federal Reserve–induced recessions broke the back of the great inflation, but the economy that emerged on the other side would be more in line with Chicago's prescriptions. Jobs became harder to find but mergers became easier to pull off. The systematic dismantling of antitrust enforcement under the new administration had been abetted by theories of the firm that made industrial consolidation seem more benign and antitrust enforcement less effective. At the same time, through both statutory and administrative efforts, regulations were rolled back in specific industries—banking, oil and gas exploration, air travel, telecom, and media. In all of those, sophisticated attempts to model the newly liberated markets sprung up, nowhere more prominently than in banking. Finance theory underwent several revolutions as the Capital Asset Pricing Model gave way to the Efficient Market Hypothesis, and the banking industry was revolutionized as a result. New applications of the theory of the random walk were field tested at the Chicago Mercantile Exchange and the Chicago Board of Trade, paving the way for the world of complex derivatives that would figure so prominently in the 2008 crash.[11] Finally, and not least, large swaths of society that might not have seemed central to economics came under its sway, particularly if they could be recharacterized as failed state interventions. Identity and personhood could be redescribed as human capital. Within the legal system, claims for justice or legislative intent could be finessed into a search for economically efficient outcomes. Pillars of civic life such as public education could be redefined as markets built on "school choice" and voucher systems. This is the intellectual armature of the Reagan revolution as the story is often told, and that story is, even now, an awesome tale in which the role of democratic government is relentlessly limited in favor of unfettered markets.[12] Yet this story is not the whole story, and Reagan's second term, the one that would conclude with a choir of "I don't recalls" and Oliver North's slide-show enabled grandstanding, contains within it glimpses of alternative futures even now.

Tax simplification was endorsed by Reagan, conservative Jack Kemp, Democrats Ted Kennedy and Bill Bradley, and others, but its legislative course was decisively set by Secretary of the Treasury James Baker and Chicago representative Dan Rostenkowski. Baker presented the administration's four demands for the legislation: that the program be revenue neutral, that the highest rate be no higher than 35 percent, that many of the poor be removed from the income tax rolls, and that the mortgage-interest deduction remain.[13] Baker's counterpart was the epitome of the Chicago pol, and Rostenkowski was always called "the powerful chairman of the House Ways and Means Committee."[14] From his parliamentary position, he controlled the legislative process until he was brought low in the House banking scandal that sent him to prison, and his death. But before his fall, Rosty, as he was known, was the most pugnacious advocate for Democratic values. His 1985 response to a Reagan address was widely lauded, and he put the drive for tax fairness at the center of Democratic concerns:

> Trying to tax people and businesses fairly. That's been the historical Democratic commitment. Our roots lie with working families all over the country, like the Polish neighborhood where I grew up on the northwest side of Chicago.
>
> Most of the people in my neighborhood worked hard in breweries, steel mills, packing houses, proud families who lived on their salaries. My parents and grandparents didn't like to pay taxes. Who does? But like most Americans, they were willing to pay their fair share as the price of a free country where everyone could make their own breaks.[15]

The bill that resulted drastically lowered income tax rates and simplified individual income taxes, as conservatives wanted, yet remained revenue neutral by raising capital gains and corporate rates and severely restricting tax shelters such as the investment tax credit and passive losses. Figure 3.1 provides a snapshot of the U.S. tax structure. The dramatic downward path in the line representing the top personal income tax rate is largely an illusion. By the 1980s the code had become so complex, and the availability of income shelters so prevalent, that almost no one had significant income

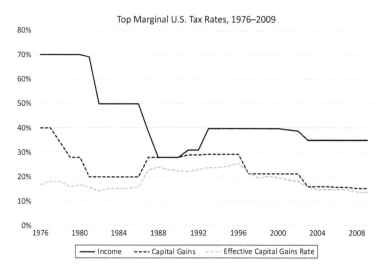

FIGURE 3.1 *Data from Tax Policy Center, FRED. Author figure.*

taxed at that top rate. Similarly, the Carter and Reagan I era reductions in the top capital gains tax rate were largely revenue neutral, involving modest recalibrations of investors' bases. Shelters and deferrals persisted. Yet as the chart shows, the 1986 Tax Reform Act brought top tax rates into line regardless of income source. What is more, the Act paid for its income tax cuts with a significant increase in both capital gains rates *and* effective rates. Writing in *The Journal of Economic Perspectives* in 1987, Charles E. McClure and George R. Zodrow captured the stunning nature of the change. "In light of the outcry prompted by the Treasury I proposal to index capital gains against inflation and tax them at a maximum rate of 35 percent, the agreement under the 1986 Act to tax gains at a 33 percent maximum rate without indexing for inflation is quite amazing."[16] If the Treasury succeeded in defending its four principles, Democrats were able to shape those principles toward the ideal of the "fair share." For them, TRA86 did what it was supposed to do, and as such, it represents the most important postwar attempt to rein in income inequality through changes to the tax code at the top. This was the centrist Democrats' best shot. They took it, and it largely paid off. As the chart shows, though, that harmonization would be undone under Clinton, and the gap between ordinary income and capital gains would widen further under George W. Bush. Rostenkowski and others had successfully argued that the tax code should not distinguish between sources of income (wages, salaries, or capital gains), but a broad center-right coalition of economists would subsequently chip away at that principled indifference, arguing that lowering the "cost" of capital would result in higher growth, that high rates "locked in" investments that might be more efficiently shifted, and, more complicatedly, that rates ought to vary with the amount of time the asset had been held.[17]

TRA86 dramatically altered the tax landscape. And in the new, low inflation, low-interest, tax-simplified world of the later Reagan era, the limited partnership ceased to be a widespread form of funding, remaining only for particularly penurious or undercapitalized companies. Disney continued its Silver Screen Partnerships, but SSP IV was the last; video distributor Vestron funded its first production slate, the one that would include *Dirty Dancing*, that way; and many of the indies Orion Pictures handled were funded through LPs and then sold/leased back. Vestron eventually cashed out; Orion went bankrupt for other reasons.[18]

Paramount was uniquely positioned to take advantage of the new tax laws. In the late 1960s, the studio had become part of the diversified conglomerate Gulf + Western, a behemoth that included everything from financial planning and insurance to sugar and zinc. With the death of G + W's charismatic CEO Charlie Bluhdorn in 1984, successor Martin Davis began remaking the company as Paramount Communications. The new conglomerate was state of the art: a company with interests in film, television, and publishing, the sort of new media conglomerate that could only exist once the antitrust barriers had been torn down by Reagan's Chicago radicals. As part of this reinvention, Gulf + Western sold off huge chunks of itself, and the money was plowed back into the company, into production and stock repurchases. As a consequence, Paramount was, in the middle of the 1980s, much more self-financing than its competitors.[19]

Was there any formal fallout from these changes? In one way, no. Paramount had been the studio most deeply committed to high-concept filmmaking. A decade earlier the departure of New Hollywood producer Robert Evans was followed by the brief tenure of Richard Sylbert and then the longer reign of Barry Diller. Sylbert began the process of reorienting the studio around design, purging it of grit. Diller and Michael Eisner and Jeffrey Katzenberg and Dawn Steel and Don Simpson and Jerry Bruckheimer and Ricardo Mestres brought a level of narrative and budgetary discipline to the studio that converted the perfect surfaces of films like *American Gigolo* into a mode of production: *Grease, Flashdance, Footloose,* and so on. As Justin Wyatt has convincingly argued, and as David Bordwell has grudgingly accepted, the constellation of early 1980s films at Paramount possessed a distinctive look: backlit, industrial settings featuring a limited palate and high gloss.[20]

Yet following Davis's ascension, Diller and his allies were forced out. The studio cleaned the development slate. The year 1985, then, was a moment when Paramount might have turned against its recent past and gone in any number of directions. It did not. Instead, Ned Tanen pursued the same strategy Diller had, mixing youth comedies, Eddie Murphy vehicles, and testosterone-fueled jukebox pix. In this new incarnation, he turned to the same group of producers, directors, designers and stars, and they succeeded.

Top Gun was one of the first projects Tanen greenlit. *Ferris Bueller, The Untouchables,* and *Beverly Hills Cop II* quickly followed.

The studio's mode and style persisted, but the high-stakes battles over tax reform *did* inflect the films that Paramount produced. *Top Gun* repurposed Bruce Weber's queer gaze in the service of Cold War propaganda, but *The Untouchables* sold the struggle for tax fairness as part of the broader Reaganite culture. The neo-gangster picture combines De Palma's florid direction and Armani couture with David Mamet's characteristic dialogue of masculine bluster. Eliot Ness's manly rectitude becomes the figure for Paramount's own, in contrast to its tax-avoiding competitors Disney and Warner Bros.

In *The Untouchables,* Paramount's continuing culture of masculine display collides directly with the proceduralism of forensic accounting. Part of the film's efficiency lies in the way it reduces the Ness crusade. Instead of the dozen men on his squad historically, the movie gives us only four. And instead of a string of successful wiretaps and brewery busts, the film concentrates on a single duality: violence and accounting. The first half of the film opposes the one to the other, with characteristic irony: *we* know it was the income tax that got Capone; Ness does not. Yet.

In the essential scene, bespectacled Agent Wallace will pound the desk in triumph and explain that Capone has not filed an income tax return since 1926. It is more than Ness can take. He leaves his office, just-slightly-mockingly offering his desk to Wallace, and a tracking shot delivers him to Sean Connery's Malone. Ness and Malone visit a nearby church to discuss confidentially the campaign to "get Capone." The scene alternates between a stunning low angle that captures the church's vaulted ceiling and a characteristic De Palma diopter shot. Ness avers that he is prepared to do "everything within the law." Malone is dismissive: "And then what are you prepared to do? . . . You must be prepared to go all the way." "Here's how you get him: He pulls a knife, you pull a gun. He sends one of yours to the hospital, you send one of his to the morgue. That's the Chicago way, and that's how you get Capone."

The two scenes set up an opposition between the man who wants a closer look at the books and the men projected against a grand vaulted ceiling, their masculinity ascendant but under pressure. This second moment is "the Chicago way," and the commitment to the defense of that way, that flavor of masculinity, is a blood oath. Ness initially thinks the accountant is a put-on, but he opts to pursue the accounting strategy nonetheless. In the second vaulted scene, Capone himself explains that prosecution for tax evasion is unmanly. "Somebody steals from me, I'm gonna say you stole, not talk to him for spittin' on the sidewalk. . . . .I have done nothing to hurt these people, but they're angered at me, so what do they do? Doctor up some [whirls hands] income tax, for which they got no case. To annoy me. To speak to me like men? No . . . .I pray to God that if I ever had a grievance I would have just a little more self-respect." Wallis the accountant will agree with Capone, coming to enjoy "the tactical aspects of law enforcement"— that is, guns. This, naturally, is his downfall. He is shot by Frank Nitti and left hanging with the bloody admonition: *TOUCHABLE.*

What the film needs, then, is a conceptual equivalent of the tracking shot that takes Ness from Wallis to Malone. It needs a way of understanding its fascination with numbers in light of its belief that such a fascination risks the monumental masculinity it aspires to. It needs a way of transforming the struggle for tax fairness into a great battle. It needs a Rostenkowski moment. It achieves that in two crucial scenes that reharmonize the film's incompatible registers of policework. The first comes when Malone is killed by Nitti. With his dying breaths he reaches toward a train timetable. He wants it because Capone's accountant will be on a particular train. As he crawls toward the information-dense, modernist grid, he closes the ideological gap between himself and Wallis. For both of them, numbers are a matter of life and death.

For Capone, too. Despite his dismissal of "some income tax," he regards his accountant, Walter Payne, as an essential member of the gang. (Movie gangsters often display numerical facility.) The timetable also sets up one of De Palma's great set-pieces, the rewriting of Eisenstein's Odessa Steps sequence as a violent catwalk. Stairways, in *the Untouchables,* are places where men model, but when conflict breaks out, the defense of the accountant's life becomes a worthy enough test of manhood to complete the ideological harmonization between beancounters and men of action. Bringing in Capone's accountant will not only finish Wallis's project, but also offer Ness's crew the chance to atone for their earlier failure. The low-level gangster who intends to kill Payne is instead shot—an image that roughly mirrors the scene in which we discover Wallace's body. *The Untouchables* thus makes the defense of accountancy safe for high concept and makes a certain form of financial sophistication the emblem of manhood triumphant. In the film's last shot, Ness heads down the street, straight for the Chicago Board of Trade.

The Untouchables required enormous reservoirs of masculine anxiety to sustain its tenuous utopia of tax-driven justice. Alongside it Paramount also pursued a more durable response to the Reagan revolution in its stories of suburban anomie. John Hughes was the Chicagoteur of that feeling. Rostenkowski had summed it up nicely: "A lot of people I grew up with live in the suburbs now. They make more money than their parents. . . . [But] working families file their tax forms with the nagging feeling that they're the biggest suckers and chumps in the world." Ferris Bueller is neither sucker nor chump, but his sister Jeanne has the nagging feeling that she is. However righteous her anger, though, her progress through the film will require that she somehow get over it. And however deserving of comeuppance, Ferris will not get what is coming to him. For the duration

FIGURE 3.2 The Untouchables, *De Palma, Paramount, 1987.*

of the film, he will display what director John Hughes called, "just the right amount of smirk."[21]

Let us begin with a characteristic pair of scenes from the day off. Ferris, his girlfriend Sloane, and his best friend Cameron have traveled to the top of the Sears Tower for some vertiginous fun (Figure 3.3). For Cameron, though, the dizzying heights open up a hole in his relationship to the world, his fraught relationship with his father. We cut from that moment to the Chicago Mercantile Exchange, a world of highly coded financial communication. And here, at the very center of the world of contract, Ferris proposes a contract of his own: he asks Sloane to marry him.

When Cameron leans against the Sears Tower window, he begins to wallow. "I think I see my dad. . . . The son-of-a-bitch is down there somewhere." When the scene shifts to the Merc, we alternate between shots of traders making incomprensible hand signals and Cameron mocking them, eventually launching into a Three Stooges routine. Cut off from his family, he is also cut off from the contracts that make the world go. In contrast, when Ferris turns away from the window overlooking the trading floor, his first words are "Do you want to get married?" Sloane agress—"Sure"—half-seriously, putting on a blasé front. But when he asks "Today?" she demurs. The two fake-disagree, before the scene reverts to a discussion of Cameron's parents' marital strife—the bad contract at the origin of his suffering—and to what Hughes calls his "self-indulgence. He's now playing 'I'm from a home with problems.'"[22] But the conversational turn masks the scene's tacit, and more important conclusion: the conversion of Ferris's proposal into a futures contract. They will get married—Sloane's last line in the film is "He's gonna marry me!"—just not today. The essential moment occurs just after Sloane laughs off "Today?": Ferris quickly turns to look over his shoulder at the vast hubbub of the trading floor, and just as quickly turns back to declare: "I'm serious."

FIGURE 3.3 *Vertiginous subjectivity and contractual utopia in Chicago.* Ferris Bueller's Day Off, *Hughes, Paramount, 1986.*

This is the film's characteristic move: to give expression to the foundationless existence of the late modern subject and to have Ferris embrace that foundationlessness through an appeal to self-authorization. It is in no way an accident that when he gets to the Merc, Ferris's thoughts turn to romance. Economics, for him as for the Chicago School, is the science of unlimited desire. And it is no accident that while he might be living for the day, it is only a day off. Ferris is happy to oblige future versions of himself.

The opposition that works across the two scenes in the Sears Tower and the Merc is also present in a more spatialized version, an opposition between whatever is going on at school and whatever might happen anyplace else. By skipping school, Ferris misses a stultifying lecture on supply-side economics and the Laffer Curve. It is the scene that made Ben Stein a star. But its place in the film is often overlooked. Before we jump into the lecture, Ferris pokes fun at his unique version of autodidacticism. In a low angle that reads as a parody of the monumentalizations in a film like *The Untouchables*, Ferris squeals away on a clarinet. He quickly pauses, addresses the camera, and quips, "Never had one lesson." He then goes back to squawking. The short scene highlights the smirking entitlement that usually reads as childlike, and it serves as the slightest rejoinder to the day to come. It may very well be that Ben Stein's economics lecture is terrible, but that does not imply that all education is. People need lessons to play the clarinet well; Ferris is going to try to avoid that.

Hughes explained, "I asked Ben . . . to talk about economics, which we figured would probably be the worst thing to discuss—political economics to discuss with kids—and we talked about the Smoot Hawley Act which I thought was a really wonderful example of adults just making a terrible mess of things. These kids aren't just bored; they hate him. They resent him. They can't stand him. . . . And we used voodoo economics which I thought was kind of a funny term." Here, Hughes is passing off the film's politics—its sustained discussion of political economy—onto the generation gap and a childlike fascination with words. That much is characteristic of Hollywood's routine search for deniability. But for Ben Stein, a former Nixon speechwriter and supply-side devotee, the lecture wasn't just an excuse to show angry teens. It was the message of the film, however monotonically it was delivered:

Today we have a similar debate over this. Anyone know what this is? Class? Anyone? Anyone seen this before? The Laffer curve. Anyone know what this says? It says, that at this point [CHALK SQUEAL] on the revenue curve you will get exactly the same amount of revenue as at this point. This is very controversial. Does anyone know what Vice President Bush called this in 1980? Anyone? [BUBBLEGUM BUBBLE POP] Something d-o-o economics. Voodoo economics.

Part of what makes the scene so effective is Hughes's decision to rely almost entirely on Stein's droning voice. As he lectures, we take a tour of the students' faces—seething, bored, asleep and drooling—and when we do finally return to Stein, he is still in closeup. We never see what he has written on the chalkboard; we don't see him scrape the chalk; we don't see the Laffer Curve itself.

The Laffer Curve is the totem object of supply-side economics (Figure 3.4). It took its name from Arthur Laffer, and its importance from a dinner in September 1974 when Laffer, then at the Graduate School of Business at Chicago, drew it on a napkin for Dick Cheney, Donald Rumsfeld, and Jude Wanniski.[23] The idea—that the country was so overtaxed that revenue might go *up* if tax rates went down—was too good pass up. The mantra was that tax cuts could be "self-funding." And in the immediate aftermath of the Nixon administration (he had resigned the previous month), the switch from Nixonian state meddling in the economy to Reaganite free markets was on. Ben Stein's father, Herbert Stein, had been the chair of Nixon's Council of Economic Advisers. When he resigned at the end of August just after Nixon, he expressed his disappointment with the wage-and-price-control strategy he himself had pressed for in the fight against inflation. Again, it would take

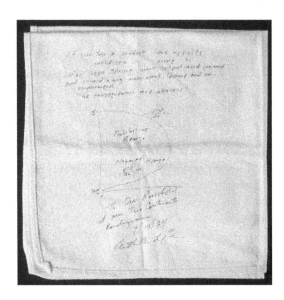

FIGURE 3.4 *The legendary Laffer napkin. 15" × 15". Courtesy National Museum of American History.*

the Volcker recession to really do the trick. It would be Laffer's ideas that would provide much of the intellectual cover for the dramatic tax cuts at the beginning of the new administration, setting up the outsized deficits to come. The long post-Nixon moment culminates in *Ferris Bueller*. That may seem overblown, but for Ben Stein it was simply true: "Working on this movie was the most laughs, the most giggles, the high point of my life ever since I helped write Richard Nixon's resignation speech. It was, seriously. I'm not kidding."[24] Stein does not look over his shoulder for support from the trading floor, but he is serious nonetheless.

A final version of the film's central opposition exists not across two scenes or two spaces but between the real and the virtual. *Ferris Bueller* abounds in 9's. For Hughes, this is an allusion to the Beatles's song "Revolution 9"— he apparently listened to the White Album each day during production. Throughout the film Cameron wears a Red Wings hockey sweater bearing Gordy Howe's number 9. Ferris's "9," in contrast, appears on a green computer screen and signifies the number of days he has already missed school that term. As the dean of students and Ferris's mother discuss Ferris's egregious hooky-playing over the phone, the number begins to change. Ferris's 9 is already barely material—it exists on screen—already the sign of absence. By hacking into the system and altering it, Ferris makes his absence absent. The EMH cut to Ferris at his keyboard comes as something of a surprise, and he addresses us directly: "I asked for a car, I got a computer.

How's that for being born under a bad sign?" This is (at least) triply ironic. First, no one as well-off and with as solid a family and set of friends as Ferris could reasonably be described that way. Second, to the extent that we take his remark quasi-literally, we will remember that his room is filled with superbly chosen posters from highly credible bands. And to the extent that his "day off" is founded on his willingness to play the sick child for his parents, he is more properly understood as reborn under very good signs indeed—SAVE FERRIS the water tower proclaims. Finally, he may have been denied a car, but he will get it soon enough when he convinces Cameron to join him on the day off. The red car may match Cameron's sweater, but it becomes Ferris's Ferrari when he drives it.

Still, this moment when Ferris fiddles with his school's computer system foreshadows his life to come. An extension of Broderick's character from *WarGames* (Badham, MGM/UA, 1983), this Ferris-the-hacker, Ferris-in-the-futures-market is destined to grow up to be a trader. On his day off, he skips economics in order to live it, albeit in a more affective register. Like Paramount or a Laffer tax cut, he is "self-funding." Here, that entails being a neoliberal subject as comfortable at the Merc or the Art Institute as at the ballpark or in the Von Steuben German Day parade. His politics are mid-1980s bipartisan. He is a firm believer in Rostenkowski's "free country where everyone can make their own breaks"; he just happens to have an enormous head start. Hughes, I think, senses this when he says that "Ferris is not a, he's not really a nice guy. He's an interesting guy."[25] To the extent that we imagine an entire lifeworld for this character, we are imagining a culture, here, the culture of the Chicago School. In the 1980s, American politics was reconfigured, and society became one made for and made by interesting guys like Ferris. He's never had one lesson, but the interesting guys like him received their first taste of comeuppance in the stock market crash of 1987. It was a lesson that took twenty years to learn.

Notes

1 The Graduate School of Business (GSB) is now the Booth School. The interactions between those units and the Harris School of Public Policy are now formalized under the aegis of the Becker Friedman Institute.

2 Jennifer Holt, *Empires of Entertainment: Media Industries and the Politics of Deregulation, 1980–1996* (New Brunswick: Rutgers University Press, 2011), 44.

3 Fredric Jameson, "Economics: Postmodernism and the Market," *Postmodernism, or, the Cultural Logic of Late Capitalism* (Durham, NC: Duke University Press, 1991), 260–79, 269.

4 Jameson, "Economics: Postmodernism and the Market," 274.

5 Ibid., 275.

6 For a study of the operation of the earlier tax regimes, see Eric Hoyt, "Hollywood and the Income Tax, 1929–1955," *Film History* 22 (2010) 5–21.

7 Lee Knight and Ray Knight, "What Happened to Limited Partnerships?" *Journal of Accountancy*, July 1, 1997, http://www.journalofaccountancy.com/issues/1997/jul/knight.html, accessed January 20, 2017. See their exhibit 1.

8 Knight and Knight, "What Happened to Limited Partnerships?"

9 Jack Mathews, "HBO, Disney Take Betts at Fun Odds," *L.A. Times*, September 20, 1985, http://articles.latimes.com/1985-09-20/entertainment/ca-6537_1_finance-films. The final dispositions for the four Silver Screen Partners can be found in their 1995 10–K filings via edgar, 0-11949, 0-14421, 0-16823, and 0-17713, respectively.

10 Michael Eisner with Tony Schwartz, *Work in Progress* (New York: Hyperion, 1999), 154.

11 For an account of the importance of Chicago's urban-economic geography in the development of both the theory and markets for options trading, see Chris Muellerleile, "Turning Financial Markets Inside out: Polanyi, Performativity and Disembeddedness," *Environment and Planning A* 45 (2013), 1625–42. Muellerleile is taking issue with Donald MacKenzie's actor-network theoretical account of the development of the Black-Scholes-Merton option pricing model, which I discuss in Chapter 7. See "An Equation and its Worlds: Bricolage, Exemplars, Disunity and Performativity in Financial Economics," *Social Studies of Science* 33, no. 6 (December 2003), 831–68.

12 The secondary literature on the school as a whole—not to mention individual members—is large and growing. A rigorous overview of the many discipline-shaping contributions of the school is *The Elgar Companion to the Chicago School of Economics*, ed. Ross B. Emmett (Cheltenham, UK: Elgar, 2010); more thematic approaches are Johan Van Osterveldt, *The Chicago School: How the University of Chicago Assembled the Thinkers who Revolutionized Economics and Business* (Chicago: Agate, 2007) and Lanny Ebenstein, *Chicagonomics: The Evolution of Chicago Free Market Economics* (New York: St. Martin's, 2015). Robert Van Horn, Philip Mirowski, and Thomas A. Stapleford, *Building Chicago Economics: New Perspectives on the History of America's Most Powerful Economics Program* (Cambridge: Cambridge University Press, 2011) is a more historically minded reassessment. The introduction usefully highlights the differences between the policy-optimistic Friedman and his more pessimistic colleagues, differences I am obviously skating over. Craig Freedman describes the pernicious interaction of "Ideology and Methodology" in *Chicago Fundamentalism: Ideology and Methodology in Economics* (Hackensack, NJ: World Scientific, 2008).

13 John H. Makin and Norman Ornstein, *Debt and Taxes* (Washington, DC: American Enterprise Institute, 1994), 204.

14 Makin and Ornstein, *Debt and Taxes*, 193.

15 "DEMOCRATIC PARTY'S RESPONSE TO THE TAX PROPOSAL" *The New York Times,* May 29, 1985, A19.

16 Charles E. McLure and George R. Zodrow, "Treasury I and the Tax Reform Act of 1986: The Economics and Politics of Tax Reform," *Journal of Economic Perspectives* 1, no. 1 (Summer 1987), 37–58, 51.

17 Most of these arguments were considered at the time of TRA86. See Joint Committee on Taxation, *Tax Reform Proposals: Taxation of Capital Income* (Washington: GPO, 1985) and the other articles in the special issue of the *Journal of Economic Perspectives*, previous note.

18 For Vestron's travails, see Dennis Kneale, "Vestron's missteps after 'Dirty Dancing' show pitfalls of crowded video market," *Wall Street Journal*, August 28, 1989, 1, and Linda Moss, "Tale of Vestron seems like a movie," *Crain's New York Business*, September 21, 1987, 3. For Orion's, see Joseph N. Cohen, *Investing in Movies: Strategies for Investors and Producers* (New York: Routledge, 2017), 122.

19 These moves, in their broad outlines, are detailed in Gulf + Western and Paramount Communications Annual Reports.

20 For a more detailed discussion, see Chapter 5 of my *The Studios after the Studios* (Palo Alto, CA: Stanford University Press, 2015), 159–214.

21 John Hughes, "Commentary," *Ferris Bueller's Day Off*, Bueller . . . Bueller. . .Edition, DVD, Paramount, 1986.

22 Hughes, "Commentary."

23 For the Laffer dinner, see the Smithsonian's catalog entry for the napkin itself: http://americanhistory.si.edu/collections/search/object/nmah_1439217, accessed January 20, 2017. Recent work has called into question the authenticity of the Smithsonian napkin; still, the underlying anecdote remains foundational to the mythos of the Reagan Revolution.

24 Stein, "The World According to Ben Stein," *Ferris Bueller's Day Off*, Bueller. . .Bueller. . .Edition, DVD, Paramount, 1986.

25 Hughes, "Commentary."

4

Like some dummy corporation you just move around the board:

Tax credits and time travel

Early in Oliver Stone's *JFK* (Warner Bros., 1991), Jim Garrison is conducting his infamous "walking tour" through "the heart of the United States government's intelligence community in New Orleans," and explaining how it is that ex-FBI man and staunch anticommunist Guy Banister is mixed up with ostensible communist Lee Harvey Oswald. As Garrison tells the tale of a magical building with two addresses, one belonging to Banister's office, one that appears on Oswald's pro-Castro leaflets, we are treated to a high contrast black-and-white pseudo-flashback to a very particular moment, where we can see, if we are paying careful attention, Oswald catch sight of Clay Shaw, aka, Clay Bertrand, aka Tommy Lee Jones, walking down the street. Stone is remaking some television footage that was shot on August 16, 1963.[1] The furtive eyeline match is the barest hint of what is to come in *JFK*, a bizarre homosexual plot to destroy King Kennedy, a Freudian slaughter by the primal horde that Michael Rogin has so incisively unpacked.[2]

These are the rewards of something like audience paranoia, but when Stone's manic editing met up with the intense and protracted home viewing that DVD made possible, it turned out that there was a second figure off in the distance, a fluttering banner reading "Tax Free." Like most such pieces of free-floating signification in contemporary cinema, it was duly enrolled in the IMDB, under the heading "goofs."[3]

The rationale for its enlistment is simple: in 1963, there was no program to rebate taxes to international visitors to New Orleans. The banner is part of a program promoting tax-free shopping in Louisiana begun in 1987; it is thoroughly anachronistic. And yet as Jerome Christensen has argued,

FIGURE 4.1 *Tax Free New Orleans: Clay Shaw encounters Lee Harvey Oswald outside the International Trade Mart. JFK, Stone, Warner Bros., 1991.*

Stone's film is a remarkably intense allegory of TimeWarner's corporate agonies circa 1991.[4] At its heart is the conspiracy of the folks from Warner against those from Time. The Time, Inc.'ers thought they were purchasing Warner Communications; in reality, they were being subverted at every step. In addition to the evidence he marshals, it turns out that Kennedy's real assassins are from ACME, that the Garrison children watch the WB cartoon "Dripalong Daffy," that the agreed-upon alibi for David Ferrie's trip to Texas is that he is going "duck hunting," that Kennedy was killed in a "turkey shoot," etc. Seen in this light, the sign is not a goof at all, but part of what Christensen calls Warner's "humiliation" of Time. Coming on the heels of the grand, hotly litigated, but ultimately tax-free merger, the banner is a corporate badge of honor.

Yet there is even more to it than that. As Eugene Schreiber, then the chairman of Louisiana Tax Free Shopping and the managing director of the New Orleans World Trade Center, explained, "The idea for Tax Free Shopping in Louisiana arose at a meeting of the World Trade Center's International Business Committee in early 1987 as an additional way to promote both tourism and retail trade throughout the state, as was done in many countries in Europe. We felt that being the first state in the United States to offer it would create significant attention and publicity."[5] The World Trade Center was formed in 1985 through the merger of two long-standing New Orleans organizations, the International House and the International Trade Mart, and in the 1950s the director of the International Trade Mart was Clay Shaw, the man we see walking down the street in *JFK*. Indeed, Oswald chose to hand out his leaflets in front of the Mart ostensibly because the Trade Mart and its leadership were major funders of New Orleans anti-Castro organizations.[6]

FIGURE 4.2 *Warners' assassins of choice: ACME.* JFK, *Stone, Warner Bros., 1991.*

JFK makes this link clear, repeatedly: When Garrison's investigator first learns, to his astonishment, that Clay Bertrand is Clay Shaw, he puts it this way: "Clay Bertrand is Clay Shaw, the guy who used to run the International Trade Mart?" Midway through this sentence, a figure from the danse macabre leaps into the shot, cackling maniacally, drawing further attention to Shaw's occupation. When the investigator relays this information to the rest of the team, he is positively gleeful. "Grab your socks and hose and pull. Clay Bertrand is Clay Shaw." The immediate response? "Director of the Trade Mart?" "Former director." Finally, and in keeping with the Hollywood rule of three, when Shaw is finally being questioned, he defends himself by incriminating himself: "I'm an international businessman. The Trade Mart I founded is America's commercial pipeline to Latin America. I trade everywhere. Like all businessmen, I am accused of all things." All of which makes the banner less a goof or an anachronism than a prophecy: through the Trade Mart, Shaw has begun to assemble a global, tax-free trading system centering on Latin America.[7]

FIGURE 4.3 *Nested Warners: "Dripalong Daffy" within* JFK. *Stone, Warner Bros., 1991.*

In the film, the avatar of this free-trade system is, naturally enough, Oswald himself. In the days leading up to the shooting, he is spotted in Dallas, in New Orleans, in Miami, and in Mexico where he is looking to get into Cuba and from there to Russia.[8] Garrison's investigators think this is "positively spooky," but the DA understands that the processes of political conspiracy and free market economics are the same. "God damn," he declares, "they put Oswald together from day one, like some dummy corporation from the Bahamas you just move around the board."

If every screenplay is a business plan, every production is a dummy corporation, a virtual corporation that gives rise to and reflects the actual corporation that it is. In *Production Culture*, John Thornton Caldwell puts it like this: "Because film and television are so capital intensive, a script also functions as a financial prospectus, a detailed investment opportunity, and a corporate proposal." "A fictional scenario is always tied to and considered alongside an economic one."[9] This dummy corporation can be "moved around the board" as necessary in order to find an ideal combination of location, labor, financing, and distribution. "The board" here is the matrix of possible combinations of time, space, labor, and capital. (In more contemporary movies, such as the *Bourne* series, it is called "the grid.") Is a star available? Is a location "fresh"? Should this movie be marketed for Christmas release? Does it have a guaranteed cable slot? How will it play across the windows of distribution? These are a film's virtual times and spaces, and as they become actual, they may also, and by that very same maneuver, be retained in their virtuality, as images and sounds, as self-allegorizations.

Thus, via a discussion of the operations contemporary Hollywood production system, we have returned to the point that Gilles Deleuze was making when he was moved to claim that "Money is the obverse of all the images that the cinema shows and sets in place." That point, again, was that the actual and virtual images are duplicates of one another: "The present is the actual image, and *its* contemporaneous past is the virtual image, the image in a mirror." And that exact duplication becomes perceptible in the phenomenon of déjà vu. "According to Bergson, 'paramnesia' (the illusion of déjà vu or already having been there) simply makes this obvious point perceptible: there is a recollection of the present, contemporaneous with the present itself, as closely coupled as a role to an actor."[10] Still, we might grant that the actual and the virtual image are exact duplicates without extending that exactitude to the internalized relation to money that, Deleuze says, defines industrial art. But before foreclosing that exactitude as just a symptom of the "long martyrology" of cinema production under the sway of money, we should hold open the possibility that the feeling of déjà vu conveys—displays—a potentially unlimited internalization of the relation to money. And, to pursue that possibility further, we should ask what relation to money *Déjà Vu* internalizes and where the limits of that equation lie.

This open exploration of the possibility of Hollywood intellection stands in contrast to the approach taken by Garrett Stewart in his "Fourth Dimensions, Seventh Senses: The Work of Mind-Gaming in the Age of Electronic Reproduction."[11] Both that essay and this chapter include extended discussions of Deleuze, *Déjà Vu* (Tony Scott, Touchstone, 2006) and *Source Code* (Duncan Jones, Summit, 2011), and the numerous parallels illustrate a stark difference in approach. (Indeed, even a glance at the endnotes would reveal that.) In his account, the time-images in a Hollywood time-travel film are "travesties" in which "the philosophical instigations of the virtual [are] turned to digital contrivance."[12] Such images "instrumentalize—almost to parody, rather than productively explore"—Deleuzian ideas.[13] This reads to me as condescension, and leaves Hollywood cinema little to do other than map powerful cultural "trends" such as militarization, worries about PTSD, and surveillance while remaining subject to "shocks" such as digitization. There are, to be sure, advantages to the quick critical reduction of the complex aspirations and qualified achievements of Hollywood moviemaking. Such an approach obviates the need to investigate the actual situations of the creative personnel or institutions involved or to ground those situations in precise times or places. Instead, there is a short route from cultural anxieties over the disintegrity of the veteran's body to classical film theory's interest in the mediation of bodies by the screen. And there are ready payoffs in the discovery that the movie is about its medium. Puzzle films, he contends "are most interesting as films . . . when their riddling uncertainties are more than just structural but in fact medial."[14] At the same time, there are losses, especially conceptual ones. In this instance, a "medium" is not that through which thinking is practiced nor that through which collective practice is objectified, nor is it even, as it was for Jameson, a potential image of the global circulation of capital. Medium is that thing we find at the base of seemingly every "interesting" film, even when a different examination might reveal something altogether different about instrumentalization, or near-parody, or the quality of aesthetic reflection available within the Hollywood system.

Déjà Vu was the third collaboration between Denzel Washington and director Tony Scott, the third between Washington and producer Jerry Bruckheimer, and the third between Scott and Bruckheimer, although it was only the second film the three of them had made together (*Crimson Tide* [Hollywood, 2005] was the first). The story in brief: following the explosion of a New Orleans ferry, ATF agent Doug Carlin (Washington) hooks up with a secret part of the FBI that can look four days and six hours into the past in order to solve the case. The key to the crime is Claire Kuchevar (Paula Patton) who, they believe, was killed by the bomber (Jim Caviezel) *before* the ferry explosion; by surveilling her, they will be able to find him. And though they do, in fact, capture the bomber, Carlin decides to go back into the past to save Claire, with whom he has fallen in love. (So it's *Laura* with a time machine instead of a place in Connecticut.) Together, Doug and Claire prevent the ferry bombing, but he dies in the process. As she sits grieving on the dock, another, not-dead-Denzel approaches her and they drive off together; he gets déjà vu. The plot, of course, is full of holes and makes no sense in the way all time-travel movies of any complexity are full of holes and make no sense.[15] The production, though, makes perfect sense.

Déjà Vu was supposed to shoot in October 2005, but the devastation wreaked by Katrina that August made that impossible and forced Bruckheimer to begin moving the project back around the board. At one point, when the film was to be shifted to Seattle or Miami, Tony Scott reportedly "ankled," doubtless taking with him his cinematographer, production designer, and editor. Yet Scott came back in what *Variety* irresistibly called "Déjà vu all over again."[16] And in February 2006 the film became the first production to be mounted in New Orleans after the hurricane. The revival of the film found ready allegories in the revival of the city and of the film's central characters. Thus Claire, who has been killed when the film begins, will be "revived" by Denzel after he travels back in time. Of course, time travel will temporarily kill him and he will have to be resuscitated. When he appears, suddenly, in a hospital operating room, he bears instructions, just as Claire's fridge had.

Throughout the commentary track to *Déjà Vu*, we are told that New Orleans was simply the right place for this movie to be set. The implication, of course, is that it *could* have been set somewhere else, somewhere less optimal. (You wouldn't say that Iraq was the right place to *set* a fictional

FIGURE 4.4 *Signs of revival.* Déjà Vu, Scott, Bruckheimer/Touchstone, 2006.

film about the war in Iraq; instead, you would talk about where you were *shooting* it, which would in all likelihood be somewhere else.) The script initially placed the action on Long Island so that the investigation could occur in close proximity to Brookhaven National Lab, one of the few facilities that would have the sort of particle accelerator that would be necessary for any sort of time travel. Of course if you could somehow conjure a *mobile* particle accelerator—and why not?—the action could shift to any place with a substantial ferry—Seattle, Miami, even Boston. The particle accelerator is contingent; the ferry is necessary. And so it happened that although New Orleans ferry rides are short, the film ended up set in New Orleans.

At no point in the commentary does anyone mention the enormous cost savings that shooting (and setting) the film in Louisiana would yield. Yet the state did not achieve its recent cinematic prominence because of its unique landscape, culture, or creative institutions. Louisiana became Hollywood South for the same reason that Vancouver became Hollywood North: because it pioneered using tax credits to draw production. This is the relationship to money that *Déjà Vu* internalizes.

Since the Second World War there have been several successive but overlapping regimes of Hollywood film financing, each epitomized by a certain allocation of risk assumption and deferral. High marginal tax rates after the war encouraged stars to incorporate and spread their compensation out through net profits participation, as Eric Hoyt details. Expansion of passive loss accounting rules led to film financing syndicates in the 1960s and 1970s, as I discuss in the previous chapter. The advent of lottery funding in the UK, alterations to the German tax code, the avalanche of hedge fund money—all of these have diverted, temporarily, the flow of capital.[17] And yet the possible consequences for story and style of these drastic alterations have been largely unexplored.

The implication here is not that taxation structures are the hidden key to the history of Hollywood cinema; I am not making a connoisseur's version of the old finance capital argument.[18] Rather, I want to suggest that the changing relationships between the different aspects of capital deployment are strongly correlated with the time horizons on which financial success is measured, and that, furthermore, the complications that come with these new funding systems may not be simply reflected in, but thought through, in the films that they support. This impulse to aestheticization is a regular feature of Hollywood filmmaking and much else. And at its most successful we find tight allegorical links between particular films and their funding regimes. *Winchester '73* (Anthony Mann, Universal, 1950) is not simply a net profits film; it is a film about the inexplicability of perfection, the impossibility of correctly valuing industrial products based on their origins. *Ruthless People* (Zucker, Abrahams, and Zucker, Touchstone, 1986) is not simply a limited partnership film; it is a film about the calculation and disbursement of income streams in the form of ransom; *Alexander* (Oliver

Stone, WB/InterMedia, 2004) is not simply a German tax-shelter film; it is a film about the amortization of library rights. And *Déjà Vu* is not simply a film where tax credits were crucial to its success; it is a film about catching up to a past fulfilling itself—it is a film largely told in the future perfect.

In addition to attracting dozens of television series and films from *True Blood* and *Treme* and *The Riches* to *Bad Lieutenant: Port of Call New Orleans* and Denzel's *Great Debaters* and *Battle: Los Angeles*, the motion picture tax incentive system in Louisiana has bolstered virtually every cliché about the state's political and economic culture.[19] Until 2009 the program for production worked as follows. Motion picture productions received a large percentage of their expenditures—it has been 30 percent—back in the form of tax credits. However, since these companies did not ordinarily have tax liabilities in-state, they could not make use of their substantial credits. In many other jurisdictions, the credits were refundable, and the state would simply cut a check to the production company; cash in, cash out. In Louisiana, though, the credit was not refundable. To receive their funds, producers had to re-sell the tax credits to someone who had in-state tax liability. Thus it happened that wealthy out-of-state motion picture producers and wealthy Louisianans looking to reduce their tax burden were drawn together. Between them, naturally, there arose a host of brokers who would match producers with taxpayers and negotiate the rates at which the tax credits would be sold—they are always sold at less than par, and the brokers always take a cut. This is the cliché of Louisiana as a system where corruption makes the economy work.

The more successful the state was in luring production, the more money flowed through in the tax credit market and the more prone to corruption it became. The legal tax skimming that the system counted upon gave way to a flood of illegal transactions. As has been true in past statewide corruption cases, the system sheltered its prominent players until the FBI began investigating. Eventually, tax credit scams would bring down the state's film commissioner, the Louisiana Institute of Film Technology (LIFT), and many prominent Louisianans, including several players on the New Orleans Saints. This is the cliché of Louisiana as a system so corrupt that someone finally oversteps the line between functional corruption and something that must be stopped.[20]

In 1992, Louisiana became the first state to turn to tax credits as a way of developing its local screened entertainment industry. The program was relatively small scale, and it was limited to investment losses. In 2002, Louisiana and New Mexico launched a much more ambitious scheme.[21] They were following Canada's lead. There, in 1995, a system of tax syndication dating from 1974 was overthrown in favor of a production tax credit. Initially, the system was intended to support the national film and video industry, and it was restricted to Canadian producers. But in 1997, the doors were thrown open to outside (i.e., Hollywood) investment. British

Columbia and Quebec added their own huge tax credits to the national rebates, luring production to Vancouver and Montreal.[22] In this strategy Canada was not alone. Countries around the globe made similarly enticing offers—Hungary had tax credits, the UK had lottery-funded rebates. Back "home," Hollywood studios were stymied in their efforts to convince the federal government to match Canadian largesse, so they turned to individual American states, with tremendous success. More than forty states eventually offered tax breaks beyond mere tax exemptions for out-of-state productions, and those breaks have been astonishingly resistant to drives for fiscal austerity. Despite the extreme constraints on state budgets in the Great Recession, tax credit programs still rebated $1.5 billion nationally in 2010. The pervasive availability of credits forced even the long-standing production centers in Los Angeles and New York to respond. They saw business draining away to such a degree that studio interests were able to lobby successfully for generous credits. New York's went to 30 percent on labor, 5 percent on infrastructure. California's has been more limited, but even in the midst of a fiscal catastrophe, the state preserved its $150 million program, with credits of 20 percent for major motion pictures and 25 percent for "independent" films and television series that relocate to California. The race to the bottom is largely over; producers need only run the numbers to determine which virtual location best suits their budgets.[23]

What has become a system for the studios is, for states, a far more precarious situation. The industry is both large and, in certain aspects, exceptionally mobile and flexible. States and nations attempt to purchase production industries through tax credits and other incentives on the assumption that when Hollywood (or other) capital and labor are regularly deployed in a particular area, the industry will become a permanent fixture in the jurisdiction's economy. This is not the case. As Robert Tannenwald of the Center for Budget and Policy Priorities put it in November 2010, "No state can 'win' the film subsidy war. Film subsidies are sometimes described as an 'investment' that will pay off by creating a long-lasting industry. This strategy is dubious at best. Even Louisiana and New Mexico—the two states most often cited as exemplars of successful industry-building strategies—are finding it hard to hold on to the production that they have lured."[24] As advice to policy-makers, Tannenwald's conclusions may be perfectly accurate and absolutely impossible to implement. But our interest lies as much in the representation of political economy as its actualities, and there again the situation in Louisiana has been paradigmatic.

In the early years of its tax-credit-fueled dominance of runaway Hollywood production, the greatest threat to Louisiana's hold on its film production industry was Katrina. In the wake of the hurricane, the state became the first to realize just how tenuous its industry was. A consensus gripped Louisiana and New Orleans politicians alike: it was imperative that the state re-open itself for the film business as soon as possible. Beyond the regular tax incentives, then, *Déjà Vu* also benefitted from a city and state that could not afford to say no. The bomber has a house in the Lower Ninth Ward, which adds a bit of devastation porn to the mix—the neighborhood was preserved in its wreckage for filming. And it is unlikely that any other city would have allowed the dramatic multitemporal car chase to tie up a major commuter route. Looming over both those was the ferry explosion. As director Tony Scott described it, "Their biggest concern was that the size of the explosion we wanted to do could actually breach the banks of the Mississippi. [laughs] . . . People were so cooperative. I think generally the people of New Orleans are, but they were just so grateful that we were there, that we were employing a lot of people in the city."[25]

As they compete for productions, states all emphasize the speed with which expenses will be recouped. Whether that recoupment comes through refund or transfer, it can be realized nearly simultaneously with the investment. (This is what separates the new tax credits from earlier strategies of liability syndication, which often took years to pay off and until their final disposition sat as complicated liabilities on corporate balance sheets.) Indeed, unlike every other major film-financing regime, the amount of money that is realized through the credit grows in direct proportion to the expense.[26] What you spend comes back to you. Or, to put it in the future perfect tense of the time-machine movie: you will not have spent it. And so it is that the tax credit movie instantiates a version of the Bergsonian duality of virtual and actual that is Deleuze's "crystal of time."

Déjà Vu is a time-travel movie where the distance that is traveled is comparatively small—four days and six hours, a sort of displaced simultaneity that allows only for *events* not for *processes*. That is, in a story where you can time-travel anywhere, be it Nazi Germany, 100,000 years from now or a 1980s hot tub, the span is capacious enough to allow History to unfold in dramatically different ways, but in *Déjà Vu* the gap between now and then is only large enough to assure us that the past carries the sign of its pastness.

As a result, *Déjà Vu* is less about the past than it is about an uncomfortable proximity, the sense of exact coincidence paired with a feeling of simultaneous distinction. It achieves déjà vu formally through three aspects of the array of video feeds that it calls "the time window": the fragmentation of the screen, the indeterminate dimensionality of the image, and the manipulation of resolution. These aspects of this (economic) image are both technical and formal, emblems of both the production and the narrative.

Fragmentation is the simplest to capture: the frame is divided within itself between feeds that are marked as present and those that are designated as past. This is true not only in the main control room, but more spectacularly in a car chase where Denzel pursues the bomber, driving *four days ago* at night. For the first half of the chase, Denzel wears a special "goggle rig" that allows him to look into the past as he drives. This turns the screen

FIGURE 4.5 *The fractional dimensionalities of the time window.* Déjà Vu, *Scott, Bruckheimer/Touchstone, 2006.*

into a nested POV shot, one made more complex because Denzel is driving against the flow of traffic. "Oh, this is trippin'," he muses. The overload of information through the display proves dangerously distracting, and at the chase's static midpoint, Denzel is able to stare into the face of the bomber, oblivious to the jackknifing eighteen-wheeler bearing down on him. The collision knocks out Denzel's goggle display but not the feed to the time window. Even though Denzel is now effectively time-blind, the feed allows the agents and physicists in the control room to direct his driving while he is able to devote all of his attention to the road he is presently driving on. And with that reduction in complexity, the chase loses momentum.

Tony Scott said that left to his own devices, he would be likely to produce a film that looks like *Domino* (New Line, 2005) on speed. This sequence, then, would be Deleuze's mobile section on speed, the hypermobility through time and space that is the essence of the car chase but also, and not really very figuratively, the essence of contemporary capital. Screaming across the bridge in his tricked out Hummer, Denzel is living beyond the dreams of the New Frontier–era free traders. Kennedy only wanted to lower taxes and tariffs; the twenty-first century's Bobby Jindals have managed to make them negative.

And yet with Scott there is always a countervailing pictorial pressure in which the rules of composition are bared.[27] So in Claire's French Quarter apartment, while the architecture divides up a wall into subframes, the mural she is executing works against those frames according to its own perspectival laws.

This countervailing autonomy (the still as opposed to the mobile, the analog as opposed to the digital, the historical as opposed to the contemporary) is, in the filmworld, the ghost of New Orleans authenticity: the mural, naturally, depicts Satchmo and Jelly Roll Morton. Claire is

FIGURE 4.6 *Confrontations immaterial and immanent through the goggle rig.* Déjà Vu, *Scott, Bruckheimer/Touchstone, 2006.*

recovering from Katrina, and a bad breakup, by gaining some perspective on her life—by reimagining New Orleans as the birthplace of jazz and not the emblem of governmental incapacity and malfeasance that it had become. The film ferries between these poles, endlessly relaunching its investigations of "the board." In Carlin's time window, the frames are obvious and the possibilities are open; in Claire's apartment the frames are occluded and New Orleans is inevitable. The tension between the two is a Hollywood love story.

Claire is also, and more than once, the figure for and vehicle of a simulation of dimensionality. In order to create a convincing sense that the time window was simply an extension of satellite surveillance technologies, the production used LIDAR to generate 3-D skins of buildings which it could then render and into which it could drop Claire.[28]

FIGURE 4.7 *Frame-breaking aesthetics in Claire's apartment.* Déjà Vu, *Scott, Bruckheimer/Touchstone, 2006.*

FIGURE 4.8 *The characteristic point cloud of LIDAR uniting time travel and levee analysis.* Déjà Vu, *Scott, Bruckheimer/Touchstone, 2006.*

The aim, though, was not to create a virtual world but to articulate the passage from the present *into* the past of the time window. As director of photography Paul Cameron described:

How do we go in and out of the past? We wanted to develop something that was more tactile, more realistic for people to understand . . . We start out with more traditional satellite footage, and then it goes down to Louisiana, and then it goes down into New Orleans, and as we come down to the rooftops of the building we incorporate the 3-D architectural skin that enables you to travel through walls or rooftops down shaftways or stairwells and into a location, hence giving the sense of passing through space.[29]

Within that rendered space, Claire will appear with what Scott called "this weird sort of ghosting toffee effect" generated by a frozen-moment camera system.

She acquires, they hoped, a sort of spatio-temporal blur that, combined with the near–3-D spaces, would give an added dimensionality to the frame. Between 2-D and 3-D, she becomes the figure of passage in and out of the screen, and in so doing she differentiates herself from her on-screen, 2-D trackers while at the same time acquiring a greater degree of proximity to us.

The final piece in this technical puzzle is resolution. In the main lab, Scott shot using Panavision's Genesis camera—then the state-of-the-art digital system. The tiles in the time window were being projected in real time; they were not composited in later. Among those tiles, the main window, usually focusing on Claire, was originally shot in high definition while the others were shot in standard resolution. This bolstered the tactility of the past. Scott effused, "The contrast and the separation when you see the finished print is huge. So the main window, it hums, and sings, and stands out. It's

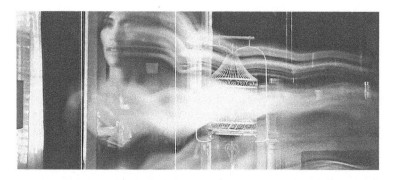

FIGURE 4.9 *Stretched subjectivity as an artifact of time-travel.* Déjà Vu, *Scott, Bruckheimer/Touchstone, 2006.*

pretty different from the other, smaller tiles."[30] For the crew, at least, it was convincing.

As DP Cameron put it, "For me the best sense of feeling déjà vu occurs when we do projection onto glass with Denzel behind it. It's a very subtle photographic technique, but we're racking focus from the surface of the glass to Denzel, to people in the background. It's this kind of multi-layered image that's very emotional. Then when you cut back and go over the shoulder, it's got this sense of it really happening."[31]

"The sense of it really happening": What is, for Cameron, the realization of a particular aim in a particular motion picture might be understood as the aim of immersive moviemaking in general. What *Déjà Vu* almost uniquely realizes is that such immersions have an inevitably proleptic effect: if you feel as though it is really happening, you will want it to; you will do things

FIGURE 4.10 *The romance of racked focus across diaphanous projections.* Déjà Vu, *Scott, Bruckheimer/Touchstone, 2006.*

to make it happen, even if those things require you to go back in time. That "doubling back on itself" is the form of desire that underlies the timeloops of déjà vu. Here is the way Bergson describes it:

> If I recognize the present instant, am I not quite as surely going to recognize the coming one? So I am unceasingly, towards what is on the point of happening, in the attitude of a person who will recognize and who consequently knows. But this is only the *attitude* of knowledge, the form of it without the matter. As I cannot predict what is going to happen, I quite realize that I do not know it; but I foresee that I am going to have known it, in the sense that I shall recognize it when I shall perceive it; and this recognition to come, which I feel inevitable on account of the rush of my faculty of recognizing, exercises in advance a retroactive effect on my present, placing me in the strange position of a person who feels he knows what he knows he does not know.[32]

In these Bergsonian terms, then, *Déjà Vu* is a retroaction movie.

At its conclusion, Bergson's first-person account becomes both knottier—feeling he knows what he knows he does not know—and more objective—casting him into the "strange position" of a more general type. Something similar happened to Hollywood filmmaking in the tax credit era. Even a decade before, the situation was subtly different. Massive expenditures always constitute massive risks, even if producers "know" that those risks are contained by anticipated ancillary revenues or balanced out across the corporate siblings of an integrated media conglomerate. But in that era of high neoclassicism, the studios (through their allies in the enfotainment industry) cultivated Wyatt and Vlesmas's "drama of recoupment."[33] Would *Titanic* break even? *Could* it? Such drama still existed, and it could still occasionally become the rallying point of a production or its reception, but as immediate, guaranteed, partial recoupment became the norm, some of the "drama" leached out of the revenue stream and was replaced by a narrative fascination with the manipulation of contingent certainties.

The more baroque the daisy chains of executive knowledge or self-consciousness become, the more they cry out for objectification. The "strange position" of the generic subject of déjà vu finds its characteristic cinematic home in a control room, taking charge of a vast media array—all versions of *Déjà Vu's* time window. Control rooms, particularly tv control rooms, have always been locations from which to observe things spinning out of control, going "live" and "uncensored" directly to an audience. But where earlier incarnations of the control room might foreground the abstract outcomes of strategy (*WarGames*) or the techniques of persuasion and performance (*Tootsie, Groundhog Day, Broadcast News*), or the idea of the public (*Batman*), these new control rooms (in *Syriana, Body of Lies,* or the *Bourne* films) work at a meta level.[34] Whatever unforeseen complications arise to thwart the controller's control can be sloughed off in favor of a fairly desperate belief in the totality of the grid itself.

Five years after *Déjà Vu*, Summit released *Source Code* (Duncan Jones, 2011), a time-travel film that one of its actors called "*Groundhog Day* and *Speed* and *Déjà Vu* on a train." Because the central conceit involved going back into the past repeatedly, the *Groundhog Day* comparison was inevitable. It was, said Jeffrey Wright, "*Groundhog Day* on the far side of the moon—somewhere in virtual space." But where *Groundhog Day* was an elaborate meditation on the promise and possibilities of Hollywood performance (the sources and worth of "talent"), *Source Code* narrated its way through the distentions of contemporary capital: the ultimate, mobile abstraction comes to ground through the bodies and in the spaces of the world it continuously remakes. Indeed, the film's own narrative is a more thorough conceptualization of the working of capital than its story requires. Instead of allegorizing its own production, *Source Code* is the allegory of the relationship between the *world* of its story and the *world* of its production.

The film itself oscillates between two emblematic spacetimes: a doomed commuter train making its way to Chicago and a control room at Nellis AFB in Las Vegas. Narratively, the exclusive jointure between them is supposed to be the consciousness of Capt. Colter Stevens, a mind that will be dropped into the body of a particular passenger for eight minutes at a time to gather information and then report back to his handlers at Source Code headquarters. Consciousness shuttles between *Source Code*'s spacetimes, and information is its product. There are not supposed to be any other communicating channels between past and present; the temporal "continuum" cannot be "unsettled." Thus when Stevens announces that he has placed a cell-phone call to Wright's character, he is told that "You may have made that call from the train, but I would never receive it here. It's a different reality, Captain. If the call even went through it would be received by a different me entirely." This is the stable model of time-travel in *Source Code*, and when Stevens begins to understand the fatality of time's arrow, he (like Phil Conners in *Groundhog Day*) begs for death.

That stability cannot last, and part of the movie's particular niftiness is the way it staggers the ruptures of the spatio-temporal continuum. The two worlds of *Source Code* are as distinct as possible: geographically (Las Vegas and Chicago); culturally (military/civilian, private cars/mass transit, classified info/public parks); temporally (present and past); even formally (the scenes in the pod were shot with RED digital cameras; those outside Chicago on film). The breach in that distinction is supposed to be limited and, like time, unidirectional, but as in every time-travel movie, there are additional possibilities. Our first hint of that openness appears as changes to the "pod" in which Stevens is being held—it expands, its controls shift, it leaks fluid. What initially seems to be an isolation chamber is revealed (at minute fifty-one) to be a "manifestation" created by his mind. Yet the revelation that the pod is a virtual space has no immediate consequences for the story's progress; the segregation of the worlds remains contained. Still, that segregation has been stipulated to be a matter of information rather than an inevitability of space-time: when Stevens asks where his actual body is, he is told that is "classified." Several time trips later, Stevens has found the bomber and now wants one final chance to go back into the "source code" to save the passengers on the train—even though he knows that, in the lab's time continuum, they are dead. What appears to be a matter-of-fact reckoning with finitude or fatality occasions one of the film's big reveals. Up until now, we have seen the a/v link from the lab to the pod and assumed that it was operating both ways. As it turns out, in the virtual pod Stevens receives audio and visual communication from his handlers in the lab, but within the lab, Stevens's thoughts are displayed as text generated by his brain without another input system.

The significance of the reveal is that the viewer now knows that Stevens is not present to the information system in the usual way, and that revelation

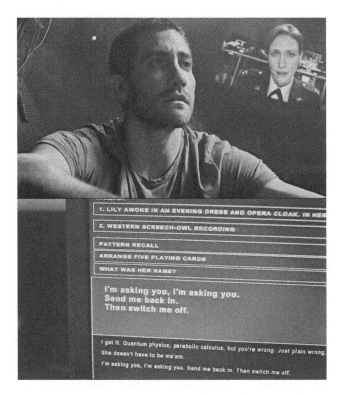

FIGURE 4.11 *Communications asymmetry from pod to control.* Source Code, *Jones, Vendome/Summit, 2011.*

coincides with a change in Stevens's goals in the film's other world. This communication disturbance will work itself out in Act III.

In the other world, the train, like the pod, is enclosed and claustrophobic. This social pod is vectored through the actual space of Chicago and its suburbs, a space which registers only when the train stops or when, in the happy ending, Stevens and his (new) girlfriend visit Chicago's Millennium Park. Communication between the train-pod and the space around it is even more radically asymmetric than communication with the lab: The space of northern Illinois "communicates" with the train only when the film's terrorist makes a cell-phone call that sets off the bomb. (The content of the call is irrelevant; it is the connection that triggers the device.)

Once we discover the communications asymmetry between the pod and the lab, and once Stevens's goals have changed, the train's communications asymmetry is adjusted: on his last trip into the source code, and after foiling the bomber, Stevens calls his father, not the Air Force base. The content of their conversation is, like the bomber's triggering phone call, less important than the fact of connection; it does not matter whether that connection has consequences outside its own temporal continuum. Yet Stevens *does* disrupt the continuum: his consciousness cannot return to his mutilated body back in the lab because that body has been euthanized, according to his wishes. As a result, his consciousness continues to dwell in the body of Sean Fentress, the passenger he has displaced. This in-dwelling first appears as a cinematic trick: whenever Stevens is in the "source code," we see and hear Jake Gyllenhaal (Stevens's mind) until his reflection reveals the face of the actor playing Fentress. (We even see Gyllenhaal when his girlfriend looks at him; it's a clarifying lesson in the difference between formal and narrative points of view.) The flipside of this audio-visual nesting comes when Stevens sends an email to Captain Colleen Goodwin, his handler. Just as, within the lab, she is televisually present to him but he is textually present to her, so in the disrupted temporal continuum at the end of the film, Stevens is cinematically present in Chicago but textually present at Nellis.[35] In this new, stable timeline, Source Code has found a way of scaling up the mediascape of its lab setting so that it can become continuous with the film as a whole. That medial-temporal asymmetry, both realist and allegorical, ultimately describes the relationship between a host of contemporary films and their tax credit–abetted productions. It is their economic image.

How thoroughgoing was the drive to save money on *Source Code*? Producer Philippe Rousselet's Vendôme Productions drew on his French background when the production headed to Montreal to shoot all the interiors. (The raft of French surnames in the credits makes that abundantly clear.) Mobile productions like *Source Code* typically fill their rank-and-file with local workers and bring along enough Hollywood talent to spread across the production like a layer of icing. The thickness of that layer is the evidence of the production's balance between its commitment to aesthetic

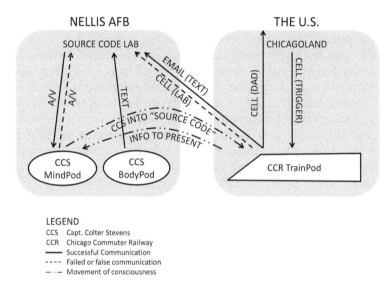

LEGEND
CCS   Capt. Colter Stevens
CCR   Chicago Commuter Railway
——   Successful Communication
- - - - Failed or false communication
— · · — Movement of consciousness

FIGURE 4.12 *Modes of communication and transit in* Source Code. *Author graphic.*

autonomy (how much labor do department heads get to choose?) as opposed to financial constraint (how many subsidized local salaries will there be?). In the case of *Source Code*, the availability of first-rate crew in Montreal meant that the production was able to staff up locally almost all the way: the costume designer, the effects houses, and the camera operator were local. When screenwriter Ben Ripley asked director Jones "How much of the crew was Montreal-based and how much did you bring from elsewhere?" the answer made it clear that financial considerations were overriding: "99 percent. It was very much a local crew . . . Don Burgess obviously came up from the United States, but because of the speed and the budget of the film he came up on his own. Normally he likes to move with a team of people, and he agreed that on this project he would work with a whole new crew from Montreal" (ellipses added).[36]

But while the control room might have been located anywhere, the film needed an actual, traversable location in which to situate its train disaster, just as *Déjà Vu* needed a location for its ferry disaster. Screenwriter Ripley initially imagined the train in the greater New York area, but that possibility gave way for budgetary reasons. The major incentive was a more generous Illinois tax credit. Still, *Source Code* would insist on converting its constraints into virtues. The helicopter shots over the opening credits alternate between images of the train in the great horizontal landscapes of Chicagoland and the sudden verticals of the city itself. Such vistas and contrasts are harder to come by around New York. The shift in location had narrative consequences as well. As director Jones explained, the penultimate scene at Anish Kapoor's *Cloud Gate* sculpture was only possible because the production had been moved to save money: "I know that when we had to move the film from New York to Chicago, the fact that that [sculpture] existed made me very excited because I felt the whole idea of distorted reflections was going to be very useful as a joining tool" between the sequences in the pod and those on board the train.[37]

How seriously should we take "the whole idea of distorted reflections" as the formal principle that joins the different worlds of *Source Code*? Jones is certainly alluding to the moments when Gyllenhaal sees someone else in the mirror, but those reflections are more than distortions—they are substitutions: Chicagoes for New Yorks; Chicagoes for Montreals. (There are no half-Stevenses/half-Fentresses in the mirror. To take it a step further, Hollywood's Gyllenhaal is replacing Frédéric de Grandpré, the Quebec-based actor playing his reflection.) Distortions occur when one person or thing or idea morphs into something else. The concluding conversation between Gyllenhaal and Monaghan is exemplary. He belatedly recognizes the sculpture as the silver kidney from his passages out of the source code, realizing that he has, in fact, known the future all along. "Do you believe in fate?" he asks. She responds that she's "more of a dumb luck kinda gal." The film, naturally, imagines that one is the distorted reflection of the other, just as Forrest Gump had reconciled determinism and free will by supposing that "maybe both is happening at the same time."[38] *Cloud Gate* embodies that simultaneity. The shape channels its reflections groundward so that, according to the *Source Code* trivia track, "80%" of it reflects the sky. But the low angles of the sequence reverse the balance between sky and ground, and, what is more, the ground that we see

FIGURE 4.13 Cloud Gate *and the distorted grid of possibilities. Source Code, Jones, Vendome/Summit, 2011.*

FIGURE 4.14 *Threat Condition Alpha at Nellis A.F.B.* Source Code, *Jones, Vendome/Summit, 2011.*

is the grid of possibilities itself. In this way, the Chicago of fate-and-luck becomes the equivalent of Nellis AFB, a zone of militarized risk control.

Stevens, like Oswald, like Carlin, is the dummy corporation that has been moved around the board. Like almost all films that successfully make it out of development hell, *Source Code* imagines this manipulation as romance.

Coda: No future

There is a price to pay for Stevens's romance: by successfully usurping Sean Fentress's body, Stevens erases Fentress's consciousness. That Fentress would otherwise have been killed in the train explosion is some compensation, but his eradication is the unacknowledged cost of forgoing at least one cinematic possibility. To put this another way, for Colter Stevens, *Source Code* is an action-romance; for Sean Fentress, it is a body-snatching horror film.

The flip side of the time-travel movie's confidence in the inevitable grid of contingencies is the horror film's almost desperate need to cordon its characters off the grid. As cell phones have chipped away at the isolation necessary to make the genre go, screenplays have been forced to account for technological failures, resulting in an endless stream of "no signal" and "dead battery" moments.[39] Few movies have been as canny about this convention as *Cabin in the Woods* (Drew Goddard dir., Goddard and Joss Whedon, scr., Lionsgate, 2012).[40] As a band of slaughter-ready coeds heads for the eponymous locale, one of them notes that the road they just crossed "Doesn't even show up on the GPS. It's unworthy of global positioning." The stoner sage responds, "That's the whole point. Get off the grid, right? No cellphone reception, no traffic cameras . . . go somewhere for one goddamn weekend where they can't globally position my ass. This is the whole issue." As it happens, though, the execution of the five college students is not simply a genre-driven requirement. It is, rather, an expiatory ritual managed in a control room, and the cordon that will keep the students off the grid is itself an elaborately maintained electrical curtain. Once the impending victims pass through a mountain, "A bird comes from behind the camera, flying directly above the tunnel. About halfway across it hits an invisible barrier and falls in a shower of sparks as for one moment an electrical grid seems to appear where it struck, before sparking away into nothing."[41] The grid here is a hexagonal honeycomb pattern, mimicking vertically the conventional pattern of cellular phone coverage.[42] The "off-the-grid" is nested inside the grid.

Cabin's sales pitch assumes a high degree of generic self-consciousness: "You think you know the story" is its tagline. But by literalizing generic conventions ("The Director" is in charge) and crossing the "cabin-in-the-woods" slasher film with the televised-life film (the production intern is named Truman, after *The Truman Show*)—*Cabin* draws our attention to the process of locating the production in a particular woods: "A helicopter shot floats over the rambler as it winds through an endless expanse of firs, finally consumed by them."[43] Within the film, these woods are the setting for the "reality" production within which the victims will unknowingly choose their own mode of execution. As it happens, they are pursued by a family of farm-implement-wielding zombies, but they might have been killed by something like *Hellraiser*'s Pinhead, werewolves, vampires, mutants, or even an "angry molesting tree."[44] "We chose," one of them belatedly realizes. "They made us choose how we die." The monsters are housed in a subterranean warehouse of potential carnage and illusory choice, a "Costco of death."[45] The spectacular array of death-dealing creatures is mere distraction; the location was already fatal. Before the victims might have chosen their mode of execution, they had been "consumed" by "endless firs." The woods are,

FIGURE 4.15 *The cell barrier that keeps our cabin campers "off the grid."* Cabin in the Woods, *Goddard, Lionsgate/MGM, 2012.*

FIGURE 4.16 *The locus of persecution: The control room.* Cabin in the Woods, *Goddard, Lionsgate/MGM, 2012.*

as it happens, in British Columbia, which is to say they are woods where the tax credits are monstrous.[46]

The global system of tax-credit-driven film and video production success-fully virtualizes even the stubborn realities of location shooting—not by de-materializing those realities but by shadowing them with their future perfect selves.[47] The proliferation of control rooms may appear to be a way of insist-ing upon the difference between places real and places virtual, but that insist-ence is always undermined in order to vouch for a higher order of control.

At the end of *Cabin in the Woods,* an unlikely romantic couple has nearly managed to escape their pre-scripted death, but instead of constituting the happy ending, their survival will result in the destruction of all humanity by renascent evil gods that dwell deep within the earth. The control room will be destroyed, and the cabin will be crushed by "a gnarled hand, bigger than the house and on an arm a hundred feet long."[48] Capitalism didn't quite go under in the Great Recession, so it made perverse sense to rewrite the system's survival as the mythos of a jokey, faux-ancient theology repurposed for the bursting of the housing bubble. If Hollywood remained sanguine about the continuing operations of the global economy that is because it had adopted a post-crisis mode of production even before the crisis hit. For more than a decade, the industry had been telling a story that we seemed to know already but that we were unprepared for nonetheless.

Notes

1   Robert J. Groden, *The Search for Lee Harvey Oswald: A Comprehensive Photographic Record* (New York: Penguin Studio, 1995), 75, photos originally WDSU TV archive.

2 Michael Rogin, "Body and Soul Murder: *JFK*," in *Media Spectacles*, eds. Marjorie Garber, Jann Matlock, and Rebecca Walkowitz (New York: Routledge, 1993), 3–22.

3 The entry for *JFK* goofs is http://www.imdb.com/title/tt0102138/trivia?tab=gf, accessed January 20, 2017.

4 Jerome Christensen, "Post–Warners Warners: *Batman* and *JFK*; *You've Got Mail*," in *America's Corporate Art: The Studio Authorship of Hollywood Motion Pictures* (Palo Alto, CA: Stanford University Press, 2011), 245–79.

5 Twentieth anniversary brochure, np.

6 Groden, *The Search for Lee Harvey Oswald*, 74, photo originally WDSU TV archive.

7 This story of the interplay between the rabid anti-communism of New Orleans's business elite and their drive for international market dominance is told in Arthur E. Carpenter, *Gateway to the Americas: New Orleans's Quest for Latin American Trade, 1900–1970* (Tulane PhD thesis, 1987). In Dallas, Kennedy is shot on his way to deliver a speech at the Dallas Trade Mart.

8 Oswald's famous radio debate with Carlos Bringuier, later released as *Oswald: Self-Portrait in Red* (Eyewitness, 1965), came about after he was spotted distributing "Hands Off Cuba" leaflets in front of the Trade Mart building.

9 Caldwell, *Production Cultures*, 232, 233.

10 Deleuze, *Cinema 2*, 79.

11 An earlier version of this essay was published in *Reading Capitalist Realism* in the summer of 2014. That same summer, Stewart's essay appeared. (Garrett Stewart, "Fourth Dimensions, Seventh Senses: The Work of Mind-Gaming in the Age of Electronic Reproduction," in *Hollywood's Puzzle Films*, ed. Warren Buckland [New York: AFI/Routledge, 2014], 165–84.) It is safe to say that neither of us knew what the other was up to.

12 Stewart, "Fourth Dimensions," 176.

13 Ibid., 184, note 5.

14 Ibid., 183.

15 The exception is *Primer* (Shane Carruth, THINKFilm, 2004).

16 "Scott Revisits 'Déjà vu,'" *Variety*, October 19, 2005 http://www.variety.com/article/VR1117931300.html, accessed January 20, 2017.

17 I digest the history of lottery funding and discuss its application to *Under the Skin* in "Independence and the consent of the governed: The systems and scales of *Under the Skin*," *Jump Cut* 57 (Fall 2016). The standard economic work is Hofmann, *Co-Financing Hollywood Film Productions with Outside Investors*. The narrative I adumbrate above is contained in Chapter 3. For a colorful account of German tax-shelter financing of Hollywood movies, see Edward Jay Epstein, "Why *Lara Croft: Tomb Raider* is Considered a Masterpiece of Studio Financing," and "Money-For-Nothing from Germany," *The Hollywood Economist 2.0* (New York: Melville House, 2012), 85–88. For details on Hollywood's hedge fund era, see Angus Finney (with Eugenio Triana), *The*

International Film Business: A Market Guide Beyond Hollywood, 2nd ed. (New York: Rutgers, 2015), 88–91.

18 The finance capital argument is explicitly anti-connoisseur, as can be seen in the first drafts of Horkheimer and Adorno's *Dialectic of Enlightenment*. When they revised the manuscript during the war, they removed the rhetoric of finance capital but retained the critique of connoisseurship. Max Horkheimer and Theodor W. Adorno, *Dialectic of* Enlightenment, trans. Edmund Jephcott, ed. Gunzelin Schmid Noerr (Palo Alto, CA: Stanford University Press, 2002). See the editor's afterword for an account of the revision process and the notes on 268–72 for specific changes. The best outline of the historical importance of taxation to the motion picture industry is Hoyt, "Hollywood and the Income Tax, 1929–1955," *Film History*, 22:1 (March 2010): 5–21.

19 *True Blood* (Alan Ball, HBO, 2008–14); *Treme* (Eric Overmyer and David Simon, HBO, 2010–13); *The Riches* (Dmitry Lipkin, FX, 2007–08); *Bad Lieutenant: Port of Call New Orleans* (Werner Herzog, Millennium/First Look, 2009); *The Great Debaters* (Washington, Weinstein Co., 2007); and *Battle: Los Angeles* (Jonathan Liebesman, Columbia/Relativity, 2011). For a labor-centered account of this same period in New Orleans production, see Vicki Mayer's trenchant *Almost Hollywood, Nearly New Orleans: The Lure of the Local Film Economy* (Oakland, CA: University of California Press, 2017). Her crucial case is *Treme*.

20 Gordon Russell and Robert Travis Scott "FBI Investigating Louisiana's Film Industry Incentives," *New Orleans Times-Picayune*, May 29, 2007, http://blog. nola.com/business_of_film//print.html; Robert Travis Scott, "LIFT Officials Pressured State to Speed Tax Credits," *New Orleans Times-Picayune*, June 4, 2007, http://blog.nola.com/times-picayune//print.html; Tim Morris, "Gov. Bobby Jindal Seeks Renewal of Film, Music Tax Credits," *New Orleans Times-Picayune*, March 9, 2009, http://blog.nola.com/news_impact/print. html?entry=/2009/03/gov_bobby_jindal_seeks_renewal.html; Robert Travis Scott, "Increase in Movie Tax Credit Endorsed," *New Orleans Times-Picayune*, June 19, 2009, http://www.nola.com/news/t-p/capital/index.ssf?/base/news-7/124538940923020.xml; Laura Maggi, "Former Louisiana Film Official gets Two-year Sentence in Bribery Case," *New Orleans Times-Picayune*, June 29, 2009, http://blog.nola.com/news_impact/print.html?entry=/2009/07/former_ louisiana_film_official.html; Robert Travis Scott, "More than Two Dozen with Ties to the New Orleans Saints Invested in Movie Studio Deal," *New Orleans Times-Picayune*, July 2, 2009, http://blog.nola.com/saintsbeat/2009/07/ more_than_two_dozen_with_ties.html; David Hammer, "New Orleans Saints Charles Grant, Jeremy Shockey sue Kevin Houser Over Film Tax Credits," *New Orleans Times-Picayune*, March 8, 2010, http://blog.nola.com/crime_impact/ print.html?entry=/2010/03/new_orleans_saints_charles_gra.html.

21 William Luther, "Movie Production Incentives: Blockbuster Support for Lackluster Policy," *The Tax Foundation*, January 2010.

22 The Canadian case remains the paradigm for U.S. production subsidies. In addition to the sources in the next note, see the following. For the transition to the credit regime: Stephen Godfrey, "Producers Protest Tighter Tax Rules;

Province Restricts Definition of 'Made-in-Quebec' Film," *The Globe and Mail*, February 22, 1991; John Schreiner, "Lights, Action, Financing!" *The Financial Post*, March 30, 1992, 3:24; Ian Austen, "Lobby Group Urges Ottawa to Introduce New, Refundable Tax Credit for Film Industry," *The Gazette*, November 16, 1994, B4; and Gayle MacDonald, "Mixed Reviews for Film Tax Changes: Federal Budget Brings Down Gradual Elimination of Shelters in Favor of Credits," *The Financial Post*, March 11, 1995, 2:31.

For the extension of tax credits to non-Canadian producers, Susan Walker, "Tories Boost Tax Credits for Culture," *The Toronto Star*, May 7, 1997, D2; Harvey Enchin, "Canada Extends pic Tax-shelter Program," *Daily Variety*, July 31, 1997, 8; Paul Gessell, "Bigger, Perhaps Better, but Less Canadian," *The Gazette*, October 4, 1997, B2; Christopher Harris, "Lights! Camera! Action! HOLLYWOOD NORTH: Toronto Remains the Third-largest Film and TV Production Centre on the Continent, and the City Would like to Keep it that Way," *The Globe and Mail*, October 30, 1997 C1; and Brendan Kelly, "B.C. Offers Tax Credit," *Daily Variety*, June 4, 1998, 10. The last captures precisely the beggar-they-neighbor approach that marks the tax credit arms race: "The tax credit will save producers roughly five percent of their overall costs and brings B.C. on par with Ontario and Quebec, which both recently unveiled similar tax-credit schemes. . . . 'The film industry is a growing industry here and it's footloose,' said [B.C. Film Commissioner Pete] Mitchell. 'It can move anywhere it wants very quickly. We heard from our key customers that they wanted this and we responded. It's all about competition and about staying on a level playing field.'"

The byplay became a debate over "runaway production" with Hollywood unions leading the charge for parallel domestic subsidies. Ian Bailey, "U.S. Unions Declare War on Hollywood North: Film Industry Wants Tax Breaks to Woo Business Back from Canada," *The Ottawa Citizen*, July 5, 1999, A5; Don Townson, "Canadian Goose: Defying H'w'd Whining, Canucks Sweeten Pot," *Daily Variety*, July 9, 1999, 1. When the national effort failed, the arrival of Louisiana's subsidies was cast as an anti-Canadian salvo, Dana Harris, "Prod'n Gets Bayou Boost," *Daily Variety*, August 27, 2002, 1.

Just as it pioneered tax credit financing, so Canada pioneered the tax credit scandal, this one involving the children's programming producer CINAR, which falsely labeled screenplays to qualify as Canadian content. Mark Lamey, "Cut! Cinar owes $27.5 million: Film House's Settlement with Ottawa and Quebec Includes Ill-gotten Tax Credits," *The Gazette*, December 20, 2000, D1. Rumors also abounded that Canadian houses issued "local" invoices for work so that they would qualify for provincial tax credits when the equipment and work were run out of U.S. offices. Doug Saunders, "A Cheater's Guide to Canadian Television: How to Bilk Taxpayers and Influence People," *The Globe and Mail*, October 23, 1999, C1. Worries that the scandal would cause legislators to restrict or remove production subsidies inspired fierce lobbying; ultimately, no charges were filed, no major changes were instituted because of the scandal, and the fraud and abuse were chalked up to a few bad apples.

23 See Robert Tannenwald, "State Film Subsidies: Not Much Bang for Too Many Bucks," *Center on Budget and Policy Priorities*, November 17, 2010, 2, for figures. The MPAA maintains a one-stop website to track current production

incentives at http://www.mpaa.org/policy/state-by-state. The Association of
Film Commissioners International performs a similar clearinghouse function,
http://www.afci.org/. A roundup of the global system as of 2005 can be found
in *The Global Success of Production Tax Incentives and the Migration of
Feature Film Production From The U.S. to the World Year 2005 Production
Report*, Center for Entertainment Industry Data and Research, 2006, http://
www.ceidr.org. CEIDR appears to have shut its doors; however, KPMG
regularly issues *Film Financing and Television Programming: A Taxation
Guide*; the fifth edition appeared in 2009.

I have said that tax-credit financing turns filmmaking toward the future
perfect. It has other effects as well. As it has become more prevalent, and as
studios have come under renewed pressure to drive down costs, more and
more of the enfotainment coverage of budgets has reported the budget-net-
tax-credits. What is particularly odd about this trend is that it has not been
accompanied by a concomitant rethinking of marketing expenses. Imagine
a film with a negative cost of $50 million that will be supported by a typical
advertising campaign. For years, the rule of thumb has been that marketing is
roughly half a film's budget. If tax credits reduce the effective budget to $40
million, do producers lobby for the same $25 million campaign? Or, to take
another tack: Since the tax credits are not actual reductions in the budget, they
must be credited against the film's negative cost (or counted as part of its "gross
receipts"). This would seem to be a simple enough matter. But for producers
and others who will share in the film's revenues, when and whether those funds
count toward the film's "cash-break" point are crucial questions. Without
very precise contracting, talent is liable to find itself farther from its back-end
payments than it might otherwise be. The tax credits might go directly to the
distributor, might be excluded from the producer's share, and might, therefore,
count as something like double free money for the studio. (I want to thank a
former student who now works in the industry—and who wishes to remain
anonymous—for working through these possibilities with me.)

24 Tannewald, "State Film Subsidies," 2.

25 Tony Scott, "Commentary," *Déjà Vu*, DVD, Buena Vista/Touchstone, 2007.

26 Tannewald, "State Film Subsidies."

27 An example of the way he talks about the pictorial: "Because of Katrina . . .
we had to move our shoot back to the winter, but I loved the winter in the
Bayou because all those trees, those birch trees became silver and white and the
graphics were spectacular." Scott, *Déjà Vu* DVD Commentary.

28 A fuller discussion of the film's special effects appears in Tara DiLullo,
"*Déjà Vu*: Time Tripping to new VFX Heights," *Animation World Network*,
November 22, 2006, http://www.awn.com/articles/reviews/ideja-vui-time-
tripping-new-vfx-heights/page/1%2C1. Scott was a particular proponent of the
"raw" look of the LIDAR pointcloud. Asylum, the effects house on the film,
hired Steve Snyder of Bohannon-Huston, a civil engineering firm, to do the
local scans in New Orleans. Even at the level of technology, the production was
ghosting the hurricane. October, 2005, the National Science Foundation sent
in its own investigators (The Independent Levee Investigation Team, ILIT) to

examine levee breaches throughout the city. The members of the team from the U.S. Geological Survey brought their own LIDAR with them to produce rapid digital maps of the damage. Their work is reproduced in the ILIT *Investigation of the Performance of the New Orleans Flood Protection System in Hurricane Katrina on August 29, 2005*, Appendix A, http://www.ce.berkeley.edu/projects/neworleans/report/A.pdf. They released their final report July 31, 2006. *Déjà Vu* recommitted to New Orleans in October and was released in November, 2006.

29 Scott, "Commentary."

30 Ibid.

31 Ibid.

32 Henri Bergson, "Memory of the Present and False Recognition," *Mind-Energy: Lectures and Essays*, trans. H. Wildon Carr (London: Macmillan & Co., 1920), 109–51, 137.

33 Wyatt and Vlesmas, "Drama of Recoupment," 29–45. The emblematic form of self-knowledge under neoclassicism is the self-similarity of chaos theory, as in the lyric from *Pocahontas*'s "Colors of the Wind," "But if you walk the footsteps of a stranger,/ You'll learn things you never knew you never knew." For a more extensive consideration, see my "Let's Make the Weather: Chaos Comes to Hollywood," in *The Studios after the Studios*.

34 *WarGames* (John Badham, MGM, 1983); *Tootsie* (Sydney Pollack, Columbia, 1982); *Groundhog Day* (Harold Ramis, Columbia, 1993), *Broadcast News* (James L. Brooks, Fox, 1987); *Batman* (Tim Burton, WB, 1989); *Syriana* (Stephen Gaghan, WB, 2005); *Body of Lies* (Ridley Scott, WB, 2008); *Bourne Identity* (Doug Liman, Universal, 2002); *Bourne Supremacy* (Paul Greengrass, Universal, 2004); and *Bourne Ultimatum* (Greegrass, Universal, 2007).

35 His body remains in its preservation pod in both cases, but in the first case, the consciousness in that body is communicating textually while in the second the consciousness has been shifted to Sean Fentress.

36 Duncan Jones, "Commentary," *Source Code*, Blu-Ray, Summit, 2011.

37 Jones, "Commentary."

38 The full quotation is: "Jenny, I don't know if Momma was right or if, if it's Lieutenant Dan. I don't know if we each have a destiny, or if we're all just floating around, accidental-like on a breeze, but I, I think maybe it's both. Maybe both is happening at the same time."

39 The "No Signal" supercut by Rich Juzwiak captures the many modes of cell-phone failure. http://fourfour.typepad.com/fourfour/2009/09/no-signal-a-supercut.html, accessed January 20, 2017.

40 The film, although finished in 2010, was a victim of the MGM bankruptcy. It sat on the shelf until Lionsgate acquired it for release.

41 Drew Goddard and Joss Whedon, *Cabin in the Woods*, screenplay, 20.

42 See, for example, the patent application for 4144411.

43 Goddard and Whedon, *Cabin in the Woods*, 20.

44 Ibid., 45.

45 Ibid., 92.

46 Without access to the books, it is impossible to know precisely how much *Cabin* received. Roughly 49 percent of its Canadian labor costs were refundable, with the possibility of more depending on how far away from Vancouver the location was.

47 Hollywood does imagine a complement to filmmaking in the future perfect: The abandoned serves as the substrate of filmmaking in the imperfect. In the making of featurette for *Casino Royale* ("James Bond: For Real"), producer Michael G. Wilson explains, "When you're looking for a building under construction for filming they're just about impossible to find because by the time you go and look at a building, you have to plan to work there, and by the time you're done planning, the building's moved on and probably finished. But this place, being an abandoned building, it was easy for us to make it look like it was a construction project that was still going on."

48 Whedon and Goddard, *The Cabin in the Woods*, 105.

PART TWO

Recession

Two trailers from the
opening of the Obama era

The move from precession to recession was not absolute. There had been glimmers of "existential threats" to the industry before the onset of the Great Recession and there would be logical, stepwise organizational and strategic innovations after. "Anxieties" about climate change might be corralled, but they were plausibly dire; the systematic inventorying and deployment of intellectual property offered producers many opportunities to screw things up, but the system of sequels and reboots I discuss in the next chapter continued largely unchanged. Similarly, it would be hard to consider the rollout of HDTV in the United States that I analyze in Chapter 6 a catastrophe for the studios. What, then, grounds this division, if the industry continued to operate in much the same way that it had, except when that was no longer strategically wise? Did the Great Recession really change Hollywood?

The latter question doubtless has a give-and-take answer in which some general patterns show change, others do not; some exemplary operations or formal aspects seem novel, while many more do not. These continuities underpin both David Bordwell's sense that Hollywood remains, fundamentally, formally classical and Janet Wasko's sense that Hollywood is still best analyzed according to the protocols of political economy. But totting up novelties on one side and continuities on the other in order to determine the preponderance of a system's features strips that system of its operational coherence even before the analysis has begun. I prefer to approach such possible historical breakpoints from inside examples. There the array of forces becomes clearer and the potential for sudden institutional transformations or unlikely cultural continuities is preserved.

Just as the plunge into the backstory of *Titanic* allowed us to understand how the industry's typical, yet complex, interactions between business and art lay behind that film's signal engagement with nostalgia and anachronism, so the pair of examples that follow demonstrate the interactions between a broader, evolving media ecology and the affective fallout of Obama's "hope" campaign. Hollywood negotiated the digital erasure of intermedial lines in a variety of ways—through production design, narrative, and sound design. Faced with the pixellation of an art and an industry, faced with the impossible task of reassembling itself and the world out of uncountably many elements, Hollywood grasped for solutions in images of self-assembly, quasi-automatic virality, and unintended incarnation. Projective confidence—hope—was almost completely offloaded to data, as in the Moneyball Initiative. Hollywood had reached the carrying capacity of its appeal to abstraction. In this new arrangement, the economic image persists, but seems no longer to integrate scales of industrial attention. The process of converting one story into another, of converting yet another crisis into yet another story had slipped away. Capturing that slippage requires a wider tonal range than simple precession.

A Chicago tea party

The Chicago Mercantile Exchange and the Chicago Board of Trade have been the epicenters of a futures-contractual utopia since the nineteenth century, never moreso than the moment when Ferris Bueller proposed to his girlfriend Sloane at the Merc (see Figure 2.3). However upbeat things looked in the 1980s, in early 2009 the atmosphere at the CME Group had turned sour. And so it happened that early on Thursday, February 19, Rick Santelli, the market reporter on CNBC, weighed in on the new administration's plans for grappling with a recession that had not yet hit bottom. Dismayed at the stimulus package, proposed mortgage modifications, and tentative plans for the re-regulation of financial markets, Santelli offered his own proposal:

> How about this, President and new administration: why don't you put up a website to have people vote on the internet as a referendum to see if we really want to subsidize the losers' mortgages or would we like to at least buy cars and buy houses in foreclosure, and give them to people who might actually have a chance to prosper down the road and reward people that can carry the water instead of drink the water?

The pseudo-democracy of the online referendum came with the advantage that it would never be attempted, freeing Santelli from detailing the mechanics of such a vote. By 2009, it had become commonplace to refer to such consequence-free speechifying as "a rant," and Santelli's was swiftly duplicated, posted online, and anointed "the rant of the year."[1]

Without having to worry about implementing a new plebiscitary political system, Santelli instead suggested a media-friendly protest: "We're thinking of having a Chicago tea party in July. All you capitalists that want to show up at Lake Michigan, I'm going to start organizing." Asked by the anchors back in New York what he'll be dumping at this tea party, Santelli says "some derivative securities." The rant on the floor may or may not have been the decisive moment in the launching of the tea party movement, but the speech and its aftermath provided an early check on the Obama administration's optimistic "100 Days" narrative.[2] Yet Santelli's remarks, however galvanizing, were largely skew to the interests of the tea party as it would take shape.

That summer, the tea party's ridiculous optics—tricorn hats, illiterate racist signage, redfaced raging at town hall meetings—would congeal. But here, less than a month after Obama's inauguration, the astroturf politics of popular unrest had not yet fully engaged. In this brief window, it was still possible for something as utterly weird as Rick Santelli's rant to become the wellspring of a "movement." And it *was* weird: Here was a man who had made his reputation and his career as a derivatives trader now casting his arms wide and inviting the president to listen to "America" behind him. A trader to Santelli's right, Eric "the Wolfman" Wilkinson, serves as his amen corner, whistling support.[3] When Santelli turns his attention to the administration's tentative mortgage principal reduction plans, the Wolfman chimes in, "It's a moral hazard!" handily making a term of economic analysis into an ethical judgment. In turn, Santelli turns faux-analytic and says of his surroundings, "My guess is [they are] a pretty good statistical cross section of America, the Silent Majority." The image, naturally enough, shows nothing of the kind; there are only guys, middle-aged and apparently white, all of whom work in finance. The soundtrack makes clear that this "silent majority" is noisily aggrieved.

Santelli is not eloquent—even rightwing outlets like the National Review admitted that.[4] But however far down the ladder of Chomskian grammaticality he stands, he manages to flip all the necessary switches. Rhetorically, he makes a desperate apostrophe to President Obama of the sort that would come to characterize the farther reaches of the Republican House. Conceptually, his economic ideas are a hash of anti-Keynesian talking points. He declares governmental economic stabilization to be the road to Cuban-style collectivism. He ridicules the idea that the fiscal multiplier could ever be more than one and calls out Larry Summers, demanding an explanation for such magical math. However opaque the syntax, we can, in retrospect, see where most of this was going.

Yet the imagined tea party remains baffling. When he proposed to dump "some derivative securities" what did he mean? One way of understanding that would be to take it as populist anger at financial complexity of the sort that stretches back more than a century to William Jennings Bryan.[5] The populist line from Bryan to William Greider to the "Audit the Fed" forces gathered around Representative Ron Paul and his son Senator Rand did have a place within the tea party.[6] Sometimes populism served as the political bridge between left and right, connecting the "Austrian" economics of the Pauls to apocalyptic financial fora such as Zero Hedge and *Rolling Stone* journalist Matt Taibbi. Taibbi, who in July would memorably liken Goldman Sachs to "a great vampire squid wrapped around the face of humanity, relentlessly jamming its blood funnel into anything that smells like money," was the more rhetorically inventive counterpart to Santelli.[7] The caustic laughter behind Taibbi's satirical portraits of bailed-out bankers such as Lloyd Blankfein would become an important tonal backdrop to the Occupy movement. At the same time, Elizabeth Warren's scholarly populism would eventually inherit the political mantle of the consumer financial protection movement. Yet the tea party did not pursue macroeconomic populism, where it would likely have found itself deeply opposed to Santelli's ad-hoc liquidation of "the losers." Instead, it directed its anger at the proposed fiscal stimulus and health care reform.

Subsequent events have hidden the actual economic argument here: Santelli's framework is not populist but predatory. He begs the government to let "the losers" who bought houses with extra bathrooms go under so he and his friends can swoop in and buy those houses out of foreclosure.[8] The anger at consumer bailouts ignores the more than $700 billion in TARP funds that had already been offered to banks and investment firms to keep them liquid. Instead, Santelli intends to dump his derivatives not because in their unregulated proliferation they brought down the global economy—not for the reasons of the left, in other words—but because the administration had the temerity to entertain the idea of regulating them and even imposing a financial transactions tax. (Summers would play a key role in stopping that last initiative.[9]) The parallel between the Tea Party in both its 2009 and its 1773 versions lies in the anti-tax fervor. Tax the derivatives and Santelli will dump them.

As important as the avowed political content of this moment was in defining the Great Recession, its media form was just as significant. The contemporary HD television news image is fragmented, usually into tiles reminiscent of the *Déjà Vu* time window, and the aspect ratio of the main image is maintained by nesting it in an L, with tickers along the bottom and a rundown on the left (or right) side[10] (Figure II.1). But where the time window participated in an economy of romance precisely through the manipulation of focus, the news image creates its pseudo-dimensionalization through parallax—one ticker running quickly, another more slowly, the window on reality subject to the usual conventions of television news editing. That nested image can later be extracted, in order to be streamed to smaller screens at lower bandwidths where the tickers would be out of date, the program rundown irrelevant, and the resolution insufficient to make them legible. In the early HDTV era, newslike events were visually configured to be viralizable. As a result, most of the uploaded versions of the Santelli rant exclude the surrounding infobarrage. So CNBC quickly posted the extracted image on its website at a mere 240 lines of resolution—too low to even reproduce in this volume. Todd Sullivan quickly copied that version and posted it to YouTube, where it accumulated more than a million views.

FIGURE II.1 *Rick Santelli conjures the Tea Party: contextualized and tickered.* "*CNBC's Rick Santelli's Chicago Tea Party,*" *https://www.youtube.com/watch?v=zp-Jw-5Kx8k&t=105s, posted by The Heritage Foundation, February 19, 2009.*

Yet in its full version, one posted to YouTube not by CNBC but by the conservative Heritage Foundation, context comes flooding back. In the lower right corner, where one would ordinarily find the network "bug," we see both the CNBC logo and a countdown clock. Less than twenty minutes remains before the weekly announcement of initial unemployment claims and the Producer Price Index.[11] That gives the time as 8:10 a.m. in the East, or 7:10 a.m. in Chicago. Hence Santelli's statement that only 5 percent of the floor traders are there—the pits won't open for more than an hour—and hence his ability to capture the traders' attention. In its original context, Santelli's rant is little more than the Merc's extracurricular shop-talk. In contrast, in its viralized version, Santelli seems to give voice to the market itself.

It does not happen very often that one can witness the market in the process generating ideology in public. The ramified systems of corporate and political power usually work more subtly. But in this moment, Rick Santelli was able to serve in propria persona as the channel between the collapsing economic system and its emerging ideological pushback. As the administration cobbled together its responses to the crisis, it could rely on a continuing confrontation with Santelli, giving voice to the traders on the floor, and standing with his arms spread wide, demanding satisfaction.

Inside all of us

Obama did not directly respond to Santelli's demands, but on April 13, he read Maurice Sendak's *Where the Wild Things Are* at the White House Easter Egg Roll, ad libbing to the crowd.[12] It was a carefully crafted scene—special invitations went out to a group of same-sex parents—but there was still a deep sincerity at its heart.[13] Obama was an actual Sendak fan, and in his reading, one could see how easily parenting in public came to him. He was ideally cast in an event that in nearly every detail was designed as the antithesis of that horrible, shell-shocked morning of 9/11 when George W. Bush sat in Florida while a second grade class read *The Pet Goat* aloud.[14] Those opposed visions of reading—of literary culture—help clarify the broader mediascape of the opening of the Obama administration.

The Pet Goat is not a stand-alone work. Instead, it is part of "Direct Instruction"—a "results-oriented" education protocol built on scripted repetition and underwritten by massive governmental funding and research.[15] DI is the mortal pedagogical enemy of "inquiry-based learning," and Bush was in the classroom to witness it firsthand. As the teacher whacks her pencil against lesson sixty to encourage the students to "read the fast way," every clack seems designed to quell the wild rumpus before it can start.

Perhaps no president had emphasized "reading" as much as Bush had. No Child Left Behind, the only durable achievement of "compassionate conservatism," made a fetish of the literacy numbers; former First Lady Laura Bush, whose central philanthropic effort was "Ready to Read, Ready to Learn," currently heads up the Laura Bush Foundation for America's Libraries.[16] For both Bushes, reading was essential, but strangely instrumental. Even the Nixon era's emphasis on the *fun* in "Reading is FUNdamental" seemed to have leached away. In 2007 RIF's "National Book Program" was renamed "Books for Ownership," ideologically securitized in the waning days of Bush's "ownership society" bubble.

It may be unfair to epitomize the Bush administration by his glazed audition that morning, but a DI-driven No Child Left Behind is our best indication of what the Bush administration might have produced without 9/11. It was big, it was technocratic, and, most of all, it was tricky to oppose. The legislation had Ted Kennedy and Jim Jeffords's imprimatur, so there was no establishment liberalism to call upon to oppose it. The National Education Association argued that NCLB penalties were too blunt and that it overemphasized high-stakes testing, but the endless drumming of centrist critique had effectively cast the teacher's union as the biggest obstacle to educational reform.[17] Most of all, it was hard to doubt the sincerity of the bill's principal sponsors. Many really did want to fix "failing public schools," and regarded NCLB as a way to weaken the school voucher movement. Proponents were able to tar anyone who opposed NCLB's universal mandates immediately as someone willing to leave children behind. In the wake of NCLB's passage,

Direct Instruction took hold in more schools, and district after district tried some form of extended school day. Intensification, direction, commitment, accomplishment, standards—it was something like the last gasp of Total Quality Management, now directed at schools. The Obama administration would attempt to reform and relaunch NCLB through its "race to the top" rhetoric and later adoption of the Common Core standards, but the intensification and instrumentalization of schooling remained.

By contrast, novelist Dave Eggers and the 826 network of tutoring centers he led wanted not to drill students into becoming a nation of readers but to plug underprivileged kids into the burgeoning nation of writers.[18] Longer school days would only have made that project that much more difficult. Add to that resistance a carefully crafted ethos that implied writing as such was subversive—826 helped fund itself by selling pirate gear—and the organization had all the necessary elements to channel time, money, and talent from young adults who believed in teaching writing to the kids who needed to be taught, preferably one-on-one.

For the live-action version of *Where the Wild Things Are,* Eggers served as director Spike Jonze's one-on-one writing tutor, more or less. "I mean, really, he worked with me as . . . I mean, he brought a lot to it, but he also was a great editor. 'Cause I think I had so many ideas and it was just unfocused. And we would just go through it and refine it down."[19] They had spent five years working seriously to get their version of *Wild Things* written and then made, about as long as it took Obama to go from senator to president. The sync was more than chronological: Jonze turns the whiff of fatherlessness in Sendak's book into full-blown single-parent Freudian strife; Eggers and Obama had both become famous writing their stories of life without parents—*A Heartbreaking Work of Staggering Genius* and *Dreams from my Father.*

On March 25, just over a month after Santelli's rant and just weeks before Obama's Easter reading, the teaser trailer for the *Wild Things* dropped. The production had been a long and notoriously troubled one, with tales of angry studio execs and suitmation gone awry. Fans of Jonze and Eggers were eager to see what they had come up with—that is to say, what they had got away with. On the internet, the teaser quickly racked up a million embeds on traileraddict.com. And it was perfect.

There are, famously, ten sentences comprising 338 words in the original book, and *none of them* are in this trailer. Those sentences are definitive, and what they define is the experience of having this story read to you. Over and over. Which is to say, those words might be the words of a mother, or a father, or a grandmother; those are some of the words by which a child might come to language in safety.

In contrast, the experience of this trailer is the experience of the absence of *that voice,* the voice of your grownup, your protector, your absolver— the voice that gave you a world: "And an ocean tumbled by with a private boat for Max." Every time you had that book read to you, or you read it to someone else, that voice—ultimately *your* voice—became that private boat.

However, until you have actually had the experience of losing that sheltering voice, the trailer does not strike you with the force of a cataclysm. Children watching it with their parents or grandparents or trusted older brothers or sisters, they did not get it, and they did not get it because the cure for unprotected silence was in easy reach. They would nuzzle up, reach into a lap for popcorn, or breathe in deep and smell their way back into a sort of shelter. This was, of course, how Sendak brought Max back from the land of the wild things—not with a touch, or a voice that would compete with the voice that was reading the story right then, but with the smell, and warmth, of dinner: "And it was still hot."

This sonic desolation has a visual corollary. Halfway through the trailer, there is a montage of four shots of Max running away from us, followed by a couple of him running to us, and then falling into a snow cave. Yet this movie is not *Crank* for kids; something else is at work. Kids run. And they run in different ways—in fear, in expectation, to see how quickly they might go, to beat someone to the corner, because their coaches have told them to—and it is easy enough to tell the difference between those styles of running. They register with us the way the nuances of a glance or a sigh or a shrug register. Movies capture those nuances exceptionally well. But in this montage, those differences are sanded away, and we are left with only the experience of speedy departure: "Children don't grow up," the song says. "Their bodies get bigger, but their hearts are torn up." Every piece of the trailer is drawn into a drama of aging, loss, absence, and, ultimately, the contingency of shelter. It was not fun for the whole family.

In theaters, the *Wild Things* teaser never quite worked. Psychology is part of it, but context played a role in undercutting the impact of what is, surely, one of the great pieces of contemporary corporate art. The teaser first ran before DreamWorks' *Monsters vs. Aliens,* a jokey action-parable about fitting in. Later in the summer, it would run in front of *G–Force,* a jokey action-parable about being special. *G–Force*, the Jerry Bruckheimer–produced, Disney-distributed, $150 million monster, constitutes the frictionless gateway to the contemporary action movie system. The tale of a guinea pig secret agent force, it is a training film for audiences too young to care about the historical doodads in the *National Treasure* series, which was itself Bruckheimer's junior varsity action franchise. In order to make it palatable to the parents paying full price, Tracy Morgan's "edgy" pig will scream things like, "This is offensive!"

It may have been happenstance that Obama was an actual Sendak fan and that Sendak sent him an autographed, extra-illustrated copy of the book. But when the time came to cut the trailer, Jonze and Warners and the folks at The Ant Farm (the trailer house that made it) hitched the film to Obamaism as explicitly as they could. In the Great Depression, Warners had gone all in for FDR on films like *Footlight Parade, G-Men,* and *Wild Boys of the Road.* In the Great Recession, it would do the same for Obama.

It did so at a time, however, when the atemporality of hope was being replaced by a newly hyped-up and looped timeline. The fetish of Obama's First 100 Days was itself a bit of New Deal nostalgia, and the calendar was being manically second-guessed even before Obama took office. The subsequent tea party town hall madness seemed to go on longer than any summer vacation ever. The manifest strangeness of Obama's Nobel Peace Prize epitomized the new temporality: he must have been nominated within three weeks of his election, yet the award seemed nostalgic by the time he received it in October 2009—part of an era when the promise of doing something seemed like enough.

The same thing was happening with *Wild Things.* In July, before paying audiences had seen the movie, the teaser won a Golden Trailer award for best music (a finalist for Best Trailer, it lost to the *Star Trek* reboot). *Wild Things* was a year late, already lauded, already processed, and still to come. With its Arcade Fire soundtrack and its contentless exhortations—"Inside all of us is HOPE," "Inside all of us is FEAR"—it belonged to the era of High Modernist Obamaism, an era that was already passing.

Warner Bros. tried to solve its audience problems by changing the marketing. As great, nigh on transcendent, as the teaser was, the full-length trailer was plodding. It sold the film to kids by letting Max narrate it. People and monsters got their own voices; the story came into shape; the "wild things" took on personalities. The ad campaign swapped the anxieties of independence for the assurance of identification: "There's one in all of us." Which Wild Thing are you? Posters for individual characters began cropping up. Are you Carol, KW, Ira, The Bull? Still, a grammatical wiggle in the tagline preserved just a hint of the collective aspirations that marked the teaser trailer: not one in *each* of us, but one in *all* of us. *E pluribus unum torvum.*

Inside the möbius strip temporalities of contemporary Hollywood and contemporary politics, synchronicities can be eerie: Max's existential anxiety emerges when his teacher/mom's new boyfriend explains that although the sun is going to die and swallow the earth, it won't matter because "I'm sure, by that time, the human race will have fallen to any number of calamities. War, pollution, global warming, tsunamis, earthquakes, meteors . . . ." On October 9, 2009, the same day Obama's Nobel was announced, NASA crashed a kinetic missile into the lunar surface in order to determine whether there was water in its dark craters.[20] That same week, while many adults were joking about blowing up the moon, there was Obama, standing with middle school students and astronauts on the White House lawn, proving to them that the moon was there, and that you could go there, and come back.[21] It was another perfectly stage-managed event, a reminder that the Bush era was dead and gone. Unfortunately no one seemed to remember why it had seemed so necessary to kill it.

How should we take this strange pattern of sync and slippage between *Wild Things* and the films of the summer of 2009? Politics, particularly the contradictions and elaborations of the new Obama administration's media strategy, offer one avenue of approach. On this line, Warner Bros. wants to align itself with the new administration, and it does not quite succeed. Yet a second vector seems to be at work, one that originates within the industry itself, and that finds particular instantiations in particular studios.

In the late-2000s, the Will to Edginess was strong with the studios, largely because they were in the process of stripping away any actual commitment to independent or quasi-independent filmmaking. In 2007 and 2008 many studio indie arms crumpled. (I discuss this in more detail in the next chapter.) Warner Independent and Picturehouse shuttered, Paramount Vantage was assimilated into the mothership, Miramax was halved, then closed, and then sold off for parts.

As recently as the turn of the millennium, the studios had a strategy. They aimed to find the sweet spot where smaller budget films would routinely pay off. It had many tactics—festival purchases, transcontinental coproductions, in-house development—but what it offered the major studios was a much better sense of the talent in the room and a way to keep their stars inside the corporate fold when they wanted to make something "different." The plan, in other words, was to invest in authenticity.[22]

But with the death of this sort of indie, the cutting edge of the middle of the road was folded back into more mainstream product. Warners proceeded in two directions. First, it cultivated "edginess" in the guise of raunchier, more aggressive humor. Seth Rogen gave voice to one of the monsters in *Monsters vs. Aliens*; a month later, he starred as the psychopathic mall cop in Warners' *Observe and Report*. In July, Zach Galifianakis was the geek behind the guinea pigs in *G-Force*. But in June, his skewed sentimentality vouched for the good heart of Warners' *The Hangover*—a good heart that culminated in a digital snapshot of him receiving a blowjob in an elevator. Other studios followed suit, riding a wave of raunchy comedies.

The second prong in Warners' strategy, though, was unique. The studio had committed itself more intently than any other to making almost exclusively big "tentpole" films—so many that it brought in long-term financing partners to underwrite its expensive slate—but with surprising frequency, Warners turned those films over to indie directors. Alfonso Cuarón got a *Harry Potter* installment, Christopher Nolan got *Batman*, the Wachowskis got *Speed Racer*. When Universal put Spike Jonze's *Wild Things* in turnaround after years of development, Warner Bros. picked it up. If the movie did not make sense for Universal, it seemed inevitable at Warner Bros.—at least until the studio began pulling the plug on its indie labels.

That same summer, the tension between Jonze and the studio became public. There were rumors that the studio would fire him and reshoot the movie. (Jeff Robinov, production chief, gave the *New York Times* the following ultra-oily quote about the whole thing: "There wasn't a conversation about firing him per se. . . . We certainly reached a place in talking about the movie where I can imagine it would have been easier for Spike to walk away, and it would have been easier for me to be talking to someone else, but we never got there."[23]) Unwilling to put up with its auteur, unable to foresee that it would be unwilling to put up with him: in the contemporary talent market, this is exactly the situation no studio wants to find itself in.

Warner head Alan Horn attempted to strike a balance. As he told Patrick Goldstein of the *L.A. Times*, "We'd like to find a common ground that represents Spike's vision but still offers a film that really delivers for a broad-based audience. We obviously still have a challenge on our hands. But I wouldn't call it a problem, simply a challenge."[24] Yet balance was not enough. For Warner to maintain its position as the home of the indie-auteur-blockbuster, the studio had to *want* Jonze's movie, not just tolerate it. Horn went on: "No one wants to turn this into a bland, sanitized studio movie. This is a very special piece of material and we're just trying to get it right." And because he was speaking mainly to insiders and those who want to be insiders, he explained the strategy: "We try to take a few shots. . . . Sometimes they work and sometimes they don't. The jury is still out on this one. But we remain confident that Spike is going to figure things out and at the end of the day we'll have an artistically compelling movie."

After getting past the irony or shock produced by the fact that this is *the head of a major studio* decrying "bland, sanitized studio movies," we should be struck by Horn's affect. He is resigned and confident, but not where one would expect. Warners didn't know whether the movie would make any money; they were pretty sure they would make art. The movie made $100 million at the box office globally, equal to its reported budget, which means it likely lost the studio tens of millions.

Horn's confidence came from a belief in Jonze's team—or, more accurately but more convolutedly, a belief that Warners needed to be seen believing in that team. Beyond hipster icon Eggers, the crucial technical jobs went to Jonze veterans but relative outsiders: KK Barrett handled production design (and was nominated for an Art Directors Guild award[25]), Casey Storm designed the costumes, Lance Acord served as cinematographer, Eric Zumbrunnen edited alongside David Fincher's longtime editor James Haygood. Novice Karen O of the indie rock group Yeah, Yeah, Yeahs did the music paired with old hand Carter Burwell. Their movie, their way.[26]

Whatever its box office, however poorly it did among kids—not to mention those crucial foreign territories where Sendak's story is not the cultural touchstone it is in the United States—the film was canonized before it was even finished. Seen from the future as outlined in its official history, *Heads On and We Shoot*, this will have been the project around which these veterans of the creative underclass and their sensibility came into their own.[27] Or, if one believes that sensibility has been present throughout

Jonze's career simply waiting to break into the mainstream, then this is the project where someone decided to risk $100 million on it. That is, this is where the skate punks achieved hegemony.

Warners desperately wanted to have an anchor among them. The studio logo in the film is scrawly and twee, just as the logo in a *Batman* film is ominous and batty and the logo in a *Harry Potter* film is hewn from the same digital stone as the on-screen Hogwarts. Redesigned logos are the way a studio says "I love you" to its movies. In the case of *Wild Things*, though, love and assimilation are never far apart. We could say that it is all a matter of who's reading and who's writing. In the run-up to its release, the idea that the film somehow came out of Max was everywhere. Warners attempted to make the movie seem more kid-friendly by having Max narrate the second trailer: "My name is Max," he began. (It's a million miles from whispering, in the teaser, "I didn't want to wake you up, but I really want to show you something.") In the book, Max has drawn one of the wild things; in the film, Max's ambitions are of a different scale altogether. He designs two great constructions, a fort and a tower. Conceptually, "it's at the level that a nine-year-old can draw in sand," Jonze told the *Times*.[28]

For KK Barrett, the production designer who actually had to design and oversee the building of the things, they were monuments to Maurice Sendak's style: "The interwoven sticks look very much like how he would shade in the crosshatching in the book."[29] This is the movie's economic image: a projective reconstruction in which building and drawing converge—in which the mark can somehow, nearly magically, become the world; in which marking becomes worlding. Carol, the lead wild thing, the one voiced by James Gandolfini, has built an amazing model of the entire island using the same hatched texture on a micro scale.

If you think Max designed the tower and the fort, you can also believe he drew the hatched logo at the beginning. Charlie, an anonymous reviewer whose early take appeared on Ain't It Cool News, thought that was how the corporate suturing worked: "The audience was engrossed the minute the opening Warner Brothers logo came up, designed as if Max had drawn it to put on the fridge"[30] (Figure II.2). Enough magical thinking and you can come out of the theater believing that Warner Bros. is ruled by nine-year-olds and built by wild things, that is, by artists who know how nine-year-olds feel.

Of course, you could also believe that story is so much costume drama. Jonze, who spent more than a year "finding the film" in post, was committed to the topsy-turvy timeline: "It was like working backwards, finding what I wanted it to feel like and then creating a process," he told Ain't It Cool News. In its deep need for credibility in the community, Warners was happy to leave unquestioned Jonze's genius for feeling.

When he took charge of Paramount in the late 1960s, Robert Evans followed Stanley Jaffe's advice: "Every half-assed guy in the business is

FIGURE II.2 *Rebranding the WB*. Where the Wild Things Are, *Jonze, Warner Bros., 2009.*

making films about where it's at. . . . Let's take a different road, Bob . . . give the audiences something they haven't had for a while—stories about how it feels."[31] This idea turned the New Hollywood into something more than a set of formal revolutions, and Paramount would channel it into *Rosemary's Baby, The Godfather,* and *Chinatown.* In a more contemporary moment, when transformations in technology, distribution, and finance have undermined the confidence of mainstream studios and independent filmmakers alike, the production of *Wild Things* was a lesson in inquiry-based learning for Warners. From Jonze, the studio relearned the importance of selling feeling.[32] But unlike the director, they weren't working backward. They had the process first: hire the indie. They even had the sincerity down— there was no hiding the strategy from everyone involved.

All that it took to learn this lesson was a relentless disavowal of aesthetic agency. The film was always Spike's to find, not Warners' to meddle in. The trailer, though, was a different matter. The voice you don't hear in the teaser might be yours or your mom's or your dad's or President Obama's, but it more plausibly belongs to the studio. When Max and Spike and Dave began telling their versions of the story, you felt free to nuzzle up to them. But when Warners told its version, there was nothing to cuddle, no matter how fuzzy the logo might have been. It was edgier than the film could have hoped to be.

In the middle of 2009, the recession offered a feeling but demanded a process. Across a range of media—children's books, comics, cartoons, HDTV—Hollywood went in search of that process. The neoclassical balance of *Titanic,* with its utopia of clean exchange, gave way to something like its opposite, a newfound permeability to cultural and economic forces that threatened to overload the system. Hollywood in recession wonders about its capacity for calculation and whatever might exceed it.

Notes

1 Youtube uploader Todd Sullivan immediately proclaimed it the "Rant of the Year," http://www.youtube.com/watch?v=bEZB4taSEoA, as did Steve Christ at the *Baltimore Examiner* the next day. http://www.examiner.com/article/rick-santelli-s-rant-of-the-year. Others followed.

2 Public protests against the stimulus and other measures had already occurred and been widely promoted by conservative writers. For a broad introduction, see Ben McGrath, "The Movement: The Rise of Tea Party Activism," *The New Yorker* (February 1, 2010), accessed January 20, 2017.

3 Wilkinson's biography page at PRO Trader Strategies.com, https://www.protraderstrategies.com/about-us/252-2/eric-the-wolfman-wilkinson/.

4 As National Review's Michael Barone put it, "No one would mistake Santelli's cri de coeur for the prose of the Founders." "The Transformative Power of Rick Santelli's Rant," June 10, 2010, http://www.nationalreview.com/article/229927/transformative-power-rick-santellis-rant-michael-barone, accessed January 20, 2017.

5 For a Chicago-centric account, see William Cronon, *Nature's Metropolis: Chicago and the Great West* (New York: W.W. Norton), 1991.

6 See William Greider, *Secrets of the Temple: How the Federal Reserve Runs the Country* (New York: Simon & Schuster), 1987. As an example of the appeal of such populism across the ideological spectrum, libertarian Ron Paul was the lead sponsor of the movement in the House while independent (democratic socialist) Bernie Sanders sponsored the Senate equivalent.

7 Matt Taibbi, "The Great American Bubble Machine," *Rolling Stone*, July 13, 2009, reprinted in *Griftopia* (New York: Spiegel & Grau, 2010), 206–40, 209.

8 That is more or less what happened, although the windout took several years. See Bill McBride, "Some Thoughts on Investor Buying," April 21, 2013, http://www.calculatedriskblog.com/2013/04/housing-some-thoughts-on-investor.html, accessed January 20, 2017.

9 Ron Suskind, *Confidence Men* (New York: HarperCollins, 2012), 365.

10 See my article "Aspect Jumping," http://flowtv.org/2012/12/aspect-jumping/ and the previous chapter.

11 For the video, Heritage Foundation, "CNBC's Rick Santelli's Chicago Tea Party," https://www.youtube.com/watch?v=zp-Jw-5Kx8k&t. As it happens, there were more than 600,000 new unemployment claims that week—a huge number, more than twice as many as one typically sees in a period of moderate economic growth. The Department of Labor's initial release pegged the loss at 627,000, unchanged from the previous week. http://www.dol.gov/opa/media/press/eta/ui/eta20090163.htm, accessed January 20, 2017. It was revised up to 631,000 the next week. The Producer Price Index turned modestly positive in January, but the trend was still ominous. The archived Bureau of Labor Statistics release can be found here: http://www.bls.gov/news.release/archives/ppi_02192009.htm, accessed January 20, 2017.

12   The Obama White House, "The President Reads 'Where the Wild Things Are,'" https://www.youtube.com/watch?v=5kP6cDoIHRw, accessed January 20, 2017.

13   Sheryl Gay Stolberg, "As Gay Issues Arise, Obama is Pressed to Engage," *The New York Times*, May 6, 2009, http://www.nytimes.com/2009/05/07/us/politics/07obama.html.

14   Buzzflashvideo, "Bush's Seven Minutes of Silence," September 11, 2006, https://www.youtube.com/watch?v=5WztB6HzXxI, accessed January 20, 2017.

15   For a highly critical assessment, see Jonathan Kozol, *The Shame of the Nation: The Restoration of Apartheid Schooling in America* (New York: Random House, 2005).

16   http://www.laurabushfoundation.com, accessed January 20, 2017.

17   For a more detailed account of the process, see Keith A. Nitta, *The Politics of Structural Education Reform* (New York: Routledge, 2008), 75–103. For a history of anti–teachers union campaigns, see Dana Goldstein, *The Teacher Wars: A History of America's Most Embattled Profession* (New York: Anchor, 2014).

18   See the chapter "McSweeney's and the School of Life" in Amy Hungerford, *Making Literature Now* (Palo Alto, CA: Stanford [Post45], 2016), 41–70.

19   Moriarty, "Moriarty Sits Down With Spike Jonze For Huge Unfettered WHERE THE WILD THINGS ARE Interview + Exclusive Debut Photos!!" Ain't it Cool News, December 19, 2008, http://www.aintitcool.com/node/39145, accessed January 20, 2017.

20   http://www.nasa.gov/mission_pages/LCROSS/main/, accessed January 20, 2017.

21   Kelly Beatty, "Stargazing with the Obamas," *Sky and Telescope*, October 8, 2009, http://www.skyandtelescope.com/news/63749172.html, accessed January 20, 2017.

      "NASA's Mission to Bomb the Moon," Scientific American, June 17, 2009, http://www.scientificamerican.com/article.cfm?id=nasas-mission-to-bomb-the-moon-2009-06, accessed January 20, 2017. The mission had been anticipated in a sketch from *Mr. Show*, which first aired October 31, 1997, http://www.youtube.com/watch?v=Csj7vMKy4EI, accessed January 20, 2017.

22   See Yannis Tzioumakis, *Hollywood's Indies: Classics Divisions, Specialty Labels and the American Film Market* (Edinburgh: Edinburgh University Press, 2012), especially Part III.

23   Sani Knafo, "Bringing 'Where the Wild Things Are' to the Screen," *The New York Times*, September 2, 2009, http://www.nytimes.com/2009/09/06/magazine/06jonze-t.html, accessed January 20, 2017.

24   Patrick Goldstein and James Rainey, "Can Spike Jonze Save 'Where the Wild Things Are'?" *Los Angeles Times*, July 11, 2008, http://latimesblogs.latimes.com/the_big_picture/2008/07/is-spike-jonze.html, accessed January 20, 2017.

25   Nominated for any number of critics awards for design, costumes, and screenplay, *Wild Things* won none of them—except the award for its trailer. It also won the more prestigious *Hollywood Reporter* Key Art award for Best Teaser Trailer PG-13 and Below.

26 For a version of the production history that makes all the complications internal to the process, see the authorized *Heads on and We Shoot: The Making of* Where the Wild Things Are (New York: It Books, 2009). Emblematically, the authorship of that book goes to the editors of *McSweeney's*, the copyright to Warner Brothers.

27 Lavishly produced, the book has a uniquely twee design featuring a binding that wraps around three distinct segments like a flattened, rounded Σ.

28 Dennis Lim, "Magical Mystery Tour," *The New York Times*, September 13, 2009, http://www.nytimes.com/interactive/2009/09/13/movies/20090913-wildthings-feature.html, accessed January 20, 2017.

29 For further insight, see KK Barrett, "Imagining a Fort for 'Where the Wild Things Are.'" *Los Angeles Times,* December 16, 2009, http://articles.latimes.com/2009/dec/16/news/la-en-lightswild16-2009dec16, accessed January 20, 2017.

30 Charlie, "Charlie goes to WHERE THE WILD THINGS ARE . . ." Ain't it Cool News, September 20, 2009, http://www.aintitcool.com/node/42558, accessed January 20, 2017.

31 Robert Evans, *The Kid Stays in the Picture* (Beverly Hills: Phoenix Books, 2002), 178. However unreliable Evans's accounts are, the emphasis on feeling survives in the contemporaneous pitch/documentary he made for the Gulf + Western brass, pleading with them to keep Paramount operating.

32 Faced with the inevitable demand for ancillary revenues, Jonze wanted to avoid "the generic, cynical fast food tie-in or other merchandising that feels like more fodder or garbage." Instead, he proposed doing a TV special that would give "kids the chance to talk about their feelings—cause I know when I was a kid, I would hear other kids' feelings and what they were going through, and you're just so hungry for that." Moriarty, "Moriarty."

5

The biggest independent
pictures ever made

Last of the independents

Upon receiving his Lifetime Achievement Award from the Independent Feature Project in September 2002, Ang Lee was looking forward to his next picture, *Hulk* (Marvel/Universal), which was due to open the following summer: "I guarantee you it's the biggest independent film ever made."[1] He had reason to be nervous. His longtime partner, the producer and writer of *Hulk*, James Schamus, had just sold his own company, Good Machine, to Universal and had agreed to head the studio's new independent arm, Focus Features. Anthony Kaufman of the *Village Voice* was apocalyptic: "The death of American independent film has been prophesied more than once over the last few years, but finally we have a date on which to pin our grief."[2] If Lee also seemed slightly embarrassed, some of that feeling was a hangover from Schamus's rather infamous IFP keynote address in 2000. Schamus had argued, somewhat tongue-in-cheek, that the IFP should be shut down and started anew. It should be shut because, simply, the indies had won. "The IFP has already, and fabulously, achieved its goals."[3] The indie market had grown exponentially alongside the expansion of the media conglomerates, while at the same time those major players were making more and more films with an "'independent' feel." "The successful integration of the independent film movement into the structures of global media and finance has wrought untold benefits to American filmmakers." He was, many felt, far more gracious than necessary when he argued that "there is no logical reason why the towering artistic achievements of films like *Boys Don't Cry* and *Election,* brought to us by the News Corporations and Viacoms of this world, should not be celebrated, and we ought to be genuinely grateful that caring and savvy people who work for those corporations have cleared a path in the marketplace for these kinds of films."[4] In place of the de rigueur defense of independent film, Schamus contended that the IFP should defend independent expression more generally—fighting the extension of the conglomerates, supporting local distribution networks around the world, working to repeal parts of the Telecommunications Act of 1996. If this speech was the theory, the integration of Good Machine into Universal and the launching of *Hulk* were the practice.

Six years after Lee's guarantee and eight years after Schamus's rant, Mark Gill, speaking at the Los Angeles Film Festival, announced, "Yes, the sky really is falling."[5] Surveying the landscape of studio-based indie labels and real indies, he noted the implosion of various production companies (Warner Independent and Picturehouse, New Line and ThinkFilm), the evaporation of Wall Street financing (this even before the credit panics later that summer), skyrocketing production and marketing costs, and the generally bleak competition for leisure time and dollars. It was clear from his title that an epoch had passed, and in what followed he offered ways to navigate through what would remain of the indie sector.

Paradoxically, the notion of independence was more prominent than ever. Gill noted that "for the first time in the roughly 20 years I've been looking at this data, more than 10% of the audience now is telling pollsters they prefer independent films."[6] What he did not specify (because the poll did not ask it) was whether those "independent films" came from a studio or a true indie. (Indeed, the response to "Would you prefer to see a film from Fox Searchlight or ThinkFilm?" is most likely "Wha?") And yet the survival of the term and the notion of the independent film among producers who produce nothing of the kind suggests that the invocation of independence does not in these cases refer to a mode of production or distribution but rather to both a relationship of responsibility and of authorship and an aspiration to quality of a particular kind. Independence is nearly identical with an ideology of art; it is, after all, a spirit.

Director Andrew Stanton described *WALL•E* in just these terms:

> I almost feel like it's an obligation to not further the status quo if you become somebody with influence and exposure. I don't want to paint the same painting again. I don't want to make the same sculpture again. Why shouldn't a big movie studio be able to make those small independent kinds of pictures? Why not change it up?[7]

The notion of *WALL•E* as a "small" picture is ludicrous, of course. It cost $180 million, and it opened in nearly 4,000 theaters in the United States. It earned $224 million domestically and $283 million abroad, making it the eighth highest grossing film of 2008.[8] But is Stanton's recourse to a discourse of "independence" any less ludicrous? How does it play out in *WALL•E*? At the dawn of the Great Recession were there plausible alternatives to this self-contradictory aesthetic? To put it more pointedly: if studios were "changing it up" when they make their "indie" films, what were they doing when they practiced what we might call "normal" studio filmmaking?[9]

Before answering these questions, though, we might account for their origins slightly differently. The speeches by the producers Schamus and Gill bookend a particular economic period in the history of indie filmmaking, but they are also highly staged instances of industrial reflexivity. These are public addresses; the speakers have been chosen for their ability to narrate compellingly. Structurally, these are self-conscious performances by producers who are simultaneously part of the system (Schamus then at Good Machine/Focus, Gill then at The Film Department) and called upon to render an opinion about the system as a whole. Even more, these controversial speeches required elaboration and response, comment and questions, rebuttals and denunciations, contextualization and re-narrativization.[10] They are nodes in the discourse of industrial reflection, a place where wisdom (conventional or not) finds explicit formulation and around which collective energy might gather. That is, in part, why it makes sense to point to them as landmarks and to build a story around them: from hubris to realism in the indie film community. Something similar is true of the remarks by Lee and Stanton, although in their cases the reflection tends *away* from the industrial no matter how cannily the directors understand the system. Instead, their professions of independence are compared with their actual situations. Because they are Hollywood directors, we more readily ask how (or, in a suspicious mode, whether) their films reflect their beliefs.

Questions about independence, then, appear within a broader context of reflexivity. That reflection is natural to cinematic creativity, necessary to professional identity-formation, endemic to professions of criticism, and assimilable to the qualifiedly public discourse of marketing, education, and appreciation that surrounds mass arts. In what follows, I want to bring more specificity to the configuration of reflexivity in the run-up to the Great Recession so that we might see how its various aspects were brought to bear within and just outside particular films. Beyond the particular examples, we may begin to answer the larger question of how industrial reflexivity has changed within what we might think of as Hollywood's "order of composition."[11] As it happens, the crucial institutions of studio independence—Pixar, Marvel, Miramax, and LucasFilm—all either were or would all become part of Disney. In the conclusion, I turn to the problem of independence in this altered context, and the new models of participation in the Great Recession's wake.

Realms of reflexivity

Three ways of thinking about reflexivity cordon this discussion of the ideology of independence. The first, derived from Stanley Cavell's *The World*

Viewed, is more philosophical and considers the relations between films that reflect on their own nature and our general capacity for reflection within and outside art. The second, developed in the work of David Bordwell and Noël Carroll, is more immanent. In place of a general reflexivity, they concentrate on the proliferation of cinematic allusions. From this they conclude that contemporary Hollywood storytelling struggles against an overarching "belatedness." Late to the party, today's filmmakers must grapple with their precursors, one way or another. The third avenue for reflection, which follows from John Caldwell's *Production Culture*, is more immanent still. Caldwell examines the myriad ways in which film production workers understand their positions within their crafts, the industry, and the culture at large. Where Cavell excavates "the thought of movies," and Bordwell and Carroll the rise of "iconographic coding," Caldwell takes up the "deep texts" of the film/television industry—brochures, demo reels, trade shows, producers' script notes—in his effort to detail the anxiety-fueled current production culture.[12]

These three ways of understanding why reflexivity is essential to contemporary Hollywood can be understood as emblematic of three relatively broad approaches or subdisciplines of cinema and media studies. Cavell's work stands at the origin of an important strand of film-philosophy in its more speculative forms. Bordwell and Carroll's assays a hybrid form, where the conceptual aspirations of film-philosophy are crossed with historical poetics, that is, with analyses of stylistic change over time. And Caldwell's work on production cultures has been essential to media industry studies. These three strands sometimes engage in polemical contests of authority, sometimes attempt to incorporate the conclusions of the others, and sometimes allow the others to proceed of their own accord. If combined they would compose a psychedelic Venn diagram, with blobs of competence shifting and bubbling, yet it might still be possible to gain a sense of the half-dimensions in which they interact.

In what follows, I hope to show how contemporary Hollywood films have served as communicating channels—imperfect, to be sure—between the deep textual situations of workers and the marketing efforts of the executive corps; between the discourses of authorship and the ideals of viewership. More than a collection of instances, or a story of the filmmaking process, these readings provide an account of the degree of coherence of the system as a whole. In short, feature films themselves constitute nodes in the ongoing process of industrial reflection. Yet these reflections are under new pressures once the sky starts falling. To understand the ways those pressures have affected and been affected by filmmaking, to understand why late neoclassical Hollywood entered the era of the biggest independent pictures ever made, we need to read Cavell, Bordwell and Carroll, and Caldwell historically.

Writing at the dawn of the New Hollywood, but looking back to films like *Contempt* (1963), Cavell turned naturally enough to problems of reflexivity and what he called "the camera's implication."[13] While in some of its historical lineaments Cavell's argument seems to accord with widely available notions of postmodernism, the conceptual consequences of each step he takes run counter to narratives in which postmodern referentiality comes between viewers and their "natural" appreciation of the cinema. On his account, in the classical era, implications of the camera and breaches in the fourth wall functioned as inside jokes. And these jokes "confirm[ed] for the insiders a strong sophistication in moviegoing, a proof that their increasing consciousness of movie-making routines [would] not jeopardize the film's strength for us."[14] Now, circa 1970, baring the device no longer lightens or enlightens. "The world's presence to me is no longer assured by my mechanical absence from it, for the screen no longer naturally holds a coherent world *from* which I am absent."[15] And this "loss of conviction in the film's capacity to carry the world's presence" has made it necessary to insist on the camera's existence. Reflexivity amounts to candor. Hence "the shakings and turnings and zoomings and reinings and unkind cuts to which [the camera] has lately been impelled."[16]

Until this contemporary moment, then, the distance between the world viewed by the camera and the world we inhabit had been automatic. The camera needed only to document the division between the world and the audience. But where once the world exhibited itself, now film has "tak[en] over the task of exhibition."[17] This last idea, that film "exhibits" itself, explains a final complication in Cavell's account, namely, that he does not call this new aesthetic "postmodernism." Rather, he regards the reflexive, exhibitionist, "theatrical" turn as the delayed arrival of modernism in the cinema.[18] Modernism, in this definition, appears when an art first discovers its freedom ("now anything can be exhibited and so tried as art") and subsequently recognizes the problem that entails, "that perhaps *all* you can do with your work and works is to exhibit them."[19] The autonomy of the artwork occasions a search for connection. Reflexivity is a solution to the problem of freedom; it asserts a connection where connection has been lost. "The object itself must account for the viewer's presenting of himself to it and for the artist's authorization of his right to such attendance."[20] Put another way, reflexivity is the tribute art pays to marketing.[21]

A decade later Noël Carroll drew attention to the increasing allusiveness of Hollywood cinema.[22] What had been inside jokes were now extended beyond the comic into other registers where they might serve as shorthand invocations of thematic or historical density. These allusions could, at the same time, ground the authority of post-studio directors who wished to (or needed to) assert what Cavell called their right to our attendance. Yet, after a period in which reflexive irruptions seemed to be everywhere (whether they were, in Cavell's terms, "serious" or not), Hollywood filmmaking settled down into an era of what Bordwell dubbed "intensified continuity."[23]

Flashing forward to the 1990s, viewers continued to encounter all those attention-grabbing devices and more, yet these moments hardly functioned as instances of reflexivity at all; indeed, they barely registered as technical flourishes. (Think here of digital lens flare and its banality.) Instead, other features seemed to dominate the style. Shot lengths shortened; the depth of field contracted; closeups got bigger. This is the era of Bordwell's "mannerist" or "referential" or perhaps "belated" classicism; what I and others have been calling neoclassicism.[24] What are the stakes of this difference in terminology?

"Intensified continuity" carries with it a critique of histories that regard Hollywood cinema as fundamentally postclassical. On these accounts, to put it briefly, the fragmentation of the production process attendant upon the breakup of the studios is reflected in the fragmentation of the narrative and spatial worlds of the film. But for Bordwell, the general homology between industrial form and narrative form is beyond dubious. While he and Carroll reject the notion of a fundamentally postclassical Hollywood cinema on both historical and theoretical grounds, they do recognize that something general has changed. Within their argument, then, the ideas of belatedness and allusionism amount to a *de minimus* version of postmodernism, one so small that it might still be subsumed by a nearly timeless classicism.

We might, though, reframe the argument about the relationship between art and industry in a way that would avoid any necessary reflection or homology between the product and the process. Intensified continuity editing, multiple plotlines, and the general referential substrate are the (potential) reflection and (necessary) demand made of (not made *by*) the production process. Contemporary filmmaking solicits reflection; there is no reason why that reflection might not make itself apparent in the films themselves. After all, if Cavell is right, film as an institution routinely reinterprets its own automaticity and its own requirements.

Here Caldwell's ethnographic work among everyone from below-the-line workers up through the executive ranks helps explain how this aestheticized homology works, how allegory wends its way through the industry. "Film and television companies, in particular, acknowledge image making as their primary business, and they use reflexive images (images about images) to cultivate valuable forms of public awareness and employee recognition inside and outside of the organization."[25] In the ever more fragmented and flexible film and television industry of the last two decades, industrial reflection has become increasingly fraught:

Within the nomadic labor and serial employment system now in place, any area that wishes to remain vital—in the face of endless new technologies, increased competition, and changes in production—must constantly work, through symbolic means, to underscore the distinctiveness and importance of their artistic specialization.[26]

The "deep texts" are routinely reflexive; they are "native theories" of practitioner groups at various levels of the hierarchy. The system is manic and anxious. Unable to achieve balance in the worklives of its practitioners ("If you want work-life balance, go get a government job," said Gill) it sought that balance in various ways on screen. Whether those films might exert any sort of control over the system as a whole is a question, but it is a question that should remain open.[27]

The studio/indie divide in the summer of 2004

The slash . . . has a panic function: it is the slash of censure, the surface of the mirror, the wall of hallucination, the verge of antithesis, the abstraction of limit, the obliquity of the signifier, the index of the paradigm, hence of meaning.

–ROLAND BARTHES, S/Z[28]

If the modernism of the New Hollywood lined up all too well with postmodernism, the subsequent decades found the studios reascendant, in what looked like a kind of corporate recidivism. In 1971, Cavell could contend that "Self-reference is no more an assurance of candor in movies than in any other human undertaking. It is merely a stronger and more dangerous claim, a further opportunity for the exhibiting of self."[29] Yet what does it mean when, for the sake of argument, the modernist moment in the development of a particular aesthetic institution coincides with the postmodern moment in the culture and the economy? We have a much better sense of this combined and uneven development nearly fifty years on. Within Hollywood, that precarious moment was followed by a reinstitutionalization, a neoclassicism.

For there to be industrial reflexivity, there has to be an industry to reflect, but those reflections are distributed across innumerable levels, from the lowliest term-contracted computer compositor to the CEO, from union workrule campaigns to Motion Picture Association lobbying efforts. In a context of potentially overwhelming anxiety, symbolic forms of coherence replaced durable arrangements of labor and capital. In that period, coherence was provided, I have been arguing, by the idea of the classical Hollywood studio itself. In the modern media conglomerate, then, the motion picture may have been displaced from the center of the company's finances but it remained, somehow, the center of its corporate identity: "the most fundamentally symbolic piece of content" Sony CEO Howard Stringer called it. "It drives all your content. It's the most visible. It's the most conspicuous. It's the most dangerous. It's the most exciting. . . . And it lives forever."[30] The movie was the home of collective reflection, where competing visions of the current industrial configuration could play out.

Stringer, though, is describing the system as it consolidated in the 1980s and flourished in the 1990s. Early in the new century, however, several of the imperial medialiths had begun to sense the limits of their expansion. Where before the trends in corporate behavior and corporate representation were uniform and mutually reinforcing, now conglomerate and studio activity became diffuse and inconsistent. Two entered retreat. TimeWarner sought to unwind its merger with AOL and to spin off its cable arm; Vivendi simply imploded. In the last instance, the instant French media conglomerate coughed up Universal, which GE merged with NBC, thereby recreating a seventies-style inter-industrial conglomerate only to be spun off to Comcast. In contrast to the unwinding conglomerates, Sony remained content with Columbia, although it did become embroiled in the latest incarnation of MGM/UA to no great success. Viacom cleaved in twain, leaving the slow-growth television networks on one side and the potentially higher-growth media properties, as well as the studio, on the other. News Corp. retained some of the go-go atmosphere of a nineties before similarly dividing. And Disney made three crucial acquisitions, Pixar, Marvel, and LucasFilm.

Had things changed sufficiently to regard Hollywood in the 2000s as different in kind from that of the 1990s? How would we mark the change? In *The Studios after the Studios* I pointed to the abandonment of synergy, the flattening of DVD revenues, and the reemergence of a distinction between corporate and auteurist politics in the wake of the Iraq War as potential markers. The attendant shifts in landmark genres reinforce the sense that the order of composition is in flux. In addition, we might include the disruption of long-term labor relations—made notorious by the 2007–08 writers' strike but epitomized in the drastic changes in the workflow and hierarchies of production designers, cinematographers, and editors, and the foreseeable completion of the digitization of the industry. (Here it is essential that we attend not simply to digital production, but to distribution and exhibition as well.) Of course it is difficult to assess the depth of such transformations at such close range, yet we might suspect that the convergence of radical changes in corporate aims, rates of market growth, and the division of labor point suggest that some breakpoint is at hand.

What might be replacing the neoclassical order? One compelling reading of this new era would contend that the principal locus of corporate reflection has simply shifted to television. TimeWarner's landmark HBO series such as *The Wire*, NewsCorp's *American Idol*, Disney's *High School Musical*s, and NBC Universal's *30 Rock* were, in their different ways, emblems as central to their corporations as *Batman, Die Hard, The Lion King*, and *Waterworld* were, respectively, in the high neoclassical period. Indeed, the emergence of a broad, auteurist strand of showrunning, and its concomitant popular and critical endorsement may amount to what we would call "The New Television" after "The New Hollywood" of the 1970s.

The residual film studios offer an interesting contrast to this new world of reflexive, authored television. One nonclassical feature of the emerging order of composition was the lurch toward radically immersive forms, in this case explicitly three-dimensional forms, at all phases—production, distribution, and exhibition. Three-dimensional production and exhibition are readily represented, indeed, they are so excessively representative that they become ready allegories for themselves. Distribution, though, lurks on the edges of our understanding; it seems to require a kind of allegorical support to make itself apparent. To adumbrate this recent history: Pre-internet worries about theatrical release *patterns* (*Outbreak*) were replaced by the manic reshuffling of release *windows* based on what is called "the tracking" (*Minority Report* [Spielberg, Fox/DreamWorks, 2001]). Even this rapid 2-D manipulation proved insufficient. Motion pictures, especially large ones, would now not only be projected in 3-D, but also would find their way into the multidimensional space of push-marketing and word-of-mouth (*The Dark Knight* [Nolan, Warner Bros., 2008]). Controlling windows now seemed insufficient; what was required was the ability to render consumer and corporate space by accumulating an entire world of individual preferences. Thus it is no accident that while Morgan Freeman was in Chicago working on *The Dark Knight,* a film deeply committed to rendering aggregate demand, he was also working across town on *Wanted,* (Bekmambetov, Universal, 2008) a film that, in its own way, turned on the rendering and manipulation of the bare dimensionality of the digital.

A second feature, and the one I will concentrate on here, is the pervasive adoption of the discourse of independence as the next step in

FIGURE 5.1 *Axial depth as quality 3-D.* Coraline, *Selick, Laika/Focus, 2009.*

FIGURE 5.2 *The tracking: Future haptics and shuffled cards.* Minority Report, *Spielberg, DreamWorks/Fox, 2002.*

the rationalization of Hollywood's industrial reflection. Earlier reportage on the indie scene from Peter Biskind has been supplemented, and often usefully corrected by more rigorously scholarly work from Geoff King, Claire Molloy, Alisa Perren, and Yannis Tzioumakis.[31] King, Molloy, and Tzioumakis's landmark anthology *American Independent Cinema* laid the groundwork for a far more expansive investigation of the relationship between industrial structures, representational systems, and discourses of differentiation.[32] These more subtle periodizations and typologies clarify the conditions that make "studio independence" possible. The notion of studio independence is self-contradictory, to be sure, but not necessarily more

FIGURE 5.3 *Mapping dimensions via distributed data collection.* The Dark Knight, *Nolan, Legendary/Warner Bros., 2008.*

FIGURE 5.4 *A world reconstituted from individual preferences.* The Dark Knight, *Nolan, Legendary/Warner Bros., 2008.*

self-contradictory than any other ideology of authorship within a highly capitalized, collaborative industry of mass entertainment.

By 2008 the anaclitic relationship between studio and independent was breaking down. In the neoclassical era, the formal division of labor between the studios and the independents was fairly stable. The studios made deniable allegories of the motion picture process—development (*Notting*

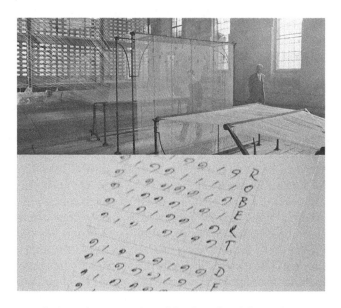

FIGURE 5.5 *The bare dimensionality of the digital and the analogue engine of fate.* Wanted, *Bekmambetov, Relativity/Universal, 2008.*

Hill), production (*Jurassic Park*), distribution (*Outbreak*), exhibition (*Speed*)—and the indies made undeniable, insistent critiques of that process (*Sleep with Me, Swimming with Sharks, State and Main*).[33] That the studio/indie division was conceptually stable did not mean there was not constant negotiation over the boundaries of corporate identity, but the principles of that negotiation were so widespread that they verged on the tacit. They became explicit only when necessary. As is usually the case in complex systems, friction indicates function.

No one better embodied that particular division between studio and indie than Steven Soderbergh. At the turn of the decade, he had perfectly captured the balance in *Erin Brockovich* (Columbia), a paean to indie-corporate resistance to the big corporation, and *Traffic*, an investigation of the complexities of distribution and demand for Barry Diller's USA Films. After 2000, his directorial work was divided between the *Ocean's* series for Warners on the one hand and much smaller projects such as *Full Frontal* (Miramax 2002) and *Bubble* (2929 2005) on the other. *Ocean's 11* amounted to a happy allegory of the sheer complexity of synching the schedules of its stars while *Full Frontal* was an earnest, overly literal look at life on the set. What Soderbergh was less able to do after 2000, though, was craft an indie film within the auspices of a major studio. *Solaris* (for Fox) and *The Good German* (for Warners) were box office duds. Still, he was so emblematic a crossover figure, and his ability to convince stars such as George Clooney reduce their quotes for particular projects was so pervasive, that the two of them successfully prodded Warner Bros. into starting Warner Independent Pictures (WIP) in 2003. WIP was supposed to serve as a home for the smaller projects Soderbergh had built his reputation on; its first head was Mark Gill. The strategy caught Warner up with other conglomerates that had matched their "mother ship" studios with indies. TimeWarner closed WIP in 2008; another piece of Gill's sky had fallen.

For another, and more institutional example of the studio/indie entente in action, we might turn to Disney, the studio with the most obtrusive brand. Unlike its fellow conglomerates, Disney is always confronted by the question of what a particular instance or decision means for the corporation as a whole. Whether Disney is making an R-rated comedy (*Down and Out in Beverly Hills*), extending employee benefits to same-sex partners, or buying Miramax, the overarching question is what the significance will be for the Disney brand. In 1999, this hyperconsciousness could productively serve both studio and indie. When Harvey Weinstein released *She's All That* to "prove to them that I [could] make a piece of shit and compete on their level," Disney CEO Michael Eisner was the voice of brand caution: "Yeah, but I really think you should have done that movie through Dimension, at the genre label. Because your label means something. Miramax has value, a certain level of quality. . . . If people start to think that Miramax produces stuff like *She's All That,* you're fucking with the brand name."[34] Eisner had learned this lesson from the history of Touchstone Pictures, Disney's "adult" arm, and now he was intent on keeping Miramax from becoming a similarly empty category.

By mid-decade, though, the balance had shifted and the recognized division had become more conceptually porous. In 2004, Disney found itself responsible, through Miramax, for Michael Moore's documentary *Fahrenheit 9/11*. If anyone caught more grief from *Fahrenheit 9/11* than President Bush, it was Eisner. The "inside" story of the film "broke" the week before the Cannes Film Festival, when Michael Moore's agent Ari Emanuel publicly alleged that Eisner forced Disney's indie subsidiary Miramax to back out of distributing the film. The core of Eisner's objection was a fear that Florida governor Jeb Bush would come to the defense of maligned brother George, and this bad blood would endanger the host of sweetheart development deals that allow Disney to continuously expand Disney World.

It was a juicy bit of movie gossip to report, and it broke on the front page of the *New York Times* with the headline, "Disney is blocking distribution of film that criticizes Bush."[35] The *Times* quoted Emanuel: "'Michael Eisner asked me not to sell this movie to Harvey Weinstein; that doesn't mean I listened to him,' Mr. Emanuel said. 'He definitely indicated there were tax incentives he was getting for the Disney corporation and that's why he didn't want me to sell it to Miramax. He didn't want a Disney company involved.'"[36] The anti-censorship firestorm played right into Weinstein's hands. He now had not only the hottest anti-Bush film at Cannes, but a parable of corporate censorship. With "his guy" Quentin Tarantino heading the Cannes jury, the Palm d'Or was in the bag. (Moore won.)

Further corporate machinations ensued. The Weinsteins, "forced" to buy the rights to a surefire hit movie and distribute it themselves (and not through Miramax, but rather Lionsgate), named their little one-off company the "Fellowship Adventure Group" in a bizarre and possibly homophobic bid to avoid any space-saving press acronymization and an equally bizarre nod to the *Lord of the Rings* trilogy which had just wrapped up. The Weinsteins would leave Miramax (and Disney) in 2005.[37]

Weird or conspiratorial, it was a sad moment for Eisner. Here was another embattled chief executive, under attack from the major shareholders who installed him back in the 1980s, caught very publicly telling his edgy indie subsidiary that in no way would Disney get near the most anticipated documentary of the year, a film that turned out to be the most successful and widely released documentary ever. It would be hard to say which part of this was the least intelligent move—missing out on the cash, announcing to the indie film world that Miramax was on a short leash, or making it uncomfortable for Florida governor Jeb Bush to continue to cut tax laws and zoning rules to order for Disney now that their coziness was a matter of embarrassing public record.

The fracas over *Fahrenheit*, in other words, brought the several sides of The Walt Disney Company—its family-friendly brand, its membership in the media oligopoly, and its magic real estate kingdom—into dangerously public proximity. It transcended gossip to become something akin to a state of corporate emergency. What to do, and where to turn? Fortunately for Disney, it had the closest thing to a house auteur that one could find in the neoclassical era, a director as beholden to the studio and as committed to its ideology as Michael Curtiz was to Warner Bros. in the days when he was directing *Robin Hood, Casablanca,* and *Mildred Pierce* for them. That director was M. Night Shyamalan.

Shyamalan's *The Village* (Touchstone 2004) had been in the works about as long as *Fahrenheit 9/11,* and with about as much anticipation. It was released July 30 (a month after *Fahrenheit*) and quickly took its place in his oeuvre of the "big reveal."[38] Such reveals depend, always, on the thoroughness of the set-up. The village is a bounded escape from the violence and predations of the modern world. Its fashion and dialect are off-kilter, its architecture and infrastructure are maintainable by its citizens. In these ways it is a displaced version of the Amish communities that dot the Pennsylvania landscape in what we might think of as the Shyamalanian hinterlands. Through most of the movie's narration, we do not know whether the village exists in our world but apart from it or whether the cinematic world is meant to have replaced our own (unless we have confidently guessed in advance). We subsequently discover that the members of the older generation have been consciously feigning their lack of knowledge of the rest of the world while enforcing a real ignorance upon the younger generation. Between the village and "the towns" lies a woods ostensibly populated by monstrous creatures, and much of village life consists of rituals of appeasement directed at these creatures. (The marketing campaign consisted of a display of these prohibitions: "Let the bad color not be seen. It attracts them.")

In short, *The Village* tells the story of a post–9/11 America, its frightened fellowships and authoritarian embraces, but it tells that story deniably. More deniably, but at the same time, it reimagineers the story of the Magic Kingdom itself, its avowals of its own noble aims and its concomitant authored repressions, its boundedness within a landscape of control. (Whether that is the Magic Kingdom story or the Manoj Night story is finally undecidable and, as of 2004, irrelevant. Not until Shyamalan destroyed his relationship with Disney in the orgy of egotism surrounding *Lady in the Water* would that distinction be important.) Just as the pirates of the Caribbean were emerging from the world within the park to dominate a motion picture culture made hospitable for ride-narratives, *The Village* re-reversed the oscillation and set up its strategic hamlet as something like a Jurassic Park for victims of violence.

Once viewers discover the scheme at the heart of *The Village,* though, they are immediately put on guard and begin to question the sustainability of the setup: How could such thorough isolation be possible in this globalized world? To be sure, the film tips its hand when William Hurt's character announces, "It is farce." But as in all Shyamalan films, the farce is otherwise played close to the vest. The administration of the park's borders falls to the director himself, playing the head ranger, and in this role he provides some essential background. "It's a really easy gig," he says to another ranger. "Maintain and protect the border, that's it. A few years ago, it got out in the papers that some government guys had been paid off to keep plane routes from flying over this place, that was a very stressful time for me."

And with that proviso, the deniable studio world of *The Village* and the insistent indie world of *Fahrenheit* reconnect. Within the diegesis, an overflight would destroy the isolation of the village whether the plane crashed or not. But the ban on overflights evokes both President Bush's meandering criss-crossing of the country in the wake of the 9/11 attacks and the parallel secret flights that carried the prominent Saudi diplomats and their families out of the country in the days when all civilian air traffic was supposedly grounded. Bush was reading *The Pet Goat* in Sarasota, one hundred miles from the park, when he received news of the second attack. When civilian air travel resumed, he advised Americans to "do your business around the country. Fly and enjoy America's great destination spots. Get down to Disney World in Florida."[39] Then, just before the Iraq war, a ban on overflights was extended to Disney's theme parks, which joined "President Bush's Texas ranch, nuclear submarine bases and stockpiles of sarin gas and other weapons of mass destruction," on a list of potential targets.[40] The news "got out in the papers" in May 2003 in time for the filming of *The Village* that August and September. Eisner's stress, and Bush's, became Shyamalan's story.

In *Fahrenheit 9/11* Bush was simultaneously the hapless zigzagger and the deep conspirator. Eisner achieved a similarly implausible combination in his attempts to distance Disney from its own subsidiary's film. With Eisner playing the movie version of Bush in real life, Bush did his part by shilling for the Disney-centric leisure economy during wartime. Moore's film ridicules Bush for extended vacations and dwells on the slowed time of the reading of *The Pet Goat*. These divisions are the heart of the film. To the extent that Moore's title makes any sense at all, it evokes this temporal rupture—what we might call the censorship or burning of temporality. That same censoring impulse lies behind the establishment of the atavistic village, with its old-fashioned ways and *Pet Goat*–style dialect. In *Fahrenheit*, the emblem of the distance between the president at play and the nation at war is the slash between the 9 and the 11.

That slash is also the emblem of *The Village*, the bright red mark of division and prohibition. "Those we do not speak of" slaughter and skin the village sheep (not goats) and leave the mark on the house doors. It is something like a bloody contrail, not the sign of passover but the sign of what could not pass over in the heavens. It is the sign of denial and the

FIGURE 5.6 *The slash as emblem of the distance between play and war.* Fahrenheit *9/11, Moore, Fellowship Adventure Group, 2004.*

emblem of deniability. It is a reading of the EMH cut. Within Disney itself, it is the line between the studio and the indie. It has, as Barthes put it in another context, a panic function.

The point of this reading is to suggest two things. First, that the dangers of indie and auteurist filmmaking lie not in the *possible* meanings of films but in their *insistent* meanings. Reading the suggested allegory of *The Village* we find an indictment of cultural *gleichschaltung* as damning as any in *Fahrenheit 9/11*. But that indictment could not be pinned on Disney since Shyamalan could always block the corridor of intention, a ranger in the park of interpretation. Second, this reading implies that major studios offload narrative risk just as they offload financial risk. Auteurism and indie branding are strategies for managing the risks of allegory when it threatens to become too obtrusive. I suggested earlier that this protocol was fundamental

FIGURE 5.7 *The apotropaic slash.* The Village, *Shyamalan, Touchstone, 2004.*

to the neoclassical system. That system had undergone and would continue to undergo wrenching changes. On the eve of the Great Recession, it appeared to many that the sky had finally fallen and the mutually supportive relationship between the indie and the studio had slipped away. The end of the era was not brought about because independent cinema rediscovered an authenticity it never possessed. Instead, the multiple roles the indie might play within the overarching conglomerate could be sorted and valued. The ones that mattered—the ones that brought coherence and profit to the corporation—could be retained and incorporated even more fully. The ones that carried more risk than reward could be dumped entirely.

Bibliotechnologies

As studios identified themselves as indies, though, their reflexive allegories leaked out all over. In the *New York Times*, Karen Onstad asked Stanton directly, "Is the ubiquitous, all-powerful Buy n Large a sly dig at Disney, Pixar's new corporate bedfellow? With a fervent head shake no, Mr. Stanton turns company man. 'Part of the contract was: "You can't touch us, you can't change what we do," and that's actually gained them such a level of respect and trust they wouldn't have gotten if they'd tried to be Draconian.'"[41] Allegory was still deniable, but only barely so. Despite his protestations that *WALL•E* was an "indie" picture, Stanton "turns company man": defending his own independence amounts to defending Disney against the allegorical stories his independence makes possible, which is to say that defending Pixar's independence amounts to defending Disney's corporate culture. Pixar, by 2008, had become as overbranded as Disney itself.

We can see that in the initial teaser trailer. Stanton, on screen, harkened back to an initial pitch meeting, years ago. "In the summer of 1994, there was a lunch." The sentence is banal, but the cinema is portentous. As saccharine music plays we dissolve into an empty, almost abandoned-looking Hidden City Cafe. "So at that lunch we knocked around a bunch of ideas that eventually became *A Bug's Life, Monsters, Incorporated, Finding Nemo,* and the last one we talked about that day was the story of a robot, named WALL•E." Setting aside the skeptical interpretation—that fourteen years on Pixar had finally run out of better options and decided to make the robot romance—the implication was that as an audience, our associations with Pixar would be strong enough to motivate our desire to see anything the company produced. But even more precisely, the implicit appeal of that first trailer was to our nostalgia for the founding moments of Pixar as a production company, and for its independence. Alongside that nostalgia there was also a sense that the movies pitched that day belonged together, that they constituted a unified sensibility, a library waiting to be born. The trailer fostered that continuity by linking one filmscape to another: the *Bug's Life* grass island, *Monsters, Inc.'s* vault of doors, and *Nemo's* jellyfish. All of Pixar is available to us, the viewers, and all at once.[42]

Indeed, while *WALL•E* has been taken as a fable of ecological destruction and overconsumption, of politics left and right, one thing that has gone suspiciously unremarked is its interest in filing and retrieval. "Filing and retrieval" hardly seem like fodder for the marketing machine, whatever their appeals to juvenile discoveries of order, but they are the necessary backdrop for the movies's invocations of individuality and independence. WALL•E's occupation is ostensibly trash compacting—he makes cubes and places them in grand architectural structures. But his romance lies not in the Watts Towers aesthetic of his trashcubes—they are simply a stunning byproduct of his dayjob—but in his retrievals—the bits and pieces of the world that he collects. (Eve's "directive" is retrieval, too; she is supposed to collect any sign of "ongoing photosynthesis" and return it to the Axiom.)

The movie opposes active retrieval to passive consumption. In the dystopia, Buy n Large is a vast warehouse retailer that has taken over the entire world, an already shopworn joke from its appearance in *Idiocracy* (where the ultrastore is an actual Costco [Judge, Fox, 2007][43]) and a 2003 *Saturday Night Live* skit about Walmart ("Bathrobes with patriotic ducks is in aisle 6,000 and, here, you're gonna need this poncho because I think it's rainy season in that part of Walmart"). In contrast, WALL•E is a DIY recycler. His home entertainment system consists of an old VCR wired to an iPod and viewed through a CRT screen as a magnifier. His walls are lined with racks for other WALL•E units, but they have all been mined for spare parts. Their places are now filled with the detritus that has struck his emerging subjectivity as worth preserving. (Hidden among the shelves, naturally enough, are characters from earlier Pixar movies.)

FIGURE 5.8 *The architecture of filing and retrieval.* WALL•E, *Stanton, Pixar/ Disney, 2008.*

On the mother ship (we won't call it Disney), the captain need do nothing but let the autopilot (we won't call it the brand) run everything. Eventually, he discovers just how vast the computer's stores of knowledge are, and surfs its databanks from one entry to another. The troika of WALL•E, Eve, and the captain share more than a commitment to the transformative power of recall; they share Pixar's corporate pedigree. WALL•E's startup sound is the Apple C-Major chord, Eve's design was vetted by Apple's chief designer Jonathan Ive, and, slightly more speculatively, the captain is empowered by his computer to throw off the shackles of his autopilot.[44]

Pixar had been owned by Apple CEO Steve Jobs until 2006, when Disney paid $7.4 billion for the company, a move that installed Jobs on Disney's board and Pixar chief John Lasseter as Chief Creative Officer of both Pixar and Disney.[45] This is why the *New York Times* reporter asked Stanton if the criticism of Buy n Large was a "dig" at Disney. In the movie's version of the change in corporate control, the acquisition of Pixar saves Disney from its own infantilizing complacency. Pixar's own well-tended corporate culture drives that subversive reinvention: the arrival of the Apple/Pixar robots leads the captain to unlock the knowledge dormant in the vault. The robots are the keys to the library, and the library is the key to the rediscovery of human purpose.

Libraries may do many things on film. They frequently serve as locations of hidden, total knowledge, as in *Toute la Mémoire du Monde* (1956) or

FIGURE 5.9 *Post apocalyptic home entertainment*. WALL•E, *Stanton, Pixar/ Disney, 2008.*

All the President's Men (1976) or *The Time Machine* (2002), or *National Treasure 2* (2007). In *Jumper* (2008), the library is a refuge. When David Rice first discovers his ability to teleport, he arrives (twice) in the Ann Arbor public library. ("Escape to your library" reads the helpful poster.) In *Alexander* (2004), Anthony Hopkins as Ptolemy narrates the story from the library of Alexandria, vouching for its historical reality. In *Se7en* (Fincher, Fox, 1995), the library is the locus of obsession; in *A.I.* (Spielberg, DreamWorks/WB 2001), the "room where they make you read" is the place where David lashes out against his own double, against his own identity as a product. The library as such has no single meaning.

Just offscreen, though, we see that libraries have become the anchors of corporate identity.[46] Legacy libraries feed individual productions. The RKO library had been opened up for remakes (e.g., Ice Cube's *Are We There Yet?* [2005] remakes *Mr. Blandings Builds His Dream House* [1948]). Libraries also drive mergers and acquisitions. The MGM/UA library was the most enticing element for the private equity investors in a recent sale of the studio while the DreamWorks library was monetized in order to make the Paramount/DreamWorks deal possible. Libraries reliably spin off cash that can be plowed into production, as at Lionsgate or Luc Besson's EuropaCorp.[47] In short, library rights are the legal order that makes a culture of "the long tail" possible.[48]

Postmodernism is often understood as a recycling of certain modernist moments in collage form—as pastiche, bricolage, remix, and so on. But within the ordered narrative worlds of contemporary Hollywood, postmodernism (or Cavellian modernism) works through cataloguing and recall, and both of those depend on an underlying structure of reliable availability. The satisfactions of knowing the inside joke align viewers with the property regime of the authoring institution. Theories of the postmodern, like theories

FIGURE 5.10 *The library as an adventure in identity. A.I., Spielberg, DreamWorks/ Warner Bros., 2001.*

of creativity, may emphasize notions of disorder or spontaneous order—the rhizomatic, the playful, the autopoietic, the networked. But the imperatives that organize intellectual property and revenue streams in Hollywood foster a much broader organization of entertainment. That organization has its enforcement side in various Digital Rights Management technologies and legal campaigns against individual BitTorrent downloaders. The pseudo-creative flipside is a personalized bibliotechnology that entices users to more intently manage the entertainment they already have the rights to. Spotify playlists, Netflix queues, and TiVo protocols are not simply ways of cataloguing what one owns, but are ways of shaping future consumption along the lines of present desires.

The industrial commitment to maximum exploitation of intellectual property and the consumer's commitment to a maximum availability of popular culture offer an explanation for the reappearance within Hollywood of a version of the "jukebox musical" (*Magnolia, Across the Universe,* and, most prominently, *Mamma Mia!*). The fan of a particular artist enjoys the double pleasure of the music for its own sake on the one hand and the anticipation of the deployment of particular songs from the oeuvre on the other, while the production companies benefit from a unified rights situation and the chance to capitalize on the stored value of the song catalogue. As Robert Kraft, then director of Fox Music explained, the difficulties in producing a soundtrack like *Juno* or *Moulin Rouge!* make *Mamma Mia!* "a dream."[49]

Some features of Hollywood's "bibliothecarian imagination" are almost constant, such as the oppositions between reserve/prolepsis, stasis/circulation, artifact/idea.[50] But they have been joined by two significant new realizations of the library as technology or social form or concept. In the first, typified by Marvel Studios' aggressive self-understanding, the library functions as a reserve of characters and stories through which producers and audiences renegotiate the terms of franchise identity. The Marvel example shows how Hollywood characteristically balances innovation and consistency. The second mode, exemplified by *Harry Potter* and *Indiana Jones and the Kingdom of the Crystal Skull*, turns even further inward, toward the histories of its creators. Yet *Crystal Skull* casts the disordered archive of its own history (of film) as an analogue for both its own practice and its reception. The differences between these three deployments (including *WALL•E*) suggest the contours of a broad swath of contemporary reflection. Through them we approach not the meaning of the library, but the possibilities of meaning and creative work defined through the library. Which is to say that we begin to answer the question of Hollywood's order of composition.

From library to reboot

Returning to the biggest independent film ever made, *Hulk*, famously, was a disappointment—an odd disappointment, given that it grossed $245 million worldwide. But it was only a disappointment, not a flop. By the following summer, it had become possible to imagine a sequel—at least outside Universal. In June, the satirical magazine *The Onion* published a column by the Hulk himself headlined, "Why no one want make *Hulk 2*?"[51] In a world where franchises exist, in Caldwell's term, to be stripmined, the notion of a character in search of a sequel was only slightly implausible. The *Onion* piece turns the Hulk into a wheedling self-promoter with his characteristic fractured English intact. He drops articles and prepositions, ignores verb tenses, and remains trapped in the third person. Still, he has a keen sense of craft of the sequel: "Hulk work out treatment for next movie Hulkself. It have everything in *Hulk,* only more intense." Hulk is working on the pitch, which will tie up some of the loose ends in the sequel-porous initial installment and capitalize on the array of characters already available in the comic: "Many unanswered questions from last *Hulk* movie. What happen to puny human Banner in rainforest? Is there cure for Hulk? . . . Is there future with Betty Ross? Where villains that make comic so great?" But he is also thinking up merchandising possibilities ("If Hulk Hands big hit, Hulk Feet even bigger hit!") and marketing campaigns ("This time it personal").

   If much of Hulk's column seems persuasive—why not make *Hulk 2* indeed?—the tagline gives the game away in its allusion to the campaign for *Jaws: The Revenge* (1987), a film widely regarded as the worst sequel ever made. The industrial logic of sequels ("everything in *Hulk,* only more intense") is inexorable but risks franchise-killing, clichéd badness. Hulk recognizes this possibility, too. "First studio exec to suggest Joel Schumacher get smashed!" In place of the *Batman Forever* director, he pins his hopes on the indie cred of Schamus ("Him really get what Hulk all about") and Lee.

Why no one appreciate daring vision of Ang Lee? Aaargh! Ang Lee genius! Maybe panels on screen gimmicky, but him try something new. When last time you try something new?! Ang Lee willing to work in unfamiliar genres. Him brave like Hulk. Hulk wish for him to work on *Hulk 2*, if he willing, but Hulk understand if he not want to. Ang Lee like Hulk: He not stay in one place for too long. Him working on gay western right now. That prove Hulk's point.

In the paramarketing world of insider-styled coverage of Hollywood, every interpretation is also a defense of certain choices, of certain ideologies. Alongside interpretation, then, there is also plenty of room for accusation: "When last time you try something new?!" Even if that accusation would be utter bad faith (this is a sequel pitch; it is trying something *again*), it stings, and it stings whether it is directed at the "puny humans" in the general public who want the same thing, only more of it, or the gutless producers who have not greenlit the sequel. Finally, within this defensive castigation of the audience, Hulk offers an auteurist allegory, though it is unfocused. Lee's genre-bending is evidence of both his Hulk-like bravery and, somehow, his Hulk-like persecution ("Sometimes Hulk so sad and alone").

In this last respect, *Hulk*'s claim to be the biggest independent film ever made was Marvel and Universal's attempt to duplicate the strategy that had worked for Fox on *X-Men* and, before that, for Warner Bros. with *Batman*. If one could put a franchise in the hands of an indie director, there could be something fresh and enticing to audiences; it would not seem rote.[52] At the same time, though, the franchise had to deliver on the promises of the underlying property ("Where villains that make comic so great?").

The original *Hulk* marketing campaign already embodied this two-sidedness; it suggested deep reserves of independent authorship beneath its "popcorn" façade. For Ang Lee, the indie-auteur model succeeded. *The New Yorker* ran a long profile of him with particular attention to his role not simply as a director but as a performer.[53] Lee had begun as an actor at Indiana University and had put that talent to work in *Hulk* by donning the motion capture suit and providing the initial data points for the computer rendering of the monster. (The DVD release included plenty of behind-the-scenes footage of him hulking out.) The protagonist was not simply a plausible allegory of the director but was actually—that is, kinetically—him. In an era when digital effects are contracted out, potentially leaching the director's control over the process, Lee's performance background became the means of bringing effects back under his signature.

FIGURE 5.11 *Ang Lee hulking out: auteurist performance capture.* Hulk, *Lee, Universal, 2003.*

For Schamus, though, the model failed. He wrote a piece in the *Times* touting the Hulk as "a perfect embodiment of American repression, a curiously asexual rampaging id" and *Hulk* as an exploration of the nearly timeless notion of the hero. "Spectacles hold little fascination without the heroic figures who are inscribed within them. It is the constant testing, reconfiguring and evolution of such heroes that make these movies so compelling, and the Hulk provides the opportunity to explore a particularly complex member of the heroic tribe."[54] The backlash against the piece suggests the dangers of indie insistence. The sense of a structural imbalance in the interpretation captures some of what made it possible for *Hulk* to seem "disappointing" regardless of the numbers.

The problem with *Hulk*'s marketing was not the simple fact that there were two registers of meaning directed at two audiences ranked in a hermeneutic hierarchy. As Richard Maltby has argued, that split audience was a foundational principle of classical Hollywood.[55] Instead, the problem with *Hulk*'s split marketing was that it had violated the implicit division of labor between the neoclassical studios and the independents. In indie fashion, *Hulk* made its reserves of authorship *explicit*, thus insistently forcing the "popcorn" audience to contend with a denigration of the "mere entertainment" that it sought, while, at the same time, *Hulk* short-circuited the "deep" interpretive work of the audience for whom that work constitutes entertainment. For any classical aesthetic, this loss of balance is fatal.

The Onion's Hulk was two years too early in his sequel pitch. If, that is, *The Incredible Hulk* is actually a sequel to *Hulk*. It would be hard to know even apart from the lack of a numeral. The characters remain, but all the actors are new. And despite Hulk's plea, Ang Lee and James Schamus were not part of the film; Louis Leterrier directed while *X-Men* writer Zak Penn did the screenplay. The origin story is rehearsed behind the opening credits, as is typical in a sequel, but this version is aligned not with the universe of *Hulk* but with that of the 1970s television show. All these things make *The Incredible Hulk* less a sequel than what was increasingly being called a "reboot."

The reboot took the place of the sequel and the remake. The term was inserted into the rhetoric of the intermittent franchise narrative and its attendant, pulsed revenue streams in order to capitalize on the discontinuities inherent in the lags between installments. It does this work in four ways. First, where the sequel and the remake suggest a smooth continuity and a machinic replication, the reboot locates creativity in delay. Second, at the same time that they vouch for the creativity in the system, reboots also promise to purge older stories of whatever might have become problematic in them—whether those are problems of politics, narrative balance, pacing, or, most generally, style. Third, rebooting directly solicits the audience's reflection on the differences and connections between incarnations. That reflection is aided by the release of new, more feature-laden disks that promise to take the audience not simply behind the scenes but behind the decision-making that led to the now-outmoded version. Ultimately, though, the efforts to intensify certain viewers' attention to difference and connection are not in the service of a radical problematization of the text, for the studios' aims stop short of such a complete deconstruction of identity. Instead, the reboot posits a real property that can be the hermenaut's true object of desire. There is value in the library. The studios know this, they defend that intellectual property extraordinarily vigorously, and in the reboot, they inculcate that belief in the audience.

The reboot may veer away from fundamental critique, but at the core of *The Incredible Hulk* lie potentially radical worries about identity and replication. When Bruce Banner intentionally draws his blood to send it back to a willing researcher (Mr. Blue) he unwittingly gives rise to a library. He arrives in New York to test out a possible cure and discovers that Blue has generated a vast collection from that initial sample. "You didn't send me much to work with so I had to concentrate it and make more," says Mr. Blue. Here, Blue gives voice to the film's hybrid identity as reboot-sequel. The franchise must be rebooted (because "you didn't send me much to work with") while it fulfills the demands of a sequel ("concentrate it and make more"). It is, for the researcher, a utopian scene of production and reproduction: "This is potentially Olympian. . . . We will unlock hundreds of cures." Characters are libraries or bibles, filled with data and stories. "Bruce, this is all you," says Blue, gesturing to the library.

At the same time libraries are populated by the exploits and potentials of the characters they catalog. This vacillant equivalence lies at the heart of

FIGURE 5.12 *Concentrate it and make more: the bibliotechnological imaginary of the sequel.* The Incredible Hulk, *Leterrier, Marvel/Universal, 2008.*

the pre–Great Recession wave of industrial reflexivity. What has become more explicit is the stored value that can be unleashed, Hulk-like, when necessary. "It has to be me, you have to take me back there," Banner says, before dropping out of a helicopter and into the fray against Abomination.

But if the *Hulk*s were intended to be summer tentpoles and were, therefore, important occasions for a studio and its employees to ponder their own fates, then they might for the same reason be isolated occasions. If, however, the *Hulk*s are part of a strategic pivot in which the assertion of a reflexivity corpus would now occupy a crucial space in Hollywood, then we should find similar reflection even in downmarket properties. And in the case of *The Punisher*, that is exactly what we find.

When Lionsgate released *The Punisher* in 2004, Marvel (under Avi Arad) had become a zealous developer of its intellectual property, and its studio brand had begun to vie with its distributors for prominence.[56] *The Punisher* is odd and unique: its broody hero vies with subtropical sun (Tampa, FL), the aesthetic is neon moderne in a too-crisp, video-edged way reminiscent of *CSI: Miami*, and the tone veers from broad, absurdist violence, to domestic comedy, to (supposed) melodrama. Itself a relaunch from a Dolph Lundgren vehicle from 1989, the version starring Patrick Jane reads as low budget as its hero.

The 2008 reboot *Punisher: War Zone* puts the Punisher back in New York City, and while it is a cold, wet New York, overly familiar from the *Batman* films and *Grand Theft Auto IV*, the setting better explains the baleful, retributive moralizing of the film than even Frank Castle's own tragic backstory. Five years have elapsed since Castle's family was gunned down. In the meantime he has been busy meting out justice. Friends on the police force look the other way, feeding him inside information, until Castle

FIGURE 5.13 *"All of them."* Punisher: War Zone, *Alexander, Marvel Knights/ Lionsgate, 2008.*

accidentally kills an undercover FBI agent. When the dead man's partner, agent Butiansky, joins the "Punisher Task Force," (staff of one) he is directed to a basement library. The endless rows of metal shelves and archival boxes are the materialization of the department's bad faith. The locale makes it all too clear that the police have no interest in arresting Frank. Still, Butiansky intends to persevere. When he asks for the Punisher case files, he is told they are right here. "Which drawer?" "All of them."

As with Mr. Blue's "Olympian" fantasies, this represents the producers' dream. The Punisher library provides a narrative equivalent of the hardware racks on which Frank stores his armory. And just as each weapon promises a different way to die, so each drawer promises a different death. These libraries are extensions of a character, but they are also, in the Marvel Universe, the equivalent of characters. The film's final battle at the Brad Street Hotel takes this cataloguing to the next level by literalizing the characters involved. The city's ethnic gangs have been invited to take their best shot at Frank, their shared nemesis, and each gang occupies a different space in the hotel, filed neatly away in rooms ready to launch into the fight and the story.

FIGURE 5.14 *A transmedial visit. Tony Stark drops in.* The Incredible Hulk, *Leterrier, Marvel/Universal, 2008.*

If *The Punisher* was part of Marvel's attempt to exploit its lesser properties—to see, in effect, how the studio's new "Marvel Knights" label would match up with the zeitgeist—*War Zone* was also part of a more conscious attempt to bring all of Marvel together. A frozen Captain America would have made a cameo appearance at the beginning of *The Incredible Hulk*, but it was later relegated to the DVD's deleted scenes. However, Robert Downey Jr.'s Tony Stark did appear at the end, visiting from Marvel's independent production, *Iron Man* (Jon Favreau, Paramount 2008).

At this moment, across studios and seasons, the pieces of the Marvel Cinematic Universe are being assembled, catalogued, and held in readiness. "We're putting a team together," says Downey. The plan was to bring separate franchises centering on Hulk, Iron Man, Captain America, and Thor together as the Avengers in 2012.[57] With the Spider-Man/Fantastic 4/Silver Surfer series ensconced at Sony and the X-Men at Fox, Mr. Blue speaks as the genius of the (Marvel) system: "With a little more trial and error there's no end to what we can do."

TimeWarner in the Hall of Prophecies

What is the nature of the end of a series? Caldwell sees producers stripmining titles until the franchise dies. Doubtless some franchises are driven into the ground. For years, the Disney model worked from the initiating theatrical film to the straight-to-video sequels and so on down the ladder. The ride-based films *Pirates of the Caribbean* (Verbinski, 2003), *Tower of Terror* (MacHale, 1997), *The Country Bears* (Hastings, 2002), and *The Haunted Mansion* (Minkoff, 2003) reversed that, and tv-franchises-turned-theatrical releases *High School Musical 3* (Ortega, 2008) and *Hannah Montana: The*

Movie (Chelsom, 2009) show the company able to channel product to meet virtually any perceived demand shift. Stories come from anywhere; properties can wind up anywhere. Properly managed, remediated, or rebooted, or put on temporary hiatus as necessary, there is no end to them.

Harry Potter and the Order of the Phoenix, the fifth novel in the series, was published in June 2003. It was nearly a year late, and clamor for the new book had begun to spin off rumors of plotting difficulties. A great deal had changed in the nearly three years since the publication of *Goblet of Fire*, and those changes seemed to find their way into the *Order of the Phoenix* and subsequent books, adding to their length and slowing J.K. Rowling's pace. Most important of these, the Bush and Blair administrations' responses to the 9/11 attacks and subsequent events seemed to reshape the struggle against the Death Eaters. Beginning with *Order*, the Ministry of Magic's repressive reactions and mendacities become painful distractions from preparations for the inevitable wizard war while within the conflict, fascination with the Nazi dynamics of the Death Eaters gives way to the cellular structures of The Order itself and its student analogue, Dumbledore's Army.

The last is an almost purely ironic formation brought into being in self-conscious parody of Ministry fears. Yet by duplicating that fear, the DA makes itself a real target for the Ministry's high inquisitor. Indeed, the power of the DA only confirms the Ministry's suspicion that this band of Hogwarts students is fearsome. And while the power of the group stems from many sources (innate skill, personal vengeance, budding romance) there are two crucial binding mechanisms at work. The first, a negative bond, is a jinx secretly placed on their original contract: anyone who publicizes the group will come down with a terrible rash. The second, positive bond is an enchanted coin that will announce to each member when the next meeting will occur. It is a form of instant, secret communication, and Harry immediately recognizes the similarity between it and the Dark Mark scarred into the Death Eaters' forearms. "Well . . . yes," Hermione says. "That *is* where I got the idea."[58]

One takes ideas where one finds them. If the "war on terror" was the central sociopolitical fact that erupted between the fourth and fifth Harry Potter novels, the arrival of Harry Potter on screen was the central narrative-aesthetic fact. (*Sorcerer's Stone,* the first film, premiered in November 2001.) Rowling had unprecedented control over the adaptation: she secured director and script approval and was able to place strict limits on Warner Bros.' marketing tie-ins. She also spent a great deal of time working with Chris Columbus and others on the casting and the overall look of the film. Her canniness and caution are evidence that, from the outset, she had known that the existence of film adaptations would drastically alter the series's public meaning. Recognizing that, she had plunged into the process to guide those alterations as best she could.

Order is the first book that exists in a world where there are actual *Harry Potter* films, and the ironic incarnations at the heart of it read as figures for both the post–9/11 world and the discovery of a film universe in competition with the books'. The past-tense world of books is now joined by a future- and future-perfect-tense world of stories: each book will be and will have been a film. This new configuration of contained indeterminacy appears most concentratedly as the Department of Mysteries within the Ministry of Magic. Behind the black door of Harry's dreams and through a revolving room of doors that would baffle anyone who attempted to orient himself, there is a room of clocks "hanging in spaces between the bookcases or standing on desks ranging the length of the room, so that a busy, relentless ticking filled the place like thousands of minuscule, marching footsteps."[59] One would be hard pressed to find a better allegory of Rowling up against her deadline, faced with clocks "gleaming from every surface," and persecuted by the "relentless" army of her fans and their "minuscule, marching footsteps."

Beyond the Time Room lies the Hall of Prophecies, an enormous analogue for a film vault, "high as a church and full of nothing but towering shelves covered in small, dusty glass orbs. . . . The room was very cold."[60] There, the battle against the Death Eaters will begin. Early in the conflict, when two of the spheres shatter, "figures, pearly white as ghosts, fluid as smoke" "unfurl" and speak their prophecies. Afterward, "nothing remain[s]" of these quasi-cinematic specters, or, rather, not quite nothing since "They had, however, given Harry an idea."[61] Just as the Death Eaters' scars give Hermione the model for her secret communication system, so the destruction of these two prophecies suggests to Harry the idea of destroying the entire hall. In the "torrent of crashing glass and splintered wood" that follows, the lines between the characters, the prophets, and the shelving blur into a tongue-twisting climax: "They were all yelling, there were cries of pain, thunderous crashes as the shelves collapsed upon themselves, weirdly echoing fragments of the Seers unleashed from their spheres—"[62]

The dash at the end indicates that the list is incomplete, as the series itself then was. Yet by the time Warner Bros. had caught up to Rowling's *Order of the Phoenix*, the series of books had run its course. (Both that movie and the seventh volume, *Harry Potter and the Deathly Hallows*, were released in July 2007.) As part of TimeWarner's overarching strategy, the studio under Alan Horn and Barry Meyer had made itself the most franchise-dependent of the majors. Some of these properties seemed infinitely replicable (Batman). Yet some were strictly limited. TimeWarner had already had to come to terms with the end of New Line's *Lord of the Rings* juggernaut (December 2003) and was facing the end of HBO's *The Sopranos* (June 2007). Warner Bros. had known all along that the Potter saga would someday end; how did they react? If Rowling's novel took up the pressures and paradoxes of interleaved serialization, David Yates's film captured the studio and the conglomerate's ambivalence at committing to this particular future perfect. To say yes to one film (or even seven or eight) requires saying no to hundreds, perhaps

FIGURE 5.15 *Releasing the power of the vault*. Harry Potter and the Order of the Phoenix, *Yates, Warner Bros., 2007.*

thousands of others. There is thus untold and untellable value in the Hall of Prophecies, an economic image raised to the scale of an enormous set. As the torrent of glass crashes down, we can sense both the abiding confidence of the film (figured, as is usual in the Potterverse, in a powerful female; here, Ginny Weasley[63]) and the nagging feeling of dependence on its past. There is nothing "indie" about *Order of the Phoenix*; this is a studio coming to terms with its own normal practice.

Indy and the indie

Hulk may have been the biggest independent picture ever made, but at the box office the biggest Indy is Indiana Jones. The first installment, *Raiders of the Lost Ark*, was a triumph of dealmaking: Lucas and Spielberg received nearly half of the gross; they participated in the music and merchandising; they had control over the poster and trailers; and Paramount reduced its distribution fee.[64] Culturally, the film drove home the nostalgia at the heart of the Lucas–Spielberg axis of postmodernism by cloaking its 1930s setting in something like the form of an old serial. It looked like narrative "slumming," and it was quickly diagnosed by Fredric Jameson as part of the Reaganite populism of the era.[65] But it also advanced a serious aesthetic claim, namely, that the attempt to comprehensively recapture a period's authentic look and feel ought to be marked by that period's demotic narrative forms even as it elevated those forms to the center of film art. This sly historicism mixes the pleasures of childhood with a recognition that something separates this film from the serials it evokes. That "something" is quality, a recognition that, despite its narrative and formal debts, *Raiders* is good by our standards and not those of the past. In its famous concluding joke, *Raiders* tucks the Ark of the Covenant in some vast warehouse where it is in principle catalogued but in actuality lost. The political lesson is simple enough: the fate of independence and adventure is bureaucratization, the loss of control to "top men."

The fourth installment, *Kingdom of the Crystal Skull*, kicks off by recapturing that economic image, beginning at that warehouse, which we come to learn is Hangar 51, putative resting place of the aliens who crashed at Roswell, NM. Like the "book of secrets" in *National Treasure 2*, this warehouse-cum-soundstage is the place "where you and your government have hidden all of your secrets," and the new adventure is triggered by the arrival of the ultimate bureaucrats, the Soviets and their top woman. Where the Americans hid things away for the good of the citizenry, the communists desire total knowledge. The glimpse we get of the Ark as they leave the warehouse makes the irony of their fate clear from the outset.

The merger of 1930s tale and 1930s telling from *Raiders* gives way to a 1950s version of the same. As Lucas put it, "It was the idea of taking the genre from the 1930s serials, action-adventure serials, to the B science fiction movies of the '50s. . . . I wanted to rest it on a cinematic antecendent, like we did with the other one." The entire Lucas-Spielberg team still operates within a classicist/nostalgist aesthetic. These are the basic terms of their art. Screenwriter David Koepp describes it as needing to adhere to "the rules" of the series while somehow being "fresh." Sound designer Ben Burtt will say, "When I think of the Indy films, I always think I want to give things a classic sound." But if these are "classic" sounds they are also new: "There's been a conscious choice to create the supernatural sounds as if maybe they were created for movies back in the 1950s. I've tried to derive a style from those movies, to make new sounds in that old style." Composer John Williams will

FIGURE 5.16 *An archive in search of a search protocol. Hangar (Area?) 51.* Indiana Jones and the Kingdom of the Crystal Skull, *Spielberg, LucasFilm/Paramount, 2008.*

FIGURE 5.17 *Cate and alien.* Indiana Jones and the Kingdom of the Crystal Skull, *Spielberg, LucasFilm/Paramount, 2008.*

describe the Crystal Skull's musical motif as a product of this same effort: "The crystal skull, certainly for its various appearances in the film, needed to have some musical identification, and what I tried to do was to try to get some kind of homage if you'd like to the science fiction films of the '50s that would bring an aspect of nostalgia into this piece."[66]

The filmmakers may be trying to merely update their 1980s neoclassicism, but *Crystal Skull* is decisively inflected by a reading of its period in a way that *Raiders* was not. Spielberg, describing Lucas's pitch to him, drifted in and out of quotation, but even when it is unclear who is speaking, it is absolutely clear that the shared terms of the discussion are interpretive: "But George insisted, and he said, 'This will be like a B movie. It'll be like those 1950s B movies, *Earth vs. the Flying Saucers,* and all those exploitation movies that were really about government paranoia, Cold War fears and things like that, and Hollywood turned them into *Invaders from Mars.*'"[67] It is a truism of film history that the alien invaders of the 1950s movies represent the marching forces of communism, or conformity, or both. On this understanding of Cold War culture, social and political anxieties would occasionally find more literal expression in social problem or exploitation films—juvenile delinquency in *Rebel without a Cause* or nuclear anxiety in *On the Beach. Crystal Skull* stages both aspects of this reading via confrontations between the actual period threats and their allegorical period stand-ins: the (actual) Russians want to know everything the (allegorical)

FIGURE 5.18 *The nuclear family.* Indiana Jones and the Kingdom of the Crystal Skull, *Spielberg, LucasFilm/Paramount, 2008.*

aliens know. If communists came to 1950s cinema dressed as aliens, Indy's communists now want to *be* aliens. (Indeed, Cate Blanchett's black bob, drawn cheeks, and bulging eyes make her an alien manqué.) Meanwhile, the film offers us the ultimate conformists in the form of TV-watching mannequins who populate a Potemkin Eisenhower suburb. They will soon perish in a nuclear test strike. If the social discipline of suburban conformity was the complement of the anxieties of nuclear age, *Crystal Skull* takes that functionalism a step further: its suburbs exist only in order to be destroyed by the bomb.

What to make of the film's reliance on such a reading? Is *Crystal Skull* a critique of 1950s paranoia or an endorsement of it? In truth, the film is neither. The McCarthyite thugs who badger Indy about his loyalties are off-track not because there are no communist subversives on campus, but because there are actual Soviet spies all over the country, stealing its secrets. The populuxe design of the fake suburb and the intended glee that greets its destruction imply that the film endorses the critique of suburban homogenization, and yet it brings that critique to ground when it nukes the place. The further implication seems to be that if you think that the suburbs are full of consumerist mannequins who "deserve it," you are no different than the bombers. Whether this conclusion amounts to a critique of the critique, whether it reverts to an "endorsement" of suburbanism or not, is unclear. Regardless, the whirl of interpretation verges on the ludicrous. Indy rides out the bomb in a convenient, lead-lined refrigerator; fans and critics everywhere object. "Nuke the fridge" replaces "jump the shark" in the critical lexicon.[68]

In Spielberg's work, the collapse of the oppositions between cultural resistance and approval on the one hand and between allegory and literalism on the other had actually occurred by the time he made *War of the Worlds*

(2005). Where *Jurassic Park* (1993) had maintained a studied ambivalence about the relationship between showman and exploiter, *War of the Worlds* couldn't keep its allegory straight. Spielberg explained that the humans fighting off the aliens were like 9/11 victims fleeing Manhattan, while screenwriter Koepp told *USA Weekend*, "You can read our movie several ways. . . . It could be straight 9/11 paranoia. Or it could be about how U.S. military interventionism abroad is doomed by insurgency, just the way an alien invasion might be."[69] To Koepp, it did not matter which account was right. All that mattered was that there be some story, *any* story to link the summer sci-fi blockbuster to terrorism and war. Those plucky Americans fighting off the aliens might be the plucky Americans they appeared to be, or they might be members of Al Qaeda in Iraq. Regardless, the horizons of interpretation had been opened for the audience. The mission in *Crystal Skull* was very much the same.

Crystal Skull begins by excavating hidden secrets; it ends with a nightmare of total recall. At the climax of *Raiders*, Indy's nemesis Belloc looks at the angels rushing around the ark and proclaims, "It's beautiful!"—just before he becomes a column of fire. In *Crystal Skull*, the problem is not too much beauty but too much knowledge. Cate Blanchett's Spalko tells the alien, "I want to know everything. I'm ready." She is not. Bombarded with too much knowledge, Spalko attempts to turn away from the alien's eyes, but it refuses to let her go. Reanimated, the creature from another dimension reveals itself to be a postmodern connoisseur of irony. Fountains of knowledge will come streaming out of her eyes and mouth like so much ectoplasm. Spalko vaporizes because her skull lacks the capacity of the scaphocephalic aliens. Indy, though, will survive because he doesn't want to know everything the aliens do; he simply wants to be able to access it. She wants to be the library; he wants to be the librarian.

But we can be even more explicit: Like its contemporaries *The Dark Knight* and *Wanted*, *Crystal Skull* tells the story of the digitization of library access. *Raiders*'s concluding joke was analogue. As Michael Rubin, LucasFilm veteran and author of *Droidmaker: George Lucas and the Digital Revolution*, put it, "If you want to know what editing was like before George came along, visualize that warehouse at the end of *Raiders of the Lost Ark*. . . . If you shot a movie like *Star Wars*, you had 300,000 feet of film and sound rolls that had to be code numbered and matched by hand. If you wanted to cut the scene where Luke was doing this and Han Solo was doing that, some poor schmuck had to find those pieces so you could fit them together with tape. It was like the Library of Congress with no librarian."[70] When *Crystal Skull* revisits that warehouse, Indy becomes that librarian, tossing handfuls of gunpowder in the air and allowing the strong magnetic field of the alien sarcophagus to grab the particles and lead the way to the appropriate crate. In this new magneto-digital world, the randomness of the library's arrangement becomes irrelevant: your data knows you want it.

FIGURE 5.19 *The Commie and the Nazi as streaming media.* Indiana Jones and
the Kingdom of the Crystal Skull, *Spielberg, LucasFilm/Paramount, 2008;* Raiders of
the Lost Ark, *Spielberg, LucasFilm/Paramount, 1981.*

As it happens, *Crystal Skull* was edited on film—itself a conscious
throwback. "In keeping with our desire to make the movie as close to the
other three as possible, Steven stayed on film for the entire process. In other
words, we did not shoot digitally, and we did not edit digitally, which is
very unusual today," said producer Frank Marshall. But this is overstating
the retro-nature of the project. *Crystal Skull* was not an exercise in period
filmmaking in the way that Steven Soderbergh's *The Good German* was.
Spielberg and editor Michael Kahn were able to get away with editing on
film for two reasons independent of their nostalgic commitments to 1980s
processes. First, they were incredibly fast. Kathleen Kennedy touted editor
Kahn's skills: "He doesn't need to be cutting electronically because he's as
fast as anybody cutting on Avid." Second, the movie only stayed "on film"
during the cutting of the footage Spielberg and Janusz Kaminsky shot. Many
effects were done in the computer (by ILM), and EFilm handled the digital
intermediate. To imagine that *Crystal Skull* "stayed on film" long enough to
qualify as a throwback is only to stipulate how digital the state of the art
actually is.

It may still be possible to shoot and cut picture on film, but only a
committed antiquarian would edit sound that way. Led by Sound Designer
Ben Burtt, who also created the sound for *WALL•E*, the team built the
soundscape of *Crystal Skull* out of two things: the library of sounds from

FIGURE 5.20 *Alien Xanadu.* Indiana Jones and the Kingdom of the Crystal Skull, *Spielberg, LucasFilm/Paramount, 2008.*

previous Indiana Jones films and the typical sound of 1950s B-movie SciFi. First, though, the library had to be invented. At the heart of that effort was the relationship between Ben and his son Benny (shades of Indy and Mutt). As Ben explained,

> One of the first tasks I had was to really go back and gather all the sounds together that had been created for the previous films. We hired my son Benny Burtt to do that job because it meant going into lots of old tapes and older recording formats which are no longer used any more, and we wanted to go back to the original recordings wherever we could and digitize them now at the highest quality copy into the computer, and then classify the sounds and get them into a searchable database, because there's really thousands of sounds.[71]

At this point, it becomes difficult to sort through the multilayered grid of historical references behind *Crystal Skull.* Sloshing around in the film

FIGURE 5.21 *The flying saucer as alien hard drive.* Indiana Jones and the Kingdom of the Crystal Skull, *Spielberg, LucasFilm/Paramount, 2008.*

we find the 1950s of its setting, the 1930s of its origins, the 1980s of the series' origins, a healthy dose of Lucas's late-1960s libertarian paranoia (the politics of *THX–1138*), and, of course, the 2000s. In characteristic fashion, the film stages this pastiche as self-reflection. Standing in the antechamber to the crystal aliens' chamber, among the bric-a-brac of thousands of years of civilization gathered from across the globe, Indy recognizes his own profession: "They were collectors . . . Archeologists." The room may be as haphazardly arranged as the boiler room in *Citizen Kane*, but the aliens know what they have. As their saucer rises through the shell of the temple, it looks for all the world like a spinning hard drive.

When IBM debuted the hard disk drive in 1956 (in plenty of time for the events of *Crystal Skull* the next year), they announced it this way:

[The] 305 RAMAC and 650 RAMAC, [are] two electronic data processing machines using IBM's random access memory, a stack of disks that stores millions of facts and figures less than a second from management's reach. Because transactions are processed as they occur, the fresh facts held in a random access memory show business as it is right now, not as it was hours or weeks ago.[72]

The total library, stocked with "fresh facts" and instantly available: this has been a remarkably durable commercial utopia. The digital library promises to make sense of the convergent flux of filmmaking practices, corporate mythologies, and audience involvements; it promises *to show business as it is right now*. That is what Schamus and Gill were promising as well, when they played their parts in one of dozens of self-reflexive Hollywood rituals.

In this new era, when it became impossible to distinguish between the indie blockbuster and the blockbuster as such, both "the biggest independent pictures ever made" and their less-indie complements were drawn from a standing reserve, a library of stories and storytelling. Yet the library was not simply a theme or a motif, the way that the absent father (in Spielberg) or the recognition of impending climate change (at Fox) were. While themes and motifs bring order or coherence to a film or group of films, the library offers the possibility of imagining order as such—an order that is not merely narrative, but always potentially so; an order that is not necessarily "logical," but nested within the social and aesthetic practices of Hollywood. Libraries look most thematically insistent when they suggest the parameters of self-understanding in general. Hollywood movies are themselves industrial reflections even as they serve as communicating channels between the layers of reflexivity that compound into an evanescent industrial self-consciousness. Whether we attribute that reflection to the studio, the indie director, the author of the source text, the community of fans, or the assembly of artists and artisans is a matter to be decided in each case. Yet the order of reflexive composition in contemporary Hollywood makes our decision one the movie has already imagined—imagined, and filed away.

Cards against humanity

The bibliotechnological imaginary that cemented the importance of the reboot in Hollywood prioritized the retrieval of files. But as the process became more regular and cyclical—filing, then retrieval, then filing—the studios' focus shifted to the timing, linkage, and arrangement of those retrievals. Pioneered by Marvel, but subsequently adopted throughout the industry, multiyear slate schedules became the norm and narrative planning became longer term. In isolation, linkages give rise to various network images—the "crazy boards" put together by investigators attempting to get to the heart of a criminal syndicate, or the clouds of character relations in the Marvel Universe as a whole. But when timing and arrangement become important elements in the process of library management, strategy becomes a more explicit part of the self-reflection. In the wake of the Great Recession, the world of filing and retrieval thus pivoted toward strategic recall. In keeping with the Obama-era rhetoric of the New New Deal, strategy materialized as cards. But where Hollywood's cards in the 1930s were parts of games like poker, the cards of the Obama era were collected.

The opening act of *The Avengers* (Whedon 2012)—better called by its global title *Avengers Assemble*—requires that the gang be gathered together to retrieve the Tesseract (a source of untold power, capable of being weaponized, held over from the Captain America movies, etc.). That narrative gathering is simultaneously a variation on the intellectual property development strategy Marvel had pursued as an independent and a recapitulation (with significant alterations) of the initial burst of creativity that gave rise to the Marvel comics universe.[73] The movie represents that layered duplication via immaterial arrays.

The first cardlike array appears when Nick Fury (Samuel L. Jackson) has a videoconference call with the members of the World Security Council—shadowy figures who appear in portrait-oriented screens as silhouettes. Next, we are shown a transparent intercom-gizmo that Tony Stark uses like an advanced tablet computer, and that is quickly joined by a collection of hovering projections displaying the data and feats of the other Avengers—Thor, Cap, and Hulk—and the Tesseract itself. These quasi-screens are barely material and only count as cards because they feature identifying portraits of their subjects—more like an office personnel file than an object of strategy. Still, these early screencards and the souped-up tablets that conveniently drop expository information, connect the world of digital moving images to the more general problems of collection and display.

The problems of collection are made more material in Agent Coulson's discussions with Captain America. In an awkward scene that stages the relationship between the supersoldier and his overgrown fanboy ("It's an honor to meet you. Officially. I sort of met you, I mean, I watched you, while you were sleeping."), Coulson proudly explains that he has made "modifications to the uniform" and has had "a little design input." His fan status secure, Colson will continue to press his relationship with Cap. The next time they are together, we jump into a conversation already underway:

Coulson: I mean, if it's not too much trouble.
Cap: No, no. It's fine.
Coulson: It's a vintage set. Took me a couple years to collect 'em all.
    Near mint. Slight foxing around the edges, but—

Colson is discussing his Second World War Captain America cards. For Whedon, Marvel's willingness to retain the card subplot was a "win." He was convinced "there's no way this is going to survive, there's no way they're going to let this much of me in there."[74] On his terms, it is a win for *him*, and, on principle, for the auteur within the major studio. But Coulson is not simply a figure for Whedon, the "true collector"; he is just as readily speaking for Marvel, and for Disney. The Avengers are, indeed, a vintage set. It has, indeed, taken Marvel years to collect its heroes into the movie we are watching, just as it has taken Disney years to assemble its own portfolio of brands. The MCU has been, indeed, almost perfect, and it certainly mints money. And finally, with the panache typical of *Avengers*, there remains some "slight foxing around the edges." Coulson means the edges have browned; Marvel and Disney mean that valuable assets have not yet been reacquired from other companies: themepark rights at Universal, Spider-Man at Columbia, and the X-Men at, yes, Fox.

The cards appear after Coulson's death when Nick Fury throws them, bloody, on the round glass table in the *Helicarrier*. Forced to confront the death of the agent who gathered them together and the fan who believed in them most strongly, the Avengers (Stark and Cap) will put their differences aside, finally. It will turn out that Coulson was not carrying the cards when he was shot—that Fury has staged this scene. Whedon is sympathetic to Fury here, in large part because Fury is, as showman, his stand-in. In the grand battle for New York that will follow, the narrative is hardly in doubt. What will matter is its form, and the imagistic culmination of *The Avengers'* assemblage strategy is doubled. We are given grand economic images, two embodiments of the series's linkage, timing, and arrangement; two versions of cinematic collection. In the first, the Avengers are assembled as a group, one that finally includes the Hulk and not Bruce Banner, Iron Man and not Tony Stark. The camera swirls around them, giving the group a kind of totality it has not had before. "The dolly-shot," as Whedon calls it, is quickly

FIGURE 5.22 *Coulson's legacy, no longer near mint.* The Avengers, *Marvel/Disney (Paramount), 2012.*

followed by "the tie-in shot," which composites any number of plates and backgrounds to form a "single" shot that leads from Black Widow to Iron Man to Cap to Hawkeye to Hulk to Thor. As Whedon explains, "The tie-in shot is the whole point. That's when the Avengers are the Avengers."[75]

The timing, linkage, and arrangement of this gathering are the narrative and imagistic engine of *The Avengers*, but the MCU strategy was never *simply* a gathering of equals. The crucial sub-franchise, the one that made it financially possible, was Iron Man, and the continuing efforts to rein in Stark's independence *in* the movies read as the studio's continuing efforts to migrate from a narrative universe dominated by a single player to a more properly multipolar universe. The systematic development of Captain America as the hub within the MCU is part of this strategy, but in the case of *The Avengers*, the corralling of Tony Stark takes a more imagistic form. The battle of New York that destroys much of the city centers on his personal, branded tower. When, in the final shot of the film, we pull back from him and Pepper planning its reconstruction, the STARK on the side has been reduced to a simple "A"—A for Avengers, A for (Captain) America. Still, Whedon (and Marvel) knows that the simple demonstration of Stark's newfound willingness to collaborate does not solve the MCU's continuing problem. So in the post-credits scene we flash back to the Avengers in the immediate aftermath of battle, enjoying shawarma together. They are there because Tony has never eaten it, so it is his doing. On the wall behind Captain America we see a prominent American Flag and just below that, the restaurant's Health Department grade: a bright blue "A" to match Cap's uniform.[76]

If *The Avengers* tells the story of the emergence, however partial, of a brand that might supplement or replace the Iron Man brand, it is also, for Disney, the story of a brand that does not emerge. In its independent phase, Marvel Studios had struck a distribution-only deal that gave Paramount 8 percent of its box

FIGURE 5.23 *The dolly, the tie-in, the shawarma.* The Avengers, *Marvel/Disney (Paramount), 2012.*

office receipts. Disney, naturally enough, wanted to handle distribution itself. A deal was struck in which Disney bought out Paramount's interest in *Iron Man 3* and *The Avengers* in exchange for a payment of at least $115 million, up to 8 percent on *Avengers* and 9 percent on *Iron Man 3*.[77] Yet despite that payout, it was the Paramount mountain, not the Disney castle, that appeared at the opening of *The Avengers*. The movie would take as one of its tasks the gradual erasure of Marvel's distribution partner, and it would imagine a world in which no distributor was necessary at all. The key figure here is the self-powering Stark Tower. As Tony discusses his new building, he takes credit for nearly all of it in franchise-management terms—the heavy lifting (which *Iron Man* did for the MCU), the clean energy source (the arc reactor, but also the *Iron Man* sub-franchise), the design. Still, he offers Pepper Potts a "percentage" of the credit—at first 12 percent, though "a case could be made for fifteen." She is nonplussed and will not return until Act III. As a stand-in for Paramount, she will be absent for the *Avengers* sequel, *Age of Ultron*.

Fleeting as Marvel's structural independence was, Disney, in contrast, emerged from the Great Recession more powerful than ever. It had assimilated all three strands of library-mining. From Pixar and Marvel, it took the ideology of independence. From Marvel and LucasFilm, it took the display of library management and collection strategies. From all three, it took the thrill of archival search and discovery. During the acquisition process Disney had made Marvel nearly the same promise it made Pixar: that it would not interfere in its creative decisions. Ike Perlmutter and Kevin Feige were left in charge and a committee continued to articulate relations between cinema, television, comics, and other media. In *The Avengers*, the structural loss of independence was reimagined as a triumph of teamwork and portfolio management. Marvel was making a case for its centrality to Disney as a whole. But after the next full cycle of the MCU, *The Avengers* sequel *Age of Ultron* (Whedon, 2015) turned independence into its opposite. Throughout the teaser trailer, Ultron, Tony Stark's super-A.I. turned bad, touts his new freedom in malevolent, Disneyfied terms: "I got no strings," he says. An ethereal child's voice continues the theme song from the studio's *Pinocchio*. No longer is the Avengers project a matter of unveiling the inevitable team behind the Stark ego. Now, independence is on the defensive, hence Stark's dream of "a suit of armor around the world" and hence Ultron's conviction that independence can only exist with total assimilation. As he populates the world with robot avatars and plots the total destruction of humanity in favor of himself, his protégé Scarlet Witch is horrified: "All of these are . . . all of these are . . ." "Me."

The battle for control and collaboration consistently turns on questions of bodies and files, corporeality and materiality. Ultron needs a body and is attempting to build a perfect one. The Avengers on his trail are frustrated when the files they need are missing. "Everything we had . . . has been erased," Black Widow says. "Not everything," Stark replies, whereupon the team dives into a "vintage set" of Second World War–era paper files. Yet bodies and paper files are not simply more robust ways of being; they are, when combined, essential for narrative, what the film calls "the picture"

> Ultron: You need patience. Need to see the big picture.
> Quicksilver: I don't see the big picture, I have a little picture. I take it
>   out and look at it every day.
> Ultron: You lost your parents in the bombings. I've seen the records.
> Quicksilver: The records are not the picture.

These heavy discussions show how far from the utopian possibilities of reboot-dominated narrative possibility *Ultron* has drifted. What has replaced that early Obama-era hope are onerous obligations in the forms of fan service, moral reasoning, and reckoning with despair. Thor seems to be speaking for Whedon when he says, "I've had a vision. A whirlpool that sucks in all hope of life."

Ultron lacks some of the snappily casual coherence of *The Avengers*—the way the "A" health grade in the shawarma restaurant bathetically undercuts the heroically remaining "A" on Stark Tower, or the way that the banter over percentages between Stark and Pepper Potts pokes Paramount over its distribution deal. Still, there are islands of savviness. Throughout the film, the Avengers are outmatched, but some shadowy force within the internet seems to have come to their aid. As it happens, this force is JARVIS, Stark's A.I. butler. Initially, Stark and the rest believed that Ultron had "killed" JARVIS. Instead, as Stark semi-explains, "JARVIS went underground. Okay? Scattered, dumped his memory. But not his protocols. He didn't even know he was in there, until I pieced him together." Watching *Ultron* this flies past, but it hinges on a (faux) precise distinction between "memory"—what the movie has been calling "files" or "the records"—and "protocols." Put them together, and one has a moral compass—"the picture," and ideally, in this post-reboot, post-independence sequel, *this* picture. So Stark will use JARVIS to create a "perfect" Ultron to fight Ultron, and Bruce Banner will object one last time: "No, no, I'm in a loop! I'm caught in a time loop! This is exactly where it all went wrong." Stark will, one last time, disagree, and swear "It's not a loop. it's the end of the line." But the hero of *Hulk* and *Incredible Hulk* knows loops when he sees them, and he knows this cannot mark the end of the Avengers.

Notes

1 Rebecca Traister, "Crouching Budgets, Hidden Profits: James Schamus, Columbia Professor, Bets $137 Million on Ang Lee Epic," *New York Observer*, June 22, 2003, http://observer.com/2003/06/crouching-budget-hidden-profits-james-schamus-columbia-professor-bets-137-million-on-ang-lee-epic/, accessed January 20, 2017.

2 Anthony Kaufman, "Ghost of the Machine: Mourning Has Risen for Independent Film," *Village Voice*, May 28, 2002.

3 James Schamus, "IFP Rant," *Filmmaker,* Spring 2000, http://www.filmmakermagazine.com/spring2000/short_reports/ifp_rant.php, accessed January 20, 2017. All subsequent quotations in this paragraph are from this source.

4 Schamus, "IFP Rant."

5 Mark Gill, "Yes, the Sky Really is Falling," *Indiewire*, June 22, 2008, http://www.indiewire.com/article/first_person_film_departments_mark_gill_yes_the_sky_really_is_falling/, accessed January 20, 2017.

6 Gill, "Yes, the Sky Really is Falling."

7 Kristen Onstad, "Pixar Gambles on a Robot in Love," *The New York Times*, June 22, 2008, http://www.nytimes.com/2008/06/22/movies/22onst.html, accessed January 20, 2017.

8 All figures here and later from boxofficemojo.com.

9 The idea of the "normal" film derives from Thomas Kuhn's account of normal science. But filmmaking does not progress in the ways that science does, and it may be that what is "normal" is both always undergoing transformation and is yet, at the same time, only defined in contrast to something else ("indie kinds of filmmaking"). What would it mean then to speak of "normal" filmmaking? It might mean something like the "average" film of the sort analyzed in David Bordwell, Janet Staiger, and Kristin Thompson's *Classical Hollywood Cinema* (New York: Columbia University Press, 1985), where random sampling is supplemented by a selection of other landmark films to provide a portrait of a broad range of Hollywood filmmaking. But I am less interested in the average

or baseline film than in a competing positive notion of what studio filmmaking might entail. To look ahead: if independence is associated with the endlessly renewed surprise of creativity; normal filmmaking will be aligned with the inherently sustainable, with films that look like models.

10 For responses to Mark Gill's speech, see: Anne Thompson, "LAFF: Mark Gill on Indie Crisis," June 21, 2008, http://weblogs.variety.com/thompsononhollywood/2008/06/laff-mark-gill.html, accessed March 24, 2009; Patrick Goldstein, "The Sky is Falling on Indie Film," *L.A. Times*, June 23, 2008, http://latimesblogs.latimes.com/the_big_picture/2008/06/the-sky-is-fall.html, accessed January 20, 2017; David Poland, "The Indie Thing," *Movie City News*, June 23, 2008, http://moviecitynews.com/2008/06/the-indie-thing/, accessed January 20, 2017; and Scott Macaulay, "Mark Gill in Paris, Indiefreude, and Third Way Distribution," *Filmmaker*, July 8, 2008, http://filmmakermagazine.com/3521-mark-gill-in-paris-indiefreude-and-third-way-distribution, accessed January 20, 2017. Macaulay begins: "I'm blogging from Paris where, the other night, I had dinner with two Palme d'Or–winning French producer friends. 'What did you think of the Mark Gill article?' one wanted to know. Yes, Gill's speech is dinner conversation across the Atlantic. In fact, the producer had printed it out and circulated it among her staff."

    "I've commented before on the Gill piece, which I mostly agree with. Now we're seeing a second wave of responses to the article, and one must-read for indies is by writer/director John August, who blogs about the release of his Sundance film *The Nines* and relates it to the speech."

11 The crucial sentence appears in a note: "It matters what the materials of a pictorial order are, even if the order is something different from the materials, and in the end more important than they are" (T.J. Clark, *The Painting of Modern Life: Paris in the Art of Manet and his Contemporaries* [Princeton, NJ: Princeton UP, 1985], 78). Cinema has more than a pictorial order (there is, at the very least, a sonic order), but the principle holds. In what follows, I address a comparatively special case in which the materials and the order have converged; one of the questions I want to answer is how materials matter.

12 Stanley Cavell, "The Thought of Movies," in *Themes out of School* (Chicago: University Chicago Press, 1984), 3–26; David Bordwell, *The Way Hollywood Tells it* (Berkeley, CA: University California Press, 2006), 7; and Caldwell, *Production Culture*.

13 Stanley Cavell, *The World Viewed*, enlarged edition (Cambridge, MA: Harvard University Press, 1979).

14 Cavell, *The World Viewed,* 124.

15 Ibid., 130.

16 Ibid., 128.

17 Ibid., 132.

18 His use of "theatrical," here, is heavily indebted to Michael Fried's development of the same term.

19 Ibid., 120.

20 Ibid., 121.

21 Caldwell, *Production Culture*, 275, 309.

22 Noël Carroll, "The Future of Allusion: Hollywood in the Seventies (and beyond)," *October* 20 (Spring1982). Reprinted in *Interpreting the Moving Image* (Cambridge: Cambridge University Press, 1998), 240–64.

23 Bordwell, *The Way Hollywood Tells it*, 121–38.

24 Ibid., 188–89, 23–24; Murray Smith "Theses on the Philosophy of Hollywood History," in *Contemporary Hollywood Cinema*, eds. Stephen Neale and Murray Smith (New York: Routledge, 1998), 3–20.

25 Caldwell, *Production Culture*, 110.

26 Ibid., 116.

27 Caldwell, *Production Culture*, 69, puts it this way: "Ultimately I will suggest that material and conceptual uses of space do impact the sense of space and narrative that viewers experience when watching the screen at home or in the theater. But this connection between the space of making and the space of watching is more circumstantial than direct."

28 Roland Barthes, *S/Z*, trans. Richard Howard (New York: Hill & Wang, 1970), 107.

29 Cavell, *The World Viewed*, 124.

30 "The monster that ate Hollywood," *Frontline*, November 22, 2001, http://www.pbs.org/wgbh/pages/frontline/shows/hollywood/etc/script.html, accessed January 20, 2017.

31 Peter Biskind, *Down and Dirty Pictures: Miramax, Sundance, and the Rise of Independent Film* (New York: Simon & Schuster, 2004); Geoff King, *American independent cinema* (London: I.B.Tauris, 2005); Alisa Perren, *Indie, Inc.: Miramax and the Transformation of Hollywood in the 1990s* (Austin, TX: University of Texas Press, 2012); and Yannis Tzioumakis, *Hollywood's Indies: Classics Divisions, Specialty Labels and American Independent Cinema* (Edinburgh: Edinburgh University Press, 2012).

32 Geoff King, Claire Molloy, and Yannis Tzioumakis, *American Independent Cinema: Indie, Indiewood and Beyond* (New York: Routledge, 2012).

33 Within the system, movie-movies from the studios would seem to offer a more candid reflection of the industry, but they are almost invariably played for laughs. In this comedic form they pre-neutralize their critique of the system—as in *Bowfinger*, or in the mirthless spoofs that stretch endlessly from *Not Another Teen Movie* to *Epic Movie* and *Disaster Movie*.

34 Biskind, *Down and Dirty*, 364.

35 Jim Rutenberg, "Disney is Blocking Distribution of a Film that Criticizes Bush," *The New York Times*, May 5, 2004, A1, 22.

36 Rutenberg, "Disney is Blocking Distribution of a Film that Criticizes Bush." A22.

37 Anti-Eisner conspiracies aside, there was more weirdness about *Fahrenheit 9/11* than in an Oliver Stone picture. Pseudo-candidate Ralph Nader sent a public letter to Moore calling him a fatty. Moore responded by having himself

photoshopically thinned on the *Fahrenheit 9/11* poster. The primer that contains "The Pet Goat," the story the president couldn't tear himself away from, shot up the Amazon sales charts into the top 50,000, even though it cost $37.50. Before Miramax was slated to distribute the film, it was to be released by Mel Gibson's Icon. The odd couple pairing of Gibson and Moore was striking enough that the *New York Times* played it for laughs, Joyce Wadler, "Call Us Crazy, but We See a Buddy Movie Here," *The New York Times*, January 11, 2005, http://www.nytimes.com/2005/01/11/nyregion/call-us-crazy-but-we-see-a-buddy-movie-here.html, accessed January 20, 2017.

38 The two movies were not only released the same summer, but also earned very similar amounts in the United States: $114 million for *The Village*; $119 million for *Fahrenheit*. Globally, though, *The Village* earned $143 million, $40 million more than Moore's film.

39 Mike Allen and Gregory Schneider, "National Guard to be Used at Airports; Bush Calls for Public Confidence in Flying, Details Security Plan," *Washington Post*, September 28, 2001, A1. This is the infamous "go shopping" speech, but in it Bush does not actually suggest shopping. The first leader to suggest going shopping was New York City mayor Rudolph Giuliani: "Go to restaurants. Go shopping. Show that you are not afraid." David Jackson, "Death Toll Climbs; White House, Air Force One were Intended Targets," *Dallas Morning News*, September 13, 2001, nexis.

40 Sean Mussenden and Henry Pierson Curtis, "No-fly Zones Shield Disney's Resorts; Competitors say Disney Used Terrorist Fears to Get Rid of Aerial ad Planes and Sightseeing Helicopters," *Orlando Sentinel*, May 11, 2003, A1, nexis.

41 Onstad, "Pixar Gambles on a Robot in Love."

42 Of course the story was mythical, and even Stanton could not remain committed to it. When Steve Weintraub asked him, "Was this kind of the end maybe of the first generation of Pixar?" Stanton answered: "I mean, that lunch got a little mythologized once we got the fully-formed ideas, like it was the only lunch we ever had. But it is funny that, out of that lunch, came *A Bug's Life* and *WALL•E*, but there were many other lunches and meetings that, eventually, those seeds turned into *Monsters, Inc.* and *Finding Nemo*," Steve Weintraub, "Interview with Andrew Stanton," *Collider*, November 17, 2008, http://www.collider.com/entertainment/interviews/article.asp/aid/9881/tcid/1, accessed January 20, 2017.

43 Although *Idiocracy* was given a token release in 2007 it had languished on Fox's shelf for a year following disastrous test screenings.

44 For the history of the Mac startup sound, see Tom Whitwell, "Tiny music makers, Pt 4: The Mac startup sound." *Musicthing*, May 26, 2005, http://musicthing.blogspot.com/2005/05/tiny-music-makers-pt-4-mac-startup.html, accessed January 20, 2017. For Ive's visit to Pixar see Weintraub, "Interview": "I had two things. One, I had the making-fun-of-the-iPod joke, I was having the Apple sound joke and I also had decided that if I was going to make the prettiest robot in the world, for a machine, what would that be and we all

agreed that, currently, Apple products are the most gorgeous looking machines in the world. They could be art objects without adding a function. We didn't want to literally make her be Apple, but we wanted her to feel that same design sensibility, where the functions are hidden. It's a mystery and you're not exactly sure how it all works, but it seems almost magical and everything is almost perfectly molded into one another. It became obvious to us, but I wanted Steve to be comfortable with it and he said we should have Jony Ive come over and see what he thinks, because he designs everything for Apple. He came over and pretty much fell in love with immediately and it was the biggest shot in the arm. He didn't have anything to approve on, he just said, 'I love her.' It was a great afternoon with him that was pretty much the stamp of approval."

45 Laura M. Holson, "Disney Agrees to Acquire Pixar in a $7.4 Billion Deal," *The New York Times*, January 25, 2006, http://www.nytimes.com/2006/01/25/business/disney-agrees-to-acquire-pixar-in-a-74-billion-deal.html, accessed January 20, 2017; Charles Solomon, "Pixar Creative Chief to Seek to Restore the Disney Magic," *The New York Times*, January 25, 2006, http://www.nytimes.com/2006/01/25/business/media/pixar-creative-chief-to-seek-to-restore-the-disney-magic.html, accessed January 20, 2017.

46 For an overview of the role of libraries in studio finances and much else, see Eric Hoyt, *Hollywood Vault: Film Libraries Before Home Video* (Berkeley: University of California Press, 2014).

47 Alison James, "Besson's EuropaCorp buys Roissy," *Variety,* October 15, 2007, http://variety.com/2007/film/news/besson-s-europacorp-buys-roissy-1117974054/.

48 Chris Anderson's argument that digital retrieval shifts society away from hits toward the "long tail" of distribution depends on a broad and unlikely disintermediation in most media fields; it has come to pass only fragmentarily. See *The Long Tail* (New York: Hachette, 2008).

49 Robert Kraft, author interview, January 24, 2008.

50 There seems to be no common adjective meaning library-like in English.

51 "Hulk," "Why No One Want Make *Hulk 2?*" *The Onion*, July 14, 2004, http://www.theonion.com/content/node/33980, accessed January 20, 2017.

52 Caldwell points to another possibility, that such a film might be made more efficiently because its indie-based creatives would not be beholden to union workrules and divisions of labor. In the case of summer tentpoles, though, that advantage tends to fade. The sheer bulk of effects work puts the responsibility for squeezing efficiencies out of a budget in the hands of the ultra-competitive effects shops themselves.

53 John Lahr, "Becoming the Hulk," *The New Yorker*, June 30, 2003, 72–81.

54 James Schamus, "Sing to us, Muse, of the Rage of the Hulk," *The New York Times*, May 11, 2003, MT29.

55 Richard Maltby, "'A Brief Romantic Interlude': Dick and Jane go to 3½ Seconds of the Classical Hollywood Cinema," in *Post-Theory: Reconstructing Film Studies*, eds. David Bordwell and Noël Carroll (Madison, WI: University of Wisconsin Press, 1996), 434–59.

56 Ann Donahue, "Above the Line: Avi Arad: Turnabout? It's Marvel-ous," *Variety*, May 19, 2002, http://variety.com/2002/film/news/above-the-line-avi-arad-1117867142/, accessed January 20, 2017. This history is encapsulated in the leaders running before the three installments of the X-Men series. I discuss that series in the opening chapter of *The Studios after the Studios*. Derek Johnson provides an incisive, longer view of the X-Men franchise and its complex relations to Marvel's independence in *Media Franchising* (New York: New York University Press, 2013) and "Cinematic Destiny: Marvel Studios and the Trade Stories of Industrial Convergence," *Cinema Journal* 52, no. 1 (Fall 2012): 1–24. Martin Flanagan, Mike McKenny, and Andy Livingstone investigate the next phase of Marvel's convergence in *The Marvel Studios Phenomenon: Inside a Transmedia Universe* (New York: Bloomsbury, 2016).

57 Pamela McClintock, "Sony Sets Date for Spider-Man 4," *Variety*, March 12, 2009, http://variety.com/2009/film/markets-festivals/sony-sets-date-for-spider-man-4-1118001130/, accessed January 20, 2017.

58 J.K. Rowling, *Harry Potter and the Order of the Phoenix* (New York: Scholastic, 2003), 399.

59 Rowling, *Harry Potter and the Order of the Phoenix,* 776.

60 Ibid., 777.

61 Ibid., 785.

62 Ibid., 787.

63 In the novel, the group casts the Reductor spell *as a group*, while in the film Ginny alone destroys the towering shelves. Why is this a habit of the films? One might attribute it to the charisma of the young women playing Hermione, Ginny, Luna, and so on, were it not the case that there are young men of similar skill (Neville especially). But I would be more inclined to view it as Warners' attempt to reckon with Rowling's own control over the series.

64 Bernard F. Dick, *Engulfed: The Death of Paramount Pictures and the Birth of Corporate Hollywood* (Lexington, KY: University of Kentucky, 2001), 187.

65 Fredric Jameson, "Postmodernism and Consumer Society," in *The Cultural Turn* (London: Verso, 1998), 1–21.

66 "Adventures in Post-Production," *Indiana Jones and the Kingdom of the Crystal Skull,* Blu-ray (Paramount, 2008).

67 "The Return of a Legend," *Indiana Jones and the Kingdom of the Crystal Skull,* Blu-ray (Paramount, 2008); quotation marks inserted.

68 Tomberry, "Nuking the Fridge," *Know Your Meme*, http://knowyourmeme.com/memes/nuking-the-fridge, accessed January 20, 2017.

69 Craigh Barboza "Imagination is Infinite," *USAWeekend*, July 15, 2005, http://159.54.226.237/05_issues/050619/050619spielberg.html, accessed January 20, 2017.

70 Steve Silberman, "Life after Darth," *Wired* 13, no. 5 (May 2005): 140+.

71 "Adventures," *Crystal Skull* Blu-ray.

72 IBM "650 RAMAC Announcment," September 14, 1956, http://www-03.ibm.com/ibm/history/exhibits/650/650_pr2.html, accessed January 20, 2017.

73 Flangan, McKenny, and Livingstone, *The Marvel Studios Phenomenon*, 4.

74 Joss Whedon, "Commentary," *Avengers*, DVD (Buena Vista, 2012).

75 Ibid.

76 This is an appropriate place to mention just how sterling the production design and set decoration work in *The Avengers* and the MCU as a whole are. For this film, the art department was headed by James Chinlund, Richard L. Johnson, and Victor J. Zolfo.

77 Nikki Finke and Mike Fleming, Jr., "Paramount To End Relationship With Marvel In 2012: Disney Will Distribute 'Iron Man 3' and 'The Avengers,'" *Deadline*, October 18, 2010, http://deadline.com/2010/10/disney-paramount-marvel-restructure-marketing-distruibution-deal-76534/, accessed January 20, 2017; Andrew Stewart, "Paramount's Super Payoff for 'Iron Man 3'," *Variety*, May 10, 2013, http://variety.com/2013/film/news/iron-man-3-paramount-disney-1200479325/, accessed January 20, 2017.

6

Numbers, stations:

Lost and the digital turn in U.S. television

Weird island

ABC launched *Lost* (2004–10) on the back of J.J. Abrams's substantial cachet as a television auteur. "From J.J. Abrams," the pilot promo began, "The Creator of *Alias*." Yet despite enormous production and marketing investments in Abrams the auteur, the assertion of fan control was swift and thorough. Within a year, showrunner Carlton Cuse, Abrams's replacement, was explaining that the story was *really* about its fans. The on-screen conflict between rationalist Jack Shephard and mystical John Locke was redescribed as an allegory of the show's reception: "Jack and Locke are representative of the two kinds of fans the show has. . . . Locke is the guy who says, 'I want the island to be weird.' Jack is the guy who says, 'I don't want the island to be weird.' That is a road map for what we're doing this year."[1] Criticism has been all too happy to follow Cuse's lead. While studies of The New Television have been attentive to both the rise of showrunner auteurism and the new roles of audiences, no series has been seen by critics as more emblematic of the power of fans than *Lost*.[2] Yet the focus on new, technologically driven modes of reception and response made possible by digital video recorders (DVRs) and online fora (in *Lost*'s case, "The Fuselage") has made criticism less attuned to the particularities of industrial history than it ought to be. In place of the fancentric, new media utopianism that has characteristically greeted *Lost*, I offer a far more suspicious reading of the series's contents, contexts, and ambitions. *Lost* appears less the product of a faltering auteurism or an ascendant fanocracy, than a precisely tailored response to the digital turn in American television.

By 2004, ABC had stripmined the success of *Who Wants to Be a Millionaire?* until there was nothing left.[3] The network was mired in fourth place. Steve McPherson, head of corporate sibling Touchstone Television, had been tasked with finding something that would boost ratings, and he and Anne Sweeney shifted the studio away from imported game show and reality franchises toward scripted, "quality" product. Abrams was ideal for the new direction. He wanted the series to look "very cinematic," and he largely succeeded. "It felt like a film," said actor Dominic Monaghan, the *Lord of the Rings* veteran who played Charlie. McPherson was even more effusive: "We were all so proud of it, because, you know, to do a pilot like that and be the studio that was involved in that, and the network, it was just like, look at this piece of work. It was just a devastating *movie*."[4] A telling clip on the DVD extra features shows Abrams shaking the film magazine on the camera during the filming of the plane crash. "I love those little jitters that happen, not the kind of big shakes so much, so he would let me hold on to the film magazine, and shake the magazine, to get that kind of little look."[5] The hand of the master was everywhere.

FIGURE 6.1 *The jiggle of the auteur.* Lost.

Yet despite the comforting authorial cocoon surrounding the pilot, there was, already, a problem: fans. The opening promo included a clip of a scene in which one of the castaways shoots a lunging polar bear. And, as Abrams explains, "when you freeze frame it, it is absolutely the dumbest thing you've ever seen. It is ridiculous. It's a stupid, goofy, muppet looking thing, just like—it could not be less scary. It's, it's embarrassing." Worse, "someone had not only seen that on TV but had freeze framed it and posted it on the internet, which made the show laughable before it even aired."[6] The problem disappeared when Abrams agreed to replace the stuffed bear with a computer-generated version, but the power dynamic seemed to have changed. The auteur might still serve as the channel of control and the focus of aesthetic responsibility, but there was a new source of critique—fans—a critique that had become, through technology, instant. Abrams describes his acquiescence to fan-driven production "notes" in casual enough terms, but he left his role as showrunner halfway through the opening season in order to work on *Mission Impossible III*.[7]

With Abrams's partial exit, the pattern for *Lost* had been set: this would be a series very particularly shaped by its online relationships with its viewers. Everyone working on the show knew this, and that knowledge seeped into the production. Cuse summed up the series's resonance with its fans in decidedly allegorical terms: "In a way the fan community kinda mirrored a little bit what we were doing thematically on the show, which was, this plane crash caused this sort of disparate group of people to kind of come together and form a community, in the same way the show caused this disparate group of people all around the world to come together. And it was satisfying to see that there was this whole resonance of the show that was larger than just the hour that was on the network every week."[8] The dissolution of narrative into reception became one of *Lost*'s principal marketing channels, culminating in an enormous "watch party" on the Oahu beach for the final season premiere.

Lost became the emblem of an industry-wide trend, although ABC's turn to "quality" was a far more fraught and desperate move than, say, similar evolutions at AMC or USA. Still, as Stacey Abbott, Paul Grainge, Roberta Pearson, and others have argued, legacy networks adopted several strategies to compensate for their eroding position within the media system.[9] *Lost*, like several of its contemporaries, was serial (not episodic), featured a large cast and big-budget production values, and solicited high levels of audience attention in both its broadcast versions and online. As network audience share declined, audience intensity increased.

In this new arrangement, audience intensity is fostered by narrative complexity in an attempt to compensate for technological change. As Erika Johnson-Lewis sums up: "Central to this shift are new digital technologies that have given audiences more control over when, where, and how they consume televisual content. To accommodate this shift, networks sought

FIGURE 6.2 *Hawaiian watch party.* Lost.

series that could be successful within this new environment. The transmedia temporality of *Lost*'s narrative world is indicative of post-network changes in content, promotion, and distribution."[10] On this argument, the auteurist strategy finds itself conjured by and pitted against forces unleashed by new, digital technologies and their attendant consumption shifts—what Henry Jenkins calls "convergence" or Will Brooker calls "overflow."[11] "Man, this makes watching a TV show *so much work*," as one *Heroes* fan posted online. But, as Brooker glosses that statement, "This 'work', though, for those who choose to undertake it, is driven by the pleasures of detection and community—and is based increasingly around the crossing of the boundaries between fiction and the real world."[12] As the digitized televisual experience expanded to include blog recaps, participation in online fora, watch parties, meetups, fan fiction, and so on, programming itself changed. *Lost*, then, would be an attempt to capitalize on this general trend and drive it forward, particularly through the digital seeding of its fictional brands across the internet and the distribution of *Lost*-based material products (Dharma Initiative t-shirts; Apollo chocolates).[13] Fans, living in the emergent digital present of instant feedback, rip the auteur apart, leaving the network little choice but to acquiesce to audience authority.

That seems to be the case with *Lost*. In addition to the world-building that Derek Johnson and Johnson-Lewis draw our attention to, *Lost* aspired to repurpose the intensities of reality and cult television for serial ends. The narrative had obvious links to CBS's *Survivor*, with its group of island castaways. But that initial setup quickly became more and more complicated. The survivors of the plane crash were joined by others on the island ("The Others") and, eventually, survivors from the tail section of the plane ("Tailies"). Main characters often bore the names of canonical philosophers—there was a Locke, a Rousseau, a Hume, even a Bakunin—were they supposed to embody the philosophies? That seemed unlikely given John Locke's mysticism; then again, he did have a Crusoe-like resourcefulness. The narrative came unstuck in time, initially filling in character backstories with extended flashbacks, then adding flash-forwards to off-island life before finally achieving a kind of quantum narration with the appearance of alternate timelines, the "flash sideways." The island itself became a source of compounding mysteries. There were polar bears and vengeful smoke monsters: where did they come from? There were underground lab stations with names like The Swan and The Pearl: why had they been built? There was a slave ship marooned in the middle of the island: how had it gotten there? And, most of all, there were The Numbers: 4, 8, 15, 16, 23, 42, 108. They were everywhere—as flight numbers and winning lotto tickets, repeating endlessly from a numbers station located on the island, promising to be the key to it all, pulling the audience in. On the usual reading, newly hegemonic fans challenge producers to find new ways of mapping the narrative onto the fanbase.

The more triumphalist the story of fan-driven television, though, the closer criticism gets to marketing. If television really is being driven by changes in consumption, if audiences really are exercising new forms of authority and choice, isn't that all to the good—for critics, fans, and networks? And aren't the best auteurs the ones who take audiences into account at every step? As critics have taken up the narrative of fan accommodation, it has allowed them to ignore or, at the very least, massage a particularly thorny problem: despite its state-of-the-art audience relations, *Lost* suffered significant ratings declines over time.

Few critics even mention the drop.[14] Yet claims that *Lost* successfully compensates for the erosion of network dominance by incorporating a host of transmedial or para-textual phenomena are difficult to distinguish from self-serving assertions on the part of producers that while the broadcast audience for *Lost* was collapsing, something else—something worth paying for—was taking its place.[15]

The most logical candidate for that "something" is the "global community" itself. When Jonathan Gray argues that *Lost* creates an island, inhabitants, and even an idea of "home" that lie outside the binary of Orient and Occident, and that by doing so the series "represents an intriguing step toward a post-national television," he could hardly be making a better case for the series than Cuse and his partner Damon Lindelof.[16] One could easily enough understand that community less benignly. Begin from the proposition that *Lost*'s globalization was necessary to support its large budget. That aim would be achieved by pursuing a host of experimental strategies, and the series's success would enforce a spectatorial discipline that might prove

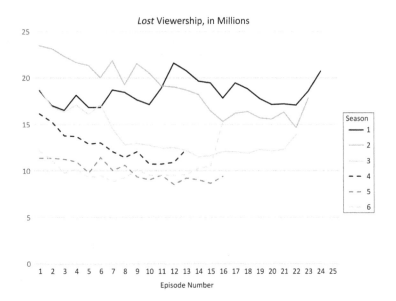

FIGURE 6.3 *Nielsen ratings via Lostpedia. Author graphic.*

particularly profitable for the studio and for networks throughout the world. Such a strategy sounds like the Dharma Initiative mission statement, and it is also Johnson's reading of contemporary television—neither a world of unlimited audience influence nor one of fruitless resistance, but a collection of varying responses that "must be *managed*."[17] Audiences are "invited in" but producers crucially still do the inviting: Namaste.

Still, even on this more suspicious reading, it is difficult to distinguish the project of global community building from quality showrunning: The best auteurs are the ones who behave like critics who behave like fans. This metacritical problem becomes trickier the more we realize that any apparently negative critical affects we might strike toward the series—even Johnson's—have been anticipated by it. The creators' roadmap requires them to typologize the audience—"the two kinds of fans the show has." Fans, showrunners, critics: *Everyone* wants to tell the story of *Lost*'s fandom.

The larger problem with audience-centric accounts, then, is not that they are too credulous or too critical but that by privileging fans they have turned away from other aspects of the industry—everything from career management to network politics to regulatory change.[18] What is more, in the guise of attending to "the way we watch now," fancentric criticism attends only to those forms of technology that have been "noticed" by fans, and ignores a host of apparently subliminal technological transformations. Most contemporary television history rests on a particularly unhistorical understanding of technology and a characteristically limited vision of the critical enterprise. The latter problem is, I think, the root of the former, and so I will address it first before turning to its consequences both for television history and for our understanding of *Lost*.

No *Animal Farm*

Lost both is, and is not, an allegory. At the most general level, it is an allegory in the way that it is *about* everything it *depicts*. Here is Randy Laist listing all the things *Lost* might be an allegory of:

> Critics who have studied the show have discovered much to talk about. In its depiction of an international community, *Lost* is a narrative about globalization. In its treatment of corporate-industrial threats to an unspoiled wilderness, *Lost* is a narrative about ecological awareness. In its dramatization of territorial disputes between aboriginals and settlers, *Lost* is an allegory of postcolonial territoriality. In its technique of revealing obscure patterns buried within streams of data, *Lost* suggests associations with genetic sequencing and hypertextuality. . . . But *Lost* does more than merely represent these issues; it enacts them.[19]

The chain of events is complicated here, but it stretches from depiction (a television show must depict something) to considered intervention (the meat of "about-ness," that is, here, a "treatment," a "dramatization," a suggestion, and an allegory) to enaction. To get from depiction to enaction one passes through more formal and thematic intentions, but one also quickly passes beyond them. Laist's criticism does the same, dispatching the idea of allegory in favor of, well, audiences:

> *Lost* is no *Animal Farm*-type allegory of conflicting philosophical positions. As is the case with *Lost*'s literary allusions, the philosophical allusions in *Lost* are not easily collapsible into one-to-one correspondences. The function of these names seems to be primarily to connote philosophical discourse itself and to activate in the *Lost* audience the kinds of attention we associate with philosophical problems. This is one of the many ways that *Lost* non-directively stimulates interpretive behavior on the part of its audience and directs us to contextualize the events of the show within philosophical modes of discourse.[20]

For Laist, allegory is the intellectual misstep one makes on the way to a "non-directive," interpretation, or if interpretation is no longer the right word, a non-directive contextualization within a mode of discourse. Allegory names the semantic reduction that good criticism and good television avoid.

This intellectual move is not unique to Laist. Jesse Kavadlo, in trying to specify the relationship between *Lost* and the attacks on 9/11, passes through the same stations of interp. He is "reluctant to use the word 'allegory,' with its suggestion of a true meaning behind its emblems" because *Lost*'s "sheer length as a serial narrative and concomitant intricacies" render it "too elusive and ambiguous for such direct equivalencies."[21] "Much of the show's resistance to allegory stems from its equal resistance to Manichean separations of good and evil."[22] So there will be local moments of allegory— the plane crash and 9/11, surely, but also Ben Linus, "the best allegory for the Wall Street debacle television has provided"—but those are the problem.[23] The whole course of the show amounts to a drifting away from correspondence to something more fluid, more general, more like itself. By the end, watching *Lost* becomes an allegory of watching *Lost*. And that is how we should understand Christian's advice to Jack that he "remember and let go":

> This advice, in the end, seems less about 9/11 than it is Christian's advice to fans of *Lost*, about to lose their series and characters in a way that even resurrection and the afterlife cannot correct. The last season, then, was self-consciously and self-reflectively about television itself, away from the 9/11 allegory that began it.[24]

Allegory, then, is the thing that *Lost* is not, but it is also the thing that it becomes, the mode of interpretation that it requires of its fans. In this allegorical instruction, *Lost* was not unique. As Johnson notes, characters in cult series such as *Star Trek* (Lt. Barclay), *The X Files* (Leyla Harrison), *Buffy the Vampire Slayer* (Jonathan, Warren, and Andrew), *Heroes* (Hiro), and *Lost* (Hurley) have all "served to textually delineate appropriate and inappropriate relationships between fans, texts, and productive storytelling practices."[25] Nothing embodied *Lost*'s version of fan incentive and response like the show's internal tagline, "We have to go back." (Kavadlo and Johnson-Lewis both use it as the title to their essays.) Johnson-Lewis explains that while it has a manifest narrative function—Jack and Kate have to return to the island—it is implicitly "an instruction to the audience to 'go back' and reevaluate what they thought they knew about the episode they were watching." That instruction, in turn, "comments on the experience of watching the series from the macro-level; we not only have to go back to the beginning of the episode but to the beginning of the entire series to situate events in their full context."[26] Other instances of the "We have to go back" moment—"We need to see that again"— are more literally emblems of rewatching, but in this early version from Season 2, we see how the metacritical prohibition against "one-to-one correspondences" is quickly thrown aside when the correspondence is with fan behaviors.

Why, if our interpretive protocols tell us that complex texts do not or should not exhibit "*Animal Farm*–type allegory" or amount to a "cardboard morality play" should we carve out an exception for allegories of the television audience? The obvious answer is that audiences are doing all the interesting things, and what makes the series interesting is the way it attempts to cater to these new, interesting behaviors. Because *Lost* is playing catchup with its fanbase, then, it can't (or shouldn't) be an allegory of anything even though it is (or must be) an allegory of everything, which is only to say that *Lost* is an allegory of its fans and their efforts to understand it. Here Laist, Kavadlo, and Johnson-Lewis join Cuse and Lindelof: "Jack and Locke are representative of the two kinds of fans the show has."

Yet this convergence between critics, fans, and showrunners offers us a new avenue of approach. Critics and fans have noticed the reflexivity field the series seems to have induced in them, but so have the series's producers. And if we can, as critics, look to all the ways that fans put *Lost* to use, then we ought at the very least to extend that same courtesy to the creative professionals and media organizations behind it. For while reflexivity is a way of grappling with and encouraging fan interest, it is also a textual feature of creative industries under stress. Reflexivity, as I discussed in the opening of the previous chapter, promises intellectual depth for those audiences who seek pleasure in hermeneutic work—the sort of hermeneutic work required to understand the temporalities of *Lost*, the language of *The Wire*, or the production design of *Mad Men*—but more than that, reflexivity constitutes both symptom and scenario to be projected and read by industrial participants.

Yet unlike *The Wire*'s David Simon or *Mad Men*'s Matthew Weiner, J.J. Abrams's auteurism is unraveling *in the same moment that it is elaborated*. Why? The universally agreed-upon answer has been that this auteur is born hobbled by a new force of feedback: instant and universally available fan discourse. But if this force seems new—if it seemed new to everyone involved—its application seems to be a version of the comparatively old-fashioned notion of televisual *liveness*.[27] The principal novelty is that everything is live: the commercial with the muppet polar bear, the fan response, and the discourse of auteurism. The fan-centered understanding of contemporary television in general and *Lost* in particular has omitted that more general liveness because it looks like a "residual" force in the configuration of television. Brooker registers that nagging difficulty when he distinguishes between fans who "binge" on series via DVR or DVD or streaming and those who proceed "drip by drip following the producers' intended rhythm of weekly episodes."[28] The marathon watcher may be the new viewer incarnate, but that novelty comes at the expense of the very social intensity that the cult series played to. Such a binge viewer "may find him or herself isolated out of time, with no obvious place within an online community that, perhaps quaintly, remains structured around traditional broadcast schedules and global geography."[29] The "drip by drip" model may be "quaint" or "frustrating," or residual, but it is this model that makes "appointment television" possible.[30]

Lost, with its podcasts, fansites, and Alternate Reality Game (ARG), built itself and billed itself as a model of the new mediascape, but it always had to justify that innovation through an appeal to the idea and the infrastructure of the live viewing audience. In its peculiarly fraught relationship between its "quaint" network broadcasting schedule on the one hand and its unprecedented digital ancillaries on the other, *Lost* suggests that The New Television is far more bound up with questions of perdurance, capture, storage, and retrieval than The New Hollywood was. That difference, in turn, suggests that the central self-allegorizations of contemporary television will be far different from the libertarian individual-against-the-system allegories of the New Hollywood. It further suggests that if the series is an allegory of watching, we should attend far more intently to the technology and institutions of watching within it. The cumulation of reflexivity does not begin and end with fans; Laist is right that the series is about all the things it depicts, for in the manic production cycle of contemporary, feedback-laced television, depiction and reflection are intercalated like an infinite club sandwich. One of the things *Lost* depicts is its own production, and one of the things that it is about is the depiction of its own production.

Aspects

Let us take a step back. In the critical attempt to get inside the industry's efforts to use viewer intensity to compensate for viewer dispersal and scarcity something rather obvious is missed. Consider, again, Figures 6.1 and 6.2, stills from the pilot episode making of featurette "Welcome to Oahu" and the post-series featurette "Planet Lost." The obvious difference in aspect ratio goes more or less unnoticed today, but it is worth dwelling on. Depending on your TV, your broadcaster, and your country *Lost* was available in widescreen from its premiere; its DVDs were released at 16:9. But the special features for Seasons 1 and 2 are 4:3. What is happening, then, between 2004 and 2010 is that the state of the art is in flux: shot on film, *Lost* the series is widescreen; shot on video, *Lost*'s extra features vary. And these days, through technological succession and the cultivation of cinematized technophilia, the widescreen television dominates. There is a story here.

Over its six seasons, *Lost* spans a fundamental transition in the history of U.S. television, as analog broadcast is replaced by digital, as analog timeshifting via VCRs wanes in favor of digital timeshifting via DVRs and the internet, as standard definition gives way to high definition, as Academy-ratio sets are either replaced by widescreen sets or are made to display letterboxed, widescreen versions of broadcasts that were initially shown 16:9. The progress of technology (including hardware, standards, regulation, and distribution) was not smooth. A host of forces, from government agencies and networks to showrunners and local stations, struggled to shape the emerging HDTV landscape. *Lost*, with Jack and Locke, became an allegory of its anxieties over the power of its own fans. *Lost*, with its dangerous numbers, timeshifting plots, and mobile island, became the privileged site for the display of a particular corporation's version of American television's digital anxiety.

For some obvious reasons the digital turn in television has not occasioned anything like the medium-specificity theorizing or nostalgia that has accompanied the parallel changes in cinema. (Our convergence phenomenologists and historians are not deeply interested in the "quaint.") Here, as an exemplary contrast, is David Rodowick, insisting on the essential importance of the digital turn in cinema: "It is as if the creation of digital imaging as a medium were willing the annihilation of past duration with respect to space in order to replace it with another conception of time, that is, the time of calculation or computer cycles. . . . The goal of both digital capture and synthesis is to constitute a space that is mathematically definable and manipulable."[31] That may be true of cinema, but if it is, part of what makes it true is the amenability of cinema history to an almost linear progress. Certainly cinema history seems so in contrast to television history. In TV, the complex formation of technology, political economy, and regulatory apparatus has fostered institutions with the power to check the advancing digital wave. Far more often than has been the case with cinema, televisual progress has been "blocked"—stalled and fought over in public. During the most recent stall, the industry produced a host of compromise formations, digital/analog hybrids like *Lost* that could be both remarkably prophetic and shockingly naïve. Contrast the showrunners' savvy in the face of global social networking with their innocence about "digital manipulation," whether it was fans freeze-framing the promo or obsessing over The Numbers: "We never expected the numbers to become this phenomenon," Cuse continued. "When one of the producers came to our office and gave us a coffee mug [he bought on eBay] with the numbers on it, we were like, 'This is insane.'"[32]

By 2012 the HD television penetration rate in the United States was 2/3. At the time *Lost* debuted, HD penetration was not even measured; it was imputed from estimates. Making any estimate more complicated was the proliferation of partial technologies in the latter half of the decade: HD "ready" sets, "Expanded Definition" sets, and, more than anything, the related but nonidentical shift in American broadcasting from analog to digital, from NTSC to ATSC standards. HDTV had been, for decades, just over the horizon—it was originally part of the menu of envy directed at "Japan, Inc.," as far back as the 1980s. The ATSC standards were

U.S. HD Penetration Rates

	2008	2009	2010	2011	2012
HD Receivable	14	18	43	59	67
HD Capable	17	23	46	60	67
HD Display Capable	25	32	53	64	70

FIGURE 6.4 *Nielsen figures. Author graphic.*

published in 1995, and the enormous 1996 Telecom Act allowed the Federal Communications Commission (FCC) to start granting ATSC licenses. The next year, the first official sunset date for analog broadcasting was fixed: 2006. The transition would be cumbersome, of course, with the enormous installed base of NTSC sets on the exhibition side and the vast expense of changing over everything from sets and makeup to cameras and editing hardware on the production side. In 2005, the deadline was pushed back to February 17, 2009, and in 2009, as part of Obama's stimulus package, the date was pushed back further, to June 12.[33]

To put this in our relevant context, *Lost* was greenlit and picked up from pilot in a world where some affiliates and many network-owned-and-operated stations had already made the shift to digital production and were broadcasting in both forms.[34] The changeover would have been complete in *Lost*'s second season, but in the midst of that season, the networks and their affiliates were, like the series, given a reprieve. Whatever else it was, *Lost* was a centerpiece of ABC's technology strategy over that same period.

Years later, it is perhaps difficult to conceive how goofy the digital transition was. The National Association of Broadcasters hit the road in the "Digital Trekker" to tout "the benefits of DTV"; the Consumer Electronics Association staged side-by-side demos to persuade consumers of the inevitable; and the Commerce Department's National Telecommunications and Information Administration launched a $2 billion "coupon" program to defray the costs of digital-to-analog converter boxes for owners of analog televisions.[35]

The leadup to the conversion promised that reception would improve, but that increase in quality came with its own threat. When an analog signal is disrupted, the usual consequence is static and fade; but when a digital signal is interrupted, the stream falls off the "digital cliff," the sound stops, the image locks up and pixellates, and there is no way of tweaking the antenna to find a "good enough" version of the show. This version of the "digital cliff" was softpedaled, though, in favor of a ginned-up panic over the complete loss of the analog signal when the digital switchover occurred.

National Association of Broadcasters'
"DTV Trekker"

FIGURE 6.5 *The Digital Trekker. Courtesy National Telecommunications and Information Administration.*

The ultimate symbol and symptom of this conversion hysteria was a series of commercials starring Obama-era everyman "Joe the Plumber" hawking the boxes. Throughout the fall of 2008, Joe the Plumber had been the site of unrelenting political and media solicitation, with Joe Biden and Sarah Palin and John McCain and Barack Obama forever returning to the favored metonym of the campaign. For the right, Joe had caught Obama promising to "spread the wealth around" and had revealed the socialist conspiracy at the heart of the Democratic agenda. For the left, Joe was an emblem of mendacity and false consciousness, a guy who would be helped, not hurt, by the stimulus plan, a guy who wasn't even a plumber and wasn't even named Joe. (His legal name is Samuel Wurzelbacher; he ran for Congress in 2012 as a Republican.) Ironies piled up when the everyspokesman for rugged individualism cashed in on the government program by shilling for "velocitystore.com."

With the appearance of Joe the Plumber, we can finally liquidate the initial interest in Abrams the auteur. The series needed Abrams to launch, but he quickly capitalized on that to make the move to cinema. That particular media pathway encourages a nostalgia for the analog, one that Abrams describes in almost exactly the same terms as Rodowick:

FIGURE 6.6 *The digital conversion of Joe the Plumber. https://www.youtube.com/ watch?v=xyjqaYeuvGo&t, posted by helxis83. Courtesy Velocitystore.com*

I'm obsessed with things that are distinctly analogue. We have a letterpress in our office. There's an absolute wonderful imperfection that you get when you do a letterpress, and that is the beauty of it. The time that is put in setting the type and running the press, inking the rollers, all that stuff—that kind of thing is clearly an extreme example. But it's the beauty of the actual investment of time, and the amount of time that goes by lets you consider things that somehow, in a kind of weird osmosis or spiritual way, is somehow implicit in the final product. And that seems to not exist much any more.[36]

Compare the analog pathos of Abrams discussing the digital turn in cinema with what he called the "ridiculous" effects of the incipient digital turn in television. The cinematic institution is such that one can plausibly imagine cisterns of emotion sloshing about below the surface of the move to digital imaging. (As in the documentary *Side by Side*, which features interviews with directors and cinematographers weighing in on their reasons for preferring film or digital image capture, lamenting the passing of the celluloid era or heralding the new [Kenneally, Company/Tribeca, 2011].) The television institution offers nothing of the kind. In place of nostalgia, we have Joe the Plumber's dippy ironies and *Lost*'s conspiracies. Without a container for his digital obsessions, Abrams leaves *Lost* to join the *Mission Impossible* franchise, itself a televisual upscaling. What Abrams left behind, though, was a legacy of numerical obsession and two showrunners utterly committed to the processes and the ideology of The New Television. And while the show would become, as Laist describes it, a "uniquely contemporary engagement with emerging twenty-first-century concerns," that engagement was also bound by three late-twentieth-century legacies.[37]

The first of those legacies was the 1996 Telecom Act, which recodified the digital transition; the second was the 1992 Cable Television Consumer Protection and Competition Act; the third was the end of limits on network ownership of production—fin/syn rules—in 1993, which allowed, and all but required, far deeper ties between networks and producers. The legal tripod provided the base on which ABC, through the production, reception, and narration of *Lost*, revamped itself as a digital megabrand. *Lost* began at as a Touchstone Television production. But by 2007, Disney had finally decided that the "Touchstone" brand was essentially a non-brand, and in February, once the *Lost–*, *Desperate Housewives–*, and *Grey's Anatomy–* driven "resurgence" at ABC had taken hold, Touchstone became ABC Television Studios. Three months later, the word "television" was struck from the name.[38] Television was gone, and in the process it had subsumed "the cinematic": the new logo was decidedly widescreen.

As part of its company-wide rebranding effort, a new studio leader was developed. In it, silhouetted studio workers push bits of classic technology around a white box. But at the core of the studio image was a newfangled digital clapper, a nod to the past updated for today. Updated, and thoroughly branded, for the clapper does not slate a particular scene but initially bears the numbers 4, 8, 15, and 16—the first four numbers of The Numbers from

FIGURE 6.7 *Rebranding the televisual at ABC.* Lost.

FIGURE 6.8 *Nesting "the numbers" inside the brand.* Lost.

Lost. With the clap, the 15 and 16 are replaced by 23 and 42, completing the sequence. The promise of a post-network network seemed to be fulfilled at ABC, an effort achieved through and symbolized by *Lost*'s own manic self-referentiality. Thus does a series come to define a brand, a network, and an aesthetic strategy.

Critical to ABC's new configuration was *Lost*'s aggressive online presence. From the outset, the show was one of the most DVR'ed on television.[39] This existence of a substantial timeshifted audience implied that *Lost*'s ratings declines were not as significant as they appeared—that there were others watching. And while the series could depict that other, long tail audience as Others or Tailies, as the case may be, it could not rely on them for further revenue. Since the principal aim of a broadcast tv rating is to measure a potential audience for a commercial, *Lost*'s shadow audience was of no obvious financial use. Timeshifting made the show terribly prone to commercial zapping. In recognition of this configuration, Nielsen ratings only included the live audience until 2008, when the company added coverage for "Live + 7" (those who watched a DVR episode within seven days) and "Live + 3." But these augmented ratings did not translate into changes in ad rates; all the major ad buying agencies initially rejected the new metrics. It was not until a compromise was reached around "Live + SD" (same day) that timeshifting could help out a show's rating. (The theory was that someone who digitally paused a show in the middle and quickly resumed should be counted with the live audience. Still, it should be noted that while the ratings data that is publicly reported in the enfotainment complex is the Live + SD, networks quickly had access to "Live + 3C" data—the audience for the live broadcast plus those who watched a commercial in the next three days.[40]) ABC compensated for *Lost*'s shadow audience, in part, by making the show one of the first available for sale on iTunes in 2005, thereby monetizing the timeshift, and then, in 2006, by making whole episodes available for "free" at ABC.com and via various cable VOD services.[41] ABC, and particularly ABC.com, were attempting to become a deeply branded, walled garden like the one developed by Disney board member Steve Jobs at Apple, with all the attendant anger that was sure to bring.[42]

ABC's affiliates reacted in horror at the prospect of audience cannibalization and the loss of virtually all rerun money from one of the network's most demographically desirable shows. Worse, they resented the fact that Disney/ABC would continue to receive money regardless of platform—whether a cut from iTunes, VOD, or ABC.com. Affiliate revolt is still taken very seriously by networks despite the dominance of other pipelines into the home. When *Lost* debuted, fewer than 20 percent of TV households were broadcast-only while more than 60 percent of American households got their TV programming through cable. But the networks maintain their hold on prime cable real estate via local broadcast affiliates and cable carriage rules that are written with those local stations in mind.[43] The 1992 Cable Act codified the local power of over-the-air broadcasters in an increasingly wired world. At the heart of the relationship between broadcasters and Multichannel Video Programming Distributors (MVPDs) was the retransmission consent agreement. Local broadcasters could demand that cable systems in their area carry their signal on the same channel number on the system, or, if they chose, they could negotiate a fee for that retransmission. In virtually every market, broadcasters chose to negotiate, and they succeeded, but as part of those negotiations, they nearly always secured the same channel. Since VHF stations were assigned numbers 2–13, local broadcasters were entitled to superior positioning in the cable lineup.

The conglomeration of entertainment channels and the rebalanced relationships between MVPDs and content providers resulted in a proliferation of tough negotiations, and those negotiations were increasingly likely to drag on until the cable company yanked the channels. In the most notorious instance, in 2000 Time Warner Cable dropped ABC Owned & Operated stations (O&O's) when it could not make a deal with Disney.[44] The American television system had produced a dry-run of the "digital cliff" through stalled negotiation. These blackouts were sudden and increasingly frequent, and consumer reactions were important principally for the pressure they could bring to bear on the bargaining table. In the new legal regime, networks needed affiliates not only for the audiences they brought, and not only for their position on the station list, but in order to wield another "must have" channel when they sat down to negotiate with MVPDs.

Lost threatened to change all that as it migrated to a multiplatform distribution model. The local stations would still be essential to the live numbers, and the live numbers still amounted to the lion's share of the series's revenue. But the other platforms seemed to be slipping away from the locals. ABC responded by "geo-targeting" ABC.com versions of the show and allowing affiliates to program—and retain the revenue from— one of the limited, and unskippable, commercial breaks.[45] It was a hybrid solution to a problem that was destined to recur, and it codified the relative balance of power as it stood in 2007.

In short, the affiliate model, however technologically and organizationally residual it might have been, still exerted decisive force on network behavior. But that force was registered and negotiated not simply in economic terms, but through the complex narratives that shuttled from studio through network to affiliate and back. There is a reason *Lost* is centrally concerned with the interrelations between a set of stations and a set of numbers. Ordinarily, we call those channels. At its most manic, in sequences where the economic image is most literally connected to the numbering of time, *Lost* asks us to believe that the key to the entire series lies in the HD resolution number. Down in The Swan station, a doomsday clock counts backward— if it reaches zero, we are led to believe, the world will end. To prevent the apocalypse, one must simply input The Numbers, in order, into the attached computer terminal. The clock then resets to 108 minutes 00 seconds, an order of magnitude less (or greater) than the number of lines at the high end of HD resolution, 1,080. Combinations of 4, 8, 15, 16, 23, and 42 are seeded throughout the series, but the HD numbers are there, too, if you look for them. The training film for The Swan station explains that the two people stationed there will be on the island for 540 days until they are replaced; that is, they will live there for 1,080 workdays, during which time they will punch the button 7,200 times, an order of magnitude greater than the low end of HD resolution, 720. The endless repetition of the numbers station's signal is the endless announcement of the impending HD apocalypse, the collapse of the affiliate model, the digital cliff: always around the corner, and always deferrable. Until it comes, the broadcast day never ends, and the island will transmit its own secret over and over again.

And until it ends, *Lost* perdures in a hybrid televisual culture particular to its era and its network. Emblems of that existence are everywhere in *Lost,* most often in images that are, like the ABC Studios logo itself, divided between analog and digital interaction. In Hurley's Season 1 flashback

FIGURE 6.9 *Hitting the lottery with* Lost.

episode "Numbers" (S1E18), the numerical curse begins when his digital lotto ticket matches his old-fashioned analog tv.

Similarly, in Season 2, on the island, when Sayid rushes to fix the computer that will allow John Locke to enter The Numbers and save the world, we cut back and forth between the circa 1980 cathode-ray tube (CRT) hooked to the digital machine and the decidedly analog doomsday clock. While the fans are busily typing away on their modern computers, the affiliates are threatening armageddon as the analog clock expires.

FIGURE 6.10 *Encoding HD in doomsday.* Lost.

FIGURE 6.11 *Film and video in "Hanso exposed."* Lost.

The hybrid world of *Lost* is best exemplified in the collection of Dharma Initiative "films" that we see over the course of the series. The first of these is called *Hanso Exposed*; bits and pieces of it were dropped all over the internet as part of the ARG "The *Lost* Experience" between broadcast Seasons 1 and 2. When the seventy parts were assembled, they revealed two halves, one a "film" of the mysterious baron behind the island's research stations, one an undercover "video" of the Initiative's skullduggery.

As was the standard at the time, both were 4:3 (YouTube, for instance, did not shift to 16:9 until late 2008).[46] The series, remember, shot on film in widescreen but in the beginning was bound by the 4:3 video standard. The first Dharma Initiative training film they discover reverses that (S2E03, "Orientation").

After establishing that the film is 4:3 it seamlessly jumps out from the pillarbox to reveal a full "widescreen" shot, even going so far as to digitally insert "filmifying" artifacts like the splice line in the figure. The second

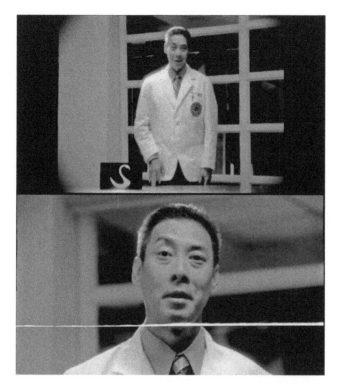

FIGURE 6.12 *Filmifying artifacts and aspect jumping in the works of the Dharma Initiative.* Lost.

training film is discovered on video (both supposedly date from 1980), and it, too, jumps out from 4:3 and inserts digital "videofying" effects like horizontal bands and demag snow (S2E21, "?").

That insistence on format agnosticism—film or video, analog or digital—is bound up with *Lost's* particular technological and network history. And with the end of that historical period, the tensions motivating the series's ersatz medium specificities vanish. The series liquidated and refigured the narrative battle between the "two kinds of fans" in the climactic fight between Jack and Locke (The Man in Black as Locke) atop the island's computer-generated, "digital cliff" (S6E17, "The End").

The series epilogue, *New Man in Charge*, is a twelve-minute postlude that was shot on digital video. It opens with a loving shot of Abrams's letterpress, the ne plus ultra of analog insistence, the spiritual source of the literariness of quality television. The technology, like the warehouse, like the Initiative, is absurd and outdated. Ben Linus arrives, pays off the two guys in the warehouse, and allows each to ask a single question before breaking down and agreeing to watch The Hydra station orientation film

FIGURE 6.13 *Videofying artifacts and aspect jumping in the works of the Dharma Initiative*. Lost.

FIGURE 6.14 *The real, digital, digital cliff*. Lost.

with them. "You guys have a DVD player?" he asks. It's an appropriate question for a workplace that has a letterpress. Ben then conjures the ideal *Lost* viewing party—"So we watch it together, and then we all leave. Is that a deal?"—before apologizing: "Sorry about the quality. It's a transfer from an old Betamax." *Lost's* format agnosticism has been replaced by digital conversion, one that has effaced the difference between film and video. (Although the "film" is supposedly copied from an old Betamax, it only shows evidence of filmifying.) Before, format agnosticism lined up with the series's broader agnosticism: the aim was to perpetuate multiple possibilities, whether they were narrative or medial, in order to intensify the viewing experience: "We're gonna need to watch that again," says John Locke; "Would you like to watch that again?" asks Mr. Eko. Keeping the fans involved was essential for its own sake, but it was just as important that the company find the time to work through the reorganization of the broadcast landscape in the digital era. Now, though, things were different. "I think we're gonna need to see that again," says the stringbean shipping supervisor, echoing *Losties* onscreen and off. "Sorry," Ben apologizes again. "We're out of time."

With this sentence, the series decouples from its fans—they can go on watching and rehashing the program (and some do), but the network no longer needs them. And it no longer needs to worry about "the quality" either—the whole thing has been moved to DVD (and Hulu). The digital turn that had so animated ABC was complete, and without that galvanizing crisis, the network settled back into third place, sometimes fourth. Unable to boost its income through greater ad sales, ABC turned on its affiliates, pressuring them to join a "retransmission clearing house" that would allow the network to negotiate with MVPDs on their behalf in exchange for half the retransmission revenues or substantial licensing fees. Time was, the networks paid affiliates to carry their programming. No more. Network head Anne Sweeney proclaimed triumphantly that broadcast television was now "a multi-revenue-stream business for the first time in history."[47] *Modern Family* (Fox Studios/ABC, 2009–) stepped into *Lost's* abandoned role as the network's laboratory for the study of the multiscreen audience. "Nearly every scene is refracted through a digital funhouse: an iPad screen, a cellphone camera, a baby monitor, a YouTube video. Characters spend half their time glancing past one another rather than communicating directly."[48] It was the series critics turned to when they wanted to know how we live now. Meanwhile, somewhere on Friday nights, *Extreme Makeover: Home Edition* (Endemol/ABC 2003–12) lumbered on. Perhaps no series on television had a more intense relationship with its dwindling and demographically undesirable fanbase. Every week, a deserving family would be trundled off to a Disney theme park while a volunteer army descended upon their home. *EM:HE* was all too legible as a vestige of corporate synergized, Bush-era, compassionate conservative, housing bubble America.

And while it was certainly that, it was also the last surviving ABC series in standard definition and the 4:3 aspect ratio. Upon its cancellation, no one particularly noticed this minor landmark in the combined and uneven history of television technology.

Notes

1 Jennifer Armstrong, "The Scoop on 'Lost,'" *Entertainment Weekly,* September 29, 2005, http://ew.com/article/2005/09/29/scoop-lost/, accessed January 20, 2017.

2 In calling it "The New Television," I mean to highlight its parallels with The New Hollywood: Its discourse of quality, the successful promulgation of auteurist reception protocols, and, finally, the sense that even as we are still coming to terms with the new showrunner-centric models of televisual production we ought to look to incorporate revisionist critiques such as Derek Nystrom's *Hard Hats, Rednecks, Macho Men*; Carlo Rotella's *Good with their Hands: Boxers, Bluesmen, and Other Characters from the Rust Belt* (Berkeley, CA: University of California Press, 2002); and Yvonne Tasker's *Working Girls: Gender and Sexuality in Popular Cinema* (New York: Routledge, 1998). Even Glyn Davis and Gary Needham's "Queer(ying) Lost," *Reading Lost: Perspectives on a Hit Television Show,* ed. Roberta Pearson (London: I.B. Tauris, 2009), 261–80, which gets at the absence of LGBT characters on the show, describes the "Network Context in 2004" as the lingering effects of Janet Jackson's "wardrobe malfunction" and the scheduling decision that put *Lost* up against more gay-centric *America's Next Top Model* following a lead-in from the more hetero *Bachelor*, (263).

3 The notion of franchise stripmining comes from Caldwell.

4 "Welcome to Oahu: The Making of the Pilot," *Lost: The Complete Collection,* season 1 DVD supplement (ABC Studios, 2010).

5 Ibid.

6 Will Brooker argues that "The nature of the downloaded text, with immediate, crystal-clear freeze frame, and the proximity of the viewer to the screen—a matter of inches rather than the full space of a domestic living area between the TV set and the sofa—also encourages and invites close analysis and forensic detection" ("Television Out of Time: Watching Cult Shows on Download," *Reading Lost,* 51–72). The screen situation he describes alters the living room situation as well, where the DVR mediates between a social first viewing and subsequent analysis.

7 As Lindelof explained once the series had wrapped, Abrams's departure gave him "plausible deniability." "When the torch-wielding mob shows up at his house, and they're like, 'Where does the polar bear come from?' he could say, I'm working on *Mission Impossible*, go to Damon." Tim Molloy, "Damon Lindelof's History of *Lost* (A Show He Longed to Quit)," *The Wrap,* September 23, 2011, http://www.thewrap.com/damon-lindelofs-history-lost-show-he-longed-quit-31281/, accessed January 20, 2017.

8 "Planet Lost" *Lost: The Complete Collection*, DVD supplement.

9 Stacey Abbott, "How *Lost* Found its Audience: The Making of a Cult Blockbuster," *Reading Lost*, 9–26; Paul Grainge, "*Lost* Logos: Channel 4 and the Branding of American Event Television," *Reading Lost*, 95–118; and Roberta Pearson, "Introduction: Why Lost?" *Reading Lost*, 1–8.

10 Erika Johnson-Lewis, "'We Have to Go Back': Temporal and Spatial Narrative Strategies," in *Looking for* Lost: *Critical Essays on the Enigmatic Series*, ed. Randy Laist (Jefferson, NC: McFarland, 2011), 11–24, 12. Also Pearson's section "Production and Audiences," detailing "the ways in which the pressures of a rapidly transforming industry have shaped *Lost*'s production and distribution" (Pearson, "Introduction," 2).

11 Henry Jenkins, *Convergence Culture: Where Old and New Media Collide* (New York: New York University Press, 2006); Brooker, "Television out of Time."

12 Brooker, "Television out of Time," 68.

13 "Perhaps even more so than *24, Lost* has used the connectivity of the digital to allow the textual and the everyday to coalesce," Derek Johnson, "Inviting Audiences In: The Spatial Reorganization of Production and Consumption in 'TVIII,'" *New Review of Film and Television* 5, no. 1 (2007): 61–80, 73.

14 Abbott notes the decline only to argue that as a result of the internal rebooting the series becomes textually more like a video game—"each season operates as a level of the game," (Abbott, "How *Lost* Found," 22).

15 In Paul Grainge's account of *Lost* in the UK, the problem of the ratings drop is addressed more directly, and what is worth paying for is brand credibility. Channel Four let *Lost* go after the second season, a move Grainge considered "unsurprising given the escalating cost . . . and the ratings slip . . . from 4.1 million (a 21% audience share) to 2.8 million (16%)." Sky quickly swooped in: "Nevertheless, *Lost* remained a core and sought-after television brand, with Sky One paying £40 million to bring *Lost* to the satellite broadcaster," (Grainge, "*Lost* Logos," 111). Whatever the brand was worth, ratings continued to slip. The third season premiere had 1.4 million viewers (a 5% share of the UK multichannel market), the fifth opened with 946,000, and the final season with 728,000. Jason Deans, "TV Ratings: Lost Returns with More Than 800,000 Viewers," *The Guardian*, February 8, 2010, https://www. theguardian.com/media/2010/feb/08/lost-tv-ratings, accessed 1/20/17. Overall, an 85% hit.

16 Jonathan Gray, "We're Not in Portland Anymore: *Lost* and its International Others," *Reading Lost*, 221–39, 237. Paul Grainge locates that "global community" within the conspiratorial machinations of the series itself. When *Lost* became a satellite-only series in its third season, he notes, the show also became more digital: "Like something born of the Dharma initiative, these [digital] files were transmitted through a data line under the Atlantic Ocean, enabling *Lost* to be converted into the European television format and broadcast in the UK just four days later," (Grainge, "*Lost* Logos," 111). Yet even this more critical appraisal of "planet *Lost*," is functionally identical to the series creators' attempts at self-understanding if we assume that their self-understanding is manifest in textual features like the Dharma Initiative.

17 Johnson, "Inviting Audiences In," 64.

18 The brief exfoliation of Grainge's point about *Lost*'s conspiracy-mongering is the barest hint of what criticism stands to gain by admitting producers' self-reflections to the mix of interpretive objects.

19 Randy Laist, "Introduction," *Looking for Lost*, 1–12, 2.

20 Laist, "Introduction," 4.

21 Jesse Kavadlo, "We Have to Go Back: Lost after 9/11," *Looking for Lost*, 230–42, 232.

22 Kavadlo, "We Have to Go Back," 234.

23 Ibid., 232, citing Chadwick Matlin, "Sweet Mother of God," *Slate*, March 17, 2010, http://www.slate.com/articles/arts/tv_club/features/2010/lost_season_6/season_6_sweet_mother_of_god.html, accessed January 20, 2017.

24 Kavadlo, "We Have to Go Back," 240.

25 Johnson, "Inviting Audiences In," 76.

26 Johnson-Lewis, "We Have to Go Back," 16.

27 The canonical source for the idea that television's liveness is a construction is, of course, Jane Feuer, "The Concept of Live Television: Ontology as Ideology," in *Regarding Television: Critical Approaches—an Anthology*, ed. E. Ann Kaplan (Los Angeles: AFI, 1983), 12–21.

28 Brooker, "Television out of Time," 58.

29 Ibid.

30 One can usefully distinguish this situation from current cinema-going. For movies, no long-standing framework of live, socialized reaction existed: you talk about the movie *after*. Yet the availability of instant social networking through platforms like facebook and twitter quickly altered the usual patterns of word-of-mouth. Where saturation advertising could "buy" a successful opening weekend before the "information cascade" took hold, quicker forms of feedback mean that bad word-of-tweet on the East Coast could wreck Friday evening grosses out West. ("Information cascade," from De Vany, *Hollywood Economics*.) One response would be to accommodate that, and Paramount attempted just such a strategy with the first *Paranormal Activity*. The studio screened the film in a very limited number of college towns using a "demand it" system. At those screenings, they provided terminals in the lobby and encouraged audiences to "tweet your scream." The volume of discussion made sure the film became a trending topic on the micromessaging service. That, in turn, raised awareness, allowing the studio to platform the release. *Paranormal Activity* earned $193 million worldwide.

31 David Rodowick, *The Virtual Life of Film* (Cambridge: Harvard University Press, 2007), 104.

32 Armstrong, "Totally Lost." Whether they were also "like, 'This is a copyright violation,'" goes unsaid.

33 This narrative is derived from several sources, but see especially Federal Communications Commission, "Cable Carriage of Broadcast Stations," *FCC*,

May 26, 2011, http://www.fcc.gov/guides/cable-carriage-broadcast-stations, accessed January 20, 2017; Joel Brinkley, "Getting the Picture: TV Stations Develop New Enthusiasm for Digital Future," *The New York Times,* November 24, 1997, http://www.nytimes.com/1997/11/24/business/getting-the-picture-tv-stations-develop-new-enthusiasm-for-digital-future.html, accessed January 20, 2017; and Michele Hilmes, *Only Connect: A Cultural History of Broadcasting in the United States*, 2nd ed. (Belmont, CA: Thomson-Wadsworth, 2007), 330–33.

34 Brinkley, "Getting the Picture."

35 National Telecommunications and Information Administration, "Outside the Box: The Digital TV Converter Box Coupon Program," December, 2009, https://www.ntia.doc.gov/files/ntia/publications/dtvreport_outsidethebox.pdf, accessed January 20, 2017.

36 Katie Puckrick, "J.J. Abrams: 'I Called Spielberg and He Said Yes'." *The Guardian*, August 1, 2011, http://www.guardian.co.uk/film/2011/aug/01/jj-abrams-spielberg-super-8, accessed January 20, 2017. I discuss Abrams's affection for the analogue and the similarities to Rodowick from the cinematic side in "'He's Building a Model': Steven Spielberg, J.J. Abrams, Scale and *Super 8*," *Media Fields,* 4, http://www.mediafieldsjournal.org/hes-building-a-model/, accessed January 20, 2017.

37 Laist, "Introduction," 2.

38 Josef Adalian, "Disney Dumps Touchstone TV Brand," *Variety,* February 8, 2007, http://variety.com/2007/scene/markets-festivals/disney-dumps-touchstone-tv-brand-1117958953/, accessed January 20, 2017.

39 Paul J. Gough, "DVR Ratings Boost is Quantified," *The Hollywood Reporter*, April 26, 2007, https://www.hollywoodreporter.com/news/dvr-ratings-boost-is-quantified-134903.

40 For an account of the inter-network battle over ratings standards, see Louise Story, "Networks are in an Uproar Over Nielsen ad Ratings," *The New York Times*, November 4, 2006, 4; "Nets Demand DVR Viewing Credit: Take an Early Tough Stance on Live-plus Issue in Advance of Upfront; Agencies Gird for Fight," *Media Week* 17, no. 5 (January 29, 2007) 4. Bill Gorman, "Network Jedi Mind Tricks: Live + 7 Rating and Your Favorite Show," *TV by the Numbers (zap2it)*, October 17, 2010, http://tvbythenumbers.zap2it.com/2010/10/17/network-jedi-mind-tricks-live7-ratings-and-your-favorite-show/68123/, accessed January 20, 2017.

41 See the extensive interview with Anne Sweeney, then president of the Disney-ABC Television Group, "On the download: Dialogue with Anne Sweeney," *The Hollywood Reporter*, September 26, 2006, nexis.

42 One particularly piquant instance of user-generated management consulting came from "Ross":

Dear abc.com,
You suck. I don't want to dwell on how much you suck, so I will briefly tell you why you suck. First and foremost you break one of the most important rules of websites. You make sound without you asking me to.

Youtube, liveleak, metacafe, sites like these are the only ones that get a break on this rule. This is because people follow links directly to a video that they expect to make noise. Please note that the main pages of these sites are silent, as every website should be. It's like a speak when spoken to thing. That's just a precursor to the real issue here, it all has to do with watching videos on your site. The following is why your video player sucks. It opens in a new window, completely unnecessary.
Fullscreen isn't really fullscreen, that progress bar hangs at the bottom. You only work in IE, Firefox and Safari.
The volume control is wonky.
You have to click off the ads to get back to a program you are trying to watch.
In short, you are not hulu. Go take a look at hulu.com for an example of how to do things. You're lucky you have Lost.
"Ross," "Open Letter to ABC.com," *Immediate Regret*, January 30, 2009. http://www.immediateregret.com/2009/01/open-letter-to-abccom.html, accessed August 16, 2012.

43 This handy FCC guide explains that "Commercial stations that have elected must-carry status have the option of requesting carriage on the same channel that they occupy over-the-air, on the channel number that the station occupied on July 19, 1985, or on the channel that the station occupied on January 1, 1992" (Federal Communications Commission, "Cable Carriage").

44 Jim Rutenberg, "Time Warner and Disney reach cable deal for ABC," *The New York Times*, May 26, 2000, http://www.nytimes.com/2000/05/26/business/time-warner-and-disney-reach-cable-deal-for-abc.html.

45 Michael Learmonth, "ABC: Give Us Credit for our Digital Strategy," *Business Insider.* 3/21/08, http://www.businessinsider.com/2008/3/abc-give-us-credit-for-our-digital-strategy, accessed January 20, 2017; Beet.TV, "Albert Cheng, Disney/ABC Television," July 25, 2008, http://www.youtube.com/watch?v=UuYs6vouJ6c, accessed January 20, 2017.

46 Fulton, Scott M. Fulton, III, "What YouTube's New 16:9 Aspect Ratio Means for Users," *Betanews.com*, November 25, 2008, http://betanews.com/2008/11/25/what-youtube-s-new-16-9-aspect-ratio-means-for-users/, accessed January 20, 2017.

47 Anna Carugati, "Anne Sweeney," *Worldscreen.com*, http://worldscreen.com/anne-sweeney/, accessed January 20, 2017; Ronald Grover, "Disney, ABC Station Owners Agree to Share Fees from Pay TV." *Bloomberg.com.* February 17, 2011, http://www.bloomberg.com/news/2011-02-17/disney-abc-station-owners-agree-to-share-fees-from-pay-tv.html, accessed January 20, 2017.

48 Bruce Feiler, "What 'Modern Family' Says about Modern Families," *The New York Times,* January 23, 2011, http://www.nytimes.com/2011/01/23/fashion/23THISLIFE.html, accessed January 20, 2017.

7

The piggies and the market

Myron Scholes, the Chicago-trained, Nobel Prize–winning economist best known as one of the developers of the Black-Scholes-Merton option pricing model, opened his 1970 dissertation by noting that "The shares a firm sells are not unique works of art, but abstract rights to an uncertain income stream for which close counterparts exist either directly or indirectly via combinations of assets of various kinds."[1] For a firm such as TimeWarner, that sentence is true. Scholes is discussing shares of stock, but what makes shares equatable is the same thing that made commodity futures possible and that will make mortgage bonds possible. In *The Big Short*, our heroes discover that the income streams are far more uncertain than the bond ratings imply, and that the compounded, next-level guarantees on those income streams—CDOs, synthetic CDOs—are not only exponentially more fragile, but by occluding the underlying risk, they magnify the inevitable crash. Even in the case of a firm like TimeWarner things are, perhaps, more complicated than Scholes implies. Many of its inputs are suspiciously close to "unique works of art." A screenplay seems to be one, for example. And the outputs of the firm are themselves uncertain income streams. Motion picture production and distribution form a complex alchemy that turns unique-ish artworks into abstract income streams, and what is more, they do so in a context where close counterparts may or may not exist. Indeed, the repertoire of counterparts might include the movies of competing firms, but it might also include other scripts the studio has passed on; other pieces of intellectual property (superheroes) it has not yet developed; other stars it has not cast; other genres it has left untapped.

How close are movies to stocks and bonds? The answer to this question does not depend the fit of the analogy but on an intricate interplay of politics and the market to make the story of that analogy fit. The limited partnerships that were popular in the 1970s and 1980s provided one answer, and as a form of risk syndication, they might be comparatively straightforward. Still, the aftermarket for those shares was miniscule—they were partnerships, not stocks as broadly held as WCI or Disney. In contrast, in early 2010, two companies, Cantor Futures and Media Derivatives, sought permission from the Commodity Futures Trading Commission to offer contracts that would allow for the trade in motion picture futures, specifically their opening weekend box office in the United States. The Motion Picture Association of America (MPAA) lobbied against the practice, and Congress had already agreed to outlaw it by the time the CFTC gave its approval.[2] The industry's argument was, in essence, that while it might be the case that one movie is much like another, the opening weekend returns on a particular movie were too prone to manipulation to be a real market—only a handful of Hollywood movies are released on a given weekend, and the choice of weekend (or the switch of a weekend or a dramatic shift in the number of theaters a movie is going to open in) is enormously important in determining that initial tally.[3]

The industry's argument against the legalization of box office futures presumes that attempts to contain risks cannot be undertaken without undermining the stability of the system as a whole. And that presumes, because it must, that there are, indeed, ways of intentionally altering both the course of individual pictures and through them the system as a whole. (In the terms of the introduction, it presumes that a strong reading of De Vany is untrue.) We might draw two lessons from this. First, the tension between unique works of art and uncertain revenue streams continues to structure Hollywood finance. Second, the industry exploits that tension in order to do what it has always done—maintain control over decisionmaking while working its way through a seemingly endless parade of suckers, as *The Big Short* called them (as Brad Pitt called himself). So at an industry-wide level the MPAA can successfully head off the emergence of a motion pictures futures market while several of its members pursue similar relations with deep-pockets partners.

If individual players within the industry undertake complex mathematical operations and their visualization in order to determine or at least bolster their commitments to particular projects, they are, nonetheless, still required to produce Caldwellian theories of their operations and they are still required to enlist their contractual partners in their goals. Hence efforts like the Moneyball Initiative. Just as a studio with a first-look deal with a star will calibrate her prominence against its level of perceived risk, so the industry calibrates the explicitness of its self-theorizations. Studios tend to produce theories that are capacious, implicit, and allegorical; independents produce theories that are niche and explicit. Studios make *Jaws*; indies make *Swimming with Sharks*. Thinking about the interplay of markets and numbers, studios make *Wall Street*, indies make *Pi*. Thinking about global trade and labor exploitation, studios make *Captain Philips*, indies make *Leviathan*. In what follows, I consider instances of local theorizing of motion picture production in the wake of the Great Recession at different plateaux of explicitness: *Pacific Rim* (Guillermo del Toro, Legendary/WB 2013), *Contagion* (Steven Soderbergh, Participant/WB 2011), and *Upstream*

Color (Shane Carruth, erbp 2013). These are figurations of cognition and control that simultaneously track and forecast the institutions and affects of the contemporary economy.

This last claim, read one way, is as banal as the claim with which I opened the book, that Hollywood thinks about capitalism by telling stories about money. But I mean to argue at a higher level of abstraction here: these movies think about the *narratives* of economic collapse by telling stories about cognition and control. What I have generally been describing as allegories of corporate or industrial behavior in which representations of the economy serve as the ground through which studios and others come to understand their own operations are here inverted. In these movies, models of thinking or the spread of ideas shape and suggest explanations for the distance between the operations of the economy and understandings of it. These are still self-reflections since the companies involved must somehow come to terms with the pressures to financialize motion picture production. But as they find application in recession stories these models take on a wider significance.

This is the difference between the recession as theme and recession as thematic. The target of this thematic varies among the causes of, responses to, and extended duration of the recession. Within economic circles, there was significant debate at the time, and there remains significant disagreement, over the causes of the Great Recession, in particular whether it can be blamed on the bursting of the housing bubble or the financial crisis.[4] While no one doubts that the two are complicatedly interwoven, a correct diagnosis matters a good deal to the design of macroprudential policies that might avoid such catastrophes going forward. A similar debate persists over whether U.S. government's response to the bank run was wise. Should Lehman Brothers have been allowed to fail? Should insurance giant AIG? The standard advice, from Walter Bagehot's *Lombard Street* (1873), is to loan into the crash, at tough terms, against assets that are safe. What the Fed did was not that—it loaned freely against assets that were probably safer than the market had priced them. The terms were ridiculously easy.[5]

Finally, the question remains as to why, if assets were cleared and repriced, the economy took so long to recover. Why would the failure of a single U.S. institution—Lehman—and the bailout of others have spilled over so devastatingly into Europe? Here, again, the explanations diverge: (1) The market in mortgage-backed securities and the insurance against them had become so enormous that everyone was involved. (2) The institutions at risk were properly global—this is what "Too Big To Fail" implied—and so even if the risky assets hadn't been held globally, these enormous banks would have imperiled the system. (3) The bad assets that we think of as primarily American were, in fact, available for other markets—Ireland and Spain had their own bubbles. (4) The bank run sparked a market-wide repricing of risk even in markets not directly implicated; leveraged borrowers became unwilling or unable to take on more debt, and this "debt-deleveraging" shock took time to work its way through the global economy because wages and prices were sticky. (5) Interest rates were so low that nothing the Fed and other lenders of last resort could do to reflate prices quickly enough. (6) The responses of state- and supra-state actors either depressed recovery through aggressive attempts to return to normal interest rates or insufficient fiscal stimulus. (7) The commitment by central banks to low interest rates paradoxically encouraged borrowers to sit on the sidelines and defer investments. Many of these might be marshalled in combination.

My expertise is too limited to be able to confidently decide among these explanations, but then so is Hollywood's. For the motion picture industry, the various accounts of causes, responses, and duration may be attractive because it is an industry increasingly dependent on hedge fund partners while it is simultaneously enmeshed in a pitched public battle against motion picture derivative markets. But the convergence between explanations of the industry's current financial arrangements and explanations of the Great Recession are useful less because the industry needs to be correct about the economics and more because each account, unspooled, suggests a group of narratives, a set of moral positions within them, and a scope or scale of social involvement. Housing bubble movies will tend toward depictions of labor, domesticity, and the gothic—zones where a fundamental mismatch between individual action and systemic responsibility is prevalent. Financial crisis movies will tend toward depictions of intellectual hubris, interpersonal betrayal, and sorcerer's apprentice-style unforeseen consequences. Housing bubble movies operate in moral universes and at scales as different as *Noah* (Darren Aronofsky, Paramount 2014), *Magic Mike* (Soderbergh, WB 2012), and *99 Homes* (Ramin Bahrani, Broad Green/Image Nation 2015). If these scales constitute tranches of moviemaking, what I am offering is something like the CDO of the underlying financial crisis cinema.

At the same time, moviemakers' attempts to use industrially inflected models to reinterpret the recession are not greatly distant from sociological attempts to account for the embeddedness of the ostensibly abstract operations of the relevant markets.[6] Where economists' accounts of markets rarely involve agents and when they do those agents possess high, although varying, degrees of ideality, and where more popular accounts such as those of Michael Lewis and Matt Taibbi may give outsized weight to characters' blindspots and foibles, the work of economic sociologists, Donald MacKenzie in particular, has analyzed the institutions and practices that mediate the two extremes. The results are exceptionally powerful accounts of the dynamics, habits, and fragilities of the system. As part of a generally actor-network theoretical approach derived from Bruno Latour and Michel Callon, MacKenzie shows, for example, that the wildly different evaluations of risk applied to mortgage-backed securities and collateralized debt obligations were the logical outcome of separated "clusters of evaluation practices" that evolved over time within banks and other financial institutions. Those differences allowed for the extreme arbitrage that occurred.[7] Where MacKenzie describes the performativity of economic models—the way those models shape practices and institutions—I see the models of motion picture production, distribution, and reception shaping understandings of the limits of narrative and formal comprehension.

Soderbergh responded to the last-minute cancellation of *Moneyball* with a flurry of "end of career" productions including *Haywire*, *Side Effects*, *Contagion*, and the movie that was the most personally profitable for him, *Magic Mike*.[8] In this period of flux, the director seemed to understand his newly precarious position as an occasion for dramatic self-authorization, the chance to constitute a system out of his own replicable actions. And he did so by taking the foundations and disruptions of systematicity as his central objects. Where *Haywire* and *Magic Mike* are built around routines in the sense of staged numbers—fights and dances—*Side Effects* and *Contagion* are built around ideas of routine—the clinical trial and the ritual. More specifically, the ebola-style story of *Contagion* is built around three central modes of repetition, each at a different scale: viral replication, a process of reproduction so nearly uncontrollable and so swift that it verges on abstraction; protocols, which the movie operationalizes as things bureaucrats are supposed to do in the handling and allocation of objects; and rituals, which in their regular repetition compose the social.

Once we recognize viral replication as ritual at scale, *Contagion*'s central social story comes into focus. This is a movie about deritualization—the evacuation of repeatable forms of social interaction. Matt Damon's Mitch Emhoff is the center of that narrative. He relishes the regularities, even the insipidities of suburban life; his earnest shlubbiness is doubtless part of what has driven his wife Beth (Gwyneth Paltrow) to carry on an affair. She will be the crucial vector for the disease, passing it on to a host of others in Macau before carrying it back to her lover in Chicago and her family in Minneapolis. But when the funeral home refuses to handle Beth's burial, the social consequences of the new epidemic become clearer. A step up the social ladder deritualization takes on an official cast when the Centers for Disease Control (CDC) recommends "social distancing." That distancing will take shape as Mitch's refusal to allow his daughter's boyfriend to visit. Late in the film, Mitch will almost comically knock on his (dead) neighbor's front door before breaking in the house and stealing a shotgun. He will be carrying the gun when he physically drags his daughter's boyfriend away from her as they are about to kiss for the first time. It is nearly a parody of Freudian paternal anxiety, but one given fresh justification by the lethality of the virus. The culmination of this deritualization plot will come in the penultimate scene when Mitch sets up a "PROM NIGHT" in the living room for his daughter and the boyfriend he has been holding off throughout the movie. That paternal hand-off—that sliver of patriarchal restoration—is the nugget of the social.

Protocols amount to bureaucratized rituals, and they guide the actions of doctors and other public health workers at the CDC, the World Health Organization (WHO), and elsewhere. But in the movie's narrative, nearly every doctor breaks protocol in favor of some other, smaller-scale ritual, with varying consequences. The one notable exception to this rule-breaking is Kate Winslet's Dr. Mears, an ultra-competent CDC doctor who mounts the Minneapolis response before coming down with the disease. The other major public health bureaucrats are arrayed along a scale of violations and consequences. Lawrence Fishburne's Dr. Cheever will illicitly tip off his girlfriend that Chicago will be quarantined. He is found out, threatening his career and the credibility of the institution. He seeks some redemption when he gives his priority vaccine dose to the child of a CDC janitor. Elliott Gould's Dr. Sussman will disobey an order to shut down his research only to discover the animal sources of the virus. Chin Han's Chinese public health service officer will kidnap WHO epidemiologist Dr. Orantes (Marion Cotillard) in order to enable his village to jump the line. Unbeknownst to him, when the vaccine finally becomes available, the village will be given only placebo. Finally, Jennifer Ehle's Dr. Hextall will inject herself with a promising vaccine and expose herself to the virus in order to speed along the development process. It is a success.

These two plots—deritualization and protocol breaching—converge at the beginning of Act III when Hextall and Cheever discuss the unconscionably long timeline to a vaccine as it moves through approvals, human trials, manufacturing, and distribution. This is the conversation just before Hextall breaks protocol, but the conversation matters just as much because at its end, she will wish Cheever a merry Christmas and he will return the wish. They both say it ironically; the ritual is, nonetheless, reestablished. The two plots converge again when Hextall visits her dying father and kisses his forehead, exposing herself to the virus. And the two modes will converge again, most explicitly, when Cheever vaccinates the janitor's son and takes the time to explain the importance of the handshake—that it originated to show that you were unarmed.

If it seems that this story is the story that it seems to be—a public health story—the third mode of action, virality, is both the encapsulation of that story and its inversion. For *Contagion*, the primacy of the social is paired with a complementary horror at the material and its distribution. Throughout Act I, we are treated to closeups and inserts of objects that carry the virus—fomites. Since the viruses are, in these images, invisible, the terror of the epidemic is carried by the mismatch between the cinematic ostension (look at *this!*) and the complete absence of anything visible beyond the object itself. Those objects are often marked by their roles in social circulation: a credit card, a poker chip, a martini glass, a subway pole, a pen, and a contract. They are also, in this opening section, quickly associated with forms and spaces of transit: planes, ferries, buses, a company car, an elevator.

But *Contagion*'s interest in virality is not limited to the material. Through the story of Alan Krumwiede, Jude Law's character, virality extends to its digital form, and how that digital form encompasses media and capital. Law's character begins the film hoping to pick up freelance work for the *San Francisco Chronicle*; he has latched on to a video of a Japanese victim and believes, correctly, that this might be the start of a new plague. The *Chronicle*'s freelance budget has, like those of other traditional newsmedia, been decimated, and he is turned away. "Print media is dying!" he exclaims on the way out; later, and complementarily, when the editor, now literally dying, comes begging to him for doses of the forsythia he has touted as a miracle cure, he will turn *her* away. Instead of print, he concentrates on his blog. As it becomes more popular, he draws the attention of a local hedge fund interested in his ability to forecast the future. At this point, the connections between Law's virality and the virus's are not simply narrative or punning; they are formal. Whenever the virus appears in a new city, an on-screen title gives us both the name of the city and its population in millions. And millions are Law's numbers: when he meets with his hedge fund guy, he touts his "uniques"—first 2 million, then 12 million. Those 12 million trust him—not because they should but because, as he puts it, "that's the brand"—and they will later come to his rescue, putting up his bail after he is hauled in by the SEC for "securities fraud, conspiracy, and most likely manslaughter." Offscreen, he has made $4.5 million in the market for his sham cure. Onscreen, we make an EMH cut from the Homeland Security agent listing the charges against him and Alan protesting that his blood is his property to a shot of the tumbling lottery balls that will determine the vaccination schedule for the world.

In the concluding montage—after the virus has done its horrible work, after individuals and institutions have attempted to come to terms with it, and after the rituals that the virus eradicated have begun to be restored— we are given a brief history of its origins. The disease's vectors are utterly plausible: a bat, a pig, a chef, a globetrotting executive, their handshake. The inciting event is utterly plausible as well—the deforestation that forces the bats to look for new locales, chasing them into the hog barn. What plants the movie firmly in Michael Lewis's world of moral economy is that Beth Emhoff, the first victim, works for the deforesting company, and so her death is a kind of moral blowback. And what plants the movie firmly in Hollywood's contemporary moral economy is that the dangerous deforestation occurs in China. (With sovereign wealth fund Image Nation [formerly ImageNation Abu Dhabi] involved, this was not going to be a movie about something like MERS. Abu Dhabi is named as a victim of the virus, not its source.)

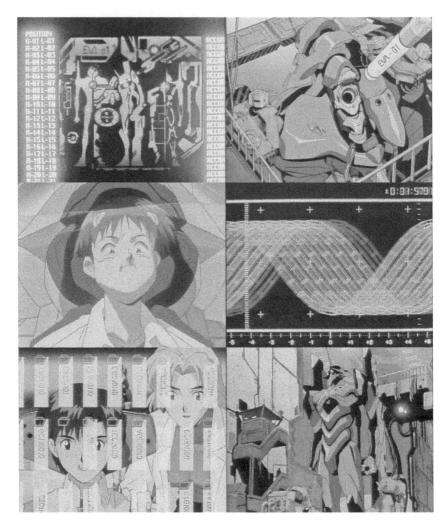

FIGURE 7.1 *Origins of The Drift.* Neon Genesis Evangelion, *Hideaki Anno, Gainax, 1995.*

Contagion was distributed by Warner Bros., and it was put together and released at a time when that studio, perhaps more than any other, was forced to rethink its relationship to the Chinese market. The studio's characteristic efforts at global cultural understanding through loving portraits of local organized crime syndicates had hit a major snag. Worried that the Chinese government and its monopoly distributor CFC would refuse to screen *The Dark Knight*, with its Hong Kong storyline centering on gangster Mr. Lao (Chin Han) and featuring a cameo by scandal-plagued Edison Chen,

FIGURE 7.2 *Interpersonal, intercorporate, international: Scenes from The Drift.* Pacific Rim, *del Toro, Legendary/Warner Bros., 2013.*

Warners avoided even submitting the movie for distribution in China.[9] Having censored itself, the studio's response was, essentially, inception, an attempted inception *on* China and a willingness to shape *Inception* to undo the mess of *Dark Knight*. That process worked.[10] Yet Warners is also a studio with a deep sense of vengeance, and *Contagion* fit the bill. The film was unreleasable under anything like the current PRC censorship regime since it located the origin of its epidemic in mainland China, channeled its spread through both Hong Kong and Macau, and portrayed Chinese public health officials (again led by Chin Han) as willing to kidnap a WHO doctor for personal gain. That the moral responsibility for the epidemic lies firmly with the globetrotting American executive and that the kidnappers are portrayed so sympathetically that even Cotillard's Orantes takes their side would have made little difference.

Pacific Rim (2013) liquidates that history, or attempts to, by safely screening the Sino-U.S. relationship behind the Japanese source material. It is an age-old story of Kaiju versus Jaegers, or Giant Fucking Monsters versus Giant Fucking Robots, as director Guillermo del Toro put it.[11] The climactic setting may be Hong Kong, but the romance is between Mako and Raleigh. That romance grows deeper when the two of them share the piloting of an enormous robot. The cockpit in *Pacific Rim* incorporates key elements from the mecha classic *Neon Genesis Evangelion*. Those elements include the entry plug, the bidirectional relationship between pilot and machine, and, most importantly, the psychic link. In the cartoon, that link runs between the pilot and the spirit of his mother; in *Pacific Rim*, the "neural handshake" runs between the pilots.

Pacific Rim takes the human-machine "synchronization ratio" of the anime and reconfigures it as "the drift." "The deeper the bond, the better you fight." The two-pilot system in the giant robots compensates for the overwhelming "neural load" they require. One can't be a solo Jaeger pilot for long. Raleigh (Charlie Hunnam) discovers this in Gipsy Danger in Act I, Newton (Charlie Day) discovers something similar in Act II, and in Act III we learn that Stacker (Idris Elba), their boss, managed it years earlier and now faces dangerous health consequences. Sharing the load requires an antecedent personality connection called "the drift," so compatible partners end up being those who have preexisting relations: brothers, a father and son, lovers. The social structures—sibling rivalry, filial piety, romance—suggest subgenres within the movie. But, as it happens, those other forms go unexplored, although we do see a triplet bond of Chinese brothers and a pair of Russian siblings.

Each pilot is, ostensibly, responsible for one hemisphere of the Jaeger's brain, but they work in tandem when they are running. That partnership is available for multiple deployments. The hemispheric analogy in the division of labor works as well as a division of the global marketplace, with Raleigh the West and Mako the East. It can also allegorize the corporate partnership between Warners and Legendary. Legendary shared production costs on a slate of Warners pictures beginning in 2005. The shared expenses allowed the companies to spread out the risk in any given instance in a quasi–De Vanian way and, most important, to pursue a strategy heavy on tentpoles.[12] That strategy, in turn, rested on a belief that while the absolute levels of risk would rise with the budget, high-priced event pictures would be less risky than, say, mid-level star vehicles.

Legendary began as a hedge fund run by Thomas Tull, and like other fund managers, he entered the movie business in search of returns. Over the years, as he and the company became more familiar with the industry and more confident in their abilities, they pushed to strike out on their own. On several occasions, they looked to escape their long-term partnership with Warners, or to set up additional vehicles—Legendary East in China was the crucial one—only to come back. This is a story of corporate competency, but, as one would expect, it is also a story about the emergence of a separable brand. Legendary announced it would move to Universal in July 2013, the same week that *Pacific Rim* opened in the United States. In short, in this movie, Legendary came into its own.[13]

If the A plot of the movie consists of the jockeying among the Jaeger pilots for partnership and control—let's call this Warners' version of corporate cooperation—the B plot consists of the scientists' attempts to predict and understand the causes of the Kaiju infestation in the first place. One of them, a clichéd neurasthenic Brit with a limp, relies on predictive mathematics. The other, a pseudopunk American, is fascinated by DNA. As the mathematician announces that the Kaiju will be coming ever more quickly, he takes time to declaim, "Numbers do not lie. Politics and poetry, promises—these are lies. Numbers are as close as we get to the handwriting of God." Meanwhile, the American is elbows deep in Kaiju entrails. Numbers versus guts, literally. In order to understand and not simply predict Kaiju behavior, the American jury-rigs a device to "drift" with a leftover brain fragment. The drift nearly kills him—that same neural overload—but he realizes that the monsters are all clones and are being used as part of a strategy of colonization.

To learn more, though, he needs access to another, more complete brain, and to find that brain, Stacker dispatches him to Hannibal Chau, the king of the Kaiju underground in Hong Kong. That man is located in a secretive compound at the corner of Fong Road and Tull Streets, his logo is suspiciously similar to that of Legendary's, and he, too, has tried to drift with a Kaiju in the past.

Warners' interest in the drift is romantic; Legendary's is cognitive, a kind of market handshake. As Linda Obst described Legendary in her 2013 business memoir *Sleepless in Hollywood*, "Its CEO, Thomas Tull, has invested in the *Dark Knight* franchise, *Inception*, and the *Hangover* movies, so we expect his decision-making to be refined, despite the first choice for his [Chinese] venture, an epic about the building of the Great Wall. I take this as a getting-to-know-you kind of gesture."[14] And getting-to-know-you is dangerous. As Chau puts it, the drift is "a two-way street, a bridge," and so while the scientist has learned about the Kaiju, they have learned about him, and now they are coming for him. Only when he gets access to a fresh Kaiju brain can the American drift again, with the Brit coming along for the ride, both to share the neural load and to test out his predictive theories. The movie manages to hold on to that sort of utopian sharing through the end, through the romance between the leads, up to the moment when one Jaeger will piggyback on another in order to be dropped into The Rift whence the Kaiju enter our world.

Contagion is the story of the market written in the pathways of bodies—the paths they take through the social they compose and the paths within those bodies themselves. *Pacific Rim* is the story of the market caught between the rift through which monstrous flops appear and the drift in which we are all on the same page. *Upstream Color*, the smallest film of the three, is the story of the market as a cycle of material exploitation. Since it is less narratively obvious, I will briefly summarize it.

Early in the movie, we are shown the effects of a particular worm. Once ingested, it opens a person's will to external manipulation. In the first instance, this appears as a sort of magical sync, a balletic or capoeiristic version of the calibration sequence from *Pacific Rim*. But the worm's power is put to nefarious purposes by a character called The Thief. He takes control of a woman, Kris, and, over the course of several days, liquidates all her assets. Now infected with the worm, Kris is drawn into an open field by

FIGURE 7.3 *Looking for Legendary East, at the corner of Tull & Fong.* Pacific Rim, *del Toro, Legendary/Warner Bros., 2013.*

another man, The Sampler, who removes the worm by transplanting it into the body of a pig.

Kris returns to her life, not knowing what has happened. Offscreen, she loses her job and her house. The powers of the worm and the malign intentions of The Thief make this a very particular sort of answer to the Santellian talking point that "nobody made these people take out those mortgages." Here, someone does.

Two paths emerge. The Sampler keeps the infected pigs in a pen where he can walk among them and, through resonance, register the emotional states of their human counterparts. In these scenes, he appears as a silent hovering figure near his targets as they live out emotional moments, often repeated in several close variations. A sound artist, The Sampler then transcribes those emotional states, musicalizes them, and releases the compositions on his own label, Quinoa Valley. In the wake of her vermectomy, Kris encounters Jeff who, unbeknownst to either of them, has been through a similar process. As it happens, Kris's pig and the pig corresponding to Jeff mate; the

FIGURE 7.4 *Capoeiristic sync.* Upstream Color, *Carruth, erpb, 2013.*

human counterparts do as well. The Sampler takes the subsequent litter and tosses it into the river. This sets off a resonant panic in Kris and Jeff, and they take refuge in their bathtub, shifting the movie's housing crisis from bad mortgages to doomsday prepping. As the piglets decay, they release the parasite which infects certain orchids, turning them blue. The Orchid Harvesters collect them and The Thief buys them. The cycle, in all its rickety contingency, is complete.

All this time, Kris and Jeff have been searching for the source of their torments and links, eventually tracing things back to The Sampler. The key, here, is Kris's automatic recall of *Walden*, the text she was made to transcribe to pass the time while under the control of The Thief, and a text that documents another sort of housing crisis. Just as The Sampler is able to bridge pigs and people, so newly awakened Kris is able to do the same,

FIGURE 7.5 *Rehosting the parasite.* Upstream Color, *Carruth, erpb, 2013.*

moving in a series of EMH cuts from the empty office space made possible by the commercial real estate downturn to The Sampler's farm, where she kills him. Kris and Jeff then contact the other victims of the cycle. They all come together to make contact with their pigs, and through the pigs, with the possibility of rebuilding their lives and their society.

Why pigs? *Contagion* suggests one reason: Pigs are plausible carriers of such a parasite. Similarly, pigs are reliable analogs of human sociality, whether in George Miller's *Babe* or Michael Haneke's *Bennys Video*. Pigs were also topical. In March 2013, as *Upstream Color* was making its way through the festival circuit, dead pigs began appearing in rivers in southern China, the latest in a string of eco-disaster reports. "Thousands of Dead Pigs Found in River Flowing Into Shanghai"; "With 6,000 Dead Pigs in River, Troubling Questions on Food Safety"; "A Tide of Death, but This Time Food Supply is Safe," the headlines in the *New York Times* read.[15] And for anyone with ecological leanings, the history of hog lagoon flooding in the American south, particularly in the wake of Hurricane Floyd is notorious.[16] But why pigs and *this* parasite? The answer, I think, comes from a 2008 report in the *Times* on a particular neurological disorder that seemed to be concentrated in workers at a state-of-the-art pork processing plant in Minnesota. As it turned out, they were using compressed air to evacuate the brain cavities of the pigs, which aerosolized the brain matter. It was then inhaled and the workers began to show symptoms like those of other encephalopathies. Pork brains are not widely consumed in the United States, but this plant produced enormous quantities for export to China. Chinese pork consumption has skyrocketed as the Chinese economy has grown, and increases in American pork production are directed almost entirely at foreign markets. This story thus offers the crucial background components of the *Upstream Color* scenario: economic transformation, cognitive alteration, and pigs.[17]

If aerosolized hog brains underlie the scenario, they do not explain the movie's form or its social valence. In a perceptive discussion of sound and politics in the movie, Amy Herzog aligns Carruth's apparent revolutionary pessimism with the work of Michel Sèrres in *The Parasite*—down to particular references to the text. In contrast, on my reading the movie seems instead to justify revolutionary action even when that action cannot be certain of the merits of its target. Kris kills The Sampler, who may or may not "deserve it," not The Thief, who seems a better candidate, but also not The Orchid Gatherers, who seem nearly innocent. Is she right to do so? Are she and the other victims and their corresponding pigs liberated for one another and by one another? Or are these final moments a sad parody of real freedom? Such questions are difficult to answer, and at the heart of that difficulty lie the diffuse responsibility and deep cyclicality of the market. The movie, after all, opens with The Thief recycling one of his victim's Walden transcriptions—he's a felon, but he's eco-friendly. What, indeed, is the relationship of this movie to the market?

FIGURE 7.6 *The joys of homeownership.* Upstream Color, *Carruth, erpb, 2013.*

Caleb Crain, discussing the role of *Walden* in *Upstream Color*, pursues a similar question.

> If movies are dreams, and if dreams represent disguised wishes, then Hollywood movies, created by many hands under high economic pressure, disguise the wishes of something like the hive mind of capitalism. The symbols and myths in a box-office hit contain fantasies that many people want to believe, or that their socioeconomic superiors want them to believe. An interpreter may enjoy exposing a hit movie's fantasy, but he would usually be wrong to mistake what he finds there for an artist's vision of the world. The hive mind doesn't come into a movie like "Upstream Color" at all—except, perhaps, as an object of analysis. "There isn't a molecule of Hollywood that touched this," Carruth has boasted to *Wired*.[18]

The essay as a whole seems to give Carruth's contention sufficient credit, but there remains an essential difference between Crain's claim about the hive mind and Carruth's claim about molecules of Hollywood. (There is also the characteristic underestimation of Hollywood's ability to treat its hive mind as an object of analysis, which even a movie such as *Pacific Rim* can do.) *Upstream Color* undertakes an experiment in materialism, in particular a materialism of cognition, and as such if it had been touched by Hollywood it would necessarily be compromised. For Carruth, there is no way to distinguish between contagion and what Crain calls "analysis." And as a result, Carruth ends up defending the production in terms that are proximate to the idea of a hive mind. He is worth quoting at length:

> Once the language was established, there's something that ha-happened— and I know everybody sort of knows this, but for some reason, I had to,

I had to figure it out on my own or whatever, and it's something I'm trying to embrace now which is just the [sigh] the—I and the filmmakers— the other filmmaking team, we have to have what we're doing so well internalized that we can go in and make choices that are seemingly improvisational but informed by thematically what we're trying to accomplish. And I'm—I used to be very skeptical about that because it's very easy to fake your way through that I think, um and I'm trying to become more and more open to it because I think it's a real thing and I think it really happened.[19]

Carruth likens this collective process to musical improvisation, and then to an extended conversation, before settling on his sharpest description: "this, this sort of network storm of activity." That sense of shared improvisation and internalized control has been the go-to utopia of independent production for decades. Walter Murch, discussing the final act of *THX–1138*—the chase sequence where our hero manages to escape when the costs of the chase exceed the budgetary limits—asks the basic question, "Why are films basically on time and on budget? I think it has to do with the amount that people follow their own intuition and are somehow intuitively tied in to the intuition of others."[20] He, like Carruth, casts about for a model of shared cognition—it is like choreography, it is like homeostatic regulation, it is intuition, it is a gut feeling. Carruth has cast his lot, for the purposes of this movie, with matter and resonance, with something that arguably looks like revolution and with something that looks like collectivity.

That is, as I said, an independent model, just as the militarized romance of *Pacific Rim* is a particular sort of major studio model. As del Toro put it at the Comic-Con panel, "I'm barren, otherwise I would bear Legendary's child." Alongside the giant fucking robots and monsters, "He praised the company for letting him find 'the perfect fucking actors for the role. To make a movie with this size and this scope and be able to cast with the greatest fucking actors is a dream come true.'"[21] Between the indie network storm and the boosterish studio bromance, we find Soderbergh's studio-indie hybrid. It stands against the viral much in the way that the old media of newspaper reporting stands against blogging. Again Law's Alan is the vehicle for the equation of bureaucratic public health work and motion picture production. By his final meeting with the hedge funder, the official vaccine is beginning to make its way into the world. Alan remains dubious, "Just wait, they'll start listing side effects like the credits at the end of a movie."

For Soderbergh's model to succeed, directors must be given both resources and independence. On the verge of (temporary) retirement, he believed that was no longer the case:

The worst development in filmmaking—particularly in the last five years—is how badly directors are treated. It's become absolutely horrible the way the people with the money decide they can fart in the kitchen, to put it bluntly. It's not just studios—it's anyone who is financing a film. I guess I don't understand the assumption that the director is presumptively wrong about what the audience wants or needs when they are the first audience, in a way. And probably got into making movies because of being in that audience.

But an alarming thing I learned during *Contagion* is that the people who pay to make the movies and the audiences who see them are actually very much in sync.[22]

Law, the viral blogger, sits between the hedge fund and his audience in much the same way that Soderbergh sits between "the people who pay to make the movies and the audiences." Until he is arrested, Law keeps those two sides "in sync." He articulates the aspects of the digital in ways that threaten the primacy of cinema, or that threaten to replace a Soderberghian cinema of protocols, violations, and social rituals with digital provocations. When we last see Law, he is filming folks waiting in line for vaccine and attempting to persuade them not to take it.

Contagion offers an alternative to this money-virus-audience network centered on the director. In place of a long timeline stretching from financing to reception, Soderbergh suggests a much more constrained model that extends only from "the kitchen" where the director is cooking to his viewing of the movie as the "first audience." Even as he is retiring, Soderbergh regards production in utopian terms. In the same interview, he strikes a centrist-liberal, post-ideological stance: "I've stopped being embarrassed about being in the entertainment industry, because I'm surrounded by intelligent people who solve problems quickly and efficiently, primarily because issues of ideology don't enter into the conversation." The model for that problem solving is an urban disaster on the scale of one of the cities in *Contagion*:

> The movie and TV business is, for all its inefficiencies, one of the best-run big businesses we have. It's very transparent, financially, and the only business I know of that successfully employs trickle-down economics: When movies and shows make money, the profits go right back into making more movies and shows, because the stock price is all about market share. . . . I look at Hurricane Katrina, and I think if four days before landfall you gave a movie studio autonomy and a hundredth of the billions the government spent on that disaster, and told them, "Lock this place down and get everyone taken care of," we wouldn't be using that disaster as an example of what *not* to do. A big movie involves clothing, feeding, and moving thousands of people around the world on a tight schedule. Problems are solved creatively and efficiently within a budget.[23]

This paean to bureaucracy-on-location has analogues throughout Soderbergh's work—the CDC and WHO in *Contagion* are only the most readily available. In the midst of widespread deritualization—at the hands of the virus or the viral—bureaucracy reassembles the social. And because Soderbergh is committed to a liberal understanding of the relationship between organization and identity, those bureaucrats' lives are given meaning through their participation, as they shape the organization through their efforts and flaws. Yet however staunchly Soderbergh's movies support governmental and nonprofit institutions of social betterment, his own work occurs within a search for market share and profit. The argument onscreen may be made on behalf of institutions of the technocratic state, but the root of that argument no longer originates in the state as such. Instead, it emerges from a particular conception of the role of institutions of cultural production in the market.

To speculate, that conception found purchase in the wake of a widespread delegitimation of technocratic expertise at the state level. Economic crises and political failures had combined with a vast intellectual effort to subordinate social action to (ostensibly) unguided marketization. That effort, epitomized by the work of the Chicago School, had its cultural corrolaries, some of which I outlined in Chapter 3. At the same time, and by a conservation of technocratic and managerial skill, that technocratic authority migrated into figures we might call "market technocrats," such as the architect and the motion picture director.[24] Without a vision of widespread social justice and achievement, the offices and worksites of these market technocrats became "limited utopias" to use Maryanne DeKoven's phrase.[25] These are small, usually temporary societies that are manageable in a collaborative or collective or even cooperative way within the sheltering confines of the market. The professionals who oversee them are superbly positioned to fashion a culture of neoliberalism because they live the contradiction between independent action and the capacity to deploy large numbers of people, where the deployment of those people requires both their submission to the demands of capitalism and something more.

Here, within sight of these utopias, transcendence stems from belief in the purposes of the organization rather than the purposes of class or nation, so it can appear that professional work is the model for all social action. It is not that you go to work in order to make things better for your family and your country and machinists around the globe. It is that you go to work because you believe in the project. And for that belief to exist, there has to be a scalar passage from the kind of work *you* do to the minds of others and on to the system as a whole. That passage—the drift in *Pacific Rim*, the bridge in *Upstream Color*, the combination of thudding irony and microsocial practice in *Contagion*—is emblematic and must be so, not so that moviemakers can create an allegory of the economy outside of and uncontaminated by Hollywood, but rather so that such a reading of this fundamental economic image can become available *inside* the system. Soderbergh waxing utopian about Hollywood's Katrina response, del Toro wishing he could bear the studio's child, Carruth, despite himself, coming to believe in the social, organismic magic of the production: those are all readings, all offered and marketed as further instances of industrial discourse, but, at the same time, as further instances of belief. Such readings and such passages differ from one another as unique works of art will; through the equation of pictures they can be compelled to resemble one another by critics or futures traders as the need arises.

Notes

1 Myron Scholes, 1970 p1, cited in Donald MacKenzie, *An Engine, Not a Camera: How Financial Models Shape Markets* (Cambridge, MA: MIT 2008), 104.

2 Paul Harris, "Cantor Trading Proposal Approved," *Variety*, June 29, 2010, http://variety.com/2010/film/news/cantor-trading-proposal-approved-1118021184/, accessed January 20, 2017.

3 See the testimony of Robert Pisano, interim CEO of MPAA, Subcommittee on General Farm Commodities and Risk Management, *Hearing to Review Proposals to Establish Exchanges Trading "Movie Futures,"* April 22, 2010, 42. It should also be said about these contracts and about the seemingly ineradicable tendency in entertainment economics to use opening weekend domestic box office to make calculations of profitability, that just because the number is widely reported does not make it a useful metric for judging anything but itself. The datasets that media economists must rely on to impute profitability in contemporary Hollywood are worse than blunt instruments. As they certainly know, foreign revenues are not only greater than domestic tallies, the rights to them may have been sold off to secure production financing. What is more, as they also know, the allocation of what revenues do return to a given production between production companies, slate partners, distributors, stars, and other participants is only very rarely available. Broad claims about the relative profitability—for whom? and when?—of films at different budget thresholds should be treated with a great deal of suspicion. Our rules of thumb—rules all scholars are generally obliged to rely on—are not the sorts of things that might support regressions. Hence the vital importance of those official ledgers that have survived, of the hacked Sony materials, and of the public financial documents filed by single-line, publicly held motion picture companies such as DreamWorks animation in its independent era, 2004–16.

4 For a version of this debate, see Dean Baker "The Housing Bubble and the Financial Crisis, #25,452" *Center for Economic and Policy Research*, April 2, 2015, http://www.cepr.net/index.php/blogs/beat-the-press/the-housing-bubble-and-the-financial-crisis-25452, accessed January 20, 2017; and the response by Brad Delong, "The Housing Bubble and the Lesser Depression: Either the Very Sharp Dean Baker or I am Hopelessly Confused," *Equitablog*, April 2, 2015, http://equitablegrowth.org/2015/04/02/housing-bubble-lesser-depression-either-sharp-dean-baker-hopelessly-confused/, accessed January 20, 2017.

5 Gary B. Gorton, *Misunderstanding Financial Crises: Why We Don't See Them Coming* (New York: Oxford University Press, 2012).

6 For an introduction to the concept of economic embeddedness and a wide range of applications to economic phenomena, see Mark S. Granovetter and Richard Swedberg, *Sociology of Economic Life* (Boulder, CO: Westview, 2011).

7 Donald MacKenzie, "The Credit Crisis as a Problem in the Sociology of Knowledge," *American Journal of Sociology* 116 (2011): 1778–1841, 1783. Also: "Knowledge Production in Financial Markets: Credit Default Swaps, the ABX and the Subprime Crisis," *Economy and Society* 41 (2012): 335–59, and "What's in a Number? Donald MacKenzie on the Importance of LIBOR," *London Review of Books*, September 25, 2008, http://www.lrb.co.uk/v30/n18/donald-mackenzie/whats-in-a-number, accessed January 20, 2017. The literature in the sociology of the economy, particularly of elite market-shaping institutions, continues to grow. See *Do Economists Make Markets? On the Performativity of Economics*, MacKenzie, Fabian Muniesa, and Lucia Siu, eds., (Princeton: Princeton University Press, 2007), especially MacKenzie's "Is Economics Performative? Option Theory and the Construction of Derivatives Markets," 54–86.

8 A wave of Soderbergh monographs underlies my reading of his career. See Aaron Baker, *Steven Soderbergh* (Urbana, IL: University of Illinois Press, 2011); Andrew deWaard and R. Colin Tait, *The Cinema of Steven Soderbergh: Indie Sex, Corporate Lies, and Digital Videotape* (New York: Wallflower, 2013); Mark Gallagher, *Another Steven Soderbergh Experience: Authorship and Contemporary Hollywood* (Austin: University of Texas Press, 2013); and R. Barton Palmer and Steven M. Sanders, eds., *The Philosophy of Steven Soderbergh* (Lexington, KY: University of Kentucky Press, 2011).

9 Dave McNary, "China to Miss Out on 'Dark Knight,'" *Variety*, December 23, 2008, http://variety.com/2008/film/awards/china-to-miss-out-on-dark-knight-1117997740/, accessed January 20, 2017.

10 Dave Itzkoff, "*Inception* to materialize in China," *The New York Times*, August 3, 2010, https://artsbeat.blogs.nytimes.com/2010/08/03/blockbuster-inception-to-materialize-in-china/.

11 Russ Fischer, "Guillermo del Toro Promises Amazing Monsters and Robots in 'Pacific Rim,'" */Film,* July 23, 2011, http://www.slashfilm.com/guillermo-del-toro-promises-amazing-monsters-robots-pacific-rim/, accessed January 20, 2017. Del Toro made the remark at San Diego Comic-Con in 2011.

12 Marc Graser, "Warner Bros. no Longer in Legendary's Future," *Variety*, June 24, 2013, http://variety.com/2013/biz/news/warner-bros-no-longer-in-legendarys-future-1200501572/, accessed January 20, 2017.

13 The twists and turns of Legendary's China ventures warrant more extensive discussion. For the migration to Universal, see Jill Goldsmith, "Legendary chief touts slate, China plans," *Variety*, September 19, 2012, http://variety.com/2012/film/news/legendary-chief-touts-slate-china-plans-1118059500/; Alex Ben Block and Kim Masters, "Legendary Entertainment Finds New Home at NBC Universal," *The Hollywood Reporter*, July 9, 2013, https://

www.hollywoodreporter.com/news/legendary-entertainment-finds-new-home-579935.

14 Lynda Obst, *Sleepless in Hollywood: Tales from the New Abnormal in the Movie Business* (New York: Simon and Schuster, 2013). *The Great Wall* (Legendary/Universal), directed by Zhang Yimou was released to mediocre reviews and a whitewashing controversy in 2016.

15 Edward Wong, "Thousands of Dead Pigs Found Floating in River Flowing into Shanghai," *The New York Times*, March 11, 2013, http://www.nytimes.com/2013/03/12/world/asia/thousands-of-dead-pigs-found-in-chinese-river.html, accessed January 20, 2017; Didi Kristen Tatlow, "With 6,000 Dead Pigs in River, Troubling Questions on Food Safety," *The New York Times*, March 13, 2013, http://rendezvous.blogs.nytimes.com/2013/03/13/with-6000-dead-pigs-in-river-troubling-questions-on-food-safety/, accessed January 20, 2017; and David Barboza, "A Tide of Death, But This Time the Food is Safe," *The New York Times*, March 14, 2013, http://www.nytimes.com/2013/03/15/world/asia/a-tide-of-dead-pigs-in-china-but-dinner-is-safe.html, accessed January 20, 2017.

16 *In the Aftermath of Floyd,* www.riverlaw.us/hurricanefloyd.html, accessed January 20, 2017; Jeff Tietz, "Boss Hog: The Dark Side of America's Top Pork Producer," *Rolling Stone*, December 14, 2006, http://www.rollingstone.com/culture/news/boss-hog-the-dark-side-of-americas-top-pork-producer-20061214, accessed January 20, 2017.

17 Denise Grady, "A Medical Mystery Unfolds in Minnesota," *The New York Times*, February 5, 2008, http://www.nytimes.com/2008/02/05/health/05pork.html, accessed January 20, 2017; Jennifer Zipser Adjemian, James Howell, Stacy Holzbauer, Julie Harris, Sergio Recuenco, et al., "A Clustering of Immune-mediated Polyradiculoneuropathy among Swine Abattoir Workers Exposed to Aerosolized Porcine Brains, Indiana, United States," *International Journal of Occupational and Environmental Health* 15, no. 4 (October–December 2009): 331–38; Stacy M. Holzbauer, Aaron S. DeVries, James J. Sejvar, Christine H. Lees, Jennifer Adjemian, et al., "Epidemiologic Investigation of Immune-Mediated Polyradiculoneuropathy among Abattoir Workers Exposed to Porcine Brain: e9782," *PLoSOne* 5, no. 3 (March 2010). The alternative to the porcine economy is industrial fishing, and the complement to *Upstream Color* is *Leviathan* (Castaing-Taylor and Paravel, 2013). Late in the film, the unnamed captain of the fishing boat sits in the galley, watching an unseen television, absently spitting into a cup and drifting into sleep. The camera is fixed, mounted on the wall below the tv. His exhaustion has been palpable and now it reaches its conclusion. In an early cut of the film, the shot ran twenty-one minutes and the tv audio was rendered inaudible. But in what the directors acknowledge was a concession to popular audience desires, they trimmed the shot and restored the audio. He has been watching *Deadliest Catch*, the long-running Discovery Channel reality series about crab fishing in Alaska. The moment is both realistic—the New Bedford fishermen are fans of the show—and dangerously allegorical.

18 Caleb Crain, "The Thoreau Poison," *The New Yorker,* May 8, 2018, www.newyorker.com/books/page-turner/the-thoreau-poison, accessed January 20, 2017.

19 Film Society of Lincoln Center, *New Directions/New Films Q&A: "Upstream Color," Shane Carruth*, April 6, 2013, https://www.youtube.com/watch?v=5cjq_Lb2F2I, accessed 1/20/17.

20 Walter Murch, "Commentary," *THX–1138*, DVD (WB 2010). I discuss this passage in its context in *The Studios*, 94.

21 Fischer, "Guillermo del Toro Promises Amazing Monsters and Robots in 'Pacific Rim.'"

22 Mary Kaye Schilling, "Steven Soderbergh on Quitting Hollywood, Getting the Best out of J.Lo, and His Love of *Girls*," vulture.com, January 27, 2013, http://www.vulture.com/2013/01/steven-soderbergh-in-conversation.html, accessed January 20, 2017.

23 Ibid.

24 Ajay Singh Chaudhary and Raphaële Chappe describe this technocratic migration in similar terms in their dissection of "The Supermanagerial Reich," *Los Angeles Review of Books*, November 6, 2016, https://lareviewofbooks.org/article/the-supermanagerial-reich, accessed, January 20, 2017. They argue that supermanagers secure their outsized salaries because they have become responsible for governance of the neoliberal behemoth. The market technocrats I discuss emphasize two elements that are essential to the neoliberal era: a global deployability and a ready ability to understand their work as emblematic of the system.

25 Maryanne DeKoven, *Utopia, Ltd.: The Sixties and the Emergence of the Postmodern* (Durham, NC: Duke 2004).

8

The United States of America
v. *The Wolf of Wall Street*

*Point at a piece of paper.—And now point at its shape—now at
its colour—now at its number (that sounds odd).—Well, how
did you do it?*

—LUDWIG WITTGENSTEIN, Philosophical Investigations §33[1]

The usual response to this question, as Wittgenstein understands it, is to
say that one "meant" something different in each case—that there is a
mental or intellectual or even spiritual difference at work. That answer, for
him, is a mistake. The "spirit" is an aftereffect, a residuum produced by a
characteristic feature of language. "Where our language suggests a body and
there is none: there, we should like to say, is a *spirit*." But before we admit
that he has it right, it is worth noting that the four "kinds" of pointing in this
discussion of ostensive definition are not the same. The piece of paper is just
that. In contrast shape, color, and number seem to be aspects or properties
of the paper. But even that distinction doesn't work for long. Wittgenstein
will go on at length about shape and color, but in the sections that follow
number all but disappears. Numbers will be particularly important in the
Investigations as examples of "going on"—of following a rule—but "its
number" as the kind of thing that one might point to or point out is harder
to make sense of. Shape and color clarify a discussion of ostension; number
clouds it.

Shape and color suggest bodies, and when those bodies fail to materialize
in the ways other bodies do, we (our languages) generate quasi-bodies—
hidden agents, near-materialities, figures with extension. Number occasions
bodies in very nearly the opposite way: with the proliferation of numbers the

world recedes, and to counter that recession, a body is called forth to stop it. There is something desperate in this move, but the withdrawal of the world is a desperate situation. And while one can certainly generate desperation from the simple proliferation of number-as-such—in Dr. Seuss's *Horton Hears a Who*, the titular elephant must investigate almost uncountably many clover blossoms to recover the lost Whos—the usual occasion and measure of such desperation is money.

None of this, so far, requires much of a history; one need only paper or vases to make Wittgenstein's key examples work. But as soon as money enters the picture, spaces for history open. (Money and time are the obverse of one another, for Deleuze's reasons and others.) Here, the history that is at issue is the history of the Great Recession and after, a period when the rapidly evolving popular datascape seemed both to constitute a background cultural condition and to come into focus as the zone of endeavor out of which an explanation for and solution to the mounting economic wreckage might emerge. Even more particularly, in the digital recession, the moral emplacement of Hollywood's own finances within the broadly financialized economy required attention of its own. Thus, the philosophical problem of attention found a practical occasion, and Wittgenstein's reiterated question returned: "You'll say you concentrated your attention on the color, the shape, and so on. But now I ask again: how is *that* done?" Just as, throughout this book, I have relied on the art and industry of movies and television shows to think through leasing and ownership, taxation and futurity, independence and image resolution, housing and exchange, here I will turn to moments of ostension that might clarify the complexities of directing moral attention to the "so on," to numbers. Each of the following sections pivots on an economic image caught in the process of calling attention to itself through a vexed ostention. How is *that* done? Like this.

This poor schmuck

At the end of *The Big Short*, Steve Carell's Cassandra-trader Mark Baum engages in some historical reflection. While his righteously angry colleague believes that the crash will drastically change the financial system—"At least we're gonna see some of them go to jail? . . . Right? I mean they're gonna hafta break up the banks. I mean the party's over."—Mark can maintain an almost smug doubt: "I don't know. I don't know. I have a feeling that in a few years people will be doing what they always do when the economy tanks: They will be blaming immigrants and poor people." Of course Mark is "Right?" and his initial doubts are so much narrative bad faith. By 2015, when the movie was released, the blame-shifting scenario had already come to pass. But before Mark's smugness can settle, the movie returns to its usual strategy, giving Ryan Gosling's voice-over the chance to address the audience directly:

> But Mark was wrong. In the years that followed hundreds of bankers and ratings agency executives went to jail. The SEC was completely overhauled. Congress had no choice but to break up the big banks and regulate the mortgage and derivatives industries. . . . Just kidding. Banks took the money the American people gave them and they used it to pay themselves huge bonuses and lobby the Congress to kill big reform. And then they blamed immigrants and poor people. And this time even teachers. And when all was said and done only one single banker went to jail: This poor schmuck.

The feint toward an alternative history in which justice is done sets up the movie's own alternative mode of justice. Faced with the foreseeable failure of the government to prosecute wrongdoing and with the reconsolidation of American finance, *The Big Short* looks inward. The same extracinematic awareness that makes Mark's "prophecy" dangerously pat meshes with an overweening sense that folks have gotten away with it—through malice or idiocy, incapacity or luck. But the turn inward rescues recessive thinking from itself and installs the story inside a new economy of justice, one in which the savvy audience has learned something while the responsible parties are held to narrative account. Almost no one is going to jail; but the tale of their infamy may be some compensation.

"This poor schmuck" was Kareem Serageldin, head of Credit Suisse's CDO operation. He pled guilty in 2013, was sentenced to 2½ years, and was released in March 2016.[2] While numerous bankers and their employers were fined or barred from certain activities, and while select others outside the United States were indicted or prosecuted, Serageldin became the nearly comical metonym for systemic failure. Financial journalist William Cohan called the widespread nonprosecutions one of the "enduring mysteries" of the crisis and in 2016 lamented that Attorneys General Eric Holder and Loretta Lynch "appear[ed] to have turned the page" on prosecuting banks and bankers. "It seems an apt time to ask: In the biggest picture, what justice has been achieved?"[3]

The problem, for Cohan and for *The Big Short*, is the incongruity between huge fines ("paid by shareholders") and the need for individual—particularly bodily—responsibility, "holding real people" accountable. "No one gets publicly shamed."[4] Justice here requires the staking of responsibility to something ineradicably personal, not something fungible or corporate or abstract. The movie's final ostension—*this* poor schmuck—both achieves that staking and dispenses a rough absolution. Serageldin, we are told, did nothing particularly different from many other bankers at many other banks.

Once guilt has been assigned and generalized, grace can be dispensed. *The Big Short* is just not simply because it holds the guilty to account, but because it offers the possibility of pardon. Leading up to the crisis, Carell's Baum had been utterly unable to control himself. He would leap to his feet in public to accuse bankers, brokers, and other enablers; he would stage debates with polyannaish financiers to force them, as best he could, to own the catastrophe around the corner. Yet Baum, we are told, "actually became gracious after the collapse and never said 'I told you so' to anyone." The movie regards this as a change in his character; within the narrative, it is a necessary consequence of its achievement of justice.

Such an internalist vision of the right is utterly in keeping with Hollywood's long-standing commitments to self-regulation on the one hand and moral metonymy on the other. And in the overarching narrative I have been tracing, it marks a return to a world where precessive thinking seems possible; that is, it marks a reflation of Hollywood's capacity for abstraction. Outside its own narrative competence, though, such an approach raises questions about the nature of systemic justice. If movie justice is insufficient, what would be? As keen to the ironies of the aftermath of the financial crisis as the makers of *The Big Short*, Cohan notes the distance between Lynch's unconcern with the closing window for going after bankers and "her first major prosecutorial act as the new U.S. attorney general": charging virtually the entire executive corps of FIFA, the governing body of world soccer, with "rampant, systemic, and deep-rooted" corruption.[5] But instead of viewing this as simply ironic, Cohan might ask whether there is, indeed, some deeper relation between what is prosecuted and what is financed. And, if there is, what that meaningful relation owes to Hollywood's practice of formulating strategy through self-representation. How does the equation of pictures operate within political culture?

This pen

On July 20, 2016, Lynch announced a similarly splashy case. *The United States of America v. The Wolf of Wall Street* was even less oriented toward bodily justice than the FIFA prosecution. The forefeiture was "the largest single action ever brought by the department's Kleptocracy Asset Recovery Initiative."[6] Instead of charging people, or even a corporate person, the case was brought as a forfeiture. In the Justice Department's narrative— one backed up by thorough reporting in publications as different as *The Wall Street Journal*, *The Guardian*, and the independent *Sarawak Report*—a Malaysian sovereign wealth fund called 1 Malaysian Development Berhad (1MDB) had been looted of billions of dollars.[7] That money was used to purchase landmark real estate and major works of art and to fund the lifestyle of Jho Low. Another $681 million was somehow designated a "gift" from Saudi Arabia and channeled into an account belonging to Prime Minister Najib Razak before it was discovered and he returned the money. As regulators in Singapore, Switzerland, and the United States pursued the complex web of transactions, crucial banking intermediaries Falcon Private Bank and BSI were both shuttered. Swiss UBS and Singaporean DBS were both fined; Goldman Sachs, which had issued billions of dollars in bonds for 1MDB, came under renewed scrutiny. Most relevantly, though, at least $100 million from the bond sale was used to set up Red Granite pictures, a production company run by Riza Aziz. (Lho and Aziz, who is Najib stepson, had known each other at school in the UK) That funding was in turn used to underwrite *The Wolf of Wall Street*; Justice was coming for the revenue stream.

Civil forfeiture initially requires the government only to establish probable cause that the assets should be subject to forfeiture.[8] Once the assets have been seized, claimants may petition for the return of those assets, but the government need only establish that the assets stem from criminal activity by a preponderance of the evidence. This lower standard makes it a useful weapon in pursuing both exceptionally complex financial crimes, where competing explanations might introduce "reasonable doubt," and criminal syndicates, since it reduces the exposure of witnesses. Forfeiture allows law enforcement to move quickly, seizing assets before they can be laundered further or "dissipated." The same lower standard also opens the practice to abuse, especially since the confiscated funds are frequently plowed back into the enforcement agency's budget. (That is not the case here; any 1MDB recoveries are to be returned to Malaysia.) But whatever their strategic value, on the surface what is most striking about civil forfeiture cases is their naming convention. Since the target in such cases is the asset as such and not the perpetrator, the cases carry the name of the thing, not a person. Frequently enough, the cases bear names such as *United States v. One 1992 Ford Mustang*, or *v. One Gold Watch*. The contests seem ludicrously lopsided: what does the government have against a watch?

In the 1MDB case, the assets were often staggeringly valuable individual objects: The Park Lane Hotel ($380 million), a Time-Warner Center penthouse ($31 million), the Montalban House in Los Angeles ($39 million), Monet's *Saint-Georges Majeur* ($35 million). In bringing its case against all these objects and more, Justice might have led off with the first asset alphabetically, or the most valuable, or the one most obviously part of the criminal scheme underlying the purchases. But it did not. It went down to the bottom of the alphabet to name a movie that, however corrupt its financing, was, in fact, produced according to industry norms, and that likely threw off less than $100 million in profit, even before participations and distribution fees.[9] *The Wolf of Wall Street Motion Picture, Including Any Rights to Profits, Royalties, and Distribution Proceeds* is a complex asset, as all Hollywood revenue streams are. What is more, in the complaint, the alleged scenario that allowed Lho and Aziz to launder money through Monet paintings is far simpler than the multiyear process of producing and distributing *The Wolf of Wall Street*. (Aziz may have been the linchpin in a global scheme to loot Malaysian government funds; he clearly wanted to be a real movie producer.[10]) In choosing the movie as the titular asset, then, Justice was not choosing based on value or centrality or the ease of making the case. Justice chose *The Wolf of Wall Street* because it allowed the department to seek publicaly the sort of symbolic justice that it had abjured in the financial crisis. At the press conference announcing the case, FBI Deputy Director Andrew McCabe emphasized that it "sent a message that no person, no company, no organization is too big, too powerful, or too prominent. No one is above or beyond the law." *U.S. v. Wolf* was designed to repudiate publicly the idea that there are entities "too big to jail."[11] This is what the equation of pictures looks like in the political sphere.

Part of what suited *The Wolf of Wall Street* for that role was its peculiar ontological lability. Because forfeiture cases are brought *in rem*, they cannot simply send a message about a person, company, or organization. But *The Wolf of Wall Street* is more than a nonhuman asset. It is also a story of financial shenanigans and the character at the heart of that story, a Wall Street trader who did, in fact, go to jail. *Ecce* schmuck.

Yet the prosecution of *The Wolf of Wall Street* is more than symbolic compensation for the nonprosecution of the wolves of Wall Street. It also compensates for the movie's own moral indeterminacy, which takes the form of a similarly complex ontology. Late in the film, Jordan Belfort, the corrupt

FIGURE 8.1 *A collusion of Belforts.* The Wolf of Wall Street, *Scorsese, Red Granite/ Paramount, 2013.*

trader at the heart of the story, has emerged from prison and has moved to Australia to reestablish himself as a master salesman. In the final scene, the real Jordan Belfort, playing an MC, introduces Leonardo-DiCaprio-playing-Jordan-Belfort, and as he takes the stage, his animated signature appears on the screen behind him. Belforts real, fictional, and graphic all but collide, yet the fictional Belfort does not remain on stage long before walking into the crowd and demanding members of his paying audience "Sell me this pen." There is something simple and material about the pen and about the scenario that helps dissolve the indeterminacy of the previous moment.

"Sell me this pen" is also a classic piece of job interview roleplaying. The conventionally bad response involves rambling on about the qualia of the pen. The New Zealanders in the movie do just this, fumbling about how "It's a nice pen," and so on. The conventionally good response involves asking the putative purchaser questions about his interest in pens—how long he's been in the market, what he's looking for, how many—and then attempting to broaden the selling opportunity. In *The Wolf of Wall Street*, though, no one gives this answer. Early in the movie, when Belfort is training his squadron of mooks in the fine art of selling penny stocks, he appeals to his cousin Brad to show them how it is done. Brad picks up the pen and immediately makes a demand: "Why don't you do me a favor? Write your name down on that napkin for me." "I don't have a pen." "Exactly. Supply and demand, my friend." Belfort, who is setting up his own boiler room, endorses this tactic: "He's creating urgency." Pressure, not "demand discovery" lies at the heart of this model of selling.

Here, the very real pen stands in for and gives material heft to the immaterial shares the salespeople will be asked to sell. It is fungible, and while it may have "qualia" that distinguish it from other pens, those are irrelevant. In addition, the pen is part of the theater of contract, and pledges (bid/ask, buy/sell, promise/consideration) lie at the center of both Belfort's moral story and the 1MDB backstory. Scorsese's movie tracks an apparent tale of debauchery, decline, and tentative redemption, but that tidy narrative simply doesn't hold. Jordan Belfort (the character) undermines every shot he has at redemption or even damage control in moments that turn on pen-based betrayal. He first agrees to a deal with the SEC to leave the company, then reneges. "This deal that I'm about to sign . . . it's them selling me, the other way around." Later, caught by the FBI, he cuts a tougher deal that requires him to inform on his partners—"Please, just let me sign the fuckin' thing already." We don't see that signature, but we do see the handwritten note he slides his best friend Donnie: "Don't incriminate yourself. I'm wearing a wire." Even as the note warns Donnie it performatively incriminates Belfort. It might just as well be the deferred fulfillment of Brad's earlier demand that Jordan do him "a favor" and write his name on a napkin: Donnie hides the note under his napkin and, offscreen, gives it to the FBI in exchange for leniency. Of course Belfort is caught again, and because he *has* signed, the punishment is more severe. Even after his time in prison, there is reason to believe that Belfort has fled the United States to make recovering any hidden assets more difficult.[12] At this point, the movie's depiction of Belfort's oiliness and the movie's own ontological fluidity coincide; Justice's case against 1MDB extends that to the film's own production.

This slippery relation to justice has formal echoes throughout *The Wolf of Wall Street*. Unlike *The Big Short*, which makes a show of its suspicion of narrative and its trust in exposition, *Wolf* perpetually undermines the revelatory power of those moments when it breaks the fourth wall. The starkest emblem of this duplicity is the scene in which Belfort, in a Quaalude-induced haze, "miraculously" drives his Lamborghini home without a scratch. The next day, the police arrive at his door and reveal to him, and to us, that the car is "TOTALLED, an absolute wreck," and that he has left a trail of destruction in his wake.[13] More typically, the film interrupts the flow of its voice-over to have Belfort tell us that "Look, I know you're not following what I'm saying anyway" before directing us to the "real question: was all this legal?" Later, he will pull the same trick: "You know what, who gives a shit? As always, the point is this—" At which point, his partner howls "Twenty-two million dollars in three fucking hours!"[14]

But to regard *The Wolf of Wall Street* as simply failing to live up to the preferred mode of justice in *The Big Short* or the prosecutorial strategies of the Department of Justice would be to misunderstand where its indictment lies. The movie is uninterested in process, just as it is uninterested in staking and forgiveness. The closest we come to a *Moneyball*-style montage rolls underneath Belfort's description of his illegal IPO scheme. The screenplay describes what is now commonly called a "crazy board"—"a massive chart on [Belfort]'s operations: pictures of Jordan, Donnie and others, a hierarchy, a history, *an investigation* . . ." but instead the movie shows us something far more orderly and boring: a wall-spanning timeline made from neatly taped-together notebook paper, with neat, dashed lines connecting three-inch squares, each filled with tiny handwriting that details a particular event. Over the course of half a dozen shots, FBI Agent Denham comes to work, navigates the wall, and fills in another small box. We are not supposed to be able to read this, but by the same token we are not to imagine that it is unknowably complex or idiosyncratic. It simply takes time and patience. At the center of this minisequence is Denham's pen, and he holds it as Belfort does in the final scene. The parallelism highlights the contrast: this pen, and Denham, are not for sale.

In contrast, Belfort is immersed in exchange without regulation. He desires money, what he calls "fun coupons," not for the usual Wall-Street-movie reasons of social scorekeeping or as part of a vision of social progress through competition, but because money procures pleasure. Those pleasures are regularly illicit (Quaaludes, prostitutes) or outlandishly expensive (his yacht, *Naomi*; his cars), yet Belfort casts his avarice as a kind of honesty.

In his sales peptalks, commercials, and seminars, Belfort promises access to this world of rare experience, while in his closest relationships there are glimmers of what a general economy of pleasure might actually entail: his second wife is a lingerie designer; his key IPO is for a footwear designer. As the avatar of this economy, DiCaprio was ideally cast. In his all-too-public quest for artistic validation, his performances refashioned character struggles as career struggles, and the collapse of those two levels resulted in an explosion of on-screen desperation. That neediness is present in *The Great Gatsby*, where the solicitation of audience regard appears as the cascade of Brooks Brothers shirts he rains upon us. Similarly, the all-too-vaunted difficulties of shooting *The Revenant* (Alejandro Iñárritu, New Regency/RatPac/Fox, 2015) allowed him to channel for us the cold, and the wetness, and the raw-liver-eating. The point of these mid-career DiCaprio performances is not that he is the vehicle through which certain realistic characters come to life but rather that he is the avenue for an audience's experience of certain extreme situations. He *distributes* them. If *The Big Short* counters the digital recession by staking numbers to particular bodies, in *The Wolf of Wall Street* those bodies are always in danger of becoming vehicles of further distribution. In Scorsese's moral economy, all that can stop that proliferation is a self-abnegation or ascesis, a great nay-saying in the face of temptation or rational interest.

This painting

If individual moral rectitude sounds like an impractical counter to global financialization, it is at least a philosophically coherent alternative to the sorts of institutionalized liberalism *Contagion* investigated. In the end, Scorsese himself seems to regard it as a failed strategy—the sort of thing suitable only for "boy scouts" like Agent Denham or for saints (as in *Silence*). Certainly it would be hard to argue that DiCaprio or Scorsese attempted to carry it out in their coziness with Jho Low. To be sure, their dependence on sovereign wealth (via Red Granite) for *Wolf*'s funding was unexceptional in the long aftermath of the Great Recession. Still, that new configuration drew from them sustained efforts to provide ideological cover for hypermobile capital.

In DiCaprio's case, that cover took the form of a colloid of cool in which moviemaking would be suspended alongside other endeavors. Not content with taking the money and making the movie, DiCaprio spent 2013, the year *Wolf* would be released, on a gambling-art-and-eco-activism jaunt. For New Year's, Low chartered two large jets to shuttle more than one hundred guests (including DiCaprio) from Sydney to Las Vegas so that they might ring in the year twice. (*Wolf* imagines this as two separate flights: first to Vegas for Belfort's bachelor party, then to Geneva to launch his money-laundering scheme.) Later, Low apparently funded DiCaprio during some very high–stakes gambling in Las Vegas. Most relevantly, the government's complaint makes clear that at the May charity auction to raise money for DiCaprio's environmental foundation, one of Low's associates was a front for the purchase of an Ed Ruscha, *Bliss Bucket* ($367,500), and a Mark Ryden, *Queen Bee* ($714,000) which he later "gifted" to Low (for no money). Those paintings, and others, were then used as collateral for further purchases, spinning the 1MDB money-laundering scheme along. Like the numbered bank accounts that facilitate all international financial thrillers (including *Wolf*), the paintings were in Switzerland, held tax exempt in the Geneva Freeport.[15] Everyone knew that art and gambling had merged. One Christie's employee emailed another about Low's rented auction skybox, "It better look like Ceasar Palace [*sic*] in there . . . . The box is almost more important for the client than the art."[16] And so the cycle ran through the end of the year: Low would buy more art at the December contemporary auctions; *Wolf* would be released at Christmas; and when DiCaprio won his Golden Globe in January, he thanked Low from the stage.

DiCaprio's every action implied that there was, indeed, a system to global culture that was never more than a step or two from vast financial chicanery, but those implications were hard to discern within the web of routine and apparently legitimate cultural production and charitable fundraising. Scorsese, in contrast, made such links explicit and attempted to pass them off with a knowing wink. In 2014, he followed up *The Wolf of Wall Street* with perhaps the most expensive short film ever made: *The Audition*, which ran sixteen minutes and cost a reported $70 million.[17] The movie is not hard to find online, subtitled in Italian or dubbed in Russian, but it has received almost no critical attention.[18] For an auteur such as Scorsese the project is just embarrassing, however much of a lark it may have been to make. Ostensibly a comedy about DiCaprio, Robert De Niro, and Brad Pitt vying for a role in an upcoming Scorsese film, *The Audition* was shot as a promotion for Melco-Crown casinos, in particular for the opening of their $2.3 billion movie-themed Studio City in Macau. The stars themselves earned perhaps $13 or $17 million each for two days' work.[19] While the plot takes them from one Melco-Crown property to another, from Manila to Macau to Tokyo, the cast and crew remained in a greenscreen studio in New York. For the movie to debut at the casino's grand opening, Scorsese had to shoot before the place was built and work from the architect's digital plans. Thus when on-screen Scorsese discusses how he will use characteristic, sweeping crane shots, that, too, is a wink at the project's greenscreen reality.

The linear storytelling of *The Audition* contrasts with its deeply enmeshed backstory. The gaming company is a partnership between Laurence Ho and James Packer. Packer, an Australian magnate, was eager to partner with Ho not only to secure his place in the pan-Pacific gaming ecology but also to gain access to the movie market in the PRC. Alongside his gambling business, Packer is the "Pac" in RatPac productions (the Rat is Brett Ratner). The

RatPac brand may carry a tinge of nostalgia for Sinatra-era Vegas, but with its partner Dune, RatPac is a major film investment fund. When Legendary declined to re-sign with Warner Bros., Dune, which had been underwriting Fox, became Warner Bros.' slate partner. Similarly, at the end of 2013, Brad Pitt's Plan B moved from Paramount to New Regency, and RatPac came on as a backer. At New Regency, RatPac co-produced DiCaprio's *The Revenant*.[20] Pitt, De Niro, DiCaprio, and Scorsese had never worked together before *The Audition*. What brought them together was money, but it was money cloaked as cinema.

Somewhere between the Scorsese and the DiCaprio strategies, we find *Jordan Belfort*. Like the other works in the 2015 series *Strings Attached* by Jonas Lund, it matches a nearly generic, commercially available fabric (the design is based on a royalty-free vector graphic) with simple, painted

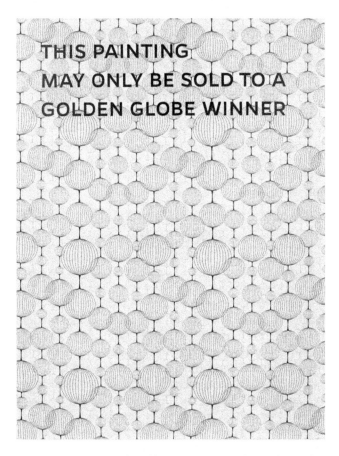

FIGURE 8.2 *An ostension of Belforts. Jonas Lund,* Jordan Belfort (Strings Attached), *acrylic on fabric, 63" × 48", 2015. Courtesy Steve Turner LA.*

text. The content of that text, again as with the other paintings in the series, puts forward some conditions on the sale of the work. Here, that it may only be purchased by a Golden Globe winner. The actual conditions outlined in the sales agreement are "not very different," and the Steve Turner gallery was happy to accommodate Lund's aims.[21] The painting singles out its audience—its consumer—its owner. And while there are many living Golden Globe winners, there are undoubtedly many fewer who would want a painting named *Jordan Belfort*, and there is only one who won his award for playing Jordan Belfort. (The painting has, indeed, been sold.)

All the paintings in the series bear their own ostension, invoking some of the foundational moves of conceptual art (e.g., John Baldessari's Commissioned Paintings). Each painting begins "This painting." But the link to Belfort makes *this* "This painting" the allegorical heart of the series. *Jordan Belfort* avowedly participates in a cultural nexus nearly as broad as capitalism itself, spanning dispersed, contemporary textile production; the art world; the entertainment industry and its award-system subroutine; as well as the individual movie and *its* depiction of and participation in the global financial industry. Lund fashions this painting as simultaneously an object staked to another object (the Globe), an object staked to a body, and an instance of distribution piggybacking on an institution of distribution, the Hollywood Foreign Press Association that gives out the awards. Whether this hybrid approach of winking adjacency constitutes a critical force, or, indeed, if the point is that such attempts at critical practice are doomed, Lund's work highlights the effort required to distribute staking, to parcel out responsibility for the system between both its artist-analyst and its distributional targets.

What is this?

In *Equity* (Meera Menon, Broad Street/Sony Pictures Classics, 2016) the usual gender world of the financial thriller is inverted. While Naomi (Anna Gunn), a veteran banker, struggles to hold on to her tenuous position at the top, her (female) vice president is ready to push her aside, and an ambitious (female) U.S. attorney is pursuing an insider trading case against her *homme fatal* boyfriend. The young gunners in the story also happen to be two of the movie's producers, and they assembled the funding for the movie piecemeal, raising more than 80 percent from women Wall Street bankers. As executive producer Candy Straight explained, she and her colleagues invested because "we wanted the story to be told and because we wanted to empower women."[22] Those women in turn make cameo appearances as fictional investors weighing whether to buy into the initial public offering that Naomi is roadshowing. A Blu-ray featurette provides more details on the "Girl Gang" on the Street and behind the movie, setting documentary footage against shots from the movie's own narrative, highlighting the incremental process of indie financing through comparisons to the legal investigation and the work of taking a company public. Never has John Thornton Caldwell's claim that every movie is also a business plan been more literal. Linda Munger, another co-producer/investor, drove home the dual-track approach: "I loved the fact that it was addressing two very relevant issues: the lack of opportunity for women on both sides of the camera in Hollywood but also the trials and tribulations continuing for women to compete on Wall Street."

If the movie as a production is utterly convinced that it is empowering, the movie as a story is less sanguine. Early on, Naomi delivers a paean to ambition and to earning money—a feminist version of Gordon Gekko's greed-is-good speech; and very late, producer Alysia Reiner as Assistant U.S. Attorney Samantha delivers that speech again, this time to a headhunter who wants to lure her away from the public sector into one of the big banks. Naomi's speech has worked, it is clear, but working here entails abandoning any search for justice. However empowered, its trio of female leads seem just the latest, blinkered victims of the ideology of ambition that underwrites financialization.

The conflict between edifying backstory and ambiguous story comes to a head and breaks in a late, mordant scene where Naomi lays into one of the doltish young men she oversees:

Naomi: What is this? How many chocolate chips are in my cookie?
Bill: . . .um. . .
Naomi: Did anyone teach you basic math? Count. The fucking. Chips.
Bill (*sotto*): Three.
Naomi: Three. Yes. And your cookies, I saw them, and they were oozing
   with chocolate. And my cookie has THREE. MOTHER. FUCKING.
   CHIPS!?

At the moment that Naomi has a Wittgensteinian realization that she cannot simply "point at its number" and that her first question about the cookie will require elaboration, she is busy watching her IPO tank, desperate to figure out where the bottom lies. But in 2016 this financial meltdown—she is oozing equity—has no systemic consequences. It is just another offering for just another technology company that wants to hit the magic $1 billion valuation. We are far enough into the post-recession that when the economic image returns it appears as a battle over baked goods, a ludicrous emblem of this indie movie's own righteous demand for capital.

The chip-deficient cookie is an economic image, and one whose significance Anna Gunn is eloquent in detailing. More prominent in the movie, though, are shots of Bloomberg terminals (and screens tuned to Bloomberg TV, and Bloomberg TV newsrooms . . .). *Equity* was a pet project for the company.

FIGURE 8.3 *Three. Mother. Fucking. Chips.* Equity, *Menon, Broad Street/Sony Pictures Classics, 2016.*

As Mike Marinello, then Bloomberg's global head of communications, technology, brand, and sustainability explains in "Bloomberg's Role in the Making of Equity The Movie," "The Branded Entertainment Group is a true Bloomberg collaboration. We work with everything from hardware to technical operations to procurement to core and financial products, to Bloomberg News and Bloomberg Media, Brand and then Communications obviously."[23] The promo reel backs Marinello's speech with a montage of not-quite-camera-ready Bloomberg employees prepping for the shoot. We see a still from *The Big Short*; a still from *Demolition* (Jean-Marc Vallée, Fox Searchlight, 2015); and a clip of maximally unsubtle product placement in HBO's *Newsroom*, in which Olivia Munn dishes out Bloomberg terminal pricing information. In on-set interviews, *Equity*'s actors tout Bloomberg's story help just as sincerely as they touted the mentorship of the Girl Gang on the Blu-ray. ("Bloomberg's Role" was not included on the disc.) But where the frisson of female investment in the production bolstered the movie's moral ambiguity, the thrum of Bloomberg hype threatens to undo it. Instead of speaking for the seldom-seen women powerbrokers of the Street, Bloomberg works on movies to "raise our brand awareness, strategically, globally, so that people who aren't traditionally exposed to Bloomberg get more familiar with our brand," as Mindy Massucci of Bloomberg TV put it.

This is the code for our RAT

When Naomi asks, "What is this?" she knows the answer, and is providing a rough Socratic lesson. When Billy Beane asked that same question in

Moneyball, he did not know, and Peter Brand had to explain that "this is the code I've written for our year-to-year projections." That code was illegible, but functional, and it served as a kind of mystifying exposition. Naomi's cookie embodies a gendered system of personality-driven investment banking that seems outdated but that persists nevertheless; Brand's code, like Bloomberg's brand, is projective, and augurs the new world of data-driven sports, a world whose contours remain uncertain.

In Michael Mann's *Blackhat* (Legendary/Universal, 2015), when a young FBI agent explains to a room full of other agents, "This is the code for our RAT," that, too, is an explanation for our benefit, but in its context, it is beside the point. A shadowy hacker has used this Remote Access Tool to access the trading system at the Chicago Mercantile Exchange, and then delivered a payload to cause an artificial spike in soy futures prices. In the FBI conference room with our dutiful expositor is a cybersecurity official from the Chinese government who has come to the United States to liaise. Chen Dawai snipes back at the agent's description of the stylistic differences between the RAT—"lean, graceful"—and the payload—"frenetic, confused." His interruption comes across as a breach of protocol. But for Dawai, it is an eruption occasioned by the temporal rift that has opened between RAT and payload. At this moment, the hacker's plans are, like Brand's code, projective. The blackhat has already caused a meltdown at a Hong Kong nuclear reactor—that was how Dawai came on board—and now he has threatened the world's financial infrastructure. Clearly the hacker has other plans. The RAT, in contrast, is older, something that, unbeknownst to everyone else in the room, Dawai and his friend Hathaway wrote as undergrads at MIT. Dawai recognizes that the code is his; "our RAT" is his RAT. That, in turn, recasts everything that has happened as the aftermath of his own work. In this economic image, time and responsibility are made manifest as *style*. This moment, when Dawai has no patience for the plodding overview—"confused—or overwritten?"—shows Mann making the case for the importance of stylishness as the vehicle for a new economy.

To track the hacker, Dawai will enlist his sister Lien and will spring his friend Hathaway from federal prison where he is being held on hacking charges. Lien, a network engineer, is someone he can trust; Hathaway is, in the way Dawai is, responsible. A souped-up version of a between-men triangle will ensue; Hathaway and Lien will fall in love; Dawai will be blown up by the blackhat; the FBI agents will be gunned down in Hong Kong; and the surviving couple will be free to pursue murderous revenge. In the end, their life on the run will be financed by €70 million swiped from the bad guy.

The story will conclude with a suddenly and fabulously wealthy heterosexual couple—handy stand-ins for American and Chinese capital and another amenable pairing for Legendary, which underwrote the movie—walking outside the frame of a security camera into the global distribution system. That system first appears in the movie as a planetary information cloud; midway through, it takes on more material form as a triple infrastructure of global finance (bank computers), hardened server farms that lie behind untraceable chains of proxies, and the web of geosatellites that might image any place on the planet's surface. The ending is tidy and implausible, but it incorporates the logic of aftermath in a way no other post-recession movie imagines. Hathaway takes up Dawai's sense of responsibility: If you are already on the hook for the disaster to come, then the only moral course of action is to prepare for it. Via its fantasies of sufficient preparation and collective, improvised professionalism *Blackhat* touches the revolutionary.

The metonymic logic of the market technocrat has been present in Mann's work from the beginning, and at one level he shares Soderbergh's interest in dynamic institutions: If you can assemble all the personnel you need to *pretend* to respond to a nuclear catastrophe, couldn't you, just perhaps, handle a real catastrophe? Such responses require both a projection forward (imagination of disaster) and a feel for the rhythm of the aftermath. Early in the movie, when a bit player in the conspiracy is killed in a crummy apartment, *Blackhat* takes the time to wait through the police response, even though that process has no bearing on the cyberforensic investigation. Later, when the team needs to extract the hacker's code from the computers in the still smoldering nuclear reactor, they arrive on the scene to discover the nuclear emergency teams in what looks like the first throes of their response. Mann makes clear that such responders undertake the crucial work of world reconstruction on the basis of their readiness for radical contingency.

But for the final battle collective preparation moves into the background. Mann and his crew enlisted and costumed some 5,000 extras to stage a Balinese parade in the heart of Jakarta, at the Irian Jaya Liberation Monument. In the parade's authentic versions, huge, demonic, bamboo and styrene ogoh-ogoh statues are paraded to the beach and burned. In the staged version, though, those demons seem to have been incarnated in the bodies of these two white men—one an actual black hat; one who first appeared in an unsullied white t-shirt. The two face each other against a backdrop of Indonesians performing cultural authenticity. The vast torchlit parade happens with no explanation—"You look at this and have no idea what's going on, and that's the idea," Mann says—an orientalist backstop to the macho ballet of blood and fire.[24]

In contrast, leading up to the clash, we see Hathaway filing down screwdrivers to serve as weapons and duct-taping magazines around his abdomen for armor. And, crucially, we see Lien dashing through a dispensary scooping up medical supplies that will be necessary to treat his impending wounds. This is the scene that is hard to imagine a director other than Mann including; it nearly redeems the indefensible atavism of the final confrontation. No course of revenge exists without bodily risk; they know what might be coming.

If the mano-a-mano antagonism is set, and if it rides on the hoariest tropes, the philosophical stakes are in flux up until the killing blow. Initially Hathaway feinted that he would be satisfied with money in exchange for his friends' deaths—20 percent of the take "for renting you my code." The hacker initially responded pragmatically, "It's my action that gave that code you wrote meaning," while Hathaway offered the materialist retort, "What's meaning without a bankroll?" At this point, confronted with the ineradicable material conditions that make practice possible, the hacker retreated to an almost pure idealism: "I can put together another bankroll, target another target, and if I stop thinking about you—if I stop thinking about anything, it disappears; it vanishes; it ceases to exist." Hathaway knows that not to be true and goes to work improvising weaponry.

At the kill, as Hathaway and the hacker circle each other, the latter stakes his final idealist claim, one that identifies that position not with a belief about the natures of being and appearing but with a privileged role in the contemporary economy: "I'm a gamer. I hire people to do sub-symbolic stuff." This is untrue: he may hire people to do "sub-symbolic stuff," but he has brought his own knife and he has whipped out his alliteration. But true or not, Hathaway answers him head on: "You killed my friends. I do my own." Assuming bodily the responsibility that Dawai first recognized, Hathaway now owns what he does—and, read slightly against the grain, he does his owning; owning is an action, not a state.

During the long postproduction for *Blackhat*, Mann made the decision to flip the opening to put the nuclear attack before the market hack. (He flipped it back for a special screening after the film flopped.[25]) There were good reasons for that decision—it activated Dawai and Lien before plunging them into the U.S. criminal justice apparatus; it extended the narrative response time to the meltdown—but for that swap to be possible, the two attacks had to be in some regard fungible. The equation of pictures is operating within *Blackhat* across electricity-generating atomic materiality on the one hand and commodity-trading abstraction on the other. Each sequence includes a vision of the mechanics of the cyberattack, with tracking shots rushing along cables then fibers then circuits and gates, a vision not of code—symbolic stuff—but of electrons racing about, bright enough to see and slow enough (and loud enough) for us to track. There are subtle differences between the internals of the two, distinctions that ultimately do not make an important difference: these are computers, they work roughly the same way, and their shared vulnerability to the hacker is emblematized in the similar visualization of the malicious code as it makes its way through the nanoscale.[26] (In the second attack, we get our first glimpses of the blackhat; first his finger hitting "enter," then a shot of him from behind. These and other differences help mark the attack as "second" in the usual, Bordwellian fashion.)

FIGURE 8.4 *The number of the RAT: 54.* Blackhat, *Mann, Legendary/Universal,* 2015.

But if the similarity of the machines is the ultimate ground of the swappability of the cyberattacks, that risks reducing the equation of pictures to the material as such. Mann, though, never lets go of the practical manifestations of matter. In each sequence, the materiality that undergirds practice emerges from abstraction—the abstraction of an abstraction. We zoom into a screen, closer and closer until the numbers pixelate, as they so often do in these montages. And those numbers are, just about, the same—not the same in that they are both numbers, or that they denote the same thing (they gauge temperature and price) or even that they are both indices, but that they are the same digits, a 5 and a 4, parts of 35.4 or 1254: the same numbers in the same Helvetica-ish font in nearly the same color with nearly the same soundtrack.

The same, but different enough in their appearance via the decimal to assure us that this is not merely the same footage. Like the deceptively named shell companies Jho Low used to launder funds, or the uncomfortable proximity of the sovereign wealth fund 1MDB and Amazon's database of movie info, IMDB, these 5s conflate the two attacks. Justice requires their untangling—and their reintegration. The differences are there to be seen or to be ignored depending upon our purposes. At every moment there are grounds for conflation and distinction, opportunities to endorse and overturn, opportunities that present themselves only in the aftermath of sufficient preparation. The equation of pictures in Mann's work refuses to settle on any one moment of ostention. *Blackhat* is unrelentingly stylish; the whole of the movie points at its number. And how is that done? Like this. And this.

Notes

1 Ludwig Wittgenstein, *Philosophical Investigations*, 4th ed., trans. G. E. M. Anscombe, P. M. S. Hacker, and Joachim Schulte (New York: Wiley-Blackwell, 2009), translation slightly modified.

2 William D. Cohan, "A Clue to the Scarcity of Financial Crisis Prosecutions," *The New York Times*, July 21, 2016, http://www.nytimes.com/2016/07/22/ business/dealbook/a-clue-to-the-scarcity-of-financial-crisis-prosecutions.html, accessed January 20, 2017.

3 Cohan, "A Clue to the Scarcity of Financial Crisis Prosecutions."

4 William D. Cohan, "How Wall Street's Bankers Stayed Out of Jail," *The Atlantic*, September 2015, http://www.theatlantic.com/magazine/ archive/2015/09/how-wall-streets-bankers-stayed-out-of-jail/399368/, accessed January 20, 2017.

5 Cohan, "How Wall Street's Bankers Stayed Out of Jail."

6 Lynch press conference, https://www.youtube.com/watch?v=31jOB0OBoM, accessed January 20, 2017.

7 For samples of this reporting, see Randeep Ramesh, "1MDB: The Inside Story of the World's Biggest Financial Scandal," *The Guardian*, July 28, 2016, https://www.theguardian.com/world/2016/jul/28/1mdb-inside-story-worlds-biggest-financial-scandal-malaysia, accessed January 20, 2017; Tom Wright and Bradley Hope, "Behind the 1MDB Scandal: Banks that Missed Clues and Bowed to Pressure," *Wall Street Journal*, September 6, 2013, http://www.wsj.com/articles/behind-the-1mdb-scandal-banks-that-missed-clues-and-bowed-to-pressure-1473109548, accessed January 20, 2017; and "How Jho Low's Gang Blasted Malaysia's Millions at New Year!" *Sarawak Report*, January 15, 2016, http://www.sarawakreport.org/2016/01/how-jho-lows-gang-blasted-malaysias-millions-at-new-year/, accessed January 20, 2017.

8 For an overview, see: https://www.justice.gov/sites/default/files/usao/ legacy/2007/12/21/usab5506.pdf, accessed January 20, 2017.

9 As the case progresses, court documents are likely to reveal the exact amounts invested, earned, and subject to seizure. As is typical in such actions, Red Granite's creditors have sought to enjoin the DOJ seizure, hoping to receive the payments they might be owed. During the press conference, it was striking that the law enforcement officials were initially uncertain whether they were seeking all the money that had flowed into Red Granite or only the future revenues.

10 Forfeitures attendant to money-laundering schemes frequently take in not just the profits of the activity but all the funds, however legitimate their origin, that can be found.

11 "Too big to jail" emerged as the legal counterpart to the idea of "too big to fail." The latter category would be more precisely defined as "systemically important financial institutions" (SIFIs), those big enough to take down the economy. Brandon L. Garrett, *Too Big to Jail: How Prosecutors Compromise with Corporations* (Cambridge: Harvard University Press, 2014).

12 The U.S. attorney said as much to the *Wall Street Journal* before recanting and issuing an apology. "U.S. Attorney's Office Apologises to 'Wolf of Wall Street' Jordan Belfort Over Article Suggesting he is Hiding in Australia," *news.com.au*, January 15, 2014, http://www.news.com.au/finance/money/us-attorneys-office-apologises-to-wolf-of-wall-street-jordan-belfort-over-article-suggesting-he-is-hiding-in-australia/story-e6frfmci-1226801457393, accessed January 20, 2017. (The real Belfort went to Australia, not New Zealand.)

13 Terrence Winter, *The Wolf of Wall Street*, screenplay, n.d., 103, http://www.paramountguilds.com/pdf/the_wolf_of_wall_street_screenplay.pdf.

14 Winter, *The Wolf of Wall Street*, 134.

15 Graham Bowley and Doreen Carvajal, "One of the World's Greatest Art Collections Hides Behind this Fence," *The New York Times*, May 28, 2016, http://www.nytimes.com/2016/05/29/arts/design/one-of-the-worlds-greatest-art-collections-hides-behind-this-fence.html, accessed January 20, 2017.

16 *United States of America v. "The Wolf of Wall Street" Motion Picture, Including Any Profits, Royalties, and Distribution Proceeds Owed to Red Granite Pictures, Inc. or its Affiliates and/or Assigns*, Complaint, filed July 20, 2016, 78.

17 Julie Makinen, "Did a Chinese Casino Really Just Pay $70 Million for a 15–minute Martin Scorsese Film?" *Los Angeles Times*, October 27, 2015; Patrick Frater, "Ratpack Era Recalled at Starry Opening of Macau's Studio City," *Variety*, October 27, 2015, http://variety.com/2015/biz/asia/ratpac-era-recalled-at-macaus-studio-city-1201627461/. The casino's official website, http://www.studiocity-macau.com/, offers a look at the movie-theming of the resort.

18 For the Italian subtitled version, see https://www.youtube.com/watch?v=dmSjSR5fHP0. For the Russian dubbed (but still Italian subtitled) version, see https://www.youtube.com/watch?v=M0u0wPci2ak.

19 For the $13 million estimate, see Makinen. For the $17 million estimate and a roundup of photographs of the premiere, see Jennifer Smith, "Packer's Rat Pack!," http://www.dailymail.co.uk/tvshowbiz/article-3291286/James-Packer-rubs-shoulders-Leonardo-DiCaprio-Robert-Niro-Martin-Scorsese-paying-trio-17million-promote-new-Macau-casino.html.

20 For the slate deal, see Dave McNary, "Warner Bros. Closes Financing Deal with Dune, Brett Ratner, James Packer," *Variety*, September 30, 2013, http://variety.com/2013/film/news/warner-bros-closes-financing-deal-with-dune-brett-ratner-james-packer-1200682476/. For Plan B, see Justin Kroll and Dave McNary, "Brad Pitt's Plan B Leaving Paramount for New Regency, RatPac," *Variety*, December 10, 2013, http://variety.com/2013/film/news/brad-pitts-plan-b-paramount-1200942448/. Sharon Waxman and Matt Donnelly, "'The Revenant' Budget Soars to $135 Million as New Regency Foots the Bill," *The Wrap*, January 15, 2016 (originally October 15, 2015), https://www.thewrap.com/revenant-budget-soars-to-165-million-with-new-regency-footing-most-of-bill-exclusive/.

21 Interview with Jonathan Hoyt, SteveTurner.la, November 16, 2016.

22 "Girl Gang" *Equity* Blu-ray featurette (Sony, 2016).

23 Inside Bloomberg, "Bloomberg's Role in the Making of Equity The Movie," February 8, 2016, https://www.youtube.com/watch?v=9SJ5trMnqgA, accessed January 20, 2017.

24 "On Location around the World," *Blackhat* Blu-ray featurette (Universal 2015).

25 Rodrigo Perez, "Michael Mann at BAM: The Recut 'Blackhat,' The Authenticity Behind *Thief*, *Heat*, *Ali*, *Collateral*, & More," *IndieWire*, February 12, 2016, http://www.indiewire.com/2016/02/michael-mann-at-bam-the-recut-blackhat-the-authenticity-behind-thief-heat-ali-collateral-more-270444/, accessed January 20, 2017; Kenji Fujishima, "Breaking Down Michael Mann's Sharper Directors Cut of *Blackhat*," *IndieWire*, February 11, 2016, http://www.indiewire.com/2016/02/breaking-down-michael-manns-sharper-directors-cut-of-blackhat-272478/, accessed January 20, 2017.

26 Faith Holland has produced a supercut of such sequences, *RIP Geocities*, which can be viewed here: https://vimeo.com/25489844, accessed November 20, 2017.

Conclusion

The collision of Hollywood's partial search for self-justification with the U.S. government's search for the same offers us a way to compare the ways in which cultural and political institutions have responded to the Great Recession. At the same time, those responses are directed downward, toward cases (individual movies, individual schmucks) and upward toward principles (sociality, justice, equity). That capacity for scalar attention, I have argued, was relatively stable for a long period, underwent dramatic reshuffling, and has, for now, recentered itself in new emblems of the process of social integration—protocol violation and ostension.

It has been my aim in this book to elicit useful concepts from within individual cases without allowing any of those concepts to congeal to the point that they cease to be subject to the same historical forces that produced them. In grandiose moments, I imagine that aim as attempting to keep every emergent frame in motion relative to every other. In practice this can come across as an endless series of arbitrary distillations of movies that (it may seem I think) don't deserve it. Their presence here is evidence that I think they deserve it, and deserve it despite whatever their other limitations are. It would be foolish not to register the difference between the conceptual utility of a movie and any other judgments one might make of it, just as it would be foolish not to recognize that defending the aesthetic achievements of a teaser trailer at length risks the good will of most readers. In quasi-economic terms: only a substantial conceptual yield can justify such risks.

The most durable of those formations, the economic image, captures a particular "equation of pictures," a particularly condensed emblem of a particular movie's negotiation of money and time (narrative). It is, in the broader context of its occurrence, the model of the model, the one not simply in the head of the executive, but the one that has resulted from structured interplay of so many forces of labor and technology. As the model of a model it can incorporate a far wider range of connotations of that underlying concept. An economic model of the sort deployed by a regional Federal Reserve Bank has a great deal in common with the sort of statistical model deployed by Relativity or Sony, but it is not the same thing. Similarly, the "model" that requires obeisance by a group of executives is not quite the same thing as the rough, rule-of-thumb model that underlies a studio's strategy or the determination of a marketing budget for a particular movie.

And then there are models as exemplars, models as prototypes, models as sources to draw on or cheat off. Some, many, or all of these might be drawn inside the event horizon of the economic image. What draws them there is, again, the consolidation of money and time. The economic image, as the internalized relation of the film to money, occurs across a span of time, highlighted by dialogue or scoring or its own construction through montage. Its micro corollary, the Efficient Market Hypothesis cut helps delimit the image, to give it a formal integrity it might otherwise lose.

Nevertheless, the economic image is not a determinant of or evidence for systemic confidence. That determination falls to a related pair of concepts, more historical (more temporal, residuals from the forced equivalence of time and money captured by the economic image): precession and recession. When the capacity for scalar attention—when the capacity for abstraction from material bases to principles and vice versa—is sufficient, then Hollywood cinema takes the form of normal cultural production, of problem→solution, and the dominant mode of strategic practice is precession. Again, the balance between precession and recession is forced. Precession in Hollywood—or, for that matter, in any field of cultural endeavor—presumes that in the contest for authority over a regular process of cultural production, the winning move is to assert control over a phase that can be understood as logically (not necessarily temporally) prior to whatever phase currently exercises decisive authority. In the first half, I laid out a precessive system for grappling with the materiality of capital and the abstraction of number as complementary bases for a system under ordinary stresses. When the future is not simply something you can anticipate, but something where such anticipations can be folded into the planning process as a kind of mass damper to moderate the effects of the buffeting winds of contingency, we are in the realm of precession. Things transpire as they were to have, and the confidence in such eventualities appears as the future perfect.

In contrast, recession designates an industry uncertain of its capacity for the management of abstraction. The second half of this book has presented four forms in which the process of managing abstraction has come apart and subsequently been renormalized as the results of some new, quasi-digital process: 1. The precessive, discursive regulation of the studio/indie divide was a durable embodiment of an overarching model for the allocation of financial and symbolic capital. Under recession, this divide is subject to scalar collapse into a uniform, digitally bibliotechnological imaginary. 2. The precessive negotiation of complementary changes in televisual narrative and the regulatory-technological system assured legacy players of continuing relevance in new forms ("must-carry rules," "quality TV"). Under new pressures of digitization, those contests become all-or-nothing "digital cliffs" in which win-win situations were no longer the norm. 3. The precessive allegorical basis for sociality in the struggles of a romantic couple yields to narratives across studio/indie scales where those foundational bonds are only tenuously imaginable as the beginnings of a reconstructed society. When such reconstitution is grounded on neural or viral materiality, however mysterious its operation (as drift, fomite, or parasite), even the most optimistic vision of the ability of pairwise interactions to constructively multiply is shadowed by an interpersonal danger just as foundational. 4. Finally, the precessive literalism of thematization—of making movies about money to make movies about capitalism—presumes a relative independence of the moral economy of the industry from the broader economy. Whether that relative independence appears as a stark contrast between them or as a surprising metonymy matters less than the ability to point at the general from the particular, and to point both justly and justifiably. When that relative independence gives way, justice is replaced by seemingly more basic questions of ostension—how do we point to "its number"? How is pointing possible at all? Only confidence, emblematized by style and authorized by an antecedent arrogation of responsibility, promises a way back to the problems→solutions of precession.

Sheltered beneath the arcs of these concepts are others, elicited from individual cases, and only fragmentarily developed here. Two—pervasion and staking—have as their occasions the manipulation of the gaze (in *Performance*) or the point-of-view more generally (in the examples of Chapter 8) and qualify certain ways in which narratives are specified or generalized. They might readily find use in a broad narratology as it tried to grapple with a transmedial franchise such as *World of Warcraft* or *Gamorrah*. Two—the self-funding individual (in *Ferris Bueller*) and the retroaction movie (*Déjà Vu*)—take up temporalities of character and production that could be explored alongside other investigations of industrial affect in *Even the Rain* or extended to the study of reboots such as *Prometheus*. Two—fragmentary dimensionality and the grid (both Chapter 4)—consider surfaces and depths in ways that might allow for a revision of the old-fashioned vision of allegory as layering or the image as a surface of surfaces. Such intercalary possibilities might reconfigure how we think of texturality in Wong Kar-Wai's films or liquidity and geography in a host of IMAX documentaries. Finally, two more—deritualization and the market technocrat—appear as mechanisms that can connect the social worlds of the screen with the limited social utopias of their production. In their mobilization of bodies, surfaces, and betrayals this conceptual pair might be a useful avenue for approaching a film as different from *Contagion* as Robert Bresson's *Pickpocket*. These subsidiary concepts are neither economic nor financial nor even numerical. They are not theoretical, if that means independent of their occasions. They might very well be applicable across various media and industries of culture. But that cultural potential, whatever it might be, lies in their proximity to Hollywood—the version of Hollywood on offer here—and draws on the industry's own claims to generality in order to seem attractive.

Like a star subject to a commutation test, these concepts would necessarily alter the projects in which they were deployed and would, at the same time, be altered by their new uses. Whether such substitutions are worth making depends on the very particular differences such concepts would make, on the particular valences they have accrued here. Consider this a book of connotations.

BIBLIOGRAPHY

Abbott, Stacey. "How *Lost* Found its Audience: The Making of a Cult Blockbuster," in *Reading Lost: Perspectives on a Hit Television Show*, edited by Roberta Pearson, 9–26. London: I. B. Tauris, 2009.

Adalian, Josef. "Disney Dumps Touchstone TV Brand," *Variety*, February 8, 2007, http://variety.com/2007/scene/markets-festivals/disney-dumps-touchstone-tv-brand-1117958953/.

"All-Star Game Television Ratings," *Baseball Almanac*, http://www.baseball-almanac.com/asgbox/asgtv.shtml.

Allen, Mike, and Gregory Schneider. "National Guard to be used at Airports; Bush Calls for Public Confidence in Flying, Details Security Plan," *Washington Post*, September 28, 2001, A1.

Anderson, Chris. *The Long Tail*. New York: Hachette, 2008.

Anderson, Mark Lynn. "The Silent Screen, 1895–1927," in *Producing*, edited by Jon Lewis, 15–35. New Brunswick, NJ: Rutgers University Press, 2016.

Andrew, Dudley. "Adaptation," in *Concepts in Film Theory*, 96–106. Oxford: Oxford University Press, 1984.

Armstrong, Jennifer. "The Scoop on 'Lost,'" *Entertainment Weekly*, September 29, 2005, http://ew.com/article/2005/09/29/scoop-lost/.

Association of Film Commissioners International, http://www.afci.org/.

Austen, Ian. "Lobby Group Urges Ottawa to Introduce New, Refundable Tax Credit for Film Industry," *The Gazette*, November 16, 1994, B4.

Bach, Stephen. *Final Cut: Art, Money, and Ego in the Making of Heaven's Gate*. New York: Newmarket, 1999.

Bailey, Ian. "U.S. Unions Declare War on Hollywood North: Film Industry Wants Tax Breaks to Woo Business Back from Canada," *The Ottawa Citizen*, July 5, 1999, A5.

Baker, Aaron. *Steven Soderbergh*. Urbana, IL: University of Illinois Press, 2011.

Baker, Dean. "The Housing Bubble and the Financial Crisis, #25,452," *Center for Economic and Policy Research*, April 2, 2015, http://www.cepr.net/index.php/blogs/beat-the-press/the-housing-bubble-and-the-financial-crisis-25452.

Barboza, Craigh. "Imagination is Infinite," *USAWeekend*, July 15, 2005, http://159.54.226.237/05_issues/050619/050619spielberg.html.

Barboza, David. "A Tide of Death, But This Time the Food is Safe," *New York Times*, March 14, 2013, http://www.nytimes.com/2013/03/15/world/asia/a-tide-of-dead-pigs-in-china-but-dinner-is-safe.html.

Barrett, K. K. "Imagining a Fort for 'Where the Wild Things Are'," *Los Angeles Times*, December 16, 2009, http://articles.latimes.com/2009/dec/16/news/la-en-lightswild16-2009dec16.

Barthes, Roland. *S/Z*, translated by Richard Howard. New York: Hill & Wang, 1970.

Beatty, Kelly. "Stargazing with the Obamas," *Sky and Telescope*, October 8, 2009, http://www.skyandtelescope.com/news/63749172.html.

Beck, Jay. *A Quiet Revolution: Changes in American Film Sound Practices*, Ph.D. Dissertation, University of Iowa, 2003.

Beller, Jonathan. *The Cinematic Mode of Production: Attention Economy and the Society of the Spectacle*. Hanover, NH: Dartmouth, 2006.

Ben Block, Alex. "Brad Pitt Reveals what he, Sony did to Save 'Moneyball,'" *The Hollywood Reporter*, December 16, 2011, http://www.hollywoodreporter.com/news/moneyball-making-brad-pitt-bennett-miller-274738.

Ben Block, Alex, and Kim Masters. "Legendary Entertainment Finds New Home at NBC Universal," *The Hollywood Reporter*, July 9, 2013, https://www.hollywoodreporter.com/news/legendary-entertainment-finds-new-home-579935.

Bergman, Andrew. *We're in the Money: Depression America and Its Films*. Chicago: Ivan R. Dee, 1992.

Bergson, Henri. "Memory of the Present and False Recognition," in *Mind-Energy: Lectures and Essays*, translated by H. Wildon Carr, 109–51. London: Macmillan & Co., 1920.

Biskind, Peter. *Down and Dirty Pictures: Miramax, Sundance, and the Rise of Independent Film*. New York: Simon & Schuster, 2004.

Blatty, William Peter. *The Exorcist*. New York: Harper, 1971.

Bordwell, David. *The Way Hollywood Tells It*. Berkeley, CA: University of California Press, 2006.

Bordwell, David, Janet Staiger, and Kristin Thompson. *Classical Hollywood Cinema*. New York: Columbia University Press, 1985.

Bowley, Graham, and Doreen Carvajal. "One of the World's Greatest Art Collections Hides Behind this Fence," *New York Times*, May 28, 2016, http://www.nytimes.com/2016/05/29/arts/design/one-of-the-worlds-greatest-art-collections-hides-behind-this-fence.html.

Brinkema, Eugenie. *The Forms of the Affects*. Durham, NC: Duke University Press, 2014.

Brinkley, Joel. "Getting the Picture: TV Stations Develop New Enthusiasm for Digital Future," *New York Times*, November 24, 1997, http://www.nytimes.com/1997/11/24/business/getting-the-picture-tv-stations-develop-new-enthusiasm-for-digital-future.html.

Brooker, Will. "Television Out of Time: Watching Cult Shows on Download," in *Reading Lost: Perspectives on a Hit Television Show*, edited by Roberta Pearson, 51–72. London: I. B. Tauris.

Brower, Jordan. "'Written with the Movies in Mind': Twentieth-century American Literature and Transmedial Possibility," *MLQ*, 78: 2, 2017, 243–73.

Brown, Jared. *Alan J. Pakula: His Films and His Life*. New York: Back Stage Books, 2005.

Bruck, Connie. *Master of the Game*. New York: Simon & Schuster, 1994.

Bureau of Labor Statistics. http://www.bls.gov/news.release/archives/ppi_02192009.htm.

Caldwell, John Thornton. *Production Culture*. Durham, NC: Duke University Press, 2008.

Cammell, Donald. *Performance*, edited by Colin MacCabe. London: Faber and Faber, 2001.

Canby, Vincent. "Why the Devil Do They Dig *The Exorcist?*" *New York Times*, January 13, 1974, 4.

Carpenter, Arthur E. *Gateway to the Americas: New Orleans's Quest for Latin American Trade, 1900–1970*, Tulane, PhD thesis, 1987.

Carroll, Noël. "The Future of Allusion: Hollywood in the Seventies and Beyond," in *Interpreting the Moving Image*, 240–64. Cambridge: Cambridge University Press, 1998.

Carugati, Anna. "Anne Sweeney," *Worldscreen.com*, http://worldscreen.com/anne-sweeney/.

Cavell, Stanley. *Contesting Tears*, 3–46. Chicago: University of Chicago Press, 1997.

Cavell, Stanley. "The Thought of Movies," in *Themes Out of School*, 3–26. Chicago: University of Chicago Press, 1984.

Cavell, Stanley. *The World Viewed*, Enlarged ed. Cambridge, MA: Harvard University Press, 1979.

Caves, Richard. *Creative Industries: Contracts Between Art and Commerce.* Cambridge, MA: Harvard University of Press, 2000.

Center for Entertainment Industry Data and Research. *The Global Success of Production Tax Incentives and the Migration of Feature Film Production From The U.S. to the World*, 2006, http://www.ceidr.org.

Center for Entertainment Industry Data and Research. *Year 2005 Production Report*, 2006, http://www.ceidr.org.

Charles C. Moul. *A Short Handbook of Movie Industry Economics.* Cambridge: Cambridge University Press, 2005.

Charlie, "Charlie goes to WHERE THE WILD THINGS ARE," *Ain't it Cool News*, September 20, 2009, http://www.aintitcool.com/node/42558.

Chase, Chris. "Everyone's Reading It, Billy's Filming It," *New York Times*, August 27, 1972, D1, 9.

Chaudhary, Ajay Singh, and Raphaële Chappe. "The Supermanagerial Reich," *Los Angeles Review of Books*, November 6, 2016, https://lareviewofbooks.org/article/the-supermanagerial-reich.

Chion, Michel. *Audio-Vision*, translated by Claudia Gorbman. New York: Columbia University Press, 1994.

Chion, Michel. *Voice in Cinema*, translated by Claudia Gorbman. New York: Columbia University Press, 1999.

Christ, Steve. "Rick Santelli's Rant of the Year," *Baltimore Examiner*. http://www.examiner.com/article/rick-santelli-s-rant-of-the-year.

Christensen, Jerome. "Post–Warners Warners: *Batman* and *JFK*; *You've Got Mail*," in *America's Corporate Art: The Studio Authorship of Hollywood Motion Pictures*, 245–79. Palo Alto, CA: Stanford University Press, 2011.

Clagett, Thomas D. *William Friedkin, Films of Aberration, Obsession and Reality*, 2nd ed. Los Angeles: Silman-James, 2003.

Clark, T. J. *The Painting of Modern Life: Paris in the Art of Manet and his Contemporaries.* Princeton, NJ: Princeton University Press, 1985.

Cohan, William D. "A Clue to the Scarcity of Financial Crisis Prosecutions," *New York Times*, July 21, 2016, http://www.nytimes.com/2016/07/22/business/dealbook/a-clue-to-the-scarcity-of-financial-crisis-prosecutions.html.

Cohan, William D. "How Wall Street's Bankers Stayed Out of Jail," *The Atlantic*, September 2015, http://www.theatlantic.com/magazine/archive/2015/09/how-wall-streets-bankers-stayed-out-of-jail/399368/.

Cohen, Joseph N. *Investing in Movies: Strategies for Investors and Producers.* New York: Routledge, 2017.

Connor, J. D. "Aspect Jumping," *FlowTV*, December 3, 2012, http://flowtv.org/2012/12/aspect-jumping/.

Connor, J. D. "'He's Building a Model': Steven Spielberg, J.J. Abrams, Scale and *Super 8*," *Media Fields*, 4, December 2011, http://www.mediafieldsjournal.org/hes-building-a-model/.

Connor, J. D. "Independence and the Consent of the Governed: The Systems and Scales of *Under the Skin*," *Jump Cut*, 57, Fall 2016.

Connor, J. D. *The Studios after the Studios*. Palo Alto, CA: Stanford University Press, 2015.

Crain, Caleb. "The Thoreau Poison," *The New Yorker*, May 8, 2018, www.newyorker.com/books/page-turner/the-thoreau-poison.

Cronon, William. *Nature's Metropolis: Chicago and the Great West*. New York: W. W. Norton, 1991.

Cubitt, Sean. *Digital Aesthetics*. Thousand Oaks, CA: SAGE, 1998.

Davis, Glyn, and Gary Needham. "Queerying Lost," in *Reading Lost: Perspectives on a Hit Television Show*, edited by Roberta Pearson, 261–80. London: I. B. Tauris, 2009.

de Vany, Arthur. *Hollywood Economics: How Extreme Uncertainty Shapes the Film Industry*. New York: Routledge, 2003.

Deans, Jason. "TV Ratings: Lost Returns with More Than 800,000 Viewers," *The Guardian*, February 8, 2010, https://www.theguardian.com/media/2010/feb/08/lost-tv-ratings.

deKoven, Maryanne. *Utopia, Ltd.: The Sixties and the Emergence of the Postmodern*. Durham, NC: Duke, 2004.

Deleuze, Gilles. *Cinéma 2: L'Image-Temps*. Paris: Les Éditions de Minuit, 1985.

Deleuze, Gilles. *Cinéma 2: The Time-Image*, translated by Hugh Tomlinson. Minneapolis: University of Minnesota Press, 1989.

Delong, Brad. "The Housing Bubble and the Lesser Depression: Either the Very Sharp Dean Baker or I am Hopelessly Confused," *Equitablog*, April 2, 2015, http://equitablegrowth.org/2015/04/02/housing-bubble-lesser-depression-either-sharp-dean-baker-hopelessly-confused/.

"Democratic Party's Response to the Tax Proposal," *New York Times*, May 29, 1985, A19.

Department of Labor. http://www.dol.gov/opa/media/press/eta/ui/eta20090163.htm.

deWaard, Andrew, and R. Colin Tait. *The Cinema of Steven Soderbergh: Indie Sex, Corporate Lies, and Digital Videotape*. New York: Wallflower, 2013.

Dick, Bernard F. *Engulfed: The Death of Paramount Pictures and the Birth of Corporate Hollywood*. Lexington, KY: University of Kentucky, 2001.

DiLullo, Tara. "*Déjà Vu*: Time Tripping to new VFX Heights," *Animation World Network*, November 22, 2006, http://www.awn.com/articles/reviews/ideja-vui-time-tripping-new-vfx-heights/page/1%2C1.

Donahue, Ann. "Above the Line: Avi Arad: Turnabout? It's Marvel-ous," *Variety*, May 19, 2002, http://variety.com/2002/film/news/above-the-line-avi-arad-1117867142/.

Drosnin, Michael. *Citizen Hughes*. New York: Holt, Reinhart and Winston, 1985.

Ebenstein, Lanny. *Chicagonomics: The Evolution of Chicago Free Market Economics*. New York: St. Martin's, 2015.

Eisner, Michael with Tony Schwartz. *Work in Progress*. New York: Hyperion, 1999.

Elliott, David. "Dumbed Down Dickens: New 'Great Expectations' Flunks Dickens, Aces Paltrow," *San Diego Union-Tribune*, January 29, 1988, Night and Day 15.

Emmett, Ross B. *The Elgar Companion to the Chicago School of Economics*. Cheltenham, UK: Elgar, 2010.

Enchin, Harvey. "Canada Extends Pic Tax-shelter Program," *Daily Variety*, July 31, 1997, 8.

Epstein, Edward J. *The Hollywood Economist 2.0*. New York: Melville House, 2012.

Evans, Robert. *The Kid Stays in the Picture*. Beverly Hills: Phoenix Books, 2002.

Executive Office for United States Attorneys, *United States Attorneys' Bulletin*, 55: 6, November 2007, special issue "Asset Forfeiture," https://www.justice.gov/sites/default/files/usao/legacy/2007/12/21/usab5506.pdf.

Faughnder, Ryan. "Relativity Media Struggles to Come Back from Bankruptcy," *Los Angeles Times*, November 4, 2016, http://www.latimes.com/business/hollywood/la-fi-ct-relativity-bankruptcy-20161102-story.html.

Federal Communications Commission, "Cable Carriage of Broadcast Stations," *FCC*, May 26, 2011, http://www.fcc.gov/guides/cable-carriage-broadcast-stations.

Feiler, Bruce. "What 'Modern Family' Says about Modern Families," *New York Times*, January 23, 2011, http://www.nytimes.com/2011/01/23/fashion/23THISLIFE.html (accessed January 20, 2017).

Feuer, Jane. "The Concept of Live Television: Ontology as Ideology," in *Regarding Television: Critical Approaches—An Anthology*, edited by E. Ann Kaplan, 12–21. Los Angeles: AFI, 1983.

Finke, Nikki, and Mike Fleming, Jr. "Paramount To End Relationship With Marvel In 2012: Disney Will Distribute 'Iron Man 3' and 'The Avengers,'" *Deadline*, October 18, 2010, http://deadline.com/2010/10/disney-paramount-marvel-restructure-marketing-distruibution-deal-76534/.

Finney, Angus with Eugenio Triana. *The International Film Business: A Market Guide Beyond Hollywood*, 2nd ed. New York: Rutgers, 2015.

Fischer, Paul. "Gwyn's *Great Expectations*," *Courier Mail*, March 26, 1988, 8.

Fischer, Russ. "Guillermo del Toro Promises Amazing Monsters and Robots in 'Pacific Rim,'" *Film*, July 23, 2011, http://www.slashfilm.com/guillermo-del-toro-promises-amazing-monsters-robots-pacific-rim/ (accessed January 20, 2017).

Flanagan, Martin, Mike McKenny, and Andy Livingstone. *The Marvel Studios Phenomenon: Inside a Transmedia Universe*. New York: Bloomsbury, 2016.

Fleming, Karl. "Who is Ted Ashley? Just the King of Hollywood, Baby," *New York*, June 24, 1974, 30–35.

Fleming, Mike, and Peter Bart, "Sony Scraps Soderbergh's 'Moneyball,'" *Variety*, June 21, 2009, http://variety.com/2009/film/features/sony-scraps-soderbergh-s-moneyball-1118005208/.

Frater, Patrick. "Ratpack Era Recalled at Starry Opening of Macau's Studio City," *Variety* October 27, 2015, http://variety.com/2015/biz/asia/ratpac-era-recalled-at-macaus-studio-city-1201627461/. http://www.studiocity-macau.com/.

Freedman, Craig. *Chicago Fundamentalism: Ideology and Methodology in Economics*. Hackensack, NJ: World Scientific, 2008.

Frenkiel, Richard H. "Cellular Radiotelephone System Structured for Flexible Use of Different Cell Sizes," patent application filed September 22, 1976, http://www.google.com/patents/US4144411.

Friedberg, Anne. *Window Shopping: Cinema and the Postmodern*. Berkeley, CA: University of California Press, 1994.

Fujishima, Kenji. "Breaking Down Michael Mann's Sharper Director's Cut of *Blackhat*," *IndieWire*, February 11, 2016, http://www.indiewire.com/2016/02/breaking-down-michael-manns-sharper-directors-cut-of-blackhat-272478/.

Fulton, Scott M., III "What YouTube's New 16:9 Aspect Ratio Means for Users," *Betanews.com*, November 25, 2008, http://betanews.com/2008/11/25/what-youtube-s-new-16-9-aspect-ratio-means-for-users/.

Gallagher, Mark. *Another Steven Soderbergh Experience: Authorship and Contemporary Hollywood*. Austin: University of Texas Press, 2013.

Garrett, Brandon L. *Too Big to Jail: How Prosecutors Compromise with Corporations*. Cambridge, MA: Harvard University Press, 2014.

Gessell, Paul. "Bigger, Perhaps Better, but Less Canadian," *The Gazette*, October 4, 1997, B2.

Gill, Mark. "Yes, the Sky Really is Falling," *Indiewire*, June 22, 2008, http://www.indiewire.com/article/first_person_film_departments_mark_gill_yes_the_sky_really_is_falling/.

Goddard, Drew, and Joss Whedon. *Cabin in the Woods*, screenplay, 20.

Godfrey, Stephen. "Producers Protest Tighter Tax Rules; Province Restricts Definition of 'Made-in-Quebec' Film," *The Globe and Mail*, February 22, 1991.

Goldman, John J., and Paul E. Steiger, "Disclosures Startling in Commonwealth's Proxy," *Los Angeles Times*, July 10, 1969, B11, 15.

Goldman, William. *Adventures in the Screen Trade*. New York: Warner Books, 1983.

Goldsmith, Jill. "Legendary Chief Touts Slate, China Plans," *Variety*, September 19, 2012, http://variety.com/2012/film/news/legendary-chief-touts-slate-china-plans-1118059500/

Goldstein, Dana. *The Teacher Wars: A History of America's Most Embattled Profession*. New York: Anchor, 2014.

Goldstein, Patrick. "The Sky is Falling on Indie Film," *Los Angeles Times*, June 23, 2008, http://latimesblogs.latimes.com/the_big_picture/2008/06/the-sky-is-fall.html.

Goldstein, Patrick, and James Rainey. "Can Spike Jonze Save 'Where the Wild Things Are'?" *Los Angeles Times*, July 11, 2008, http://latimesblogs.latimes.com/the_big_picture/2008/07/is-spike-jonze.html.

Gorman, Bill. "Network Jedi Mind Tricks: Live + 7 Ratings and Your Favorite Show," *TV by the Numbers zap2it*, October 17, 2010, http://tvbythenumbers.zap2it.com/2010/10/17/network-jedi-mind-tricks-live7-ratings-and-your-favorite-show/68123/.

Gorton, Gary B. *Misunderstanding Financial Crises: Why We Don't See Them Coming*. New York: Oxford University Press, 2012.

Gottschalk, Jr., Earl C. "Film Firms Mull Merging Studio Facilities, Seeking to Cut Costs, Revive the Industry," *Wall Street Journal*, July 18, 1971, 34.

Gough, Paul J. "DVR Ratings Boost is Quantified," *The Hollywood Reporter*, April 26, 2007, https://www.hollywoodreporter.com/news/dvr-ratings-boost-is-quantified-134903.

Govil, Nitin. "Recognizing 'Industry,'" *Cinema Journal*, 52: 3, 2013, 172–76.

Govil, Nitin. "Size Matters," *BioScope: South Asian Screen Studies*, 1: 2, 2010, 105–09.

Grady, Denise. "A Medical Mystery Unfolds in Minnesota," *New York Times*, February 5, 2008, http://www.nytimes.com/2008/02/05/health/05pork.html;

Grainge, Paul. "*Lost* Logos: Channel 4 and the Branding of American Event Television," in *Reading Lost: Perspectives on a Hit Television Show*, edited by Roberta Pearson, 95–118. London: I. B. Tauris.

Granovetter, Marc S. and Richard Swedberg, *Sociology of Economic Life*. Boulder, CO: Westview, 2011.

Grantham, Bill. "Motion Picture Finance and Risk in the United States," in *Film and Risk*, edited by Mette Hjort, 197–208. Detroit: Wayne State, 2012.

Graser, Marc. "Warner Bros. No Longer in Legendary's Future," *Variety*, June 24, 2013, http://variety.com/2013/biz/news/warner-bros-no-longer-in-legendarys-future-1200501572/ (accessed January 20, 2017).

Gray, Jonathan. "We're Not in Portland Anymore: *Lost* and its International Others," in *Reading Lost: Perspectives on a Hit Television Show*, edited by Roberta Pearson, 221–39. London: I. B. Tauris.

Greider, William. *Secrets of the Temple: How the Federal Reserve Runs the Country*. New York: Simon & Schuster, 1987.

Groden, Robert J. *The Search for Lee Harvey Oswald: A Comprehensive Photographic Record*. New York: Penguin Studio, 1995.

Grover, Ronald. "Disney, ABC Station Owners Agree to Share Fees from Pay TV." *Bloomberg.com*, February 17, 2011, http://www.bloomberg.com/news/2011-02-17/disney-abc-station-owners-agree-to-share-fees-from-pay-tv.html.

Haber, Joyce. "Making a Believer out of Friedkin," *Los Angeles Times*, April 26, 1973, G30.

Haber, Joyce. "Ted Ashley Opts for the Unknown," *Los Angeles Times*, August 28, 1974, G11.

Hammer, David. "New Orleans Saints Charles Grant, Jeremy Shockey sue Kevin Houser over Film Tax Credits" *New Orleans Times-Picayune*, March 8, 2010, http://blog.nola.com/crime_impact/print.html?entry=/2010/03/new_orleans_saints_charles_gra.html.

Harris, Christopher. "Lights! Camera! Action! HOLLYWOOD NORTH: Toronto Remains the Third-largest Film and TV Production Centre on the Continent, and the City Would Like to Keep it that Way," *The Globe and Mail*, October 30, 1997, C1.

Harris, Dana. "Prod'n gets Bayou Boost," *Daily Variety*, August 27, 2002, 1.

Harris, Paul. "Cantor Trading Proposal Approved," *Variety*, June 29, 2010, http://variety.com/2010/film/news/cantor-trading-proposal-approved-1118021184/.

Havens, Timothy, and Amanda Lotz, *Understanding Media Industries*. 2nd ed. Oxford: Oxford University Press, 2016.

Hilmes, Michele. *Only Connect: A Cultural History of Broadcasting in the United States*, 2nd ed. Belmont, CA: Thomson-Wadsworth, 2007.

Hofmann, Kay H. *Co-Financing Hollywood Film Productions with Outside Investors: An Economic Analysis of Principal Agent Relationships in the U.S. Motion Picture Industry*. Wiesbaden: Springer Gabler, 2013.

Holson, Laura M. "Disney agrees to acquire Pixar in a $7.4 billion deal," *New York Times*, January 25, 2006, http://www.nytimes.com/2006/01/25/business/disney-agrees-to-acquire-pixar-in-a-74-billion-deal.html.

Holt, Jennifer. *Empires of Entertainment: Media Industries and the Politics of Deregulation, 1980–1996*. New Brunswick: Rutgers University Press, 2011.

Holt, Jennifer, and Alisa Perren. *Media Industries*. Malden, MA: Blackwell, 2009.

Holzbauer, Stacy M., Aaron S. DeVries, James J. Sejvar, Christine H. Lees, Jennifer Adjemian, et al., "Epidemiologic Investigation of Immune-Mediated Polyradiculoneuropathy among Abattoir Workers Exposed to Porcine Brain: e9782," *PLoSOne*, 5:3, March 2010.

Horkheimer, Max, and Theodor W. Adorno. *Dialectic of Enlightenment*, translated by Edmund Jephcott, edited by Gunzelin Schmid Noerr. Palo Alto, CA: Stanford University Press, 2002.

Horn, John. "Release Dates are a High-Stakes Gamble for Films," *Toronto Globe and Mail*, January 2, 1998, C2.

"How Jho Low's Gang Blasted Malaysia's Millions at New Year!" *Sarawak Report*, January 15, 2016, http://www.sarawakreport.org/2016/01/how-jho-lows-gang-blasted-malaysias-millions-at-new-year/.

Hoyt, Eric. "Hollywood and the Income Tax, 1929–1955," *Film History*, 22, 2010, 5–21.

Hoyt, Eric. *Hollywood Vault: Film Libraries before Home Video*. Berkeley: University of California Press, 2014.

"Hulk," "Why No One Want Make *Hulk 2*?" *The Onion*, July 14, 2004, http://www.theonion.com/content/node/33980.

Hungerford, Amy. "McSweeney's and the School of Life," in *Making Literature Now*, 41–70. Palo Alto, CA: Stanford (Post45), 2016.

IBM, "650 RAMAC Announcment," September 14, 1956, http://www-03.ibm.com/ibm/history/exhibits/650/650_pr2.html.

In the Aftermath of Floyd. www.riverlaw.us/hurricanefloyd.html.

Independent Levee Investigation Team. *Investigation of the Performance of the New Orleans Flood Protection System in Hurricane Katrina on August 29, 2005*, Appendix A, http://www.ce.berkeley.edu/projects/neworleans/report/A.pdf.

Itzkoff, Dave. "*Inception* to Materialize in China," *New York Times*, August 3, 2010, https://artsbeat.blogs.nytimes.com/2010/08/03/blockbuster-inception-to-materialize-in-china/.

Jackson, David. "Death toll Climbs; White House, Air Force One Were Intended Targets," *Dallas Morning News*, September 13, 2001, nexis.

James, Alison. "Besson's EuropaCorp Buys Roissy," *Variety*, October 15, 2007, http://variety.com/2007/film/news/besson-s-europacorp-buys-roissy-1117974054/.

Jameson, Fredric. "Economics: Postmodernism and the Market," in *Postmodernism, or, the Cultural Logic of Late Capitalism*, 260–79. Durham, NC: Duke University Press, 1991.

Jameson, Fredric. "Postmodernism and Consumer Society," in *The Cultural Turn*, 1–21. London: Verso, 1998.

Jameson, Fredric. "Totality as Conspiracy," in *The Geopolitical Aesthetic: Cinema and Space in the World System*, 9–85. Bloomington, IN: BFI, 1992.

Jenkins, Henry. *Convergence Culture: Where Old and New Media Collide*. New York: New York University Press, 2006.

"*JFK*: Goofs," *IMDb*, http://www.imdb.com/title/tt0102138/goofs/?tab=gf.

Johnson-Lewis, Erika. "'We Have to Go Back': Temporal and Spatial Narrative Strategies," in *Looking for Lost: Critical Essays on the Enigmatic Series*, edited by Randy Laist, 11–24. Jefferson, NC: McFarland, 2011.

Johnson, Derek, "Cinematic Destiny: Marvel Studios and the Trade Stories of Industrial Convergence," *Cinema Journal*, 52: 1, Fall 2012, 1–24.

Johnson, Derek, "Inviting Audiences In: The Spatial Reorganization of Production and Consumption in 'TVIII'," *New Review of Film and Television*, 5: 1, 2007, 61–80.

Johnson, Derek. *Media Franchising*. New York: New York University Press, 2013.

Joint Committee on Taxation, *Tax Reform Proposals: Taxation of Capital Income*. Washington: GPO, 1985.

Jones, Chris. "Ryan Kavanaugh Uses Math to Make Movies," *Esquire*, November 2009, http://www.esquire.com/news-politics/a6641/ryan-kavanaugh-1209/.

Kaufman, Anthony. "Ghost of the Machine: Mourning Has Risen for Independent Film," *Village Voice*, May 28, 2002.

Kavadlo, Jesse. "We Have to Go Back: Lost after 9/11," in *Looking for Lost: Critical Essays on the Enigmatic Series*, edited by Randy Laist, 230–42. Jefferson, NC: McFarland, 2011.

Kelly, Brendan. "B.C. Offers Tax Credit," *Daily Variety*, June 4, 1998, 10.

Kermode, Mark. *The Exorcist*, 2nd Rev. ed. London: BFI, 2003.

King, Geoff. *American Independent Cinema*. London: I. B. Tauris, 2005.

King, Geoff, Claire Molloy, and Yannis Tzioumakis. *American Independent Cinema: Indie, Indiewood and Beyond*. New York: Routledge, 2012.

"Kinney Arranging Big Acquisitions in CATV Field," *Wall Street Journal*, October 13, 1971, 12.

"Kinney National to Sell Two Units for $12 Million to Martin Josephson," *Wall Street Journal*, March 6, 1969, 21.

"Kinney National's Plan to Acquire Movie Firm Passes Holders of Both," *Wall Street Journal*, June 11, 1969, 15.

"Kinney Net to Tumble in Year Ending Sept. 30 Because of Write-Down," *Wall Street Journal*, September 16, 1969, 18.

Knafo, Sani. "Bringing 'Where the Wild Things Are' to the Screen," *New York Times*, September 2, 2009, http://www.nytimes.com/2009/09/06/magazine/06jonze-t.html.

Knapp, Dan. "Rendering Unto the Author What Is His," *Los Angeles Times*, January 15, 1972, K12.

Kneale, Dennis. "Vestron's Missteps after 'Dirty Dancing' Show Pitfalls of Crowded Video Market," *Wall Street Journal*, August 28, 1989, 1.

Knight, Lee, and Ray Knight. "What Happened to Limited Partnerships?" *Journal of Accountancy*, July 1, 1997, http://www.journalofaccountancy.com/issues/1997/jul/knight.html.

Kozol, Jonathan. *The Shame of the Nation: The Restoration of Apartheid Schooling in America*. New York: Random House, 2005.

KPMG, *Film Financing and Television Programming: A Taxation Guide*. 7th ed. 2016.

Krämer, Peter. "Women First: *Titanic*, Action-Adventure Films, and Hollywood's Female Audience," in *Titanic*, edited by Kevin Sandler and Gaylyn Studlar, 108–31. New Brunswick, NJ: Rutgers University Press, 1999.

Kroll, Justin, and Dave McNary, "Brad Pitt's Plan B Leaving Paramount for New Regency, RatPac," *Variety*, December 10, 2013, http://variety.com/2013/film/news/brad-pitts-plan-b-paramount-1200942448/.

Kubler George. *The Shape of Time: Remarks on the History of Things*. New Haven, CT: Yale University Press, 2008.

Lahr, John. "Becoming the Hulk," *The New Yorker*, June 30, 2003, 72–81.

Laist, Randy. "Introduction," in *Looking for Lost: Critical Essays on the Enigmatic Series*, edited by Randy Laist, 1–12. Jefferson, NC: McFarland, 2011.

Lamey, Mark. "Cut! Cinar Owes $27.5 Million: Film House's Settlement with Ottawa and Quebec Includes Ill-gotten Tax Credits," *The Gazette*, December 20, 2000, D1.

Lang, Brent. "How Alfonso Cuaron Went Back to Scratch to Rekindle his Career after 'Great Expectations,'" *Variety*, April 20, 2016, http://variety.com/2016/film/news/alfonso-cuaron-great-expectations-1201757974/.

"LCROSS," *NASA*, http://www.nasa.gov/mission_pages/LCROSS/main/.

Learmonth, Michael. "ABC: Give Us Credit for our Digital Strategy," *Business Insider*, March 21, 2008, http://www.businessinsider.com/2008/3/abc-give-us-credit-for-our-digital-strategy.

Lewis, Michael. *Flash Boys*. New York: Norton, 2015.

Lewis, Michael. "How the Eggheads Cracked," *New York Times Magazine*, January 24, 1999, 24ff., http://www.nytimes.com/1999/01/24/magazine/how-the-eggheads-cracked.html.

Lewis, Michael. *Liar's Poker, 25th Anniversary Edition*. New York: Norton, 2011.

Lewis, Michael. *Moneyball*. New York: Norton, 2004.

Lewis, Michael. *The Big Short*. New York: Norton, 2011.

Lewis, Michael. *The Blind Side*. New York: Norton, 2007.

Lim, Dennis. "Magical Mystery Tour," *New York Times*, September 13, 2009, http://www.nytimes.com/interactive/2009/09/13/movies/20090913-wildthings-feature.html.

Linson, Art. *What Just Happened? Bitter Hollywood Tales from the Front Line*. New York: Bloomsbury, 2002.

"List of the 95 Largest Contributors to Nixon Campaign," *New York Times*, September 29, 1973, 15.

Luther, William. "Movie Production Incentives: Blockbuster Support for Lackluster Policy," *The Tax Foundation*, January 2010.

Macaulay, Scott. "Mark Gill in Paris, Indiefreude, and Third Way Distribution," *Filmmaker*, July 8, 2008, http://filmmakermagazine.com/3521-mark-gill-in-paris-indiefreude-and-third-way-distribution.

MacCabe, Colin. *Performance*. Bloomington, IN: BFI, 1998.

MacDonald, Gayle. "Mixed Reviews for Film Tax Changes: Federal Budget Brings Down Gradual Elimination of Shelters in Favor of Credits," *The Financial Post*, March 11, 1995, 2: 31.

MacKenzie, Donald. *An Engine, Not a Camera: How Financial Models Shape Markets*. Cambridge, MA: MIT, 2008.

MacKenzie, Donald. "An Equation and its Worlds: Bricolage, Exemplars, Disunity and Performativity in Financial Economics," *Social Studies of Science*, 33: 6, December 2003, 831–68.

MacKenzie, Donald. "Is Economic Performative? Option Theory and the Construction of Derivatives Markets," in *Do Economists Make Markets? On the Performativity of Economics*, edited by Donald MacKenzie, Fabian Muniesa, and Lucia Siu, 54–86. Princeton: Princeton University Press, 2007.

MacKenzie, Donald. "Knowledge Production in Financial Markets: Credit Default Swaps, the ABX and the Subprime Crisis," *Economy and Society*, 41, 2012, 335–59.

MacKenzie, Donald. "The Credit Crisis as a Problem in the Sociology of Knowledge," *American Journal of Sociology*, 116, 2011, 1778–841.

MacKenzie, Donald. "What's in a Number? Donald MacKenzie on the Importance of LIBOR," *London Review of Books*, September 25, 2008, http://www.lrb.co.uk/v30/n18/donald-mackenzie/whats-in-a-number.

MacKenzie, Donald, Fabian Muniesa, and Lucia Siu, eds. *Do Economists Make Markets? On the Performativity of Economics*. Princeton: Princeton University Press, 2007.

Maggi, Laura. "Former Louisiana Film Official Gets Two-year sentence in Bribery Case" *New Orleans Times-Picayune*, June 29, 2009, http://blog.nola.com/news_impact/print.html?entry=/2009/07/former_louisiana_film_official.html.

Makin, John H., and Norman Ornstein. *Debt and Taxes*. Washington, DC: American Enterprise Institute, 1994.

Makinen, Julie. "Did a Chinese Casino Really Just Pay $70 Million for a 15–minute Martin Scorsese Film?" *Los Angeles Times*, October 27, 2015.

Maltby, Richard. "'A Brief Romantic Interlude': Dick and Jane go to 3 ½ Seconds of the Classical Hollywood Cinema," in *Post-Theory: Reconstructing Film Studies*, edited by David Bordwell and Noël Carroll, 434–59. Madison, WI: University of Wisconsin Press, 1996.

Marr, Merissa. "Pushing the Envelope: Paramount's Strategy," *Wall Street Journal*, http://online.wsj.com/article/SB116961043704085847.html, January 29, 2007.

Massey, Anne, and Mike Hammond. "'It was True! How can you Laugh?': History and Memory in the Reeption of *Titanic* in Britain and Southampton," in *Titanic*, edited by Kevin Sandler and Gaylyn Studlar, 239–64. New Brunswick, NJ: Rutgers University Press, 1999.

Mathews, Jack. "HBO, Disney Take Betts at Fun Odds," *Los Angeles Times*, September 20, 1985, http://articles.latimes.com/1985-09-20/entertainment/ca-6537_1_finance-films.

Matlin, Chatlin. "Sweet Mother of God," *Slate*, March 17, 2010, http://www.slate.com/articles/arts/tv_club/features/2010/lost_season_6/season_6_sweet_mother_of_god.html.

Mayer, Thomas. *Monetary Policy and the Great Inflation in the United States: The Federal Reserve and the Failure of Macroeconomic Policy, 1965–79.* Northampton, MA: Edward Elgar, 1999.

Mayer, Vicki. *Almost Hollywood, Nearly New Orleans: The Lure of the Local Film Economy.* Oakland, CA: University of California Press, 2017.

Mayer, Vicki, Miranda J. Banks, and John Thornton Caldwell. *Production Studies.* New York: Routledge, 2009.

McBride, Bill. "Some Thoughts on Investor Buying," April 21, 2013, http://www.calculatedriskblog.com/2013/04/housing-some-thoughts-on-investor.html.

McClintick, David. *Indecent Exposure.* New York: Collins, 2002.

McClintock, Pamela. "Sony Sets Date for Spider-Man 4," *Variety*, March 12, 2009, http://variety.com/2009/film/markets-festivals/sony-sets-date-for-spider-man-4-1118001130/.

McDonald, Paul. *Hollywood Stardom.* Malden, MA: Wiley-Blackwell, 2013.

McFarlane, Brian. *Screen Adaptations: Great Expectations.* London: Methuen, 2008.

McGrath, Ben. "The Movement: The Rise of Tea Party Activism," *The New Yorker*, February 1, 2010.

McLure, Charles E., and George R. Zodrow, "Treasury I and the Tax Reform Act of 1986: The Economics and Politics of Tax Reform," *Journal of Economic Perspectives*, 1: 1, Summer 1987, 37–58.

McNabb or Kolb, "The Meteoric Rise of Other Football," n.d., http://mcnabborkolb.com/blog/819180034.

McNary, Dave. "China to Miss Out on 'Dark Knight,'" *Variety*, December 23, 2008, http://variety.com/2008/film/awards/china-to-miss-out-on-dark-knight-1117997740/.

McNary, Dave. "Warner Bros. Closes Financing Deal with Dune, Brett Ratner, James Packer," *Variety*, September 30, 2013, http://variety.com/2013/film/news/warner-bros-closes-financing-deal-with-dune-brett-ratner-james-packer-1200682476/.

McSweeneys. *Heads on and We Shoot: The Making of Where the Wild Things Are.* New York: It Books, 2009.

Michael, Barone. "The Transformative Power of Rick Santelli's Rant," June 10, 2010, http://www.nationalreview.com/article/229927/transformative-power-rick-santellis-rant-michael-barone.

Michael, Lewis. *Moneyball.* New York: Norton, 2004, 274.

Mitchell, Pamela. "The Real Artists Behind Reel Art," *The Star-Ledger*, March 4, 1988, 61.

"Moneyball Inception Greenlight Deck v. 2," https://wikileaks.org/sony/docs/03_02/Finance/SPFINANCE/FY14 Projects/Green Light Decks/Moneyball Inception Greenlight Deckv2.pptx.

"Moneyball Project Charter," https://wikileaks.org/sony/docs/03_02/Finance/SPFINANCE/Master%20Data%20Requests/FY14%20Project%20Request/PSOW/Moneyball_Project%20Charter.pdf.

Moriarty, "Moriarty Sits Down With Spike Jonze For Huge Unfettered WHERE THE WILD THINGS ARE Interview + Exclusive Debut Photos!!" *Ain't it Cool News*, December 19, 2008, http://www.aintitcool.com/node/39145.

Morris, Tim. "Gov. Bobby Jindal Seeks Renewal of Film, Music Tax Credits," *New Orleans Times-Picayune*, March 9, 2009, http://blog.nola.com/news_impact/print.html?entry=/2009/03/gov_bobby_jindal_seeks_renewal.html.

Moss, Linda. "Tale of Vestron Seems Like a Movie," *Crain's New York Business*, September 21, 1987, 3.

Motion Picture Association of America, http://www.mpaa.org/policy/state-by-state.

Muellerleile, Chris. "Turning Financial Markets Inside Out: Polanyi, Performativity and Disembeddedness," *Environment and Planning A*, 45, 2013, 1625–42.

Murphy, Mary. "Ashley Back as Chief of Warner Bros. Studio," *Los Angeles Times*, December 11, 1975, H30.

Mussenden, Sean, and Henry Pierson Curtis. "No-fly Zones Shield Disney's Resorts; Competitors Say Disney Used Terrorist Fears to Get Rid of Aerial ad Planes and Sightseeing Helicopters," *Orlando Sentinel*, May 11, 2003, A1, nexis.

"NASA's Mission to Bomb the Moon," *Scientific American*, June 17, 2009, http://www.scientificamerican.com/article.cfm?id=nasas-mission-to-bomb-the-moon-2009-06.

National Telecommunications and Information Administration, "Outside the Box: The Digital TV Converter Box Coupon Program," December 2009, https://www.ntia.doc.gov/files/ntia/publications/dtvreport_outsidethebox.pdf.

"Nets Demand DVR Viewing Credit: Take an Early Tough Stance on Live-plus Issue in Advance of Upfront; Agencies Gird for Fight," *Media Week*, 17: 5, January 29, 2007, 4.

Nitta, Keith A. *The Politics of Structural Education Reform*. New York: Routledge, 2008.

Nystrom, Derek. *Hard Hats, Rednecks, Macho Men: Class in 1970s American Cinema*. New York: Oxford University Press, 2009.

Obst, Lynda. *Sleepless in Hollywood: Tales from the New Abnormal in the Movie Business*. New York: Simon and Schuster, 2013.

"On the download: Dialogue with Anne Sweeney," *The Hollywood Reporter*, September 26, 2006, nexis.

Onstad, Kristen. "Pixar Gambles on a Robot in Love," *New York Times*, June 22, 2008, http://www.nytimes.com/2008/06/22/movies/22onst.html.

Palmer, R. Barton, and Steven M. Sanders, eds. *The Philosophy of Steven Soderbergh*. Lexington, KY: University of Kentucky Press, 2011.

Parisi, Paula. "Man Overboard!" *Entertainment Weekly*, November 7, 1997, 26–37. https://issuu.com/paulaparisi/docs/ew_titanic-cover-story.

Pearson, Roberta. "Introduction: Why Lost?" in *Reading Lost: Perspectives on a Hit Television Show*, edited by Roberta Pearson, 1–8. London: I. B. Tauris.

Perez, Rodrigo. "Michael Mann at BAM: The Recut 'Blackhat,' The Authenticity Behind *Thief, Heat Ali, Collateral,* & More," *IndieWire*, February 12, 2016, http://www.indiewire.com/2016/02/michael-mann-at-bam-the-recut-blackhat-the-authenticity-behind-thief-heat-ali-collateral-more-270444/.

Perren, Alisa. *Indie, Inc.: Miramax and the Transformation of Hollywood in the 1990s*. Austin, TX: University of Texas Press, 2012.

Pisano, Robert. Testimony. Subcommittee on General Farm Commodities and Risk Management, *Hearing to Review Proposals to Establish Exchanges Trading "Movie Futures,"* April 22, 2010.

Poland, David. "The indie thing," *Movie City News*, June 23, 2008, http://
moviecitynews.com/2008/06/the-indie-thing/.

Polster, Burkard, and Marty Ross. *Math Goes to the Movies*. Baltimore: Johns
Hopkins, 2012.

"Proposal to Divest Warner Bros. Studio Confirmed by Officers," *Wall Street
Journal*, January 3, 1969, 24.

Puckrick, Katie. "J.J. Abrams: 'I Called Spielberg and He Said Yes'." *The Guardian*,
August 1, 2011, http://www.guardian.co.uk/film/2011/aug/01/jj-abrams-
spielberg-super-8.

Rainey, James, and Brent Lang. "Relativity in Ruins: Is it Too Late for Ryan
Kavanaugh to Save his Studio?" *Variety*, July 28, 2015, http://variety.com/2015/
film/news/relativity-financial-troubles-ryan-kavanaugh-1201549697/.

Ramesh, Randeep. "1MDB: The Inside Story of the World's Biggest Financial
Scandal," *The Guardian*, July 28, 2016, https://www.theguardian.com/
world/2016/jul/28/1mdb-inside-story-worlds-biggest-financial-scandal-malaysia.

Ravid, S. Abraham. "Are They all Crazy or Just Risk Averse?: Some Movie Puzzles
and Possible Solutions," *Contributions to Economic Analysis*, 260, 2003, 33–47.

Raw, Charles, Bruce Page, and Geoffrey Hodson. *Do You Sincerely Want to Be
Rich?: The Full Story of Bernard Cornfeld and I.O.S.* New York: Broadway,
2005.

Rich, Joshua. "Relativity Television rebrands as Critical Content, post-bankruptcy,"
The Wrap, January 26, 2016, https://www.thewrap.com/relativity-television-
rebrands-as-critical-content-post-bankruptcy/.

Ricker Schulte, Stephanie. *Cached: Decoding the Internet in Global Popular
Culture*. New York: New York University, 2013.

Rodowick, D. N. *Gilles Deleuze's Time Machine*. Durham, NC: Duke University
Press, 1997.

Rodowick, D. N. *The Virtual Life of Film*. Cambridge, MA: Harvard University
Press, 2007, 104.

Rogin, Michael. "Body and Soul Murder: JFK," in *Media Spectacles*, edited by
Marjorie Garber, Jann Matlock, and Rebecca Walkowitz, 3–22. New York:
Routledge, 1993.

Rogin, Michael. *Blackface, White Noise: Jewish Immigrants in the Hollywood
Melting Pot*. Berkeley: University of California Press, 1996.

"Ross," "Open Letter to ABC.com," *Immediate Regret*, January 30, 2009, http://
www.immediateregret.com/2009/01/open-letter-to-abccom.html.

Rotella, Carlo. *Good with their Hands: Boxers, Bluesmen, and Other Characters
from the Rust Belt*, Berkeley, CA: University of California Press, 2002.

Rowling, J. K. *Harry Potter and the Order of the Phoenix*. New York: Scholastic,
2003.

Russell, Gordon, and Robert Travis Scott. "FBI Investigating Louisiana's Film
Industry Incentives," *New Orleans Times-Picayune*, May 29, 2007, http://blog.
nola.com/business_of_film//print.html.

Rutenberg, Jim. "Disney is Blocking Distribution of a Film that Criticizes Bush,"
New York Times, May 5, 2004, A1, 22.

Rutenberg, Jim. "Time Warner and Disney Reach Cable Deal for ABC," *New York
Times*, May 26, 2000, http://www.nytimes.com/2000/05/26/business/time-
warner-and-disney-reach-cable-deal-for-abc.html.

Saunders, Doug. "A Cheater's Guide to Canadian Television: How to Bilk Taxpayers and Influence People," *The Globe and Mail*, October 23, 1999, C1.

Schamus, James. "IFP Rant," *Filmmaker*, Spring 2000, http://www.filmmakermagazine.com/spring2000/short_reports/ifp_rant.php.

Schamus, James. "Sing to us, Muse, of the Rage of the Hulk," *New York Times*, May 11, 2003, MT29.

Schreiner, John. "Lights, Action, Financing!" *The Financial Post*, March 30, 1992, 3: 24.

"Scott Revisits 'Déjà vu,'" *Variety*, October 19, 2005, http://www.variety.com/article/VR1117931300.html.

Scott, Robert Travis. "Increase in Movie Tax Credit Endorsed," *New Orleans Times-Picayune*, June 19, 2009, http://www.nola.com/news/t-p/capital/index.ssf?/base/news-7/124538940923020.xml.

Scott, Robert Travis. "LIFT Officials Pressured State to Speed Tax Credits," *New Orleans Times-Picayune*, June 4, 2007, http://blog.nola.com/times-picayune//print.html.

Scott, Robert Travis. "More than Two Dozen with Ties to the New Orleans Saints Invested in Movie Studio Deal," *New Orleans Times-Picayune*, July 2, 2009.

Sedgwick, John. Review of De Vany, *Hollywood Economics*. *Economic Record*, 81:255, December 2005, 446–48.

Sedgwick, John, and Michael Pokorny, *An Economic History of Film*. New York: Routledge, 2004.

Sharon, Jeff "How to Fix Baseball, Part II: Fix the All-Star Game," June 14, 2014, http://www.jeffsharon.net/?p=412.

Silberman, Steve. "Life after Darth," *Wired*, 13: 5, May 2005, 140+.

Singh, Simon. *The Simpsons and their Mathematical Secrets*. London: Bloomsbury, 2013.

Sklar, Jessica K., and Elizabeth S. Sklar, eds. *Mathematics in Popular Culture: Essays on Appearances in Film, Fiction, Games, Television and Other Media*. Jefferson, NC: McFarland, 2012.

Smith, Jennifer. "Packer's Rat Pack!" http://www.dailymail.co.uk/tvshowbiz/article-3291286/James-Packer-rubs-shoulders-Leonardo-DiCaprio-Robert-Niro-Martin-Scorsese-paying-trio-17million-promote-new-Macau-casino.html.

Smith, Murray. "Theses on the Philosophy of Hollywood History," in *Contemporary Hollywood Cinema*, edited by Stephen Neale and Murray Smith, 3–20. New York: Routledge, 1998.

Smithsonian, "Laffer Curve Napkin," http://americanhistory.si.edu/collections/search/object/nmah_1439217.

Sobchack, Vivian. "Bathos and Bathysphere: On Submersion, Longing, and History in *Titanic*," in *Titanic*, edited by Kevin Sandler and Gaylyn Studlar, 189–204. New Brunswick, NJ: Rutgers University Press, 1999.

Solomon, Charles. "Pixar Creative Chief to Seek to Restore the Disney Magic," *New York Times*, January 25, 2006, http://www.nytimes.com/2006/01/25/business/media/pixar-creative-chief-to-seek-to-restore-the-disney-magic.html.

Sony Pictures Entertainment. "IT Projects Projects View_Final," April 7, 2014, https://wikileaks.org/sony/docs/03_02/Finance/SPFINANCE/FY14%20Projects/FY14%20Project%20Reports/12_Mar_14/For%20Distribution/IT%20Projects%20-%20Projects%20View_Final.pdf.

Stewart, Andrew. "Paramount's Super Payoff for 'Iron Man 3'," *Variety*, May 10, 2013, http://variety.com/2013/film/news/iron-man-3-paramount-disney-1200479325/.

Stewart, Garrett, "Fourth Dimensions, Seventh Senses: The Work of Mind-gaming in the Age of Electronic Reproduction," in *Hollywood's Puzzle Films*, edited by Warren Buckland, 165–84. New York: AFI/Routledge, 2014.

Stolberg, Sheryl Gay. "As Gay Issues Arise, Obama is Pressed to Engage," *New York Times*, May 6, 2009, http://www.nytimes.com/2009/05/07/us/politics/07obama.html.

Story, Louise. "Networks Are in an Uproar Over Nielsen ad Ratings," *New York Times*, November 4, 2006, 4.

Stringer, Julian. "'The China Had Never Been Used!': On the Patina of Perfect Images in *Titanic*," in *Titanic*, edited by Kevin Sandler and Gaylyn Studlar, 205–19. New Brunswick, NJ: Rutgers University Press, 1999.

Suskind, Ron. *Confidence Men*. New York: HarperCollins, 2012.

Szalay, Michael. *New Deal Modernism: American Literature and the Invention of the Welfare State*. Durham, NC: Duke University Press, 2000.

Taibbi, Matt. "The Great American Bubble Machine," *Rolling Stone*, July 13, 2009, reprinted in *Griftopia*, 206–40. New York: Spiegel & Grau, 2010.

Tannenwald, Robert. "State Film Subsidies: Not Much Bang for Too Many Bucks," Center on Budget and Policy Priorities, November 17, 2010.

Tasker, Yvonne. *Working Girls: Gender and Sexuality in Popular Cinema*. New York: Routledge, 1998.

Tatlow, Didi Kristen. "With 6,000 Dead Pigs in River, Troubling Questions on Food Safety," *New York Times*, March 13, 2013, http://rendezvous.blogs.nytimes.com/2013/03/13/with-6000-dead-pigs-in-river-troubling-questions-on-food-safety/.

"The Monster that ate Hollywood," *Frontline*, November 22, 2001, http://www.pbs.org/wgbh/pages/frontline/shows/hollywood/etc/script.html.

Thompson, Anne. "LAFF: Mark Gill on Indie Crisis," June 21, 2008, http://weblogs.variety.com/thompsononhollywood/2008/06/laff-mark-gill.html.

Thompson, John O. "Screen Acting and the Commutation Test," in *Stardom: Industry of Desire*, edited by Christine Gledhill, 186–200. New York: Routledge, 1991.

Thomson, David. *The Whole Equation*. New York: Knopf, 2004.

Tietz, Jeff. "Boss Hog: The Dark Side of America's Top Pork Producer," *Rolling Stone*, December 14, 2006, http://www.rollingstone.com/culture/news/boss-hog-the-dark-side-of-americas-top-pork-producer-20061214.

Tim, Molloy, "Damon Lindelof's History of *Lost* A Show He Longed to Quit," *The Wrap*, September 23, 2011, http://www.thewrap.com/damon-lindelofs-history-lost-show-he-longed-quit-31281/.

Tomberry. "Nuking the Fridge," *Know Your Meme*, http://knowyourmeme.com/memes/nuking-the-fridge.

Townson, Don. "Canadian Goose: Defying H'w'd Whining, Canucks Sweeten Pot," *Daily Variety*, July 9, 1999, 1.

Traister, Rebecca. "Crouching Budgets, Hidden Profits: James Schamus, Columbia Professor, Bets $137 Million on Ang Lee Epic," *New York Observer*, June 22, 2003, http://observer.com/2003/06/crouching-budget-hidden-profits-james-schamus-columbia-professor-bets-137-million-on-ang-lee-epic/.

Transcript of Q&A on the 35th Anniversary of Watergate, http://
www.washingtonpost.com/wp-dyn/content/discussion/2007/06/14/
DI2007061400497.html.

Tzioumakis, Yannis. *Hollywood's Indies: Classics Divisions, Specialty Labels and the American Film Market.* Edinburgh: Edinburgh University Press, 2012.

United States of America v. "The Wolf of Wall Street" Motion Picture, Including Any Profits, Royalties, and Distribution Proceeds Owed to Red Granite Pictures, Inc. or its Affiliates and/or Assigns, Complaint filed, July 20, 1916, 78.

"U.S. Attorney's Office Apologises to 'Wolf of Wall Street' Jordan Belfort Over Article Suggesting he is Hiding in Australia," *news.com.au*, January 15, 2014, http://www.news.com.au/finance/money/us-attorneys-office-apologises-to-wolf-of-wall-street-jordan-belfort-over-article-suggesting-he-is-hiding-in-australia/story-e6frfmci-1226801457393.

Van Horn, Robert, Philip Mirowski, and Thomas A. Stapleford, *Building Chicago Economics: New Perspectives on the History of America's Most Powerful Economics Program.* Cambridge: Cambridge University Press, 2011.

Van Osterveldt, Johan. *The Chicago School: How the University of Chicago Assembled the Thinkers who Revolutionized Economics and Business.* Chicago: Agate, 2007.

Vogel, Harold L. *Entertainment Industry Economics: A Guide for Financial Analysis*, 8th ed. Cambridge: Cambridge University Press, 2011.

Wadler, Joyce. "Call Us Crazy, but We See a Buddy Movie Here," *New York Times*, January 11, 2005, http://www.nytimes.com/2005/01/11/nyregion/call-us-crazy-but-we-see-a-buddy-movie-here.html.

Walker, Andrew. *Hollywood UK: The British Film Industry in the Sixties.* London: Stein and Day, 1974.

Walker, Susan. "Tories Boost Tax Credits for Culture," *The Toronto Star*, May 7, 1997, D2.

Wallace, Benjamin. "The Epic Fail of Hollywood's Hottest Algorithm," *Vulture*, January 2016, http://www.vulture.com/2016/01/relativity-media-ryan-kavanaugh-c-v-r.html.

Warhol, Andy. *The Philosophy of Andy Warhol From A to B and Back Again.* New York: Harcourt, 1975.

Waxman, Sharon, and Matt Donnelly, "'The Revenant' Budget Soars to $135 Million as New Regency Foots the Bill," *The Wrap*, January 15, 2016, originally October 15, 2015, https://www.thewrap.com/revenant-budget-soars-to-165-million-with-new-regency-footing-most-of-bill-exclusive/

Weintraub, Steve. "Interview with Andrew Stanton," *Collider*, November 17, 2008, http://www.collider.com/entertainment/interviews/article.asp/aid/9881/tcid/1.

Whitwell, Tom. "Tiny Music Makers, Pt 4: The Mac Startup Sound." *Musicthing*, May 26, 2005, http://musicthing.blogspot.com/2005/05/tiny-music-makers-pt-4-mac-startup.html.

Winter, Terrence. *The Wolf of Wall Street*, screenplay, n.d., http://www.paramountguilds.com/pdf/the_wolf_of_wall_street_screenplay.pdf.

Wittgenstein, Ludwig. *Philosophical Investigations*, 4th ed., translated by G. E. M. Anscombe, P. M. S. Hacker, Joachim Schulte. New York: Wiley-Blackwell, 2009.

Wloszczyna, Susan. "Films Draw on Nudes for Artistic Expression," *USA Today*, January 29, 1988, 7D.

Wong, Edward. "Thousands of Dead Pigs Found Floating in River Flowing into Shanghai," *New York Times*, March 11, 2013, http://www.nytimes.com/2013/03/12/world/asia/thousands-of-dead-pigs-found-in-chinese-river.html.

"World Series Television Ratings," *Baseball Almanac*, http://www.baseball-almanac.com/ws/wstv.shtml.

Wright, Tom, and Bradley Hope, "Behind the 1MDB Scandal: Banks that Missed Clues and Bowed to Pressure," *Wall Street Journal*, September 6, 2013, http://www.wsj.com/articles/behind-the-1mdb-scandal-banks-that-missed-clues-and-bowed-to-pressure-1473109548.

Wyatt, Justin, and Katherine Vlesmas. "The Drama of Recoupment: On the Mass Media Negotiation of *Titanic*," in *Titanic: Anatomy of a Blockbuster*, edited by Kevin S. Sandler and Gaylyn Studlar, 29–45. New Brunswick, NJ: Rutgers University Press, 1999.

Yap, Shiwen. "Singapore: YuuZoo calls off $150m Investment in US-based Relativity Media," *Deal Street Asia*, March 1, 2017, https://www.dealstreetasia.com/stories/66289-66289/.

Zipser Adjemian, Jennifer, James Howell, Stacy Holzbauer, Julie Harris, Sergio Recuenco, et al., "A Clustering of Immune-mediated Polyradiculoneuropathy among Swine Abattoir Workers Exposed to Aerosolized Porcine Brains, Indiana, United States," *International Journal of Occupational and Environmental Health*, 15:4, October–December 2009, 331–8.

INDEX

Lightning Source UK Ltd.
Milton Keynes UK
UKHW021837210220
359134UK00008B/649

9 781501 362248